EVALUATION
AND
DECISION MAKING
FOR
HEALTH
SERVICES

D1318661

EVALUATION AND DECISION MAKING FOR HEALTH SERVICES

BY JAMES E.VENEY
ARNOLD D. KALUZNY

BeardBooks
Washington, D.C.

Copyright © 1998 by the Foundation of the American College of Healthcare Executives
Originally published 1998 by the Health Administration Press
Third Edition reprinted 2004 by Beard Books, Washington, D.C.

ISBN 1-58798-230-7

Printed in the United States of America

PREFACE

Evidence-based management like evidence-based medicine has come of age. Whether the particular approach involves general management strategies such as continuous quality improvement or the use of balance score cards to assess overall performance, or the implementation of various programmatic or clinical initiatives, such as wellness programs or case managers to improve quality, these interventions are being challenged to document their relevance, effectiveness, sustainability, impact, and whether there is value added to the organization. To meet the challenge managers, clinicians, and the larger health services community are required to evaluate new approaches (as well as assess existing approaches) and in so doing are in need of usable knowledge of evaluation methodologies.

This book was first published in 1984 and revised in 1991 and 1998 as an effort to provide a comprehensive framework for assessing health programs and provide managers, clinicians, and the health services research community with the basic methodologies for evaluation. The need remains and has grown more acute as health care organizations are faced with increasing challenges and demands for accountability. The emphasis is on value added and the relationship between quality and cost that meet the needs, demands, and expectations of not only the providers of the service but the demands and expectations of the purchaser, the consumer, and the larger community.

Health care and its delivery continue to undergo unrelenting change, and the increased focus on information technology is likely to increase the expectations that ongoing and newly implemented initiatives will have been or are undergoing some form of evaluation. Failure to provide such evidence is likely to challenge the credibility of those involved and/or place them at risk of administrative malpractice.

To meet this challenge our book is divided into seven sections. The first section provides a framework for decision making that stresses the importance of evaluation in the entire managerial process of program planning, implementation, and control. Issues of relevance, progress, adequacy, efficiency, effectiveness, sustainability, and impact are presented with special attention to the operational issues of how and by whom evaluation is carried out and how best to use the results of evaluation efforts.

The remaining sections center on major evaluation techniques, monitoring, case studies, survey research, trend analysis, and experimental design. The final section is devoted to basic methods that are important for each of the evaluation techniques including general measurement issues in evaluation, the measurement of utility, sampling, operations research techniques and interpretation, and cost benefit, cost effectiveness, and cost utility analysis.

We hope that the book will be a useful guide to improve decision making for health services organizations, clinicians, and managers as well as our health services research colleagues. The challenges are great, and hopefully the information provided will better equip those responsible for improving the provision of care to deal with the barriers inherent in any improvement effort, ss well described by Machiavelli many years ago:

> "There is nothing more difficult to take in hand, more perilous to conduct, or more uncertain in its success, than to take the lead in the introduction of a new order of things, because the innovator has for enemies all those who have done well under the old conditions, and lukewarm defenders in those who may do well under the new."
>
> Machiavelli, The Prince

James E. Veney
Arnold D. Kaluzny
December 1, 2004

TABLE OF CONTENTS

PART VII Basic Methods

I

INTRODUCTION

FRAMEWORK FOR IMPROVED DECISION MAKING

T he provision of health services is undergoing unprecedented change. Consider some changes that just a few years ago were thought unlikely, if not impossible:

- the conversion of many well-established not-for-profit healthcare organizations to for-profit corporations;
- the increasing and explicit recognition that health is not synonymous with medical care and thus a growing interest in the development and implementation of "health and wellness" programs; and
- the incorporation of managed care as a fundamental framework through which care is provided even among the most prestigious and specialized tertiary facilities.

Central to each change are the questions—either implicit or explicit—to the decision-making process:

- Did the change make a difference? If yes, why? If no, why not?
- Was the change conducted efficiently given available resources and time?
- Was the change relevant to the issues of the day?

The rate and scope of change will likely not slow in the years ahead. Thus, managers and all personnel are likely to be judged on their ability to provide clear evidence that the changes are relevant to the issues at hand and have met the proposed objectives in an efficient and timely fashion. All this leads to the conclusion that evaluation continues to be serious business.

The objective of this chapter is to define evaluation and describe its role in the organization, specifically within the managerial process. Emphasis is given to identifying the challenges of evaluation in a changing healthcare system and to providing a framework for considering the various functions and different types of evaluation and their relationships to improved decision making.

What Is Evaluation?

Evaluation incorporates a broad range of activities with different objectives, procedures, and expectations. Because of the multiplicity of these activities, a tendency is to make evaluation more complex and mysterious than it need be. Although evaluation uses various quantitative and qualitative methods for data collection, analysis, and interpretation, and many of these are borrowed from the social and management sciences, its basic thrust is central to the managerial process, and its application is often intuitive in nature. For the purposes of this book, evaluation is defined as the collection and analysis of information by various methods to determine the *relevance, adequacy, progress, efficiency, effectiveness, impact,* and *sustainability* of a set of program activities. These activities may involve a range of initiatives including monitoring, case studies, survey research, experiments and quasi-experiments, and time-series analysis.

The following discussion considers the components of evaluation previously listed and provides examples to illustrate the kinds of issues involved in each component. Table 1.1 provides a definition for each of the components (Veney and

TABLE 1.1

Components of Program Evaluation

Evaluation Component	Component Definition
Relevance	Evaluation of the appropriateness or equity of a program or the correspondence between the program and the needs for the program that is based specifically on a priori judgment.
Adequacy	Evaluation of the extent to which a program is likely to be able to address the entire range of a problem that is based specifically on a priori judgment.
Progress	Evaluation of the extent to which scheduled activities occur on time, in the manner expected (e.g., according to professional standards), and at the budgeted cost and produce expected outputs.
Effectiveness	Evaluation of the extent to which the program has produced expected intermediate outcomes (effects). Assumes a causal connection between the program and the effect.
Impact	Evaluation of the extent to which the program has produced expected ultimate outcomes (impact). Assumes a causal connection between the program and the impact.
Efficiency	Evaluation that assesses the relationship between input and outcome, either intermediate (effects) or ultimate (impacts).
Sustainability	Evaluation of whether a program can capture the needed resources to sustain itself after the withdrawal of external support.

Gorbach 1993). The various methods and their relationship to the functions of evaluation, along with their role in managerial decision making, are discussed later in the chapter and in considerable detail in the respective sections of the book.

Relevance refers to whether the program or service is needed. This issue determines the basic rationale for having a program or set of activities to meet the health needs or service demands of a community. The development of relevance as a legitimate evaluation topic in health services is a recent phenomenon. Historically, health services were considered relevant a priori; critical questions concerned the delivery of services. In more recent years, however, delivery and extent of use have been supplemented by concern for the underlying rationale for a specific activity. The very basis of a program in terms of objectives, scope, depth, and coverage becomes the problematic issue. Questions central to this type of evaluation include:

- What problem does the program address?
- Does that problem need attention?
- How accurate is the information about the problem?
- How adequate is the definition of the problem?
- How adequate is the definition of the program?
- Is the program appropriate for the defined problem?
- How does the program fit with the overall strategy of the organization?

Adequacy refers to the a priori assessment of the extent to which the program may be expected to address a given problem at a level that will be meaningful (i.e., is the program adequate in size and scope to make a difference?). Often programs are available within health services but are only a symbol to the outside community that the organization is involved in an area without any truly substantive commitment. Specifically, does the program address the entire breadth and depth of the problem?

Progress refers to the tracking of program activities. Progress deals with analysis efforts made to assess the degree to which program implementation complies with the plan for it. This type of evaluation has long been considered an integral part of the management process. Illustrative questions concerning progress include:

- Are appropriate personnel, equipment, and financial resources available in the right quantity, in the right place, and at the right time to meet program needs?
- Are expected products of the program actually being produced? Are these products of expected quality and quantity? Are these outputs produced at the expected time?

Efficiency refers to whether program results could be obtained less expensively. Questions of efficiency concern the relationship between the results obtained from a specific program and the resources expended to maintain the program. Efficiency as an evaluation focus is gaining attention. The recognition that resources are limited and that programs must compete for them will increase the role that evaluations of efficiency have in determining whether new programs are funded or not funded, continued or terminated, expanded or reduced. Questions that evaluations of efficiency raise include:

- Are program benefits sufficient for the cost incurred?
- Are program benefits more expensive or less expensive per unit of outcome than benefits derived from other programs designed to achieve the same goal?

Effectiveness refers to whether program results meet predetermined objectives. Emphasis is on program outputs or the immediate results of program efforts and whether these outputs are as expected. Evaluations of effectiveness are aimed at improving program formulation and thus have a relatively short-term perspective. The questions central to this type of evaluation include:

- Did the program meet its stated objectives?
- Were program providers satisfied with the effects of program activities?
- Were program beneficiaries satisfied with the effects of program activities?
- Are things better as a result of the program's having existed?

Impact refers to the long-term effects of the program. The issue of impact is concerned with changes observed over time in characteristics that the program is ultimately designed to influence. While evaluation of effectiveness focuses on intermediate program outcomes, impact focuses on the long-term improvements expected in health status, quality of life, or general well-being. A program may prove both efficient and effective in producing short-run outcomes, yet have minimal long-term outcomes. Illustrative questions for this type of evaluation include:

- Did a particular program produce the observed effect?
- Could the observed effects occur in the absence of the program or in the presence of some alternative program or set of activities?

Sustainability refers to whether the effects of the program are likely to continue after initial funding; thus, any evaluation is directed at determining whether a program is likely to be able to capture the needed funds and resources to maintain itself after the withdrawal of the initial external support. Specifically:

- What is the likelihood of the program to be self-sustaining?
- What opportunities are available to continue the program after its initial funding has ended?

Why Evaluation?

For healthcare organizations to be successful in the future requires that they acquire new knowledge (Batalden and Stoltz 1993) and that this knowledge generates new initiatives to better meet the challenges of a rapidly changing environment. Peter Senge describes so well the "learning organization" as:

> an organization that is continually expanding its capacity to create its future. For such an organization, it is not enough merely to survive. "Survival learning" or what is more often termed "adaptive learning" is important—indeed necessary. But for a learning organization, "adaptive learning" must be joined by "generative learning, learning that enhances our capacity to create." (1990, 14)

To accomplish this requires that the organization be committed to evaluation to continually learn about the programs and services it provides to ensure that they are working, to keep track of program and service activity, and to be able to report to any increasingly complex and demanding constituency. While all this is quite reasonable, the purpose of evaluation as taken by this book can be stated much more simply: The purpose of evaluation is to make better decisions about program activities.

The key point is improved decision making. Evaluation is not an activity to be undertaken without referent. It is fine, for example, to find out more about a given program, but that additional knowledge must be directed toward a decision about the program. If no decisions are to be made, or the decisions are not ones that can be improved with the addition of information, evaluation is meaningless.

Many programs are implemented for political rather than technical reasons (Westphal, Gulati, and Shortell 1997) and operate according to political rather than technical criteria. Under such circumstances, evaluation is likely to be of little use. The possibility exists that in a highly political arena certain issues remain primarily technical and a legitimate subject for evaluation, or that in a basically technical arena certain issues remain political and not subject to evaluation. This is fine, but the evaluator must know which issues can be evaluated and which cannot; otherwise the effort may produce little of value.

Frequently, evaluations are undertaken without a clear understanding or definition of what the decision points are. This is simply bad management. No evaluation activity should be initiated without a clear statement of which decisions will result from the information obtained. The decision might be as seemingly simple as determining whether a program works and thus needs no modification, or that the state of the program requires that some action is taken. In either case the decision area must be known a priori. Evaluation is undertaken to provide information for some decision process. If no clear decision-making process is served by the results, the effort may be an excellent piece of academic work, the design well thought out, the data collection thorough, and the analysis inspired—but it is not evaluation.

Even in the best of all possible worlds, of course, many well-planned and well-executed evaluations that were clearly aimed at decision making will remain unused. If a conscious effort is made at the outset to define the decisions to be made, however, information generated by evaluations will likely be used. A major purpose of this book is to increase the likelihood that such evaluations will be part of the decision-making process.

Evaluation and the Managerial Process

All managers are forced daily to make judgments and plan actions on the basis of what are essentially evaluations. These evaluations may deal with such apparently mundane affairs as determining whether program resources and personnel are in the right places at the right time (progress), or with more glamorous issues, such as whether a program has made any difference (impact). Any activity aimed at making decisions about the following, however, is essentially evaluation:

- whether or how a program should be implemented;
- how the program should be carried out;
- whether program activities are being pursued in a timely manner;
- if the program is producing expected outcomes;
- whether the outcomes are as desirable as anticipated at the initiation of the program; and
- how the program can be improved.

Evaluation may range from highly structured, planned, and formalized activities to highly informal activities, many of which may verge on the intuitive. Whether structured or intuitive, evaluation is an integral part of the management cycle.

Figure 1.1 shows a feedback or "cybernetic" model of planning, implementation, and control as three interconnected activities. Norbert Weiner (1948) originated the word "cybernetic" to refer to the type of controlling mechanism that uses information about the state of a system to continually move the system closer to a desired state. A familiar example of a cybernetic system is a thermostat, which assesses the temperature of a house to provide information for activating the heating and cooling system in such a way as to move the temperature of the house closer to some desired temperature. In the same sense, evaluation uses information about the state of an organization or program system to continually move the organization or program closer to the organization's desired process and objectives. In this sense, evaluation occurs during all phases of the management cycle. Evaluation, for example, may accompany the planning and design stage of a program and be directed at such issues as the current state of the system to be affected by the program, the specific nature of problems that the program is to address, and alternative approaches to solving these problems. Such evaluation basically deals with whether a program is needed, how it should be structured, and what kinds of problems it should solve. This evaluation concerns the question

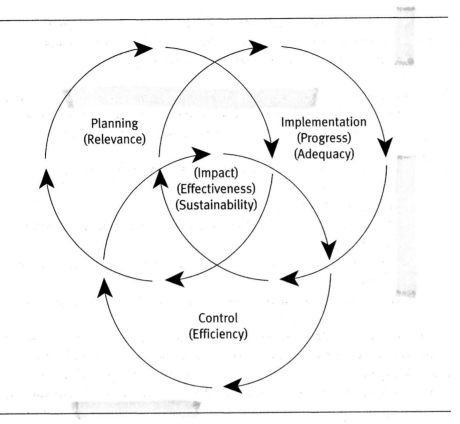

FIGURE 1.1
Cybernetic
Model of
Program Planning,
Implementation,
and Evaluation

of program relevance, although relevance cannot entirely be decided a priori because a major aspect of relevance is evaluation of program impact. The clear decisions to be made at the level of planning and design include whether to implement a program and, if so, what type to implement.

Also integral to planning and design is whether a particular problem should be solved. To a certain extent, this question is one that can be addressed by evaluation. The basic issue is whether the problem involved is one that by virtue of its widespread impact or importance requires a solution. Surveys of selected populations can provide information about the prevalence or incidence of disease and associated morbidity and mortality that can, on a comparative basis, help to identify problems that may merit solutions or efforts at solutions. In a situation of limited resources, not all health problems merit the same attention.

After a program or service has been designed and implemented, a number of other evaluation issues arise, many of which involve monitoring and improvements. General questions are whether the program is in fact implemented and whether the process works as expected relative to addressing the scope of the problem:

- Do resources (e.g., funds, doses of vaccine, students to be trained, medical supplies, or other types of inputs) arrive at the proper place, on time, and in sufficient quantity?
- Are activities undertaken in a timely manner and in proper order?

- Do various components of the program interrelate properly?
- Do various personnel in the program coordinate appropriately?
- Is it possible to improve the process over time?

These and many other questions are part of program monitoring. The point of such monitoring is to detect breakdowns in the process and the operation of the program and to take the decisions appropriate for corrective action:

- After the program or service has been implemented, is it effective and efficient?
- Are the costs of the program reasonable?
- Do results expected from the program appear in the projected time frame?
- Are there other cheaper or more timely ways of producing the same results?
- Are the results of the program meeting predetermined objectives?

These questions are often studied by more formal evaluation, such as cost-benefit analysis, as well as fairly elaborate operations research and comparative studies. Particularly during the start-up phase of a program, trying several alternative program structures to compare costs, timeliness of results, and effectiveness may be feasible. Questions also important at the implementation stage of a program include:

- Are the desired results achieved and are they sustainable?
- Has the problem that the program was designed to solve been solved or is it being solved on a continuing basis?
- Would the problem have been solved in the absence of the program?
- Could any other program have solved the problem?

This is the appropriate area of summative evaluation. If the problem has not been solved, other questions arise:

- Is the structure of the program adequate for solving the problem?
- Are the inputs adequate?
- Is the definition of the problem itself adequate?

Effectiveness, impact, and sustainability are the ultimate tests of a program or set of activities. If a program has no effectiveness or impact, decisions about the importance of the problem or relevance of the program for the problem, monitoring of program processes, and judgments about reasonableness of cost and sustainability are all basically irrelevant. Yet effectiveness and impact of a program are often the most difficult aspects of the program to assess. That is, has the program caused the expected result to occur? Very often, no good objective criteria to measure the expected result exists.

Who Does Evaluation?

All managers do evaluation, and an increasing cadre of social scientists have the skills necessary to conduct evaluations. The extent of involvement of both groups depends on the degree to which formal evaluation and research techniques are involved and the extent to which the manager collaborates with individuals skilled in evaluation techniques.

Figure 1.2 presents a continuum showing the various levels of involvement by managers and evaluation personnel. At one end of the continuum the manager has the most influence. There, emphasis is on evaluation focusing on relevance and program progress. At the other end of the continuum researchers have the most influence, and emphasis is on assessing impact. Evaluations at that end involve the most sophisticated methodological approaches and techniques.

In reality, evaluation must involve all personnel in collaboration with and facilitated by those with specific training in relevant research and evaluation methodologies. Recently described as "empowerment evaluation" (i.e., the use of evaluation concepts, techniques, and findings to foster improvement and self-determination) (Fetterman 1996), this approach requires substantive changes in the way that both researchers and managers function.

For managers, collaboration requires recognition that they do not know whether program X will be effective or whether it is even relevant to the many problems faced by their organization. Instead of advocating a particular solution, the manager needs a better understanding of the basic functioning of the organization and the economic, political, social, and financial context (Mintzberg 1989;

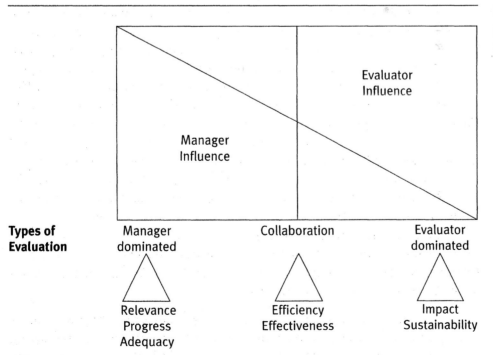

FIGURE 1.2
Manager-Evaluator
Collaboration

Batalden and Stoltz 1993) and needs to present solutions as a series of options and develop ways to assess them as they affect the community as well as the organization. As first described by Campbell, this approach requires a

> . . . shift from the advocacy of a specific reform to the advocacy of the seriousness of the problem, and hence to the advocacy of persistence in alternative reform efforts should the first one fail. The political stance would become: "This is a serious problem. We propose to initiate policy A on an experimental basis. If after five years there has been no significant improvement, we would shift to Policy B." By making explicit that a given problem solution was only one of several that the administrator or party could in good conscience advocate, and by having ready a plausible alternative, the administrator could afford honest evaluation of outcomes. Negative results, a failure of the first program, would not jeopardize his job, for his job would be to keep after the problem until something was found that worked. (1969, 410)

Within the world of health services, this approach is very difficult, yet possible through the idea of firm research—that is, research conducted within an institution in which patients and providers are randomized to assess the effectiveness and efficiency of various managerial and clinical interventions (Goldberg and McGough 1991; Neuhauser 1998).

For example, over the years a number of evaluative issues have been addressed concerning physician behavior. The availability of clinical guidelines in isolation has generally failed to promote a voluntary change in practice patterns. The ability to randomize clinic practices provides an opportunity to determine the effectiveness of academic detailing and continuous quality improvement teams as two approaches to increasing compliance with national guidelines for primary care of hypertension and depression (Goldberg, Wagner, Fihn et al. 1998). In this trial, academic detailing modeled after methods used by pharmaceutical sales representatives in which physicians or pharmacists are trained to offer providers one-on-one education and feedback was compared with continuous quality improvement interventions in which the participating multidisciplinary teams were empowered to make changes in suboptimal processes and monitor with locally collected data as to whether goals were achieved. Analysis revealed that we have not discovered the "magic bullet" yet that provides the opportunity to provide real world tests of interventions and move us from the world of "advocacy" to the world of "evidence-based management."

Moreover, the very essence of management centers on improvement and the utilization of new knowledge to manage processes in a way that assures continual renewal of the organization to meet the challenges of a changing environment. As we have learned from industry,

> to facilitate the renewal process, top managers must take on a new role— one that disturbs the organizational equilibrium. We are not suggesting that top managers' job is to create chaos. Their role as shapers of the corporate purpose still means they must provide direction and coherence.

But we are saying that top managers must also direct some of their energy into more disruptive pursuits. (Ghoshal and Barlett 1995, 94)

For social scientists, an equally important shift must occur. The challenge to the social scientist is not just to disseminate information to the managerial community to enhance program operations but also to work collaboratively with managers to achieve a clear understanding of the problem and its implications. This must be accomplished with a sense of timing vis-à-vis the managerial decision process and without the use of jargon or excessive theoretical conceptualization. This is not to say that the social scientist must abandon "rigor" or "theory," but only that it must be placed within the context of operations and be presented as underlying, often implicit, principles. Moreover, the education of both managers and social scientists involved with evaluation requires a rethinking of the educational process. As proposed for healthcare providers (Batalden 1998), but equally applicable to managers and social scientists, is the need to address the education process as a means of advancing the implementation of quality and value in the provision of healthcare. The educational process provides the opportunity for managers and evaluators to acquire new knowledge and skills and through their application ensure the continual renewal of the organization in a changing environment.

Uses, Misuses, and Nonuses of Evaluation

Evaluation is an integral part of the managerial process and provides useful information for decision making. It is also a part of a larger political context that influences the decision-making process. Information derived from evaluation efforts can be used to affect decisions at all stages of the managerial process: planning, implementation, and control. But for various reasons, evaluation may frequently be used, or be misused, in the processes of planning, implementation, and control. Following are some of the factors that lead to the use, nonuse, or misuse of evaluation in the decision-making process.

Timing

Although all programs can be evaluated, there is often merit in delaying any substantive evaluation and engaging preliminary assessment of the program's basic design. Specifically, evaluability assessment determines whether:

- program objectives are well-defined. Have the individuals in charge of the program defined the objectives in terms of quantifiable measures of performance and are data on these measures obtainable at a reasonable cost?
- program assumptions and objectives are plausible. Is there evidence that program activities have some likelihood of meeting the objectives?
- intended uses of evaluation information are well defined. Have those in charge of the program defined any intended uses of the information generated by the evaluation? (Wholey 1979)

Answers to these questions provide a basis for determining which programs are most likely to benefit from a more substantive evaluation activity. Evaluation resources, like program resources, are limited and should be allocated to those program activities likely to benefit from the evaluation.

Scope

Evaluations are inevitably carried out with specifically defined goals or objectives and often overlook important outcomes or results from program efforts that are guided by a series of philosophies, principles, values, and political orientations.

In trying to broaden the basis of evaluation and ensure that evaluation results are not so narrowly defined that major and important unintended consequences of programs are overlooked—or, further, to try to consider results of programs that are intended but difficult to assess—the evaluator is in an extremely difficult situation. Evaluation must be relevant to the issues with which decision makers are concerned. At the same time, evaluation must not be so narrow as to miss important aspects of programs that may be either unforeseen and unintended or that cannot be measured on an objective or quantitative basis.

One approach is to actively develop a theoretical model to assure that the evaluation identifies the full range of potential impacts (Browne and Wildavsky 1987) and based on this range narrows the focus on those that are most likely to have important managerial implications. While the theoretical and managerial may be of "different worlds," they are not mutually exclusive. As described so well by Lawler (1985, 4):

> Theory and practice are not competing mistresses. Indeed, research [evaluation] that is useful to either the theoretician or to the practitioner is suspect. If it is useful to the practitioner but not the theoretician then one must wonder whether it is a valid finding and whether it has addressed the correct issue. If it is useful to the theoretician but not to the practitioner, then one must wonder whether the research is capturing a critical issue. Indeed, it can be argued that we should always ask two questions about research [evaluation]: Is it useful for practice and does it contribute to the body of scientific knowledge that is relevant to theory? If it fails either of these tests, then serious questions should be raised. It is a rare research [evaluation] study that can inform practice but not theory or vice versa.

Interests and Perspective

Practicing managers often do not see the work of researchers or evaluators as relevant to their decision-making needs (Boyle 1989; Petasnick 1989). This situation is illustrated by the classic contrast between formative and summative evaluations. *Summative evaluation* refer to activities associated with more long-term efforts of a program, whether the program had an effect on some given indicators of performance. *Formative evaluation* refers to activities associated with the ongoing activities of the program. In general, summative evaluations seek a single decision that the program is good and should go on or that it is bad and should be terminated. Unfortunately, these decisions are almost invariably reached after the fact and are irrelevant to the decision-making process of program managers.

Evaluation must shed light on questions of interest to program managers as they go through the decision-making processes necessary to directing the program. Information presented six months after the termination of a program is of little practical consequence. On the other hand, evaluation data suggesting to the manager that program activities have not been up to expected standards for the past two weeks or that the program is not using resources at the level expected will be much more valuable for program management and decision making. Administrators clearly need continual information feedback about how a program is progressing. It may, in certain circumstances, lead to less than optimum results over the long term, but the information derived will be relevant to the decisions that program administrators must make. Moreover, given the dynamics of the field, interests—and the conditions that determine interest—change, providing evaluation activities with a relatively narrow window of opportunity.

A classic example of an extremely costly evaluation that in retrospect may not have been worth the effort in the long run is the Rand Corporation experiment to assess the effect of various types of health insurance coverage on use of services (Rand 1988). Begun in 1972, this project has produced a wealth of information and although a well-designed, experimental study, it has had little influence on policymaking with regard to any national health insurance scheme as the whole issue has been overwhelmed by the larger political environment and the emergence of managed care.

One conclusion from this example is clear: For evaluation to be useful to managers, it must provide information when they require it and relevant to their current interests. This does not necessarily mean that evaluation cannot be scientific, systematic, or formal; however, the evaluator must recognize the needs and interests of administrators for information that they can use as the program develops. Evaluators must be willing to abandon the notion that they can deal only with summative evaluation of the overall contribution of a program and be willing to make observations and judgments about the quality of a program as it progresses.

Information

Information based on some form of evaluation is not the only source of knowledge about program and service activities and their effectiveness. As described by Mintzberg, "organizational effectiveness does not lie in [the] narrow minded concept called 'rationality,' it lies in a blend of clear-headed logic and powerful intuition" (1989). Similarly, as Lindblom and Cohen in a classic distinction point out:

> Information and analysis constitute only one route among several to social problem solving. And [evaluation] is one method among several of providing information and analysis to the extent that they are required. Information and analysis provide only one route because . . . a great deal of

the world's problem solving is and ought to be accomplished through various forms of social interaction that substitute action for thought, understanding or analysis. Information and analysis are not a universal or categorical prescription for social problem solving. (1979, 10)

Lindblom and Cohen go on to indicate that a significant portion of decision making depends on ordinary knowledge, social learning, and interaction.

Ordinary knowledge refers to knowledge that does not owe its origin, testing, degree of verification, truth status, or currency to distinctive professional social inquiry techniques but rather to common sense, causal empiricism, or thoughtful speculation and analysis. Decision making regarding any health and social welfare program will always depend heavily on ordinary knowledge.

Social learning refers to the actual participation in ongoing social phenomena through which individuals learn new behavior. In many situations, information generated from evaluation is likely to be of little use until required learning occurs. It may, however, be useful to supplement social learning by answering questions that arise after, or as a result of, such learning.

Interactive problem solving refers to the resolution of problems by actions rather than by thought. Through this method, solutions are introduced to resolve a problem or improve a situation without any understanding of it or systematic assessment of remedies or preferred outcomes. Instead, the problem is resolved by various forms of interaction among people, in which what they do rather than what they or anyone else thinks (or understands or analyzes) about the problem moves toward the solution or preferred situation.

Evaluation efforts must take intuition and these other sources of information and methods of resolving problems into account. Intuition, ordinary knowledge, social learning, and interactive problem solving are real approaches, yet each can be supplemented by information generated by systematic evaluations when the evaluations are designed with the decision maker in mind.

Climate of Evaluation and Decision Making

In the best of all possible worlds, evaluation is a rational process that provides valuable information for decision making at all levels of the organization. No conscientious manager could oppose evaluation; there is a growing belief that no program or process should be without evaluation, that it should be designed into the process at the outset to ensure that the program will reach its established goals.

The real-life situation is quite different. Increasingly these decisions are made in an environment of resource scarcity, unrelenting pressure for productivity, and secrecy, limiting the amount of institutional learning that is possible. Decisions involve risk and over time these larger pressures shape the decision-making process and normalize decisions that in retrospect may be disastrous to the organization (Vaughn 1996). As if this is not complex enough, politics pervade the evaluation process and must be understood if the evaluation is to have any serious impact on program activities. At least five aspects of the political climate of evaluation must be understood. These include ambitious program objectives, explicit versus implicit objectives, externally imposed evaluation, evaluation as a political process, and evaluation as the intervention.

Ambitious Program Objectives

Programs and service activities develop as part of a political process and are likely to survive or fail on the basis of political, as opposed to technical, rationality. Programs and services that are the focus of evaluation have emerged from the rough and tumble of political support, opposition, and bargaining (Weiss 1975, 1989). Attached to them are the reputations of legislative sponsors, the careers of administrators, the jobs of program staff, and the expectations of the clients. In this environment one is naive to assume that the criterion by which program decisions are made is technical rationality based on some clear and rigorous evaluation process.

The politics involved in the establishment of a particular program are such that it is necessary for the program to perhaps exaggerate its potential contribution to meet the expectations of the various constituent groups. For example, General Motors used an astute political strategy during 1996 to launch a program for measuring health status and identifying health risks within its large U.S. work force (Mays, Miller, and Halverson 1999). The program centered around a voluntary, self-administered health appraisal form sent to all current employees as of mid-year 1996 and to all new employees thereafter. The corporation's primary interest in this program was to achieve the ability to anticipate health service needs and expenditures within its work force. With this information, the corporation could compare projected health service needs with actual utilization rates and thereby evaluate the efficiency and effectiveness of its healthcare plans and providers.

To secure the support of labor unions and healthcare providers, however, the corporation needed to stress the program's potential for fostering meaningful improvements in employee health and well-being. General Motors emphasized that health appraisal information would enable the corporation to target work site health and wellness programs that would promote health and well-being within the work force. Clearly, these objectives were ambitious and difficult to obtain. Nonetheless, this approach was successful in convincing labor unions, health plans, and providers to support the program by encouraging General Motors workers to complete and return their health appraisals.

Moreover, program objectives may need to be ambitious simply to assure the very initiation of change. For example, in 1995 the veterans' healthcare system initiated a reorganization that was unprecedented within the Veterans Health Administration (VHA). Focusing on the veteran patient as customer, the VHA has outlined a "Prescription for Change" (Kizer 1995) in which a critical component is service (or product) line management. The overarching objective is for the VHA to move its component organizations toward focusing on outcomes of the care process rather than the inputs to that process. These are "stretch" objectives for any organization as large and complex as the VHA, and they require sustained leadership and commitment throughout the organization.

While the objectives are indeed ambitious, preliminary analysis suggests that most medical centers are developing service line activities in a uniform format. Continued evaluation is required, yet, given the objectives, the organization appears to be moving along (Kilpatrick et al. 1997).

Explicit versus Implicit Objectives

The second climate problem confronting evaluation is the issue of explicit versus implicit program objectives. Regardless of the high-sounding, altruistic, or rational statements made for the existence of a program, the basis of any program may be hidden goals that are acknowledged only rarely and very seldom in public or may not even be recognized at all. As Kierkegaard observed, "Philosophy is perfectly right in saying that life must be understood backward. But then one forgets the other clause—that it must be lived forward" (1967). Mintzberg (1987) has applied that perspective to much of what happens within the managerial process. He has suggested that managers may have to live strategy (programs) in the future, but they must understand it through the past.

Even when goals are understood they are likely to be viewed differently by a variety of important constituent or stakeholder groups and may have multiple and potentially conflicting sets of activities. Organizations are composed of coalitions or stakeholders, each having a claim on a particular problematic activity. For example, program X may be viewed by one constituency or set of stakeholders as enhancing the overall quality of the service provided, yet viewed by another as an opportunity to gather a larger market share within the community. Similarly, programs may have a series of goals that are not easily combined. For example, in clinical research a program may aspire to diffuse state-of-the-art therapy and affect national mortality and morbidity levels. Similarly, within such programs a need to emphasize both prevention and treatment strategies may exist, thus raising the potential for conflict as they compete for limited resources and attention.

Second, any evaluation effort needs to recognize that program objectives are not a priori developed in a totally rational and deliberate process but can also be viewed as an emergent process evolving from the very dynamics of the organization over time. As described by Mintzberg (1987), strategies (program objectives) can form as well as be formulated. In other words, they need not be planned but can emerge in response to an evolving situation.

Consideration must also be given to situations in which program personnel may be characterized as "true believers." True believers are committed not only to a goal or set of goals but in general are also committed to a specific process for achieving those goals. Improving the health of the U.S. population may be a desirable goal, but many physicians in private practice are likely to believe that it should not and cannot be done by providing medical services through public financing. Certainly they are apt to agree that providing medical services under public control cannot do it. The physician is a true believer in the efficacy of the private pursuit of and payment for medical care services.

The belief that providing more medical services will in itself improve health status is another aspect of the true believer phenomenon. A recent well-reasoned paper concludes that there is only a minimal contribution of medical care services to health status as broadly defined (Bunker, Frazier, and Mosteller 1994). In the case of medical services, however, not only are program providers—physicians, hospitals, and clinics—populated by true believers, but the served population itself also tends to be a population of true believers.

Evaluation is almost impossible in programs in which true believers are in control. Because they believe a priori in the efficacy of a particular process, they are unwilling to allow that process to be subjected to evaluation. Moreover, they are likely to be unaware of the fact that the views they hold about the efficacy of a particular process are even subject to the possibility of evaluation. In such circumstances, the evaluator is likely to have substantial difficulty in affecting program activities.

Externally Imposed Evaluation

An external agent or agency may represent a higher-echelon decision-making level to which a program director reports; this level may be an outside resource important in terms of funding or an expert in evaluation working within the program itself. In any case, the politics of the situation are such that the evaluator will be in the position of power and authority with regard to the program. Few people, including managers, are so ingenuous as to welcome a free scrutiny of their affairs no matter how benign, uncritical, or even helpful that scrutiny is meant to be. If the data-gathering phase of the evaluation is successful, the evaluator is in possession of a great deal of information about a program that may have serious ramifications for its continuation and for the positions of the people in it.

If the evaluation is imposed from the top, program personnel are immediately on the defensive. They are likely to view the evaluation as an effort of the superordinate agency either to control program operations or to find reasons and excuses to modify or terminate the program. In this case, the evaluator is already at a clear disadvantage.

Even if the evaluation is not imposed from the top down or from the outside in, even in that highly desirable circumstance where the manager personally requests the evaluation or where evaluation has been built into the program at the outset, a problem that is basically political and that affects the use of evaluation results still exists. Evaluators are apt to be people who consider themselves professionals in the realm of evaluation. As professionals, they must demonstrate their expertise, which means that the evaluation must be both methodologically elegant and conceptually comprehensive. The evaluator is probably trained in one of the social sciences, partly because social science training usually includes a large measure of work in research methodology and statistics. Although this training is highly appropriate to evaluation efforts, it may be quite different from training that would lead logically to the ability to view the program from a manager's perspective. One problem of social science training, for example, is the fact that simplifying a research effort so that it confronts issues specifically of interest to and relevant for decision making is extremely difficult. Social scientists have a long tradition of launching large-scale research efforts without much thought about specific information requirements or the ability or desire to limit the amount of information gathered. As a result, many evaluation efforts become overblown and miss an opportunity to contribute to important management questions.

Large-scale studies launched without much thought about how the information will be used or with little effort to limit the activity to essentials may be acceptable for academic endeavors but are highly inappropriate for evaluation. Not only are the audiences to whom the evaluation is addressed likely to question the relevance and value of this specific evaluation, and hence the relevance and value of every such effort, but managers will probably also be quite unhappy about being required to cooperate with and perhaps participate in an activity they do not understand. The politics of evaluation are often such that there is conflict between the evaluator and manager. Successful evaluation requires the evaluator to begin with the agenda of the manager and those individuals involved with service delivery.

Evaluation as a Political Process

Those involved in evaluation often prefer to deny the reality of politics vis-à-vis their evaluation activity, yet the fact that evaluation is an integral part of the management process places it squarely in a political context. Weiss (1989), for example, discusses three ways in which politics and evaluation are related:

1. The programs being evaluated are by definition political: They have legislative sponsors and supporters, administrative careers attached to them, and the support of program staff, clients, and interest groups.
2. Evaluation reports are fed into a political arena and by definition become part of the political decision process.
3. Evaluation reports themselves by definition take a political position even if they claim to be objective.

Programs that are evaluated are the result of a long and complicated political process in which winners, losers, and various important constituents exist. Moreover, each group has its own perceptions of what the program is trying to accomplish, independent of its explicit goals. Evaluation results must fit into this ongoing process and must take into account the shifting in alliances and expectations that occur between the onset of the evaluation and its report of findings.

Finally, the evaluation itself implicitly assumes a political position. Presenting results, no matter how well designed and executed, has political overtones. For example, what is selected or not selected for study has important consequences because the unexamined program or program aspect has not become the focus of political debate centered on the allocation of scarce resources (Palumbo 1987). Moreover, programs may be in trouble even before evaluation occurs. It is precisely when programs are in trouble—particularly when the trouble is a threat to funding—that evaluators are invited to assess the program (Gurel 1975). Visualizing the chilly reception that evaluation and the evaluator are then likely to receive from program managers takes little imagination.

For example, administrators of the public hospital and primary care system serving Los Angeles, California, spent almost 30 years discussing the system's inefficiency and ineffectiveness in addressing community health needs. Administrators were ultimately forced to consider a program for restructuring the system in mid-year 1995 when federal officials denied almost $600 million in Medicaid claims submitted by the system. A massive federal bailout of the system ultimately averted financial crisis, but it came with the stipulation that the county conduct a thorough evaluation and reorganization of the system (Margolin 1996; Friedlub 1997).

The political environment of evaluation leads even the most optimistic evaluator to doubt the probability of having a useful impact on program decisions and operations. Certainly, if evaluators are to be effective, they must have a fundamental understanding of the political climate surrounding the evaluation effort in which they participate. Evaluators will probably be more effective if they recognize the characteristics of decisions that may result from evaluation efforts. An understanding of these categories can be useful to the evaluators in trying to make the work meaningful to program managers.

Evaluation as the Intervention

Finally, the evaluation itself may be the intervention. Programs that are purported to be put in place to accomplish a desirable goal often have weak, underfunded, or unclear interventions—a question of adequacy. What is not unreasonable in a situation such as this is for the existence of the evaluation, particularly the initiation of the evaluation activities, to become the force that focuses attention necessary for program activities to be undertaken. This may be fine in terms of the goals of the program initiators—they want something to happen. If the intervention does lead to program activity, however, it will never be possible to separate the effect of the program from the effect of the evaluation itself.

Plan for This Text

Figure 1.3 presents the basic structure of this book. The intent is not to make the reader an expert in either methodology or various types of evaluation but to give health professionals a better understanding of, and a set of basic tools to deal with, the evaluation problems frequently confronted in the provision of health services. This chapter defines the various types of evaluation and its relationship to the organization and the managerial process. Chapter 2 presents a model of evaluation and illustrates its application to continuously improving program and organizational decision making.

Chapters 3 through 12 outline various strategies appropriate to different types of evaluation and are divided into five major sections: monitoring, case studies, survey research, trend analysis, and experimental design. Chapters 13 through 17 represent methods that are useful in several of the evaluation strategies: general measurement issues, utility measures, sampling, operations research, and cost-benefit/effectiveness/utility analysis.

FIGURE 1.3
Plan for This Text

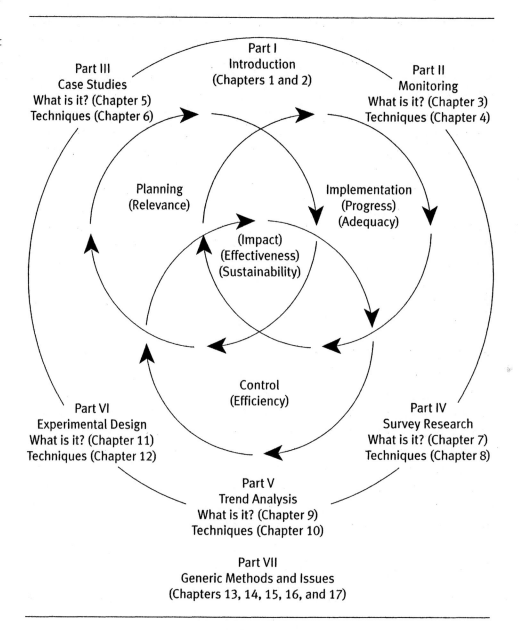

Part I
Introduction
(Chapters 1 and 2)

Part III
Case Studies
What is it? (Chapter 5)
Techniques (Chapter 6)

Part II
Monitoring
What is it? (Chapter 3)
Techniques (Chapter 4)

Planning
(Relevance)

Implementation
(Progress)
(Adequacy)

(Impact)
(Effectiveness)
(Sustainability)

Control
(Efficiency)

Part VI
Experimental Design
What is it? (Chapter 11)
Techniques (Chapter 12)

Part IV
Survey Research
What is it? (Chapter 7)
Techniques (Chapter 8)

Part V
Trend Analysis
What is it? (Chapter 9)
Techniques (Chapter 10)

Part VII
Generic Methods and Issues
(Chapters 13, 14, 15, 16, and 17)

The first chapter in each section defines the strategy, its limitation and the type of data required for its use, and the application of the approach to the various functions of evaluation. The second chapter outlines various techniques appropriate to that strategy and illustrates their use in different health services situations. The presentation of respective strategies does not imply that any one strategy is to be used to the exclusion of others. In fact, any well-designed evaluation requires multiple strategies, as Denzin describes: "No single method ever adequately solves the problem of rival causal factors—because each method reveals different aspects of empirical reality, multiple methods of observation must be employed. This is termed triangulation" (1978, 28).

In reality, the use of multiple methods is somewhat idealistic given limited funds, short time frames, and the political constraints affecting most evaluative activities. Thus, the evaluator is forced to select one particular strategy and supplement it with others, time and resources permitting. Following is a brief consideration of the strategies presented in Parts II through VII.

Part II deals with *monitoring* and begins with Chapter 3, which is concerned with monitoring program progress and improvement, whether necessary inputs are being provided, and if the program is operating as projected. In many settings monitoring is an overlooked and underrated aspect of the evaluation process; it is often the total evaluation, however. Chapter 3 deals with the appropriate setting in which monitoring should be conducted and outlines the types of data most appropriate for the monitoring task. Chapter 4 presents the analytical techniques that may be used with data collected for monitoring. The chapter deals with a variety of program-planning techniques such as PERT (Program Evaluation and Review Technique), Gantt charts, and critical path method, as well as a variety of quality improvement techniques such as control charts and run diagrams.

Part III presents the *case study* approach to evaluation. Chapter 5 discusses the appropriate setting for case studies, types of data that can be used, and various applications of case study results to program evaluation. Chapter 6 describes a series of analytical techniques helpful in using case studies as an evaluation strategy, offers various illustrations, and emphasizes how the interpretation of case studies may facilitate or impede program decision making.

Part IV focuses on *survey research* as an evaluation approach, with particular emphasis on its use in addressing questions of efficiency, effectiveness, and program impact. Chapter 7 defines survey research and discusses the appropriate settings in which it can be applied to evaluation, plus the type of data that can be used in this approach. Chapter 8 discusses various data analysis techniques appropriate to survey research, including the use of contingency tables, regression, and structural equations. The chapter concludes with an interpretation of survey data and the application of survey results to program decision making.

Part V deals with *trend analysis*. This approach combines characteristics of monitoring, case studies, and survey research and can be particularly useful in the absence of an experimental design in providing information about program effectiveness and impact. Chapter 9 defines trend analysis and outlines the appropriate settings for it and the types of data required for its successful application. Chapter 10 focuses on the analytical techniques that can be employed in trend analysis and builds on techniques initially outlined in Chapter 9. Emphasis will be given to regression techniques and methods.

Part VI deals with *experimental design* as an evaluation format. Experimental design is the most powerful evaluation strategy, particularly when directed to evaluation issues of impact. Chapter 11 defines various experimental designs applicable to different health service settings. The chapter considers the appropriate conditions for experimental design as well as types of data required for useful results. Special attention goes to various evaluation projects that have used experimental design to illustrate problems of interpretation and their overall impact on decision making. Chapter 12 discusses various analysis techniques appropriate to experimental designs, with emphasis on analysis of variance and the general interpretation of results and their use in decision making.

Finally, Part VII focuses on some *generic methodological techniques* basic to all evaluation approaches. Chapter 13 deals with general measurement issues often encountered in evaluation projects. It defines measurement and describes the process by which measurement rules are developed and applied and the types of scales and techniques used in scale construction. Chapter 14 focuses on a specific measurement issue that is assuming increasing importance in the health services field, the measurement of utility. It discusses several different strategies for measuring utilities, including standard gamble, time trade-off, rating scales, and paired comparisons, and concludes with a discussion of quality adjusted life years (QALYS) and disability adjusted life years (DALYs) as utility measures applied to populations. Chapter 15 discusses various sampling techniques. The chapter outlines basic issues and concepts of sampling and problems of sampling in different evaluation strategies; specific recommendations for sample selection appropriate to monitoring, case studies, surveys, trend analysis, and experiments are presented. Chapter 16 presents various operations research techniques and their application in decision making. Attention is given to model building, simulation, mathematical programming and queuing, and particularly their relevance to health services. Chapter 17 deals with cost benefit and cost effectiveness. Techniques involved in cost benefit and cost effectiveness and their applications to various health service settings are described. Readers not familiar with these basic issues are asked to acquaint themselves with this material before reading material on the various evaluation strategies, beginning with Part II and ending with Part VI.

Discussion Questions

1. Select a health service program with which you are familiar and define the types of issues resolved by the various types of evaluations: relevance; adequacy; progress; efficiency; effectiveness; impact; and sustainability.
2. Distinguish research from evaluation. What features are common to both activities? What features are unique to each activity?
3. Under what conditions is it advisable to undertake an evaluability assessment? Is it equally applicable to all types of evaluation? Why or why not?
4. What are some problems that evaluators experience when they work with program managers? Why do managers experience some of these problems when they work with evaluators? Consider mechanisms to use in overcoming these problems.

EVALUATION AND THE DECISION-MAKING PROCESS

Many, if not most, managers deny—or are at the very least skeptical of—anything as abstract as a "decision model." In reality, however, managers are always being influenced by information, or lack thereof, that implicitly or explicitly forms the basis of their decisions about the nature of a problem and about the effects of some program and/or service activity implemented to address that problem. The purpose of this chapter is to describe what will be referred to as the *evaluation-based decision model*, a model that formally incorporates information into the decision-making process about the problem being studied and the effects of program and service activity on that problem.

This chapter is presented in four sections, each dealing with an aspect of the decision-making process. The first section describes the evaluation-based decision model and how this model relates to other decision models that may be used to make program decisions or other types of decisions and the criteria appropriate to guide the use of these models. The other three sections of the chapter describe components of the evaluation-based decision model: needs assessment, program implementation, and outcomes assessment.

As shown in Figure 2.1, each phase of program operation is generally associated with particular types of questions in program evaluation and with related evaluation techniques. Needs assessment, for example, is most closely related to the issue of relevance and adequacy; it adopts survey-related techniques such as random sample surveys, Delphi studies and solicitation of expert opinion, and use of available data. Program implementation is most closely related to the issue of progress and adopts techniques like monitoring and related operations research techniques. Results assessment is related to issues of efficiency, effectiveness, outcomes, and sustainability and adopts, again, survey techniques, cost-benefit and cost-effectiveness analysis, time series analysis, and experimentation. The detailed discussion of these methodological techniques is the major focus of the subsequent sections of the book.

The Evaluation-Based Decision Model

Central to the evaluation-based decision model is the idea of "cybernetics" (Weiner 1948). The term cybernetics has become popular as a way of defining a methodological approach to a wide variety of scientific and management endeavors

FIGURE 2.1

Schematic View
of Components
of Evaluation

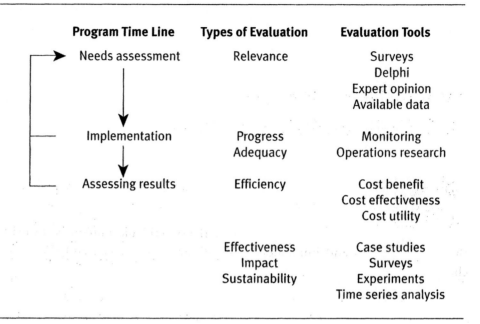

Program Time Line	Types of Evaluation	Evaluation Tools
Needs assessment	Relevance	Surveys
		Delphi
		Expert opinion
		Available data
Implementation	Progress	Monitoring
	Adequacy	Operations research
Assessing results	Efficiency	Cost benefit
		Cost effectiveness
		Cost utility
	Effectiveness	Case studies
	Impact	Surveys
	Sustainability	Experiments
		Time series analysis

and is closely linked with general systems theory and its applications in the social, organizational (Scott 1998; Senge 1990), and management sciences (Deming 1986, 93). The idea of cybernetics is intuitively simple (Hage 1974) and is characterized by two major components:

- There exists a system of interrelated variables that represent some production process—in the broadest sense, a process for accomplishing an end. These variables include inputs, throughputs, and outputs.
- Some of the variables in the input-throughput-output system are being regulated and controlled by decisions made on the basis of the feedback of information about the state of the system.

The essence of the evaluation-based decision model is shown in Figure 2.2. This figure is a schematic of the input-throughput-output model showing the

FIGURE 2.2

The Evaluation-
Based Decision
Model

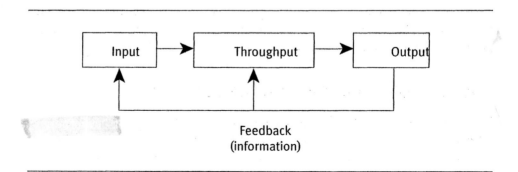

Feedback
(information)

feedback of information that leads to control where control is based on communication of information in any system, whether complex or simple. This view of cybernetics and its application within the evaluation-based decision model is the fundamental basis of managerial decision making.

The conceptual basis of the model is relatively simple. It begins with the assumption that verifiable ends (outcomes) exist that are expected to result from the activity. The extent to which the activity has been successful in producing these verifiable ends can thus be evaluated at various points in time during the life of the program and at its completion. The information about the gap between the expected outcomes and the actual outcomes is then used to modify either inputs or process, during program operation or before a similar program is launched in the future, to attempt to reduce the gap between the verifiable expected outputs and the actual outputs. If no verifiable outcomes do exist, the very initiation and implementation of such activity can and should be challenged.

Alternate Decision-Making Models

The evaluation-based decision model is but one of the four models available to managers and must be viewed in the context of the other three alternatives: random-walk decision making, traditional decision making, and mechanistic decision making. Figure 2.3 presents the four types of decision making as defined by the four cells of a two-by-two means/ends table. The horizontal axis is defined as a verifiable (i.e., to know when a process has been successful is possible) versus a nonverifiable end and on the vertical axis by whether the means to obtain the end is accepted or not accepted. Accepted or not accepted means that in a given setting a particular decision process and, hence, course of action would generally be expected to produce the desired outcomes in a direct, linear manner with no error along the way. An accepted means is essentially a recipe for moving directly to the desired output with no mistakes.

It should be understood that these decision-making modes are ideal types. By that, we mean that in virtually no real decision-making situation will the ideal type that we described be the only method that is likely to be brought to bear.

	Ends	
	Not Verifiable	Verifiable
Not Accepted	Random Walk	Cybernetic
Accepted	Traditional	Mechanistic

FIGURE 2.3
Means-Ends
Decision Table

Further, we do not claim that the ideal-type decision models we are going to suggest are totally exhaustive of all decision models. Nevertheless, it is useful to suggest these types as a point of departure.

To understand this typology, consider the category "accepted means and verifiable end." This is the *mechanistic model* of decision making (Deutsch 1968). Mechanistic decision making occurs when the ends are verifiable and the appropriate decision process (the means) is known and accepted. This is the realm, for example, of linear programming. If a hospital wishes to maximize its dollar profits from a course of action (a verifiable end) subject to a set of constraints, the decision process, and thus the course of action, can be determined by a widely understood and accepted mathematical algorithm. The means is accepted, and at some point the fact that the result of the set of decisions is the optimum result can be verified. Yet trying other alternative decisions in this context is generally not necessary because the linear programming model is the model known to produce the optimum result.

When a nonverifiable end or set of nonverifiable ends is desired, and no accepted means of reaching these ends exists, the decision process is in the realm of the *random walk*. Because the goals or ends are not verifiable and the appropriate decision process, and thus course of action, for reaching the nonverifiable goals are not accepted or specified, any decisions will be as good as any others. In essence, a random decision process is adequate. The random process may ultimately arrive at a desired result, but it will not be verifiable, in any case.

Appropriately, managers are uncomfortable with random decision making. What very often happens during this situation of being uncomfortable is that a particular means is institutionalized even in the absence of verifiable ends or confirmation that the accepted means will produce a verified desired end. This is the mode of *traditional decision making.* In this mode of decision making decisions can be made for long periods of time without ever being subjected to any further scrutiny than that they adhere to a particular institutionalized decision-making process. In effect, the process becomes the product.

If program goals or ends can be stated in ways that achievement of the ends can be verified but no accepted means to obtain the ends exists, the decision-making process may be in the realm of *cybernetic,* or *evaluation-based decision making*. In this form, information about the extent to which a particular decision or set of decisions brings the program closer to the verifiable ends can be used to modify the decisions next taken. By doing this, an effort can be made to assure that the result comes ever closer to the desired ends.

When ends are not verifiable or the necessary effort to verify them is not likely to be made (the realm of random walks or traditional decision making), evaluation cannot proceed because evaluation refers specifically to the assessment of the extent to which ends are reached. Further, no reason to conduct evaluation would exist. In the absence of verifiable ends no information will be produced that can be used for making better decisions than the ones already being made.

Decision Mode Drift

Despite the efforts and good intentions of both managers and evaluators, much of decision making follows closely either the random walk model or the traditional model. Much of what goes by the name of evaluation is actually a process of examining decisions that are made either on the basis of random walks or of tradition. To the extent that this is true, much that goes by the name of program evaluation is wasted effort because in both situations the ends are not verifiable.

A number of reasons can be cited for why decision making tends to drift toward the random walk mode, and particularly toward the traditional mode. The ability to verify that an end has been achieved is the central problem. What may begin as a clear effort to operate within the evaluation-based decision realm (i.e., clearly defined and verifiable ends available to assess results of decisions and courses of action through feedback) may quickly drift to either the random walk mode or to the traditional mode of decision making since verifiable ends are not easily accessible.

Decision mode drift may happen for several reasons. Program managers may decide that the cost of verifying program ends is greater than expected or greater than the value of verification. This perception is usually accompanied by a stated or unstated rationale that is something like "I know that this is the right course of action, so it is not reasonable to spend 25 percent of my program delivery budget on evaluation that will only confirm what I already know." In fact, this is probably often true.

Originally specified and verifiable goals may not express the full range of results expected from a program. It is unfortunate that verifiable goals may often be relatively trivial in the context of a program—the goal of a training program may be to impart the ability to deliver a complex skilled service, but the only verifiable (measurable) goal for the training program may be that a certain number of persons have been subjected to training. As goals become more complex, the decision-making process drifts toward the traditional or random walk modes.

Results that managers see from a program may not be as attractive as they had hoped. In this situation, there is a tendency to kill the messenger by dismantling what might be a fairly serious cybernetic decision effort and falling back into the random walk or traditional modes, in which the lack of attempts to verify achievement of ends will not be a threat to program personnel or continuation of the program itself.

Mechanistic decision making, which is an appropriate realm of evaluation only to the extent that continued verification of the efficacy of a particular decision process is desired, may also drift toward traditional modes of decision making as ends become more complex. What may be a straightforward, mechanistic decision process in the presence of a relatively simple set of goals (e.g., a linear programming model to maximize hospital profits) may revert to traditional decision making as the goals become more difficult to measure (e.g., improved community health status). The ideal situation would be that the mechanistic decision process would retrench at cybernetic decision making, but this will happen only if the necessary steps are taken to specify in measurable terms and to verify the more complex ends.

Evaluation-Based versus Mechanistic Decision Making

Why is the evaluation-based model—implying feedback of information about the extent to which a given decision results in achievement of a given goal—the proper realm of evaluation, while evaluation is likely to be redundant in a setting in which mechanistic decision making—implying both a verifiable end and an accepted way to reach the end—is used? As a simple example, consider the problem of finding the square root of a number. The square root of a number is defined as that number which when multiplied by itself will give the original number. Today, with the widespread availability of battery-powered calculators that provide square roots to ten decimal places at the push of a button, hardly anyone thinks of finding square roots as a decision problem, except possibly in the most trivial sense (i.e., "to find the square root of a number, enter the number into the hand calculator and push the square root button").

Not too long ago, however, finding a square root for a large number was far from a trivial matter. Tables of square roots were published in mathematics texts, but they always required approximation. People learned to use logarithms to find square roots, but these also usually required approximations. Anyone going to school before the 1960s probably learned a tedious method for extracting square roots, which most have long forgotten. This was a mechanistic method in the sense that if people learned the necessary steps and followed them faithfully without making any mistakes in arithmetic, they could produce the square root of any number to any number of decimal places desired without ever checking to see if the process was producing the right result. The result was assured by the decision-making process.

The square root of a number can also be found by a purely cybernetic decision process (i.e., feedback method) that many of us hit upon independently when we first had access to electrically powered mechanical calculators that would multiply relatively quickly but that would not take square roots directly. With this method, memorizing an accepted decision process was not needed. All that was required was to make a first guess at the square root of the number and then multiply the guess by itself. The result, however wrong it may have been, was compared to the original number for which the square root was desired. If the result was bigger than the original number, then the original guess at the square root was too large and had to be adjusted down. If the result was smaller than the original number, the original guess at the square root was too small and had to be adjusted up. The size of the adjustment in either direction depended on how bad the first guess was. On the basis of this adjustment, a new number to approximate the square root was selected and the process repeated. This could be done as many times as necessary to obtain the accuracy required by the application.

In effect, this method used feedback of information (evaluation) about the difference between what was produced and what was desired to make a decision about what to do next. This was an evaluation-based decision process and was within the appropriate realm of evaluation. To determine which method was best in this situation is unnecessary. Either method produced a usable result. Many situations exist, however, in which no mechanistic method of decision making is available. In such settings, only cybernetic decision making and evaluation are likely to produce the results desired.

Using Decision-Making Models

Given the complexity within which evaluation occurs, what criteria are appropriate in the use of each model? Three tests are available for managers and can be applied in a variety of situations: instrumental, efficiency, and social tests (Thompson 1967, 84–87). The appropriateness is a function of the degree of clear formulation or ambiguity of standards of desirability and the completeness or incompleteness of cause-and-effect relationships. Table 2.1 presents the relationship of these tests to our four decision-making models.

Instrumental Tests

As shown in Table 2.1, instrumental tests are primarily appropriate for decision making within the evaluation-based model. Here the standards of desirability are reasonably clear, and the cause-and-effect relationships are uncertain. For example, will national health insurance produce greater access to health services for all people? Will managed care programs contain costs of providing services to various segments of the population, and do consensus conferences as a means of technology assessment change physician practice patterns? These are essentially technical questions in which the major criterion is to ascertain only whether the desired ends were achieved, without considering resource utilization or the exact means by which this was accomplished.

In this area the evaluator can make the most important contributions to program decision making. The tools available to the evaluator—measurement techniques, sampling, survey designs, experimentation—are all techniques that conform to the instrumental approach to information. As long as an issue is basically technical, the evaluator is in the most effective realm, although the evaluator is always at risk of challenge if the results do not conform to the expectations of important constituent groups.

For example, in a randomized clinical trial of coronary care units, an initial report showing a greater death rate for those treated in hospitals than those treated

	Decision Models				
Criteria	Cybernetic	Mechanistic	Traditional	Random Walk	
Instrumental	X				
Efficiency		X			
Social			X	X	

TABLE 2.1
Decision Models and Criteria

at home was mistakenly reversed. When these data were presented to a group of cardiologists, they demanded that the trials be declared unethical and the study be stopped immediately because the results did not conform to their expectations. When the mistake was identified and the data presented correctly, the same group could not be persuaded to declare the trials unethical but found all sorts of problems with the study sampling and measurement procedures (Cochrane 1972).

Not all questions can be answered on the basis of instrumental tests. Many questions of belief and values are simply not subject to technical verification or refutation. Even in those areas where technical criteria (empirical verification) can apply, measurement may be so difficult or complex that arriving at even a technical answer is impossible. Furthermore, the myriad of desirable ends that a particular program is to accomplish and the difficulty of objectively measuring all these ends usually make hoping that technical rationality alone can resolve all decision-making problems for program operation impossible.

Efficiency Tests

Where instrumental criteria in the broad sense raise the question of whether demonstrating empirically that the means employed produces the ends desired is possible, efficiency criteria tackles the question of whether the specific means employed is the most efficient means for producing the ends desired. This is critical to the mechanistic model, in which cause-and-effect relationships are well understood. The assumption is that alternative means exist by which a particular end may be reached or, at the very least, that the program has the option of producing a certain amount of a desired end and that the means will be exercised only to the extent that the cost of producing the amount of the end desired is acceptable.

Again, if evaluation is limited to the aspect of technical rationality that may be seen as economic rationality, evaluators are generally on firm ground. Cost-benefit analysis, cost-effectiveness analysis, and optimization techniques available from operations research are all capable of producing useful information about the most efficient means of realizing desired ends.

Social Tests

As shown in Table 2.1, social tests are appropriate to random walk and traditional decision-making models, where standards of desirability are ambiguous regardless of cause-and-effect relationships. Under these conditions, criteria are validated by authority or consensus.

Abortion, for example, is technically an effective means of birth control. Yet in many countries both its legal and social acceptability remain in contention. Many genetic defects and genetically transmitted diseases could be effectively controlled from a technical standpoint through programs to control procreation. Again, in most societies these programs would be neither legally nor socially acceptable. Substantial questions could be raised as to whether the notion of primary healthcare as currently promoted by the World Health Organization (WHO) and the United Nations Children's Fund (UNICEF) is technically the most rational way to approach the goal of "health for all by the year 2000." This modality, which relies heavily on local self-help and to a great extent on lay practitioners, has a substantial degree of social rationality for many of the developing nations in which it is to be implemented. On the other hand, because of the continuing restrictions on what non-physicians may legally do in many of these societies, the legal rationality of the primary care programs may still be subject to question.

Similarly, a given program may be more a means of controlling resources, maintaining a particular elite in power, or providing a hope to special interest groups or disgruntled portions of the population than a way of actually eliminating or reducing the problem to which the program is manifestly addressed. Every large-scale program, despite its true relationships to desired ends from the technical standpoint, is likely to have a substantial component of political rationality in its formulation. For example, recent federal and state programs designed to regulate the utilization management practices of managed care plans offer prime illustrations of political rationality in program design. Some of these programs require managed care plans to offer minimum hospital stays for certain medical procedures such as childbirth, while others specify the conditions under which certain medical procedures can be performed on an outpatient basis.

Clearly, to implement governmental programs and regulations that established standards of practice for every possible medical procedure and condition would be impossible. Consequently, the existing piecemeal programs are unlikely to have a significant effect on the quality of care delivered through managed care plans. Nevertheless, these programs serve the political purpose of appeasing the healthcare consumers and providers who express concerns about quality of care within managed care plans.

When the prevailing criteria of program planners and managers are primarily social, the evaluator may have little effect on decision making. In fact, the evaluator's findings will probably be largely irrelevant to decision making because decisions are being made on the basis of criteria that are not essentially technical and that cannot be verified empirically. In this case, the evaluator may provide useful insights to decision makers about the technical characteristics of the program and perhaps clarify political trade-offs but cannot expect the work to have a significant impact on the decision. The evaluator should be aware of the appropriate tests within each decision model. Failure to apply the appropriate tests within each model will limit the ability of the evaluation to influence the decision-making process—as well as elucidate the evaluator's own role in that process.

Components of the Evaluation-Based Decision Model

Needs assessment, implementation, and assessing outcomes are critical elements in the evaluation-based decision model. Following are descriptions of each component, their respective approaches, and their challenges.

Needs Assessment

Needs assessment is the first stage in program implementation and is the process of determining the nature and extent of the problems that a program is designed to address; it is the assessment of the relevance and adequacy of the program. In particular, this means that information about the problem—a gap between the desired state of some verifiable end and the actual state of that verifiable end—is used as the basis on which to structure, direct, and assess the adequacy of a program. This information may include:

- the nature of the problem;
- its extent;
- who or what it affects;
- where and when it occurs;
- its frequency; and
- any other salient information.

But it is information about the problem on which the nature of the program is based, not particularly on guesses about the problem (random walk decision making) or the assumption in the absence of data that the problem fits into a previously defined mold (traditional decision making).

A needs assessment may possibly indicate that the problem is amenable to solution by one or another systematic decision-making technique, such as linear programming. This decision in itself, however, should be made within the context of information about the actual nature of the problem.

At least two reasons exist why evaluation-based decision making may fail to be used in determining the problem that the program is to address and how it will be addressed. The first of these reasons is the problem of institutionalized (previously accepted) means, and the second is expert bias. Institutionalized objectives limit effective needs assessment, particularly as they restrict the range of issues that a program may be permitted to address. Expert bias refers to the basic misconception that many experts may have about what the actual problem may be.

The issue of institutionalized objectives is one in which the problem is stated in such a way that only one or a limited number of program solutions can be adopted. For example, use of family planning services in a country may be a function of the quality and extent of training of service providers. The use will also be a function of the political situation, the degree to which people desire family planning, the availability of supplies and equipment and attractive clinics in which to provide services, and a host of other factors. If the institutionalized means of training is the driving force behind the needs assessment, it is likely that the needs assessment will find that more training of service providers is needed, even if other interventions may have a greater effect on contraceptive use.

Institutionalized objectives are often determined by agencies that fund programs; no matter how good the needs-assessment effort may be in a technical sense, it may not, by the very nature of institutionalized objectives, be useful in improving the situation relative to selected verifiable ends.

Expert bias is the problem that those who are expected to carry out the needs assessment—the "experts"—may have predetermined notions about what the needs assessment should show. For example:

- Physicians assessing emergency medical care in a community may well determine that what is needed is expanded and improved medical services in emergency rooms.
- A representative of a law enforcement agency may conclude that the problem was the need for better control of highway accidents.
- The ambulance service may conclude that what is needed is a better distribution of emergency vehicles.
- A social scientist may conclude that the problem is the need to control domestic violence.

This is different from the problem of institutionalized means because in the case of institutionalized means a serious and detailed effort to examine the problem may exist, but only from the standpoint of a single or limited number of programmatic aspects. In the case of expert bias, the problem may never actually be examined at all, but simply be assumed to exist by an expert doing the assessment, who by virtue of expertise itself may not recognize the need to empirically verify the assumed problem.

A number of strategies exist that can be used in the conduct of a needs assessment and in the determination of the relevance and adequacy of a program intervention. These include survey research, use of available data, Delphi and nominal group techniques, and expert judgments. Survey research techniques are presented in detail in Chapters 7 and 8. The use of available data, Delphi and nominal group techniques, and expert judgments are presented in Chapter 6. The steps of the needs assessment process include:

Approaches to needs assessment

1. Develop a general statement of what the program is expected to accomplish.
2. Determine the degree and nature of the problem that the program is expected to address and determine the level of accomplishment that may actually be realized.
3. Determine the strategies that should be employed by the program to address the identified problem.

Following is an illustration and discussion of each step.

The first step in the needs assessment is to develop a general statement about what the program or service activity is expected to accomplish. For example, in the area of maternal and child health services:

1. Developing program expectations

- Is the program expected to produce a set of activities to slow the rate of increase in the growth of the population?
- Is the program expected to reduce the number of unwanted pregnancies?
- Is the program expected to reduce the incidence of maternal and neonatal mortality and morbidity through child spacing?

- Is the program expected to increase the number of first-time acceptors of family planning methods?
- Is the program expected to increase the prevalence of family planning use?
- Is the program expected to increase the number of women who have favorable attitudes toward the use of family planning services?

In fact, the program organizers are likely to say that the program is expected to do all the things indicated in the preceding list, and more. Herein lies the first barrier for evaluation-based decision making, however. Managers are unlikely to be willing to expend the resources necessary to define adequately, and then to measure routinely, each possible end previously indicated. A few of the ends may be measured and the rest are left to faith, and to the traditional—or perhaps worse, random-walk—decision mode. Agreement on the ends is only the first step in the needs assessment, however.

2. Determining the nature and degree of the problem

To realistically determine what is to be accomplished by the program requires a combination of techniques including a review of existing data, survey data of risk factors, community-based interviews, and an inventory of available healthcare resources within the community. Specifically:

- *Review of existing state, local, and national health data.* Existing sources of data provide important yet often overlooked data sources to assess geographic, economic, and demographic characteristics of the community. These sources provide important insights to the principle causes of morbidity and mortality and utilization of health services within the community.
- *Telephone survey of behavioral risk factors.* While secondary data provides the base for determining need, assessing what people within the community think about their own health status and determining the health risk factors that may affect their health in the future is also important. This information can be obtained through a random telephone survey of a representative sample of the community. The survey should include a broad range of topics including levels of physical and mental health and levels of healthcare coverage.
- *Community focus group interviews.* These interviews are conducted to gain information on the perceptions of citizens' focus groups and to provide an opportunity to gain insight into health concerns of the community beyond that revealed in interview surveys. Focus groups must have a good representation of the community, including adolescents, business leaders, parents, senior citizens, homeless citizens, and other special population groups.
- *Healthcare resources inventory.* To determine the level of health resources available in the community, interviews need to be conducted with health professionals and community leaders. Information should

include issues dealing with health insurance, types of providers available, and the overall availability of healthcare within the community.

A third step in the needs assessment is to determine what programs or service activities should be employed to address the problems specified. One approach that has proven useful is the application of a rating technology using a computer program known as "Option Finder" (Flexner 1995; Halverson 1995). This approach involves all the relevant participants and stakeholders and provides an opportunity to vote interactively in the following sequence:

3. Determining strategies

1. Review risk factors and their definitions and, taking one risk factor at a time, rate each factor on its perceived "seriousness" using a scale of 1 (little impact on community health) to 7 (major impact on community health).
2. Given the risk factor ranking relative to "seriousness," rate the risk factor list again on "willingness," or likelihood that the community can work together on addressing this particular risk, using a scale of 1 (little willingness to collaborate) to 7 (high willingness to collaborate).
3. Figure 2.4 displays a grid for comparing and identifying those factors that fell in the various quadrants giving a sense of the highest priorities to be addressed.

At this point, participants are encouraged to explore possible explanations for the data and why certain factors had been rated high and others low. The technology allowed facilitators to display the spread of votes and degree of variation in votes on each factor of special interest (as in high-impact risk factors that the group believed would not enlist high community effort, such as smoking).

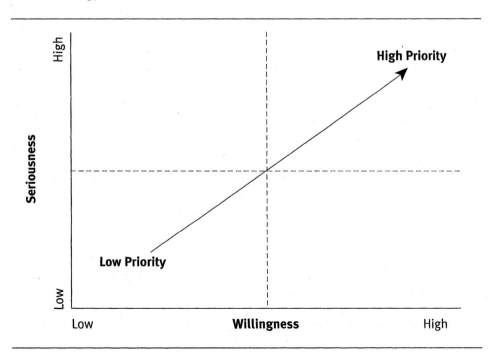

FIGURE 2.4
Community Health Priority-Setting Grid

4. Focusing on risk factors in the High Priority quadrant, participants compare all risk factors two at a time (Paired Comparison), until a final priority list has been developed. For example, participants may arrive at a final list of priority risk factors that are of high impact and that they are willing to address: alcohol and drug abuse; parenting skills; access to healthcare; prenatal care; low-immunization levels; and seatbelt use.

5. Finally, a list of perceived health system gaps are identified and rated one by one, first by perceived "potential to improve community health in the county" (1 = little potential to 7 = high potential), then by perceived "feasibility to successfully implement necessary changes" (1 = not feasible to 7 = highly feasible). For example, health system gaps identified as being in the High Potential, High Feasibility quadrant may include services to prevent or deal with substance abuse, health system coordination, services to improve parenting skills, public information and education about health and health services, physician recruitment and distribution within the county, dentist recruitment and distribution within the county, and allied health worker recruitment. Given this listing, these gaps are compared two at a time to arrive at a priority listing.

Program Implementation

Given the priority of activity established by the needs assessment, the major issue of implementation is to ensure that the identified program activities are in place and on track. This is the issue of progress. While managers and evaluators often assume the extent of implementation, implementation varies by site, over time, and even among program recipients, as their characteristics interact with the attributes of the intervention (Scheirer 1989).

Assessment of progress is generally considered to be an issue of monitoring. For example, the program is expected to have progressed to a certain point by a certain time. The point to which the program is expected to have progressed will be associated with the assurance of anticipated funding; the delivery of program equipment; the construction of a facility; the hiring or training of personnel; and the provision of services to a client population. Figure 2.5 depicts the province of monitoring as an evaluation activity.

In general, what is monitored in the assessment of progress is the provision, deployment, and use of program inputs. Figure 2.5 shows a generalized view of program implementation from the standpoint of program inputs, process, outputs, and outcomes. This may be considered an expanded view of the implementation process presented in Chapter 1 and illustrated in Figure 1.1. Program

FIGURE 2.5

Schematic of Program Inputs, Process, Outputs, and Outcomes

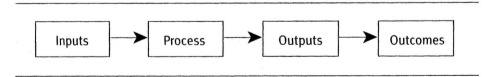

monitoring as an evaluation activity is concerned particularly with program inputs and process. The questions raised in program monitoring will be particularly questions of whether such critical inputs as funding, equipment, facilities, and personnel have been made available in the quantities and at the times specified by the program plan. Program monitoring will be concerned with whether the process of the program—which will include the way in which inputs are deployed and expended, and the timing of this use—conforms to the program plan. It also will be concerned with determining whether the persons expected to be served by the program have actually been served in the quantity and with the level of quality expected, and how the program can be improved.

In all of these monitoring activities, the evaluation-based approach to decision making has a clear role. The verifiable ends are, in this case, the inputs and deployment of inputs (program process) specified by the program plan, or evolving on a real-time basis in the minds of the program managers. Evaluation in this context is concerned with determining whether the actual deployment of resources fits the existing or evolving plan. If it does not, it is the responsibility of the program managers to make those decisions necessary to assure that the deployment and use of resources do fit the plan. Statisticians speak of type one error, the finding of a program result when none actually exists, and of type two error, the finding of no program result when a result does exist. Program evaluators also speak of a type three error, the assumption that a program was implemented when in fact it was not. Monitoring serves the purpose of allowing the manager to make the decisions necessary to assure that a program is implemented as expected and also serves the purpose of providing the basis for its continuous improvement. Monitoring fits into the evaluation-based mode of decision making, with the verifiable ends being the program plans for provision and deployment of inputs. Chapters 4 and 5 provide further discussion of the relevant strategies and approaches.

Results Assessment

The assessment of program results includes the three categories of evaluation—efficiency, effectiveness, and outcome. Efficiency and effectiveness are program characteristics that may be assessed in large part while the program is ongoing. Outcome is concerned with the long-term effects of a program and, in particular, program influence on such difficult-to-measure concepts as quality of life. In each category of evaluation, however, the evaluation-based approach to decision making should be very relevant to the managerial process.

Differences exist between the use of the evaluation process in the case of program results as compared to program implementation. Often with program implementation, evaluation information (i.e., results of program-monitoring efforts) will be available and may produce changes in a program, on a real-time and continuing basis. In the case of program results, evaluation information (i.e., assessments of efficiency, effectiveness, and impact) may come too late in the life of a program to inform decisions for significant changes in the program itself, but rather may be most valuable in decisions about how a similar program should be structured the next time.

Effectiveness Effectiveness concerns the question of whether the expected program outputs are produced. In Chapter 1, one of the questions raised as being of the type that may be addressed in an assessment of effectiveness was: Did the program meet its stated objectives? This is perhaps the central feature of an evaluation of effectiveness. From the standpoint of the evaluation-based decision-making model, a critical feature of this question is whether the objectives of the program are stated in such a way as to allow the evaluator to assess whether the objectives have been met—in short, to verify the achievement of program ends. If, for example, a family-planning program has been upgraded for the expressed purpose of increasing the length of time that women continue to use contraceptives, the verifiable program end is an increase in the length of time that women who begin family planning actually continue use. Legitimate questions can be raised as to how much of an increase in length of time is actually an increase; this is in part a technical question that can be resolved by recourse to statistics. After that question is resolved, getting data on continuation from records that are almost certain to be available in family-planning clinics should be relatively easy.

If the stated objective of the program is to increase the quality of care provided in the clinics, however, devising a verifiable measure of quality of service provided may be very difficult. The quality of training of providers and their knowledge and skills at training may be assessed, but these are essentially program inputs; what is to be assessed are outputs. Quality of service, as provided, may be assessed through the technique of observation or demonstration. This, however, is not only a costly activity, requiring a substantial amount of time in observation of the providers, but it also requires specifications of precisely what service provision actions are to be assessed, how they are to be assessed, and what measuring instruments are to be used. In the absence of such specifications, which is not a trivial matter, any decisions that result from the evaluation effort will have drifted back into either the traditional or the random-walk decision modes.

Although effectiveness concerns program outputs, this does not always mean that evaluation of effectiveness comes only at the end of the program. Efforts to determine whether the program inputs are associated with greater continuity of contraceptive use may reasonably occur during the course of the program life, and the determination that no increase in continuity of use was occurring may lead directly to a decision to modify the program. The downside to this is that decisions to change a program in midcourse can have significant and unexpected results in terms of the determination that the program—as opposed to other factors, including the changes in the program—was actually the causal agent in the change in outputs. In this regard, assessment of effectiveness can also be seen to occur on a real-time basis and to have an input on decisions made about program operation.

A number of ways exist in which effectiveness may be assessed, depending on the nature of the program itself and on the nature of the verifiable end under assessment. With varying degrees of internal validity, these include case studies (discussed in Chapters 5 and 6); trend analyses (discussed in Chapters 7 and 8); surveys (discussed in Chapters 9 and 10); experiments (discussed in Chapters 11 and 12); and simulation techniques (discussed in Chapter 16).

Efficiency

The issue of efficiency is essentially one of whether the verifiable ends of the program are sufficient to justify the costs incurred. This may also be considered in the context of the question of whether the verifiable ends are realized through the program under assessment at a lower cost than they may be realized through another program. Both issues imply that the ends have in fact been reached, and that they can be verified. Assessment of the cost of increasing the length of time that family-planning acceptors continue to use family planning can move forward relatively easily if a way is found to determine the costs of the program. However, efforts to assess the cost of increases in quality in the same program depend on the ability to determine costs and on the other problematic issue of how to determine that quality has increased. In either case, however, to speak of the efficiency of a program that had failed to meet the verifiable ends specified would make little sense. Moreover, if program outputs cannot be stated as verifiable ends, assessment of efficiency is simply not possible.

On the strength of the possibly optimistic assumption that program ends can be stated in ways that allow them to be verified, the assessment of efficiency, like the assessment of effectiveness, has the potential to provide input to decisions made about the program at two times: while the program is under way, comparing actual costs to expected costs or to costs realized under some other scheme; and at the end of the program, with the same types of comparisons. Decisions taken as a result of the evaluation effort may influence the nature of the program as it is ongoing or may be used to determine how a future program to produce similar results should be structured. In either case, the assessment of efficiency is usually subsumed under the topics of cost-benefit or cost-effectiveness analysis. Chapter 17 is composed of these topics.

Outcome

The evaluation of outcome stands in a somewhat different position relative to the evaluation decision model than do the other four aspects of evaluation. Outcome refers to the long-term results of the program—in particular, improvements in health and quality of life. The word outcome itself—while achieving almost spiritual meaning within the health services research and evaluation literature and frequently invoked by funding agencies, planners, and managers as the standard toward which all activity is to be judged—seems much too dramatic to describe even long-term results to be expected from most programs. The next section addresses some challenges associated with the use of outcomes as the gold standard in decision making.

Long-term effect and sustainability

Outcome must be thought of as the long-term effects of program activities. This definition itself makes an interest in an assessment problematic for the program manager. In general, managers are—and should be—concerned with decisions, and thus evaluations that bear on the decisions they will make about the continued progress of the program. They should do so to ensure that the results of the program are as expected, or—at the very least—to ensure that they can demonstrate where the program failed to meet its short-term objectives. The manager's job is not to ensure that two, five, or ten years after the program ends salubrious changes in health or education or quality of life will exist. In any case, program funders are not going to include the necessary resources to do such an assessment and thus ensure the sustainability of the program. On the basis of long-term outcomes, any assessment of outcomes seems clearly challenging, if not problematic.

Verifiable ends   The utility of the evaluation decision model depends on the specification of verifiable ends against which the results of the program can be assessed. A few items are in the nature of such long-term outcomes of a program as improved health, welfare, or quality of life. One is that to reach consensus on what the components of these things are is difficult (e.g., what goes into a measure of quality of life?). Another is that the components, even if agreed upon, are difficult or impossible to verify. For example, in the classic concept of health as expressed by WHO, the WHO constitution defines health as a "state of complete physical, mental and social well-being . . ." (WHO 1981). How many different aspects of complete physical, mental, and social well-being would we have to specify to assure that we had all the important ones? When we had them, how would we measure them? The likely recourse would be to fall back on specific indicators like infant-mortality rates as a measure of well-being. Why not admit that the purpose of the program is to reduce infant-mortality rates, which is a verifiable end?

Discussion Questions

1. Select a healthcare program and illustrate the type of decision making that would be carried out under each decision-making model: random-walk, evaluation-based, traditional, and mechanistic.
2. Illustrate the types of information required in each of the five steps of a needs assessment for a selected health services program. How readily available is this information? If not available, how would you propose to obtain the information?
3. Why is implementation a problem for both managers and evaluators?

PART

II

MONITORING

3

MONITORING AS AN EVALUATION STRATEGY

Program monitoring as an evaluation strategy may be one of the least discussed but most important aspects of program evaluation. Although often considered mundane or nonscientific, monitoring is a critical component of evaluation. Monitoring is particularly important to formative evaluation, and critical to the evaluation of progress and continuous improvement. The objective of this chapter is to describe monitoring as an evaluation tool. Consideration is given to the type of data on which monitoring is based, its application in various health settings, and its relationship to the various types of evaluation and improved decision making.

What Is Monitoring?

Monitoring is the comparison between program operations and expectations, and involves the continuous endeavor to learn about all aspects of a process and to use that knowledge to improve the operations of the program. When the plan and expectations do not coincide, three courses of action can be taken: the plan can be modified; the process can be modified; or steps can be taken to change expectations. In each case, data generated by the evaluation are critical to the decision.

A useful way to perceive monitoring is to view it in the context of general program activity. Figure 3.1 presents the five stages of program activity that are the primary subjects of monitoring as an evaluation activity: problem identification; program planning; program implementation; program output; and feedback.

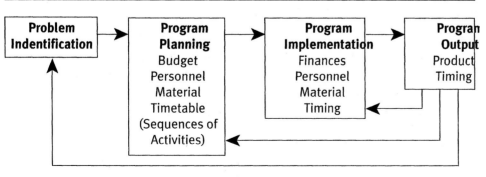

FIGURE 3.1
Stages of Program Activity Subject to Monitoring

Problem Identification and Program Planning

Monitoring has little to do with problem identification, but after a problem is identified and a program plan initiated, the issue of monitoring becomes critical. Any program plan is likely to address the six questions of *what, where, how, why, who,* and *when.*

- What is the program?
- Where will the program be implemented?
- How is it to be implemented?
- Why is it necessary?
- Who is to carry out the program?
- When will they carry out the program?
- How can it be improved?

Monitoring is particularly concerned with the questions of how, who, and when. The issues associated with these questions center on the specific sequence of activities that make up the program. A program to train a new type of ancillary service personnel, for example, a nursing assistant, may begin with the identification or establishment of institutions to provide the appropriate training, the definition and establishment of specific course content, and the identification of faculty to teach the courses. These activities may be followed by the admission of students to the curriculum, the actual training period itself, and the students' subsequent graduation. A continuing training program may then repeat the steps of student admission, training, and graduation any number of times.

This is a very simple, but fairly clear, sequence of activities that must occur if a training program is to be carried out effectively. Obviously, admission of students to a program that does not yet exist or graduation before training would be nonsensical. Any program plan must specify how the program is to be carried out—and hopefully how it can be improved.

The monitoring issues associated with the question "who" center on available resources (i.e., what resources will be allocated to reach the goals of the program?). Resources are generally defined in terms of a projected budget but will also include structures, material, and personnel. A program plan to train such personnel, for instance, must specify who will do the training and the amount of budget allocated to purchase training materials and training space. Monitoring efforts provide an opportunity to track whether these resources were allocated as originally planned.

Finally, the monitoring issues associated with the question "when" center on the actual timing of program activities. Specific techniques for planning, monitoring the timing of activities, and improving activities are the Gantt chart, PERT, or CPM, and various statistical monitoring techniques discussed in detail in Chapter 4.

Program Implementation and Impact

With the program plan constructed, including the budget, specification of personnel, specification of other resources, sequence of activities, and a timetable, the monitoring aspect of evaluation can be carried out. As the program is implemented, finances are acquired and expended in a specific manner, personnel are deployed, and material is used. All is done according to a specific sequence of activities and a specific timetable. Finally, through the implementation of the program, program output is generated. A specific product or products are produced, again according to an anticipated time schedule.

Monitoring is thus the activity of determining whether:

- the finances are available according to the budget;
- the personnel of the program meet the personnel needs of the plan;
- other available resources meet the plan specifications;
- the timing of activities follows the timetable of the plan; and
- the program output is produced as the plan projects.

Few monitoring efforts consider all aspects simultaneously.

Monitoring is critical to the implementation process and extent of implementation. Extent of implementation can be measured by counting the number of times a program is used, by counting resources consumed by the program, direct observation, activity logs, written questionnaires for providers and recipients of service, interviews with providers and recipients, or a combination of these.

Equally important, monitoring must focus on the implementation process and use that knowledge to change the process and thus improve overall service. Here, attention is given to the identification of specific processes involved in the overall program that represent opportunities for improvement. For example, within a hospital, monitoring activities may be directed toward continually improving the nurse-response time on various nursing units, or reducing the antibiotic intravenous waste in central services.

In monitoring these processes, distinguishing between what the quality improvement literature describes as special causes and common causes of variation is important (Kritchevsky and Simons 1991; Johnson and McLaughlin 1994). Common causes result from variations within the system. These are random variations even if the process is operating in accordance with its fundamental design. Special causes are deviations from the intended process specifications that are due to controllable, attributable, and non-random events. The role of management in the monitoring process is to distinguish between special and common causes of variation and to redesign the system to reduce variation in common causes (Deming 1986; Berwick, Godfrey, and Roessner 1990; Deming 1993). As described so well by Deming, "The problem is in the system and the system belongs to management" (1986).

Limitations

Although monitoring is an important aspect of evaluation, its application to health service programs is subject to several limitations. These limitations are in part generic to the monitoring process and in part a function of the unique characteristics of health services. First, monitoring is dependent on the development of information systems, and organizations are investing unprecedented sums of money to develop and implement systems as a function of the growing recognition that improved outcomes of care and decision making are dependent on such enhanced information—as well as the recognition that a number of external agencies such as JCAHO's Oryx/Oryx Plus initiative, NCQA's HEDIS, and other report card marketing efforts (McGlynn 1997) require such activity if their organization is to be competitive. Paralleling these efforts, however, is a general malaise among many managers that, despite this investment, it will make little difference in overall operations (Appleby 1997). As described by DeLuca and Cagan (1997) ". . . one of the biggest fears that executives have regarding their information technology investment is that providers and physicians simply will not use it."

In the health services area, monitoring most program activity is not easy. Despite a significant effort to develop guidelines, information systems, and a variety of review procedures for a range of service delivery activities (and thus monitor performance against these guidelines), the actual practice of medical care is rooted in the idea that professionals are responsible people, and that a certain amount of clinical judgment is required in some, if not all, service delivery activity. This idea, while clearly under siege by the development of managed care and the redefinition of healthcare as an economic good, has historically represented a significant challenge in efforts to monitor many program activities.

A second and related challenge is that monitoring is at best inconvenient and at worst uses up time and resources that providers feel can be better devoted to "practice." These difficulties have a direct effect on the monitoring process applied to health services.

First, much of what may be considered monitoring may be carried out in a highly informal manner. Frequently, a manager will be aware of the finances and personnel available to the program, materials needed, and the timetable for conducting various tasks. If program inputs, process, or outputs do not adhere to the plan, the manager will probably intuitively recognize any discrepancy and consider this good management rather than evaluation. In programs that are not exceedingly complex or that involve a limited number of actors, no formal monitoring activity may be undertaken or, for that matter, needed.

As programs and services become more complex, as they involve more resources, and as their expected products become more extensive or diffuse, program monitoring becomes increasingly important. With a large, relatively complex program, a single program manager, or even several managers, may find exceedingly difficult the task of informally maintaining the body of information needed to keep the program on track. Under such circumstances, formal monitoring systems and networks must be established to facilitate the task of program management and decision making.

A second problem of monitoring is that although more complex programs are likely to require sophisticated monitoring efforts, the resources, timetable, sequence of events, personnel, and finances involved in a large complex program are likely to be much more difficult to measure and thereby monitor. Unfortunately, the dilemma is often resolved by ignoring or giving only limited attention to monitoring activities. A more realistic approach would be to focus on those areas where monitoring is feasible. For example, the budget specified for program activities, personnel, and most resources will likely be critical to program outputs, and thus should be of concern in program monitoring. What may be less clear is that a specific sequence of activities, a specific timetable, or even certain outputs are either necessary or sufficient to produce longer-range outputs and outcomes that are desired from the program.

Third, monitoring of activities may become a substitute for program performance. Evaluators who are actively involved in program monitoring must be careful not to make monitoring a substitute for the actual products desired by the organization. In the area of family planning, for instance, monitoring the number of condoms dispensed may be useless if they are never used. Monitoring the number of contraceptive pills distributed may also be useless in attempting to ensure the expected outcomes of a program if they are used for a few days or weeks and then abandoned, or are used in a highly irregular fashion. Monitoring the number of community hand pumps installed may be useless for ensuring the success of a safe-water program if the people expected to be served by a particular water source continue to use unsafe water supplies. Finally, monitoring the number of clean needles distributed in an HIV prevention or needle exchange program is useless unless they are used by the targeted population.

A clear relationship must exist between what is monitored and what is desired as a program outcome. In many instances, the outcome must be assumed even though it is not demonstrated clearly; every effort should be made to monitor those aspects of the program related to desired outcomes. When monitoring occurs, the propensity to gather too much information or information in too great detail exists. The evaluator should be conscious at all times of the need for economy. Monitoring should refer to those aspects of the program directly relevant to decision making and not be conceived of as a general data collection activity to cover all aspects of program operations; this aspect is particularly critical, for data collection is expensive and always time consuming.

Appropriate Data for Monitoring

Data required for monitoring can be conceived of as being related primarily to inputs, process, or outputs. Figure 3.2 is a restructuring of Figure 3.1 that focuses specifically on inputs, process, and outputs. Inputs are the resources and guidelines necessary to carry out the program. Process is the specific set of activities, their sequencing, and timing for the sequencing, which actually represents program operation. Outputs are the products of the program, which consist of direct outputs, intermediate effects, and long-run, ultimate effects, or outcomes.

To specify data needed for monitoring is a difficult task. Our first inclination is to say that data should be available about all aspects of program operation

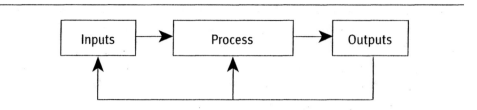

that bear on decision making. Such a statement requires clarification, however. On one hand, the term "all" may not be descriptive enough to be useful in decisions about what specific items of information should be maintained. On the other hand, taking the term "all" literally may result in the collection and maintenance of data that will be irrelevant to decision making, either because such data simply do not bear on decisions required for the program, or the collection of large amounts of data may overwhelm the evaluator's ability to process, analyze, and use it. Data needs for program monitoring within the areas of inputs, process, and outputs follow.

Data for Monitoring Inputs

All inputs to a program can be considered the resources by which the program is carried out. Resources, however, can be divided into a number of different categories.

Finances. Maintaining records of the amount of money budgeted and, subsequently, of the amount actually allocated can be useful.

Personnel. Information to be maintained in regard to personnel may include the number of positions required to carry out the project and qualifications required for positions. Such a listing may involve specification of approved positions and the number under recruitment, characterized as either full-time and part-time positions or as full-time equivalents.

Transportation and space (capital and rental). Transportation and space may best be characterized in terms of dollars available for transportation and for capital construction or rental. The category may also include specifics of expected trips—durations, costs, and times. Space requirements may be specified in terms of offices, laboratories, treatment rooms, or other categories germane to the project.

Equipment and supplies. The category of equipment and supplies will be quite program specific. The list of equipment and supplies as inputs to a primary care program will be quite different from the list for the establishment of an emergency medical services program or a managed care program. Nevertheless, certain categories are probably germane to any program-monitoring effort. In general, equipment will be considered relatively nondisposable, whereas supplies are primarily disposable items. Categories for classifying equipment and supplies may include clerical equipment (e.g., typewriters and dictating machines); disposable supplies (e.g., paper, envelopes, and pencils); laboratory equipment and supplies (e.g., microscopes, slides, and test tubes); service delivery equipment and supplies (e.g., syringes, vaccines, bandages, well-drilling machines, insecticides, or whatever other equipment and supplies may be necessary to a specific program).

Information guidelines. Guidelines are standardized specifications for care developed by a formal process that incorporates the best scientific evidence of effectiveness with expert opinion (Leape 1990).

Specific ways in which finances, personnel, transportation, space, equipment, supplies, and guidelines are broken down within categories and specific information kept within categories will be highly program specific. An important task of the evaluator will be to work with program planners to determine which categories of inputs are or will be useful for monitoring purposes, which information should be maintained, which categories will not be important in a monitoring effort, and which information can be disregarded.

Data for Monitoring Process

The major pieces of information for monitoring program process will probably include specific activities to be carried out in completing the program, the sequence in which they are to be carried out, and their timing. The timing specification, for example, should also include the specification of use of resources, such as when specific expenditures will be made; when a certain number of inoculations should have been given; when a certain number of fields sprayed; or when a certain number of hospital expansion plans reviewed. Again in the category of process, the actual specific data elements to be maintained will be highly program specific. The program evaluator must work closely with program planners and managers to ensure that important activities are specified, that their sequence is well specified, and that they agree on the timing of this sequence.

It is also important that every effort should be made to limit the amount of information to be collected and maintained to those pieces of information that are actually important in ensuring the operations of the program and its continual improvement. For example, in a hospital, the food-delivery process is one component of the larger dietary program. In the process, a patient completes a menu card which is sent by nursing personnel to the dietary department. Dietary workers check the menu card with diet prescribed by the patient's physician and complete a food production sheet. The food production sheet is sent to the kitchen. The kitchen staff then prepares the food, assembles the patient tray, and loads the delivery cart. The cart is taken by dietary personnel to the patient's floor via the service elevator. The ward clerk checks the food on the tray against the order tray, and the tray is distributed by nursing personnel to the patient.

Throughout this apparently simple process are various designated inputs, actions, outputs, and indicators. For example, the patient and physician provide input in the form of menu cards and diet orders. The menu cards and diet orders result in actions, such as sending the card to dietary, and the comparison of the card with the diet order with the output being a food tray. The criterion end point is the patient with needs and expectations that the food will be hot, correct, and on time. Available indicators may include the number of cold food complaints, disagreements with the menu card, and variance from scheduled delivery time.

Data for Monitoring Outputs

The outputs are the results of the program. Outputs can be classified in three types:

1. *Direct outputs.* Specific services or goods provided by the program, such as immunizations.
2. *Intermediate effects of direct outputs.* Results of the direct outputs, such as a person or population that is immunized.
3. *Ultimate effects of direct outputs.* The purposes served by, or the usefulness of, the impact, such as avoidance of economic and other costs of the disease against which the persons have been immunized. (Schaefer 1987)

Direct outputs and the data necessary for monitoring them are usually quite obvious. They are the actual items that the program is to produce. In the case of an immunization program, they will be the number of immunizations; in the case of a birth control program, they may be the number of condoms dispensed or IUDs inserted; in a cancer-screening program, they will be the number of mammograms provided.

Depending on the particular program, data to measure the intermediate effects or impacts of direct outputs may be relatively difficult to obtain in a form useful for monitoring purposes. If the intermediate effect of an immunization program is an immunized person or population, for example, several factors may intervene between the actual number of immunizations given (direct outputs) and the existence of an immunized population (intermediate effects). For immunizations to be effective, a sequence of actual inoculations given at properly spaced intervals or to children of appropriate ages is required. Acquiring and obtaining the data necessary to ensure that this sequence is carried out may be difficult. Similarly, a discrepancy between inoculations given and immunized persons will likely exist (e.g., an immunization program may inoculate a number of children more than once). Consequently, other persons may not receive immunizations. For example, if 30,000 inoculations are given in a population consisting of 30,000 children, to say that only 90 percent of the children have actually been immunized is still possible. A serious effort to monitor intermediate effects of even a straightforward program such as immunization requires a sophisticated record-keeping system.

Consider another type of program—for instance, one in family planning and birth control efforts. The direct output may be numbers of condoms distributed, IUDs inserted, or pills distributed. The intermediate effect is the actual use of these birth control procedures or materials in an effective way. In one sense, a measure of the extent to which these birth control activities were used effectively may be derived from the ultimate effect or outcome for such a program: a change in the birth rate. Monitoring effective use is possible, however, by conducting an interview survey once, or at several intervals, on a sample of the population receiving birth control support. This interview could provide information about the proper and continuous use of birth control methods as a way of monitoring intermediate effects of the program.

Monitoring the effects of managed care programs presents a different set of challenges (Halverson, Kaluzny, and McLaughlin 1998). Often, these programs are implemented with the intent of enhancing the efficiency with which health services are delivered to defined populations, while also maintaining and improving quality of care. Under these programs, managed care organizations assume the responsibility for providing or arranging for a comprehensive set of health services that may be needed by a defined group of individuals during a specified benefit period. These organizations typically face financial incentives to reduce healthcare expenditures for their groups of beneficiaries. However, these organizations are also held accountable for the health outcomes experienced by their beneficiaries. Monitoring efforts for managed care programs must therefore examine the direct, intermediate, and ultimate effects on health services efficiency and quality.

State and local public health agencies often maintain authority for monitoring managed care programs operating within their jurisdictions, especially those programs that serve beneficiaries of public health insurance programs. An important direct output is the number of eligible beneficiaries who are enrolled in the managed care program. As enrollment grows, so does the potential for the managed care program to produce desired effects on efficiency and quality. However, enrollment provides only a limited amount of information about program effects. If sound utilization-management processes are not in place, beneficiaries may enroll in the program but continue to receive wasteful, duplicative, and inappropriate services. Similarly, if processes for assuring the quality and accessibility of health services are not in place, beneficiaries may enroll in the program but fail to receive needed health services.

Intermediate effects provide more insight regarding processes used for service delivery and management within managed care programs. These effects include:

- rates of hospitalization and lengths of stay for specific diagnoses;
- rates of referral to specialists; numbers of physician encounters per beneficiary; emergency room utilization rates;
- rates of prenatal care delivery;
- childhood immunization rates;
- age-appropriate cancer screening rates;
- utilization rates for cost-effective clinical practices such as vaginal births after cesarean section or beta-blocker prescriptions after heart failure;
- patient satisfaction ratings; and
- rates of disenrollment.

Many of these intermediate effects may not be directly comparable across organizations or over time due to differences in the types of individuals who are enrolled in managed care organizations at any given point in time. Therefore, many monitoring efforts use statistical risk-adjustment processes to account for these differences.

Ultimate effects indicate the performance of managed care programs in containing healthcare expenditures and improving health outcomes. Financial effects typically include aggregate measures of annual healthcare expenditures for program beneficiaries. Health outcome effects typically reflect conditions that substantially affect the health and well-being of program beneficiaries and that are sensitive to health services delivery and management processes. These effects include: age-specific mortality rates and years of potential life lost; low birthweight rates; rates of vaccine-preventable diseases; rates of communicable diseases such as tuberculosis and sexually transmitted diseases; and survival rates for cancers that are sensitive to early detection and treatment. Risk adjustment processes are also applied to these ultimate effects to facilitate comparisons.

Monitoring Morbidity and Mortality

Despite these difficulties, discussing some of the data that may be involved in monitoring outcomes is still useful. These types of data usually focus on some aspect of health status. Health status is a difficult concept to define and is even more difficult to measure. Nevertheless, we can talk about some specific proxy measures that provide approximate indicators of health status. The most readily accessible indicator, and the one often considered a proxy outcome measure, is mortality or mortality rate and its refinements, such as age-, sex-, and perhaps race-specific mortality rates. For example, this measure is used by the Healthcare Financing Administration (HCFA) in the release of hospital-specific mortality rates to identify outlier hospitals whose overall or diagnosis-specific death rates are higher than expected by chance after controlling for case-mix severity.

A second general category of information useful for measuring health status is morbidity. In general, morbidity data will not be as readily available or as accurate as mortality data. Clearly, to maintain any type of accurate record on such items as venereal diseases or malnutrition conditions, items that may have a substantial impact on overall health and quality of life but that are almost impossible to measure effectively, is difficult. On the other hand, maintaining certain disease-specific morbidity data, particularly for diseases likely to be reported to public health or other authorities or diseases or conditions likely to be relatively clear at the onset may be possible. Diseases and conditions in this category may include various cancers, stroke, tuberculosis, and trauma. Other such indicators include disability and functional status (Lohr 1988). Disability indicators, including measures of premature retirement days of disability and work loss, are useful in tracking the impact of large-scale programs. Functional status indicators focus on overall health, attempting to assess physical and psychosocial dimensions of daily living.

If data on morbidity are maintained, it is desirable to have age-, sex-, and race-specific morbidity data for monitoring purposes. In addition, as disease data are maintained, it is useful to maintain them either as incidence or prevalence data. *Incidence* refers to the specific onset of a disease; *prevalence* refers to its actual existence in a population. Diseases of relatively short duration may have high incidence but low prevalence; diseases of long duration, on the other hand, may have low incidence and high prevalence.

In monitoring the outcomes of a program, it would be possible to maintain morbidity and mortality data over time and to examine continually the changes, if any, that occur in these data. Although not a highly scientific test of the ultimate effect of a program, the data provide at least some indication of whether the program does have an ultimate effect. While useful, outcome indicators must be approached with caution (Healthcare Advisory Board 1993). Some complexities include the facts that:

- *Indicators are not equally relevant to all procedures.* A critical indicator for one program activity may be meaningless for another. For example, mortality as a primary outcome indicator for coronary bypass patients because a meaningful chance of death exists is irrelevant for tonsillectomy patients because few patients die from this procedure.

- *Indicators may not be equally relevant due to differing treatment goals.* One patient may prefer to maximize length of life while another may prefer to maximize quality of life. For example, some women may choose radical mastectomy to eliminate fear of recurrence of cancer, while others may choose lumpectomy to minimize disfigurement.

- *Indicators may have different definitions depending upon institutional context.* For example, infection rates as an intermediate indicator vary across institutions due to nonstandard definition of infections.

- *Some events (e.g., complications) as an intermediate indicator may be difficult to identify, thus affecting the consistency of data collection.* For example, some incidences of stroke may be so short-lived that they are missed by the physician.

- *Critical data is often difficult to track without linked data systems (e.g., inconsistent patient identification numbers and system linkages hamper flow of information).* For example, the unanticipated return to the ER is an excellent intermediate outcome indicator but can only be tracked if the ER visit is captured by a central data source.

- *Some indicators are impossible to track without a community database.* For example, repeat procedures and readmissions are valuable intermediate indicators but are easily undercounted if the patient goes to a different hospital or physician.

- *Linking outcomes to providers' actions can be difficult.* A range of factors, such as family history, environmental condition, and so on, may be important factors affecting outcomes. For example, family history of heart disease is potentially more telling of the patient's likelihood of coronary disease than is patient management.

- *Risk factors necessary to adjust for mortality are different than factors necessary to adjust for major complications.* For example, surgery patients' co-morbidity may create risk of a complication, but no greater risk of death.

- *Inconsistent definitions applied to coding of certain medical conditions minimizes the comparability of data.* For example, one hospital may code a lower level of infection as an intermediate outcome indicator of a major complication.

- *Outcomes data that are tracked and monitored are limited to major complications and mortality.* Many clinically meaningful variables and outcomes such as lab test results and procedure-specific complications are not captured.

Data for Monitoring from Two Different Settings

To illustrate the type of data appropriate for monitoring, consider two different programs. Although differing in scope of activity and in purpose, each can benefit from various types of monitoring activity.

Illustration: Community Clinical Oncology Program (CCOP)

The program is an organizational network initially designed to increase participation in National Cancer Institute (NCI) clinical trials composed of three major components: the individual community clinical oncology programs (CCOPs), the designated research bases, and the National Cancer Institute Division of Cancer Prevention and Control (DCPC) (Kaluzny, Warnecke and Associates 1996).

The CCOP is the organizational unit for cancer control and treatment research at the community level. Specifically, a CCOP is a working group of hospitals, physicians, and support staff, which can range from as few as one or two physicians and staff affiliated with a single hospital or office to as many as 50 physicians and staff affiliated with many hospitals and offices.

Research bases can be NCI-funded cooperative groups, core-grant cancer centers, or state health departments. Each CCOP may affiliate with up to five eligible research bases, only one of which may be a national multi-specialty cooperative group.

The Division of Cancer Prevention and Control is a constituent part of the National Cancer Institute, one of the National Institutes of Health. The division is responsible for overseeing the CCOP program through its associate director for centers and community oncology. The DCPC cooperates with the Division of Cancer Treatment in the protocol approval process and with other committees and units in NCI to oversee the quality and accountability of patient care for NCI-approved studies.

The CCOPs are led by a single clinician-principal investigator or co-investigators who are responsible for the conduct of the CCOP activities. They are assisted by a data manager, usually a nurse specializing in oncology, who helps recruit patients and manages the flow of information and data between the research bases and the clinicians and the record-keeping sections of the component facilities. Additional nurse managers or coordinators are sometimes funded through the program, depending on the projected patient enrollment. One of the incentives built into the CCOP funding is support for travel expenses for the investigators, data managers, and other staff to attend the scientific and organizational meetings of the research bases. These meetings present opportunities for the staff to develop skills and provide scientific input to the development of specific protocols, and they reinforce CCOP commitment to the clinical-trials network.

The goals of the program are fivefold:

1. Bring the advantages of treatment and other cancer control research to individuals in their own communities by having practicing physicians and their patients participate in clinical treatment and other cancer-control research protocols.
2. Provide a basis for involving a wider segment of the community in cancer control research, and investigate the impact of cancer therapy and control advances in community medical practices.
3. Increase the involvement of primary healthcare providers and other specialists (e.g., surgeons, urologists, gynecologists) with the CCOP investigators in treatment and other cancer control research approved by NCI.
4. Reduce cancer mortality by accelerating the transfer of newly developed cancer prevention, detection, treatment, and continuing care technology to widespread community application.
5. Facilitate wider community participation (including minority groups and underserved populations) in future treatment and other cancer-control research approved by NCI.

The overall evaluation of the program focuses on three areas:

- the implementation of the program in the selected areas;
- the impacts of the program within the communities; and
- the characteristics of CCOPs, research bases, the NCI, and their interaction that affect implementation and impact.

The evaluation is a four-year longitudinal study examining environmental and organizational factors that affect the implementation of treatment and cancer control research in the CCOP network, and the impact of these activities on diffusion of state-of-the-art cancer care into community practice (Kaluzny et al. 1989). Implementation is measured by the ability of CCOPs to accrue patients to NCI-approved treatment and cancer control research protocols, the relative efficiency by which this is achieved, and the extent to which programs are institutionalized within their respective communities. Impact is measured by changes in practice patterns for selected disease sites (e.g., breast, colon, and rectum) and the readiness of primary care physicians to participate in cancer-control research.

To ensure that any changes documented in practice patterns or readiness of primary care physicians, or both, are in fact a function of the CCOP and not part of larger secular trends, CCOP community practice patterns are being compared to practice patterns in non-CCOP communities participating in the Surveillance, Epidemiology, and End Results Program of the NCI. Likewise, a national sample of primary care physicians is being surveyed and compared with primary care physicians located in the CCOP communities.

A range of organizational and environmental factors is being examined to characterize CCOPs, their designated research bases, and their interaction with NCI/DCPC to determine how these characteristics affect selected aspects of implementation and impact. Environmental factors include urban/rural setting, competition among local oncologists and hospitals, and basic demographic data about the community within which the CCOP is located; organizational factors focus on the structures and processes characterizing these organizations and their relationships.

This is obviously a complex program involving various approaches to evaluation. Monitoring is one part of the overall design. What are the pieces of information that may provide useful data for such monitoring vis-à-vis inputs, process, and program outputs?

Inputs Initially listed in terms of finances, personnel, transportation, space, equipment and supplies, and information, inputs are not all equally relevant to a monitoring strategy. In terms of the community clinical oncology program, finances may be important only to the extent to which some programs are able to receive additional resources from other sources, such as endowments. Because this is an NCI-funded grant, all participating programs receive resources to fund a required set of personnel, provide for transportation, and pay for data processing costs. In this particular case, however, the critical input is the availability of protocols from research bases. While each CCOP is expected to accrue a certain number of patients to treatment and cancer control protocols, this accrual is contingent on the actual availability of such protocols to individual CCOPs. Thus, the principal investigator of a CCOP and the administrator of the overall program as part of a monitoring strategy would maintain a clear record as to the availability and timing of these protocols. Clear decision information from this particular monitoring effort would include the availability of the protocols, the lag times required for local clearance by respective institutional review boards, and whether they remain open for sufficient time for the individual CCOPs to accrue patients. For example, if few protocols are available and the individual CCOP has difficulty clearing these protocols within the local institutional review board process, corrective action may be required at both the research base and the local CCOP. Failure to take such action would result in protocols being closed before patients can be placed on protocols in local communities.

Process monitoring for this community clinical oncology program is somewhat more complicated. At one level, it is simply to monitor the extent to which patients are in fact being accrued to available protocols within the individual CCOP. At a more complex level, however, is the ability to accrue patients vis-à-vis the number of eligible patients for particular protocols; this requires a clear understanding of the number of eligible patients within the geographic area being served by the CCOP. Data here would therefore include cancer incidence and demographic information for the CCOP communities.

Process

The primary output of the program is a change in physician practice patterns with respect to treatment of cancer patients within the local community. Three tracer conditions (i.e., five breast, one colon, and one rectum) have been selected, and data are abstracted from the medical records within a subset of CCOPs. Specifically, data are collected for:

Outputs

- women older than age 50 with localized breast cancer (Stage I–III), positive nodes, and ERA negative, and whether they are receiving chemotherapy;
- women younger than age 50 with negative nodes and ERA positive, and whether they are receiving hormonal therapy;
- women with localized breast cancer, and whether surgery is performed;
- women younger than age 50 with negative nodes and ERA negative, and whether they are receiving chemotherapy;
- women younger than age 50 with positive nodal status, and whether they are receiving chemotherapy;
- men and women with operable Duke's B and C colon cancer, and whether they are receiving chemotherapy; and
- men and women with operable Duke's B and C rectal cancer, and whether they are receiving chemotherapy and/or radiation.

Illustration: Early Detection in Primary Care

Physicians in primary care generally do not perform recommended prevention and early-detection services. Many barriers influence the inability of physicians to provide such service. In 1991, the NCI funded a 4-year study to evaluate an office systems approach to improve preventive care activities in primary care offices. The goal of the project was to assist practices in developing office systems to improve preventive care (Kaluzny, Harris, and Strecker 1991; Leininger et al. 1994).

The study involved a randomized, controlled trial of 69 primary care practices in North Carolina. Baseline and follow-up data was collected on NCI-recommended preventive care procedures: mammography, clinical breast exam,

Pap, fecal occult blood test, sigmoidoscopy, and smoking cessation counseling for patients who smoke. All practices were provided feedback from the baseline data before randomization to an early intervention or experimental group, or a late intervention or control group.

The intervention group—in addition to receiving their performance rates for each screening procedure based on chart review of continuing care patient 50 years and older—were encouraged to establish practice-wide policies relevant to the preventive services. Each intervention practice was encouraged to meet with trained facilitators to assist the practice in assessing its current system for providing screening services and to plan revisions of its system to increase performance. The intervention practices were also encouraged to adopt tools for tracking and prompting (e.g., flow sheets, chart prompts and stickers, wall posters, card files, and patient held records) and for patient education (e.g., brochure listing recommended preventive care for age and gender groups) to facilitate the implementation of their office system plans. Tailored material was created and supplied to the practices over a 12- to 18-month period. Throughout the period, facilitators kept in close touch with the practices to provide ongoing support and assistance as needed.

Monitoring the provision of preventive services within a primary care setting is a task of considerable complexity (Leininger et al. 1994). As with the CCOP, illustration monitoring should focus on inputs, process, and outputs.

Inputs Inputs involving the provision of prevention and early-detection services in primary care center on the fundamentals of finances, personnel, space, equipment and supplies, and information. Accordingly, the evaluation of resource use and cost focuses on two main categories of costs:

- the costs incurred in implementing the Office Systems for Preventive Care (OSPC), which include costs incurred by the intermediary organizations (IOs), the Area Health Education Centers (AHECS), and the practices; and
- the costs incurred in conducting cancer early-detection activities on an ongoing basis, which include costs incurred by the practices and patients (and any other group on an ongoing basis).

The general strategy for measurement of most of the costs is to obtain measures of resource use in units such as time expended, and then to estimate costs by attaching a dollar value to the time spent. (Exceptions to this process are some of the indirect costs, such as space used, or capital expenditures such as the purchase of a computer for monitoring screening needs.)

The costs of implementing OSPC or a similar system by practices on their own is obtained in two ways: 1) by using records and other reports from the IO and AHEC staff; and 2) through a questionnaire completed by the practice business manager or by a practice physician if there is no business manager (e.g., in the case of a solo practice).

The costs of conducting cancer early-detection activities on an ongoing basis will be measured primarily by the use of questionnaires completed by practice physicians and staff. These questionnaires will focus on the amount of time spent by physicians and staff in conducting the full realm of activities related to cancer early-detection activities. Data were not collected on three additional categories of cost: patient time, other direct costs (e.g., supplies and equipment used), and indirect costs (e.g., office space). Instead, these costs were imputed. For example, estimates of changes in patient time were calculated based on observed changes in the frequency of the conduct of cancer early-detection activities and valued at the minimum wage. Estimates of other direct and indirect costs were obtained from other sources, including the National Ambulatory Medical Care Survey and the analyses conducted by the Physician Payment Review Commission.

Two points should be kept in mind. First, the costs of implementing the OSPC were one-time costs for the most part that can be amortized over a future period of time. Therefore, the key costs of interest are those of conducting (rather than implementing) the cancer early-detection activities. Second, the implementation of an OSPC program by a practice will not only increase the rate at which the practice conducts early-detection activities, but it also increases the efficiency with which the practice conducts the activities (e.g., greater use of support staff for some of the functions that the physician does not have to perform). Therefore, we have measured physician and staff time and have used imputations for many of the other costs.

Process

At least three major areas of process involving the provision of early-detection and prevention services deserve monitoring efforts:

- the sequencing and time schedule for providing the early-detection and prevention services;
- the protocol specifying how and who should be expected to provide this service; and
- a continuing examination of the use of resources.

The specification of a sequence for implementation and continuing provision of prevention and early-detection services is a major component of any monitoring effort. Within the project the specification was based on guidelines presented by the NCI and were focused on men and women 50 years or older who had at least one visit to the practice and did not have a previous diagnosis of cancer. For example, data on the performance of breast cancer screening were collected through a cross-sectional review of randomly chosen medical records of eligible patients at two points in the study, pre-intervention and post-intervention.

The specification of how and who should be expected to provide the service is particularly challenging in the provision of services because a number of factors may be involved. For example, the physician may advise the patient to reduce smoking but not record this in the medical record. Similarly, in breast cancer screening the physician may do a clinical exam and order a mammography but not record this in the medical record. Thus, the data collected must be very specific. For example, in breast cancer screening, information collected from the medical record included patient age, race, insurance status, number of visits to the practice, receipt of mammography and clinical breast exam (CBE), and the presence and use of a preventive-services flow sheet. For mammography, data were recorded in two ways: mention of the test in the visit note and actual report of the test result, regardless of where the test was done and who did it. Thus, mention of mammography includes all those reported plus others in which the note indicated that mammography was considered. This permitted credit being given to the practice for a physician recommending the procedure to the eligible patient, even if the patient did not follow through on the recommendation. For CBE, data were recorded in only one way, giving credit for either completion of CBE or mention of CBE recommendation.

The continued monitoring of resources focuses on the cost incurred in conducting early-detection activities on an ongoing basis. Appendix 3.1 shows a draft data collection form for breast cancer screening. A similar form was developed for cervical, colo-rectal screening, skin screening, and smoking-cessation counseling (Stearns 1991).

Output Monitoring the outputs of providing prevention and early-detection services within a primary care practice can be discussed in terms of direct outputs, their intermediate effect, and their ultimate effects of outcomes. Monitoring per se will focus most on the direct outputs.

The single most important direct output is whether the program increases the number of recommended screening and early-detection services within the primary care practice. Analysis revealed that no substantial difference in the use of prevention and early-detection services exists between the intervention and control group of primary care practices on the following factors:

- age;
- race;
- number of physician office visits in the last year;
- proportion with a health maintenance visit in the last year;
- percentage who currently smoke;
- percentage on Medicaid; or
- proportion without health insurance.

The project did develop a number of practice-level indicators based on medical-record review and physician questionnaires, and found that in breast cancer screening:

- 50 percent or more of the medical records in a practice have an entry on a preventive care flow sheet in the last year.

- 50 percent or more of physicians in a practice report to have a written preventive care policy.
- 50 percent or more of the physicians in a practice report that nurses frequently or sometimes identify patients who are due for mammograms.
- 50 percent or more of the physicians report that they frequently use flow sheets, tickler files, or computerized reminders to identify patients due for mammograms.
- 50 percent or more of the physicians report that nurses frequently or sometimes recommend mammograms to patients who are due. (Kinsinger et al. 1998)

Intermediate effects of direct outputs, that is, intermediate effects of the provision of the screening activity, may be reflected in the actual detection of disease. This information can be obtained from continued monitoring of the medical record. While this was not the objective of the study, this type of information would be available through the medical record.

The availability of outcome data is more problematic and is usually associated with an end point such as mortality. While the evaluation was not designed to assess mortality as an outcome of early detection, such information would be available to the extent that patients could be followed over an extended period of time. The challenges here are the nature of the disease process and the fact that considerable time is involved between detection and death from the disease, making monitoring difficult.

Application to Decision Making and Types of Evaluation

Monitoring as an approach to evaluation and its associated techniques are no more than good management. In fact, evaluation using monitoring techniques is a component of good management. Types of decisions that can and should be made as a result of a well-designed program-monitoring effort are the types of day-to-day management decisions that program managers are required to make during the course of a program to ensure its operations and continual improvement. These decisions include: that the program has available and uses all the resources necessary for its operations and improvement; that the sequence of events is correct and appropriately ordered; and that anticipated short-term results are being generated. The relationship of monitoring to each of the types of evaluation—relevance, adequacy, progress, effectiveness, efficiency, impact, and sustainability—is discussed in the following sections.

Relevance

In general, monitoring as an overall format and specific monitoring techniques have little impact on decisions about relevance. As discussed in Chapter 1, relevance primarily concerns the particular problem that a program should consider, how well-defined the problem is, whether the appropriate agency is attacking the problem, and whether the planned program will actually have an impact on the problem. Monitoring is relatively weak in confronting any of these issues seriously. It can provide limited output data that may serve to shed light on whether the program can produce a solution to the problem, but monitoring is not capable of providing information about whether alternative programs would have produced better results, unless the alternative programs are also in place.

Adequacy

Monitoring can provide important information on the extent to which a program or set of activities is able to address a particular problem. Tracking the resources being used in the initiative and/or monitoring activities within the initiative provides insight into whether the program is capable of addressing the breadth and depth of the problem. Often programs are present and managers are able to point to the presence of a set of activities designed to address some problem, but an examination of the resources allocated to its operation would suggest that they are not adequate, given the demands of the problem the program is attempting to address.

Progress

Monitoring can and does provide information for decision making about program progress. In fact, monitoring activity is primarily directed to program progress and efficiency. Monitoring provides systematic information about whether a program is going according to plan and is on schedule, the expected activities are being carried out in the manner they should be and at the appropriate time, and resources are being expended as they should be. Again, this may seem simply an aspect of good management. Although possibly true, programs designed as part of more technically sophisticated evaluations involving applications of survey research or experimental design must be monitored to make certain that they are carried out as specified. The importance of this point is reviewed in the following discussion.

Suppose that a relatively sophisticated experimental design has been devised to test the effectiveness and impact of a way of instituting and implementing primary healthcare as opposed to an alternative method. Such an experiment may involve undertaking the two alternative strategies in a sample of different communities or within selected areas in the same communities. A result that showed no difference between the two approaches—or, perhaps more importantly, between the effort to establish a primary healthcare program and no activity at all—can have two quite different meanings. Such a result can mean that, in fact, the programs are not different—or that having a program is no different from having no program. Alternatively, it is possible that the primary healthcare program efforts were not carried out as designed. A good evaluation study of the experimental type must provide for a monitoring of the program activities that will at least indicate the extent to which the programs have been carried out in the manner specified. Otherwise, negative results cannot be adequately understood.

Effectiveness and Efficiency

Monitoring can provide important information for decision making about effectiveness. If effectiveness is considered the production of direct outputs, monitoring provides extensive information about whether expected outputs have been produced. As so well described by Freeman and Rossi (1981, 364):

> In the human services field, when evaluation after evaluation indicated that programs more often failed to have any significant effects than to be successful in achieving their intended purposes, attention began to be given to an earlier question whether programs were being delivered as intended. After all, if a program is not being delivered, or is being delivered with changes that undermine its effectiveness, then it is no wonder that experimental or quasi-experimental evaluations arrive at the diagnosis of ineffectiveness. In human service after human service it was quickly found that program implementation was problematic; indeed, some programs were found not to exist at all after supposedly having been implemented; others were delivering treatments at such weak levels or in such transformed modes that the program could not be said to exist.

The monitoring format can also produce information regarding efficiency in the sense that it may be possible, if adequate records are kept, to determine average cost of a program for immunizations, or the average cost of getting someone to schedule a clinic appointment under a form of communication. From the standpoint of efficiency, cost can be perceived as finances, time, or other resources.

Impact and Sustainability

The monitoring approach provides little or no information about program impact and sustainability. In general, most programs are under way for a long period of time before any assessment of impact can be made. Moreover, an impact evaluation assumes the ability to compare program outcomes with outcomes of alternative programs, or of no program. Monitoring is not an evaluation strategy that can be used to compare alternative programs or program to no-program.

In short, the importance of monitoring is that it can be used:

- to detect when a program is not progressing or improving as designed, either in terms of inputs, process, or outputs;
- to provide limited information about effectiveness and efficiency to the program; and
- in particular, to ensure that the program is carried out in the manner in which it was designed.

Two valuable results of the use of monitoring are that monitoring allows the evaluator's decision making to keep the program on track and permits a more adequate evaluation of effectiveness, efficiency, and impact via more sophisticated approaches of survey research or experimental design by assuring that the program was actually implemented as designed.

Discussion Questions

1. Why is monitoring often excluded as an approach to evaluation?
2. What are the strengths and limitations of monitoring as an evaluation strategy?
3. Select a health service program (e.g., an outreach program or well-baby clinic) and identify the critical input, process, and output indicators. How is this information helpful in program management?

This form should be completed if you you have indicated that you screen your patients for breast cancer. For each of the following activities, please indicate:

- whether you personally conduct the activity;
- the average amount of time in minutes that you spend on the activity per patient when conducted;
- whether you use staff to conduct the activity, when conducted; and
- your estimate of how much staff time is used per patient.

	You Perform Activity? (Y or N)	Minutes You Spend on Activity	Staff Performs Activity? (Y or N)	Minutes Staff Spends on Activity
1. *Monitoring Patients for Screening Needs*				
a. Use a paper file tracking system to notify patients of their need for a breast exam	Y N	_____	Y N	_____
b. Use a computerized tracking system to notify patients of their need for a breast exam	Y N	_____	Y N	_____
c. Review a flow sheet in the chart to check the need for a breast exam	Y N	_____	Y N	_____
d. Review the x-ray section of the chart to check the ned for a breast exam	Y N	_____	Y N	_____
2. *Conducting Breast Cancer Screening*				
a. Perform the clinincal breast exam (CBE), including explanation of the process	Y N	_____	Y N	_____
b. Discuss CBE results with patients with abnormal results	Y N	_____	Y N	_____
c. Determine whether to do a mammogram	Y N	_____	Y N	_____
d. Charting and dictation		_____		_____
3. *Follow-up Activities for Breast Cancer Screening*				
a. Check to see whether mammogram was done	Y N	_____	Y N	_____
b. Notify the patient of the mammogram result	Y N	_____	Y N	_____
c. Spend time explaining abnormal or indeterminate results	Y N	_____	Y N	_____
d. Aid in referral, including explanatory letter to referral physician	Y N	_____	Y N	_____
e. Charting and dictation	Y N	_____	Y N	_____

4

MONITORING TECHNIQUES AND INTERPRETATION

Monitoring may be done without using any formal data analysis methodology. Its primary analytical effort centers on a comparison of expectations to actual results. This area may seem intuitive, and monitoring is possible on a relatively informal basis. However, a set of related techniques is useful mainly in monitoring and evaluating the sequence of events by which a program progresses and, to a lesser extent, in monitoring the costs involved in the sequencing of events. The objective of this chapter is to present these methodologies and illustrate their use in various health service programs.

Gantt Charts

A Gantt chart can be a significant aid in monitoring program activities in a way that will be useful and effective for decision making about that program. It provides a means of visually indicating the sequence of events or activities that make up a project as it proceeds through time.

Figure 4.1 shows an example of a Gantt chart. The chart illustrates the schedule of events that take place in the implementation of a multi-component intervention in primary care medical practices. The overall objective of the project was to improve performance of selected cancer screening activities among primary care physicians (Ransohoff, Harris, Kinsinger, and Kaluzny 1997). To meet this objective, applying a clinical improvement approach to breast cancer screening, colorectal cancer screening, and smoking cessation counseling was necessary.

As the chart indicates, the clinical improvement process for preventive care requires approximately nine months. The wide horizontal lines represent the conduct of each specific activity to be carried out as part of the improvement process. The first week of the nine-month process is devoted to giving the practice feedback regarding their performance of preventive care activities by the coordinator and lead faculty. The second week is devoted to team assembly. The end of the first month and beginning of the second month are devoted to setting up a practice-wide preventive care policy. The beginning of the third and fourth months begin with analysis of the current information system, which continues intermittently through the sixth month. Concurrent with the evaluation of the information system, but beginning in the latter part of the third month of the project, the process analysis (which includes observing the practice's patient and staff flow,

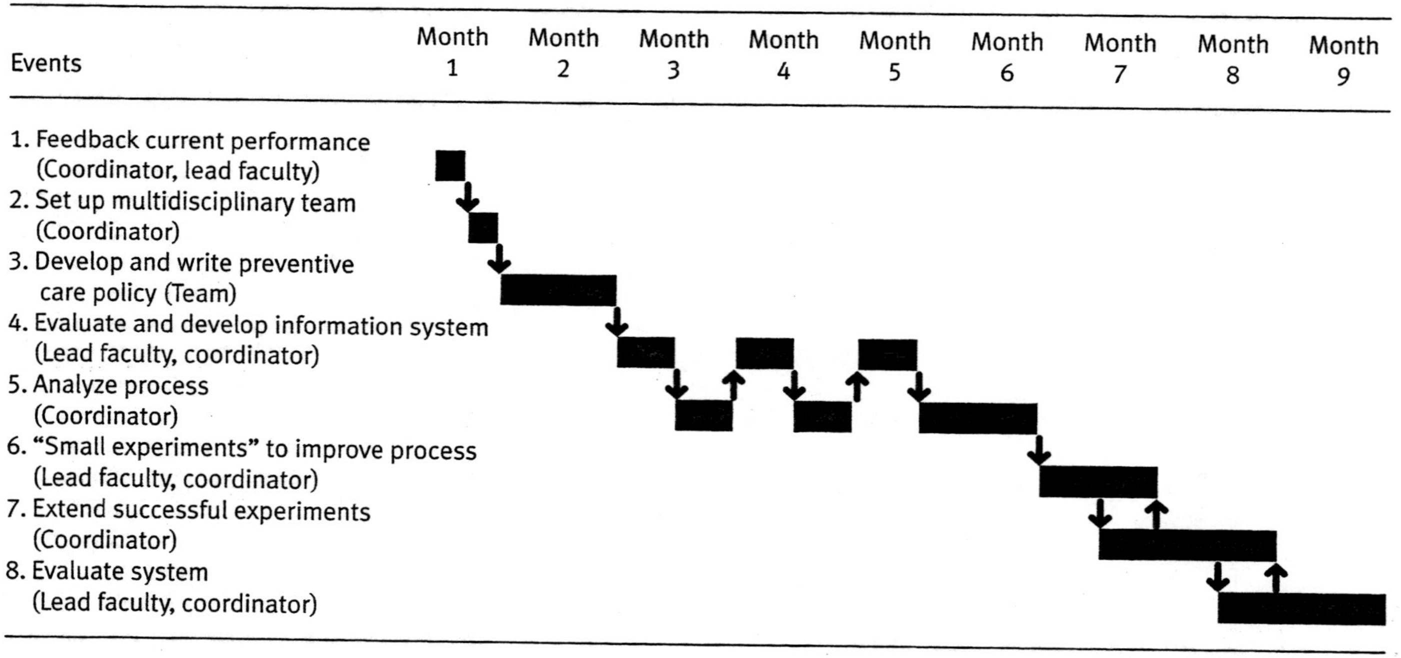

FIGURE 4.1
Sequence of Events for the Clinical Improvement Process for a Single Primary Care Medical Practice

Events

	Month 1	Month 2	Month 3	Month 4	Month 5	Month 6	Month 7	Month 8	Month 9

1. Feedback current performance
   (Coordinator, lead faculty)

2. Set up multidisciplinary team
   (Coordinator)

3. Develop and write preventive
   care policy (Team)

4. Evaluate and develop information system
   (Lead faculty, coordinator)

5. Analyze process
   (Coordinator)

6. "Small experiments" to improve process
   (Lead faculty, coordinator)

7. Extend successful experiments
   (Coordinator)

8. Evaluate system
   (Lead faculty, coordinator)

feeding back this information to the practice, team meetings, and so on) will begin; more or less, a free flow of information between the evaluation of the information system and analysis of the process will exist. The end of the sixth month and beginning of the seventh month will be devoted to a trial period for small experiments, and re-analysis of the process will begin. Again, input will be given from the lead faculty about how the experiment affects the process and what areas need improvement or implementation into the system. After experiments are successfully integrated into the system, evaluation of the entire process will begin the end of the eighth month and continue into the ninth.

Figure 4.1 is an idealized statement of how the process should be carried out. By tracking specific events, this figure serves as a useful monitoring tool. For example, if the total clinical improvement process is to be completed in nine months, analysis work must be completed by the sixth month if small experiments are to be executed and evaluated. Other specific milestones of the project have similar relationships. Thus, a major value of the Gantt chart is to allow the project decision maker to easily see the state of project progress at any point in time. To the extent that progress deviates from the projected schedule, modifications and adjustments can be made to meet that schedule.

If a Gantt chart is prepared primarily to serve or to impress an external funding agency, or as a requirement for the submission of a proposal, the chart will probably have little value in monitoring the project. If, on the other hand, it is prepared with serious attention to the problems of carrying out the aims of the program or project and a realistic schedule or timing of events, the chart can be used for serious monitoring purposes. Construction of such a chart does not require any special expertise, but a fair understanding of the project, how it is to be carried out, and the realistic relationship of the various events are required.

A Gantt chart also assumes a substantial degree of control over project and program activities. Regardless of how realistic or well planned the activities and milestones may be, serious treatment of them for progress monitoring may be useless if the program coordinator is not actually in total control. In the clinical improvement process example, the project coordinator needed to rely on faculty members—who have their own agendas and priorities—for policy development, evaluation of information systems, and influencing cycles of change via small experiments. Consequently, a great deal of the actual conduct of the project is beyond the control of the project coordinator, and adherence to the specifics of the schedules for an individual clinical improvement process is difficult.

PERT and CPM

Natural extensions of the Gantt chart are PERT (Program Evaluation and Review Technique) and CPM (Critical Path Method). Both PERT and CPM are scheduling tools represented as a network of circles representing discrete events (such as the beginning of the project, the end of a specific activity, or the completion of a report) and arrows that represent activities. While similar to the Gantt chart, PERT and CPM provide additional information not provided by the Gantt chart, specifically information about which activities must be completed on time if the entire project is to be completed on time, and which activities may be allowed to slip in time if resources are limited or overextended. PERT was originally developed by the U.S. Navy to control a Polaris missile project; Dupont developed CPM. Both PERT and CPM begin with exactly the same type of information as the Gantt chart. Although PERT and CPM have somewhat different origins, they are now quite similar in application and both deserve discussion.

While the Gantt chart is based on a graphic display that shows relative starting and ending points in time, the PERT and CPM applications are based on networks that represent the project activities over time. To employ either PERT or CPM as an evaluation tool, the first step, as with the construction of the Gantt chart, is to break the project into a series of relatively self-contained activities. The breakdown of activities shown in Figure 4.1 is a reasonable classification to begin to develop a PERT network. Two activities, evaluation and development of information system and process analysis, however, are each divided into three components in the Gantt chart. In discussing the development of the PERT chart, what may make sense is to see each activity within evaluation of information system and process analysis as separate activities.

After the project is broken into a set of relatively self-contained activities, the next step is to develop a precedence table for them. If we concentrate on the clinical improvement process as shown in the Gantt chart as an example, the precedence relationships for that project may be as shown in Table 4.1. Activity A is feedback current performance (i.e., telling the practice how the practice and providers are doing in terms of reaching eligible patients with selected preventive care activities). Activity B, setting up a multi-disciplinary team, must be, according to this formulation, preceded by feedback to the practice; presumably the structure of the team would depend on how the practice perceives its performance. Activity C, development of a practice-wide preventive care policy, would necessarily follow team assembly, because the policy affects how the entire team proceeds with the clinical improvement process. Activities D and E, information system evaluation and development and process analysis, could presumably begin at the completion of the policy development.

Phase 2 of information system evaluation and development would follow phase 1, as phase 3 of process analysis would follow phase 2 of information system evaluation and development. Evaluation of the entire system must follow the testing with small experiments and the extension of these successful experiments.

With such a precedence relationship established, a PERT network can be produced. Figure 4.2 shows an example of how events and activities are designated in PERT. The circled numbers 1, 2, 3, and 4 represent discrete events. For example: 1 may be the beginning of the project; 2 may be the specific point at which a first activity of the project is completed and other activities may begin; and 3 and 4 may again be points at which specific activities are completed.

Arrows represent the activities. Activity A requires two weeks, activity B requires five weeks, and activity C requires one week. Activities B and C cannot begin until activity A is completed. This is the basic framework of the PERT

Activity	Description	Required Preceding Activities
A	Feedback current performance (Coordinator, lead faculty)	None
B	Set up multi-disciplinary team (Coordinator)	A
C	Develop and write down preventive care policy (Team)	B
D	Evaluate and develop information system (phase 1) (Lead faculty, coordinator)	C
E	Analyze process (phase 1) (Coordinator)	C
F	Evaluate and develop information system (phase 2) (Lead faculty, coordinator)	D
G	Analyze process (phase 2) (Coordinator)	E, F
H	Evaluate and develop information system (phase 3) (Lead faculty, coordinator)	F
I	Analyze process (phase 3) (Coordinator)	G, H
J	Encourage "small experiments" to improve process (Lead faculty, coordinator)	I
K	Extend successful experiments (Coordinator)	J
L	Evaluate system (Lead faculty, coordinator)	J, K

TABLE 4.1
Precedence Relationships in Clinical Improvement

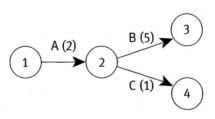

FIGURE 4.2
Example of PERT Events and Activities

network. The length of the arrow is not related to the time that the activity will require, as is the length of the horizontal line in a Gantt chart; rather, the length is arbitrary and selected simply for the construction of the network.

Using the PERT network conventions for events and activities and relying on the precedence relationship shown in Table 4.1, a PERT network can be constructed for the clinical improvement process in primary care medical practice. Such a PERT network may be as shown in Figure 4.3. According to the precedence relationships in Table 4.1, activity A must precede B, as the network in Figure 4.3 shows. Activity C can begin after activity B has been completed.

FIGURE 4.3

PERT Network for One Clinical Improvement Session

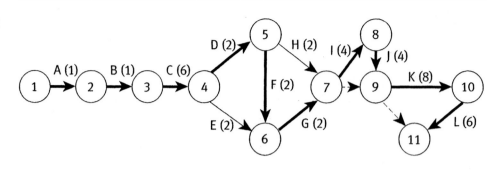

Activities D and E can begin after activity C has been completed. Activity G may begin after activities E and F have been completed, and so on. The length of time required for each activity is shown in parentheses. The broken lines from event 7 to 9 and 9 to 11 are known as *dummy* activities. Their function is only to designate a precedence relationship; they require no time and no resources. Broken lines in PERT networks always represent dummy activities.

The major value of the PERT network is the ability to determine a *critical path*. The critical path represents the sequence of activities and events that determines the longest time from the start of the project to its end. The critical path for the clinical improvement process is shown in the PERT network in Figure 4.3 by the heavy, directed line. The critical path for this intervention is 36 weeks.

Two advantages to knowing the critical path exist. First, given knowledge of the critical path, recognizing the critical path activities that must be completed on time if the project is to be completed totally within the 36-week period is possible. Furthermore, if one of the critical path activities extends past its projected deadline by two weeks, other things being equal, the project will require 38 weeks.

A second advantage of identifying the critical path is that the project coordinator can recognize activities not on the critical path. Activities not on the critical path, such as activities E or H, are activities that provide a certain amount of slack to the project in terms of time and other resources. The critical path from events 4 to 6, for example, is 4 weeks. Activity E, which must follow event C and precede event G, requires only two weeks. This means that, theoretically, activity 6 can be stretched over a four-week period if carrying out the activity on a part-time basis is possible, or if it can take place within any two-week segment of the four available weeks. Either strategy may release personnel or financial or other resources, which can then be made available to ensure that the critical path activities are completed on schedule.

Use of the clinical improvement project to introduce the PERT and CPM methodology is reasonable because it is simple enough for the relationships and sequence of events to be perceived easily. In real-life situations, PERT would probably be employed only in settings where the number of activities was so great and their precedence relationships so complex that the critical path activities and the set of non-critical path activities could not be determined by casual observation. Using computer programs designed to analyze PERT-type data would then be quite helpful.

Several modifications to PERT or CPM provide additional information to the planner and the evaluator. One approach to PERT, for example, uses a pessimistic time period for task completion, an optimistic time period, and a probable time period, thus providing a range for the project and for the value of the critical path. In many ways, this is a more realistic approach than a straight, single-time estimate. CPM goes further and estimates the cost of completing specific activities within the estimated time period or the cost of *crashing* the activity by putting excess resources into the project and completing it in a shorter time period.

Regardless of the specific additions made to the basic PERT or CPM approaches, they have much the same value for evaluation as the Gantt chart approach (i.e., as a framework against which project directors, monitors, or decision makers can determine whether the project is moving forward in a timely fashion). To the extent that activities are not completed on time, the evaluator decision maker has the option of redistributing resources to ensure the completion of various activities, particularly critical path activities, or of redefining the project.

Disadvantages of Gantt, PERT, and CPM

On the surface, Gantt charts, PERT networks, and CPM networks appear to be useful tools for program monitoring, are requested by many funding agencies, and apparently are widely used in various types of project development. They do have some fairly clear shortcomings, however. First, to produce a realistic Gantt chart, PERT, or CPM network successfully, program planners or managers must have a clear-cut idea of how to proceed from beginning the program or project to completing it. Despite all the planning tools and the best intentions, often the activities that make up a project are so poorly understood or poorly specified that any Gantt chart, PERT, or CPM network constructed on the basis of that understanding will be highly inaccurate. In this case, the manager must eventually try to reconcile the true state of affairs with the original plan. If unaware of the inaccuracy or naiveté of the plan, the manager may be tempted to make adjustments in the project to adhere to a totally unrealistic plan.

A second problem of Gantt charts, PERT, or CPM networks is that they are often constructed not for the purpose of program planning and subsequent monitoring but to impress a funding agency or higher-level management. Under such circumstances they are unlikely to have real value as a monitoring tool.

Input/Effort Analysis

Data from certain kinds of monitoring efforts may best be analyzed in terms of percentage of activity. Using these simple calculations, budget allocation by category can be compared to actual appropriations by category, which can be compared to expenditures by category. Again, such a comparison, particularly at the point of expenditures, would be most valuable if a type of timing for expenditure of funds could be built into the budget or allocation. Major divergences between allocations and budgeted amounts, or between expended amounts and allocated amounts, could be readily detected and corrective action initiated. This situation can be achieved by:

- establishing the cost of all resources mobilized for those services;
- determining the work hours available of key professionals;
- reflecting these costs or hours as a capacity to serve some number of clients per period of time; or
- a combination of the preceding actions.

Illustration of Input/Effort Analysis

An outpatient clinic has just been established in a hospital with an approved budget. Some staff members were transferred to the clinic and some were hired, equipment was purchased, and services were offered. At the end of the first six months, the monthly cost of operation can be determined by accounting for all salaries, fringe benefits, medical and office supplies, utilities, travel, educational materials, maintenance, and so on. The expenditures may be compared to the budget, the professional work hours available may be compared to the expected work hours, and the capacity to serve may be compared to the intended capacity.

A number of factors may have intervened, with the result that all did not appear to proceed as expected. Certain categories of staff may not have been transferred immediately; hiring new staff—particularly those in short supply—may take three to nine months; stocking materials and supplies may temporarily inflate costs; and other start-up expenses may produce irregularities in monthly costs.

In such a clinical setting, the ability to serve will depend on key professionals and the mix of those professionals. A particular service model may require that one receptionist, two physicians, six nurses, and one secretary be present 40 hours each week. If one physician is not present, the ability to serve clients may be cut in half. If one or two nurses are not present, serving the same number of clients for a brief period may be possible, but record-keeping may suffer badly. The capacity of the service is therefore closely linked to particular professionals (i.e., the physician or the nurse) and less so to others. For example, if a norm for a clinic service is assumed to be five clients per physician-hour, the capacity can be computed as

2 physicians × 40 hours/week × 5 clients/physician-hour = 400 clients/week

The number of clients who make appointments and come to the clinic, the mix of presenting symptoms, the experience and style of the professionals, the scheduling system, and other less critical factors will affect the actual number of clients served in any week.

This form of input/effort analysis suggests what the clinic is capable of doing, indicates a commitment to a level of service, and provides information for control purposes. For example, a seventh nurse must be hired if, on average, only five are present in the clinic at one time, but six are needed. This analysis does not guarantee that clients will be served at the capacity-to-serve levels; directly take into consideration quality of services (e.g., if the norm were to be lowered to four clients per physician-hour, the inference is that the quality of services would be higher); or consider treatment outcomes.

Performance Measurement Systems

Health service programs are more than a sequence of inputs that need to be monitored over time. Health services involve a complex set of input, process, and output activities, along with a set of expectations for what should be achieved by each activity. Moreover, these services are being provided within an increasingly competitive environment where solid information regarding quality, efficiency, and financial performance is paramount.

Performance measurement systems provide the opportunity for monitoring various types of service delivery activities. While a variety of measurement systems are available and are in the process of development, following is a description of the system developed by the Greater New York Hospital Association in response to a growing number of inquiries from member institutions for precise, valid, and reliable comparative information concerning quality, financial, and efficiency performance.

Illustration: Greater New York Hospital Association (GNYHA) Quaesitum Measurement System (QMS)

Quaesitum Measurement System (QMS) is the Greater New York Hospital Association (GNYHA) performance measurement system, which was developed in response to the growing demand of the GNYHA member institutions for better comparative performance information. As shown in Figure 4.4, QMS analyzes key quality, financial, and efficiency indicators for institutions overall, and has the capability of customizing reports by clinical service line, select product lines, specific procedures and diagnostic-related groups (DRGs), and payor groups to provide a comprehensive picture of institutional performance. Another unique feature of the QMS reporting capability is that providers can create competitor benchmarks by comparing their performance indicators with those of an aggregate group of relevant peers.

All performance measures are risk adjusted according to two risk-adjustment indicators: mortality rates and complication rates (post-surgical and post-obstetrical). Periodic QMS reports provide comparative information concerning the performance of each hospital over time and comparisons with select peer groups, offering hospital CEOs and other senior hospital administrators important temporal and competitive performance-monitoring capabilities. Finally, this information can be used to identify opportunities to improve quality of care and operational efficiency, and to assist with managed care contracting.

FIGURE 4.4

Sample Report: Quaesitum Measurement System (QMS)

The performance measurement system developed by Greater New York Hospital Association

Hospital name: _____

Operating Certificate Number: _____

QMS Performance Measure: Risk-Adjusted Post-Surgical Complications Rate
Clinical Service Line: Oncology/Surgery

	Total Number of Cases	Actual Complications		Expected Complications		Risk-Adjusted Complications Index (actual: expected)
		Rate (%)	S.D.	Rate (%)	S.D.	
Hospital X	125	10.5	—	10.9	—	.96
Peer Group	982	9.8	2.3	10.5	2.1	.93
Benchmark Group	1,115	9.5	1.9	11.1	1.7	.86*

	Total Number of Cases	Actual Mortality Rate		Expected Mortality Rate		Risk-Adjusted Mortality Rate Index (actual: expected)
		Rate (%)	S.D.	Rate (%)	S.D.	
Hospital X	125	4.7	—	5.2	—	.90*
Peer Group	982	5.1	2.3	5.0	2.1	1.02
Benchmark Group	1,115	4.9	1.9	5.1	1.7	.96

	Total Number of Cases	Actual Average Length of Stay		Expected Average Length of Stay		Risk-Adjusted Average Length of Stay Index (actual: expected)
		Rate (%)	S.D.	Rate (%)	S.D.	
Hospital X	125	9.2	—	8.3	—	1.11*
Peer Group	982	8.7	2.3	8.5	2.1	1.02
Benchmark Group	1,115	8.8	1.9	8.5	1.7	.96*

	Total Number of Cases	Actual Cost		Expected Cost		Risk-Adjusted Cost Index (actual: expected)
		Rate (%)	S.D.	Rate (%)	S.D.	
Hospital X	125	9,189	—	8,759	—	1.05*
Peer Group	982	8,749	1,997	8,875	2,148	.98
Benchmark Group	1,115	8,970	2,498	9,174	1,979	.98

*Statistically significant at $p = .05$

Limitations of a Performance Measurement System

Many of the strengths of a performance measurement system are also its major limitations. First, the initial design and the establishment of explicit goals can be extremely difficult. The natures of health services and health professionals require compromise, so goals are often general enough to foster a consensus, but are too general to be used to develop specific performance indicators.

Second, the amount of data collected and its level of detail are time consuming and, for many health professionals with an aversion to data collection, the effort required is overwhelming. The latter may not be a fatal flaw, because support systems may be introduced to gather appropriate data; the complexity of the system may adversely affect its adoption and ultimate use by critical decision makers within the organization, however. This point is particularly critical because many of these individuals are veterans of earlier versions of monitoring systems, such as management by objectives (MBO) or program budgeting system (PBS), and are skeptical—if not cynical—about the applicability of these approaches to health service programs. Finally, the quantification of goals limits the amount of improvement that the system can achieve (Deming 1986).

Quality Improvement Techniques

Monitoring provides an opportunity for assessing progress and facilitating improvement. To show how quality improvement techniques may be applied, following are examinations of several such techniques as they may be applied to the delivery of noon meals in five hypothetical nursing units over a two-week period. The techniques discussed in the following sections include the run chart, the control chart, the checklist, the Pareto chart, the cause-and-effect diagram, and the flow diagram.

Run Chart

Delivery of a noon meal or any meal should be done at approximately the same time every day. If the optimal time for a patient to receive and eat his or her meal is noon, hopefully, on average, meals would be delivered at noon. One mechanism for examining whether patients are, in general, receiving their meals at noon is the run chart.

A *run chart* is a simple display of the average time of the occurrence of the event of interest displayed over time. Table 4.2 shows the daily average delivery time of the noon meal across five hypothetical nursing units for each day of a 15-day period. These data may be converted to a run chart as shown in Figure 4.5. The run chart provides a very simple view of the average daily variation in the provision of food to patients in these nursing units. As shown on the run chart, the last Sunday in the period was characterized by apparent late delivery of food. An examination of the run chart also reveals the less obvious fact that no clear pattern in variation of delivery time exists. For example, delivery on the first Monday was early, while on the second Monday it was late. Delivery on the first Saturday was also early, but on the second Saturday it was virtually on the average.

TABLE 4.2

Food Delivery
Process: Noon
Meal Delivery Time

Day of Week	Delivery Time
Monday	11:30
Tuesday	11:35
Wednesday	12:00
Thursday	12:15
Friday	11:45
Saturday	11:32
Sunday	12:00
Monday	12:15
Tuesday	11:58
Wednesday	11:50
Thursday	11:45
Friday	12:03
Saturday	11:57
Sunday	12:56
Monday	11:35

Source: Data used with the permission of West Paces Ferry Hospital

FIGURE 4.5

Food Delivery
Process: Run
Chart for Noon
Meal-Delivery
Time

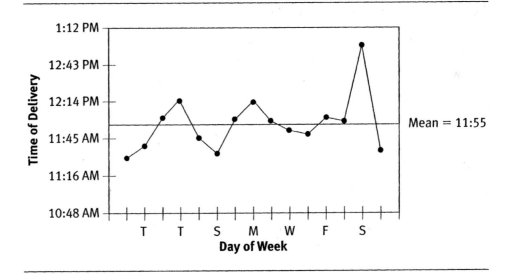

Control Chart

A *control chart* is an extension of the run chart that includes a statistically determined upper and lower limit for the normally expected variation. This was introduced in Chapter 3 as common-cause variation, which may also be reasonably assumed to be variation associated with random events. Variation that is outside the normally expected range may be considered to be variation that has been caused by an identifiable factor, and may be controlled in the future if that factor is known. Construction of a control chart for the noon meal delivery time begins with the same data used to create the run chart. However, the control chart depends on the mean delivery times, as well as the variation in delivery time.

The entire data set for noon meal deliveries is shown in Table 4.3. Section 1 in Table 4.3 shows the actual delivery time of the noon meal for each nursing unit for each day of the 15-day period, along with the average delivery time ($\overline{X}$) and the range or earliest and latest delivery times for each unit ($\overline{R}$), in minutes. Section 2 is a demonstration of the calculation of the process average ($\overline{X}$) and the

TABLE 4.3
Control Chart for the Process Average of Food Delivery Process: Noon Meal Delivery Time

1. Calculation of the Average and Range of Each of the 15 Subgroups:

Day of Week	Delivery Time					Average Time $\overline{X}$	Range R
	Unit 1	Unit 2	Unit 3	Unit 4	Unit 5		
Monday	10:45	11:01	11:27	11:55	12:22	11:30	1:37
Tuesday	10.45	11:11	11:41	12:05	12:13	11:35	1:28
Wednesday	11:11	11:37	12:02	12:30	12:40	12:00	1:29
Thursday	11:29	11:45	12:24	12:42	12:55	12:15	1:26
Friday	11:09	11:16	11:51	12:07	12:22	11:45	1:13
Saturday	10:46	10:58	11:39	12:02	12:15	11:32	1:29
Sunday	11:12	11:50	12:04	12:20	12:34	12:00	1:22
Monday	11:30	11:54	12:20	12:40	12:51	12:15	1:21
Tuesday	11:15	11:42	12:03	12:20	12:30	11:58	1:15
Wednesday	11:11	11:21	11:38	12:20	12:40	11:50	1:29
Thursday	10:59	11:25	11:48	12:10	12:23	11:45	1:24
Friday	11:17	11:39	12:04	12:30	12:45	12:03	1:28
Saturday	11:16	11:30	11:47	12:27	12:45	11:57	1:29
Sunday	12:10	12:46	12:57	1:17	1:30	12:56	1:20
Monday	10:48	11:13	11:38	12:00	12:16	11:35	1:28

2. Calculation of the Range Average ($\overline{R}$) and Process ($\overline{X}$):

$\overline{X}$ = (11:30 + 11:35 + ... + 12:56 + 11:35)/15 = 11:55
(Average of $\overline{X}$ column in 1 above)

$\overline{R}$ = 1:37 + 1:28 + ... + 1:20+ 1:28)/15 = 1:25
(Average of R column in 1)

3. Calculation of Control Limits:

$2UCL_{\overline{x}} = \overline{X} + 2\overline{R}/d_2\sqrt{n}$
$\quad = 11:55 + 2*1:25/2.326*2.236$
$\quad = 12:28$
$3UCL_{\overline{x}} = \overline{X} + 3\overline{R}/d_2\sqrt{n}$
$\quad = 11:55 + 3*1:25/2.326*2.236$
$\quad = 12:44$

$2LCL_{\overline{x}} = \overline{X} - 2\overline{R}/d_2\sqrt{n}$
$\quad = 11:55 - 2*1:25/2.326*2.236$
$\quad = 11:22$
$3LCL_{\overline{x}} = \overline{X} - 3\overline{R}/d_2\sqrt{n}$
$\quad = 11:55 - 3*1:25/2.326*2.236$
$\quad = 11:06$

(Where n is the number of observations at each time)

4. Table of Factors for Calculation of Control Chart

Observations in subgroup	2	3	4	5	6	7	8	9	10
d_2 factors	1.128	1.693	2.059	2.326	2.534	2.704	2.847	2.970	3.078

Source: Factors in section 4 taken from Gitlow et al. (1989, 588).

range average ($\overline{R}$). Section 3 shows the calculation of two and three standard deviation control limits based on these values and the factors shown in section 4.

Control limits are statistical properties of the sequence under examination, which in this case are noon food-delivery times. The basic notion is that in a stable process, events that are likely to occur by chance only infrequently would be considered to have occurred for a cause. The cause then would be sought out and eliminated. In the context of statistical testing, probabilities of .05 (1 chance in 20) or .01 (1 chance in 100) are usually taken as the criteria by which an event is assumed not to have occurred by chance. These probabilities relate in small samples (e.g., 15 days of observation) to approximately two and three standard deviations from the process mean, respectively. In consequence, control limits are usually set at two or three standard deviations from the mean. Gitlow et al. (1989) and Plsek (1992) favor three standard deviations because they feel the acceptance of two standard deviations can lead to unnecessary alarm about essentially stable processes and consequent unproductive tinkering. However, Tedaldi et al. (1992) suggest that both limits are useful, the two standard deviation limit being particularly useful because it may suggest that a process may be about to go out of control. While two standard deviations are used in practice (e.g., Schriefer 1995), setting the limits at three standard deviations is probably best, especially in a setting where many control charts are being used.

Two types of control charts are observed in practice. The first—and apparently somewhat less common in the health field—is the control chart that is based on a series of sample observations. Control limits can be calculated several ways, with the alternative ways giving slightly different results.

Figure 4.6 shows the control chart for the noon meal-delivery time including expected upper and lower limits. This allows the assessment of the variations in delivery time relative to an expected level of variation. As shown in Figure 4.6, all delivery is within expected limits except the noon meal on the last Sunday of the study period.

FIGURE 4.6
Food Delivery
Process: Control
Chart for Noon
Meal-Delivery
Time

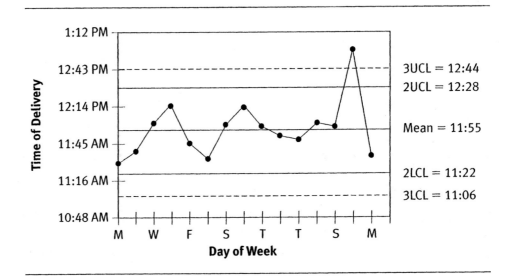

Checklist

The checklist is a form on which all apparent reasons for the occurrence of a particular problem can be recorded. For example, Figure 4.7 shows what may be a typical checklist for the food-delivery situation for the nursing unit on floor 4 East. Putting a mark in the appropriate category each time that a problem in food delivery occurs completes the checklist. Control and run charts provide data to track a process over time. The checklist provides information to assess why a particular run chart process may be occurring and what the important contributing factors are.

Pareto Chart

Data that are provided by the checklist can be used to prepare a *Pareto chart*, which is a bar graph used to arrange information in such a way that priorities for managerial action can be established. Shown in Figure 4.8 is a Pareto chart for the food-delivery process showing the reasons that patients received cold food during a hypothetical January. The chart shows that nursing unavailability was the primary factor, followed by patients being unavailable. The Pareto chart includes a line graph that shows that all reasons for cold food are included in the chart.

Cause-and-Effect Diagram

The cause-and-effect diagram is a graphic tool used to display all the factors that may produce a given effect. Often referred to as an Ishikawa diagram, this display

FIGURE 4.7
Food Delivery Process: Checklist

Date: 1/13/96–1/19/96
Floor: 4 East

	M	T	W	T	F	S	S	Total
Production sheet inaccurate	I	I			I			3
Menu incorrect	I		I		II		I	5
Diet order changed	I				I		I	3
Wrong order delivered	I		I		I	I		4
Patient asleep	III	I	IIIII	I	II	III	I	16
Patient out of room	IIIII	III	II	I	I	II	II	16
Doctor making rounds		II	IIII	I	I	II	I	11
Patient not hungry	I	I	II	I	III	I	IIIII	14
Cart faulty					I	I	I	3
Plate warmer broken	II	II	III	III	III	I	II	16
Heating unit broken	I	I			I		I	4
Thermometer miscalibrated	I				I			2
Nursing unavailable	III	II	III	III	III	III	III	20
Cart unavailable	II	III	II		II		II	11
Elevator malfunction			II	III	I			6
Tray mislabeled					I	I	I	3
TOTAL	22	16	25	14	22	18	20	137

FIGURE 4.8

Food Delivery
Process: Pareto
Chart

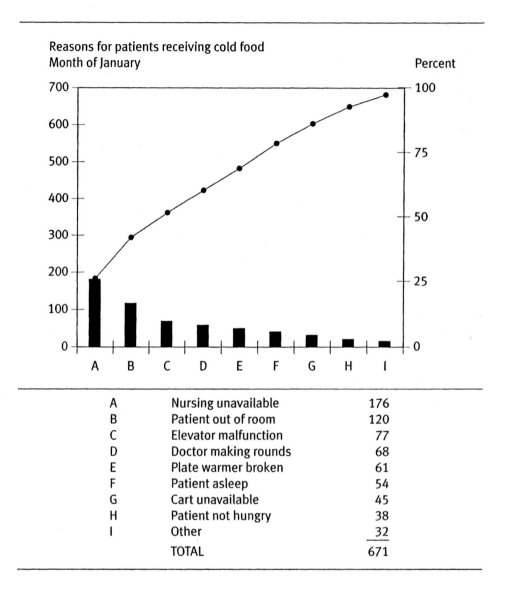

Reasons for patients receiving cold food
Month of January

A	Nursing unavailable	176
B	Patient out of room	120
C	Elevator malfunction	77
D	Doctor making rounds	68
E	Plate warmer broken	61
F	Patient asleep	54
G	Cart unavailable	45
H	Patient not hungry	38
I	Other	32
	TOTAL	671

provides information about the major contributing factors in any process variation. Figure 4.9 presents a cause-and-effect diagram focusing on food service delivery and outlines the major contribution factors associated with the patient receiving cold food. As shown in the diagram, major contributing factors include food reorder required, tray delivered late, food arriving cold, and patient unavailable. Each is further broken into subfactors.

Flow Diagram

The flow diagram is a graphic representation of the flow of all actions involved in a given process. Such a diagram provides a detailed picture of specific activities involved in a process under study. Figure 4.10 outlines the flow chart for the food-delivery process, providing insight into major events in the process. In the diagram, starting and ending points are indicated by elipses, activities are indicated by rectangles, and decision points are indicated by diamonds. At each

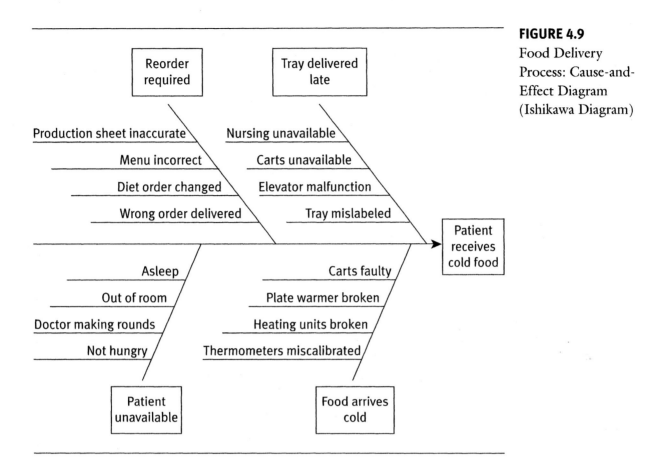

FIGURE 4.9

Food Delivery Process: Cause-and-Effect Diagram (Ishikawa Diagram)

decision point, the flow diagram may branch in two directions, either proceeding along the flow diagram or repeating one or more steps in the process, depending on the decision at that point. The primary benefit of a flow diagram is to make absolutely clear the steps required to successfully complete a process.

Quality Improvement Techniques in a Clinical Setting

While quality improvement techniques have been widely used in a variety of administrative settings, increasingly these approaches are being used to improve the provision of care within a clinical setting (Blumenthal and Scheck 1995; Neuhauser, McEachern, and Headrick 1995). Following is one illustration of the application of basic monitoring techniques to improve cardiac care provided to patients in the emergency department.

Illustration: Improving Thrombolytic Therapy

The AHA standard for delivering thrombolytic therapy to chest pain patients is within 30 to 60 minutes after patient presentation to the emergency department. Three acute hospitals within an integrated system in northern California collected data in 1994 measuring their own compliance with the standard (Mitchell et al. 1996). Analysis revealed that hospitals were falling short of the standard with

FIGURE 4.10
Food Delivery Process: Flow Chart

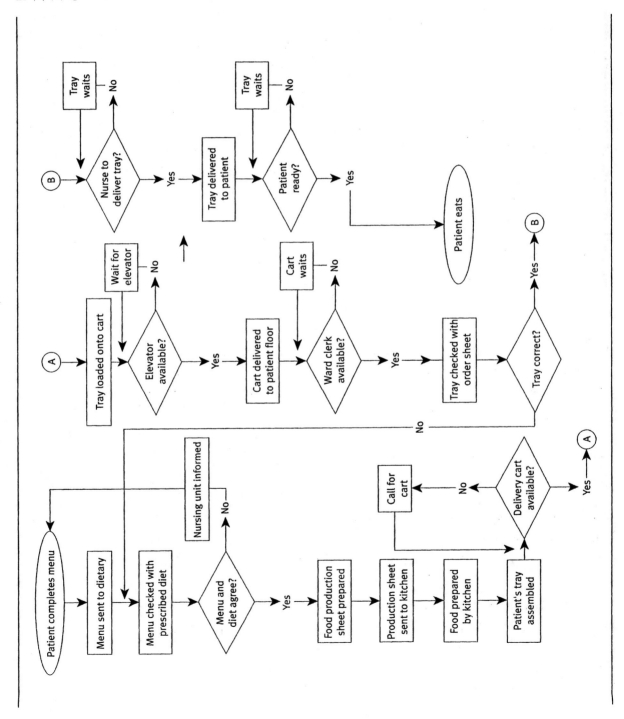

FIGURE 4.11
St. Dominic's
Hospital's Time
Frame for
Thrombolytic
Administration

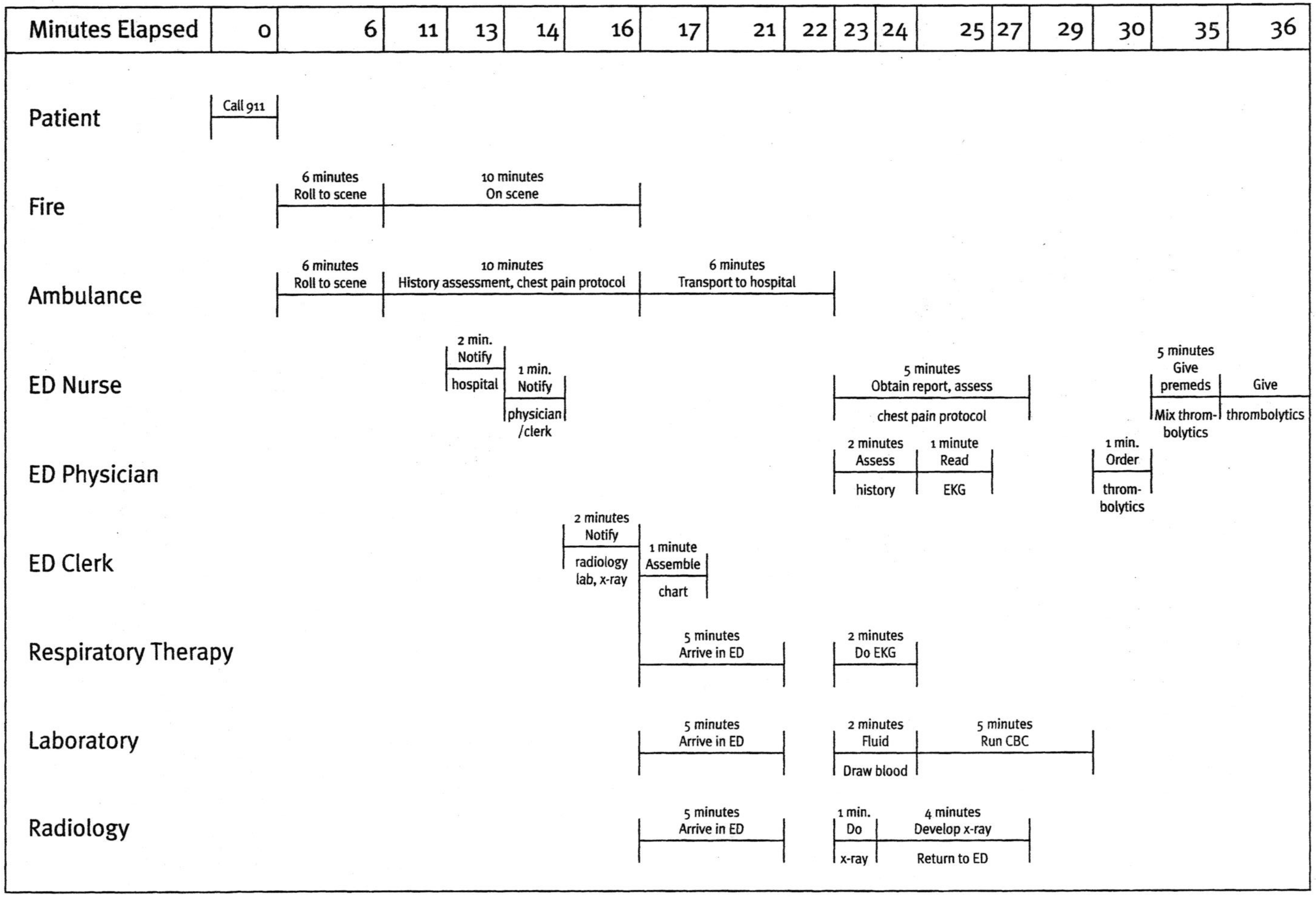

Minutes Elapsed	0	6	11	13	14	16	17	21	22	23	24	25	27	29	30	35	36

Patient — Call 911

Fire — 6 minutes / Roll to scene — 10 minutes / On scene

Ambulance — 6 minutes / Roll to scene — 10 minutes / History assessment, chest pain protocol — 6 minutes / Transport to hospital

ED Nurse — 2 min. / Notify hospital — 1 min. / Notify physician /clerk — 5 minutes / Obtain report, assess chest pain protocol

ED Physician — 2 minutes / Assess history — 1 minute / Read EKG — 1 min. / Order thrombolytics — 5 minutes / Give premeds — Give — Mix throm-/ bolytics — thrombolytics

ED Clerk — 2 minutes / Notify radiology lab, x-ray — 1 minute / Assemble chart

Respiratory Therapy — 5 minutes / Arrive in ED — 2 minutes / Do EKG

Laboratory — 5 minutes / Arrive in ED — 2 minutes / Fluid / Draw blood — 5 minutes / Run CBC

Radiology — 5 minutes / Arrive in ED — 1 min. / Do x-ray — 4 minutes / Develop x-ray / Return to ED

Source: Joint Commission on Accreditation of Healthcare Organizations. 1996. *Joint Commission Journal on Quality Improvement* 22 (6): 386.

hospitals well above the 30- to 60-minute standard. Participating institutions had well-developed quality improvement programs and each proceeded to use improvement tools and data to monitor their performance and improve the process.

The quality improvement team evaluated existing algorithms and protocols to identify delays in the thrombolytic administration process. For example, a Gantt chart (Figure 4.11) tracks the timeline of thrombolytic therapy and helps develop recommendations for improvement, including:

- cross-training emergency nursing personnel to perform electrocardiograms;
- developing thrombolytic standing orders assuring that the thrombolytic administration occurs in the emergency department, not the intensive care unit; and
- doing 12-lead electrocardiograms in the field and transmitting them to the emergency department prior to patient arrival.

Finally, Figure 4.12 shows an example of a statistical control chart used to track times of patient arrival to start thrombolytic therapy to help staff monitor progress of the improvement process. As shown in the control chart, considerable progress was made in meeting the standard of 30 to 60 minutes.

FIGURE 4.12
Time Line of Acute Myocardial Infarction Patient Arrival to Thrombolytic Administration (March 1994– March 1996)

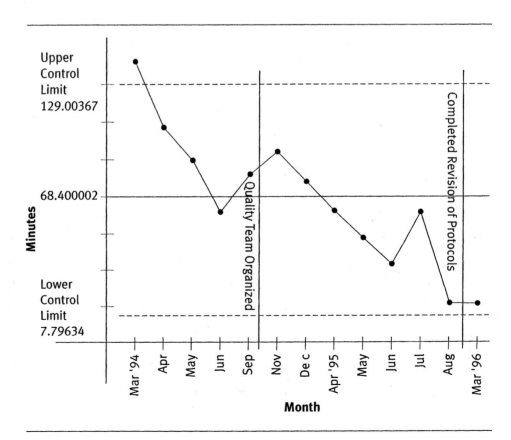

Discussion Questions

1. What are the similarities and differences between performance measurement systems and quality improvement techniques?
2. Select a health service program—or set of activities that you have been associated with—and develop a Gantt chart displaying critical activities.

III

CASE STUDIES

CASE STUDIES AS AN EVALUATION STRATEGY

The amount and speed with which change is occurring in health services is unprecedented. Managers are constantly faced with the challenges of making decisions with limited data. While it is desirable to have program or service data based on an experimental design or on a representative sample from which one could make statistically valid generalizations, the reality is that most decisions are made from data that are at best based on a series of case studies. While case studies come closer to art than science, they provide important information for improved decision making and may provide the basis for more defined and refined evaluation strategies. The purpose of this chapter is to consider the appropriate setting for case studies, what can be learned, and what decisions can be made as a result of such an approach.

What Are Case Studies?

A *case study* selects a single, unique activity, organization, or entity for observation or selects one example from a number of entities, activities, or organizations for observation and bases conclusions on the observation. This process greatly increases the amount and depth of information that may be collected over certain other evaluation approaches, but it limits the kinds of conclusions and decisions that case studies can produce. Even though case studies are essentially qualitative in nature, they use a variety of data collection methods and provide valuable insight into more quantitatively based evaluations. Following is a brief illustration of the case study as an evaluation tool.

Illustration: Improving Preventive Services

Increasing evidence exists that the most effective way to improve preventive services in primary care is to establish and maintain organized preventive-service systems and that these systems can be best established through the learning and application of continuous quality improvement (CQI) concepts and methods. The design, implementation, and evaluation of a CQI intervention within a primary practice setting and the understanding of factors facilitating or impeding that process is a complex undertaking. Using field interviews with key informants, supplemented with data from the larger study, a series of case studies (Fischer 1998) were conducted to supplement the quantitative evaluation in two ways:

1. by describing the process of change ongoing within the participating clinics; and
2. by providing insight into why things happened the way they did within the clinics (by identifying causes or determinants of such change).

Program While preventive-service systems may be the means to improve the utilization of preventive services, considerable interest surrounds CQI concepts and techniques as ways that healthcare organizations can improve their main work processes. In 1993, the Agency for Health Care Policy and Research (AHCPR) funded an evaluation to test the hypotheses that by promoting an agenda for preventive services and by working through an alternative process of planned organizational change called CQI, an HMO (or MCO) can stimulate its primary care clinics to develop and maintain systems to routinely deliver the preventive services described in the Healthy People 2000 goals (Solberg et al. 1995). The trial is called IMPROVE (Improving Prevention through Organization, Vision, and Empowerment). The intervention was conducted from September 1994 through June 1996 and consisted of three parts organized by the clinic management:

- *leadership involvement and commitment,* as expressed by the written agreement that clinic management would identify and support an internal multidisciplinary process improvement team to work on the eight targeted preventive services, the appointment of a leader and facilitator for the team, the establishment of clinic-wide guidelines for the designated preventive services, and the provision of a problem and mission statement for the team;
- *team training in prevention system and process improvement,* including a six-hour orientation session and subsequent workshops over a six-month period, along with the development of materials and manuals; and
- *facilitation and consultation* as appropriate to the designated teams during the course of the project.

Evaluation design The overall design was a prospective pretest, posttest, and experimental study of a sample of 44 primary care clinics contracting with two large managed care organizations, Blue Cross and Health Partners, that manage medical care for approximately 25 percent of the population in metropolitan Minneapolis/St. Paul. Clinics were randomly assigned to an intervention or control group. Personnel in all 44 clinics completed surveys prior to and at the end of the intervention to measure the adoption of the improvement process along with chart audits to assess practice patterns over time. In addition, case studies were conducted in 6 of the 22 clinics that participated in the IMPROVE intervention to address the following questions:

- How do clinic environments stimulate and/or impede the innovation process?

- How does organizational culture affect a process of directed innovation?
- How do the qualities of individual leaders influence the change processes?
- How does a quality improvement team actually implement the change process?
- How do clinics change as a result of a quality improvement process?

What Can Be Learned?

The data generated from the case studies provided important supplemental data to the overall evaluation (Fischer 1998). While the more quantitative evaluation is ongoing (Solberg et al. 1996) and initial analysis suggests that with training and assistance interested primary care teams will establish functioning CQI teams that will produce a substantial increase of functional preventive processes (Solberg, Kottke, and Brekke 1998), the case study material provided important insights into the challenges faced by the participating practices. Specifically, the case study analysis revealed many hazards of the implementation process including the clear documentation that the change process is tedious and cumbersome, the pay-off in either improved quality or reduced long-term investment is unclear at best and nonexistent at worst, and the intervention itself is a dynamic process that evolves and adapts over time.

The case study also documents benefits to the primary care process that are difficult to quantify. Specifically, the process created cross-departmental functioning teams that without the intervention would not have to be created; throughout the practices, a heightened awareness centered on the importance of improvement and of preventive services.

Appropriate Settings for Case Studies

The case study is a way of acquiring a great deal of information about a single program, either as a representative of a type of program activity or as the only one of a kind. In either instance, the case study will generally be carried out in a single organization or program. Case studies may be undertaken at any time. Unlike experiments or survey research strategies, case studies need not be planned or anticipated at the beginning of a program or started at the time of program implementation. A case study is a particularly useful tool when evaluators and practitioners want an insight into the entire working of a program. In this form, the case study provides both detailed and extensive knowledge of selected aspects of a program or their operations and a broad overview of the total program.

A case study, unlike other forms of evaluation, is often exploratory. Very little may be known about a particular program by people or organizations that must make decisions regarding its level of funding, staffing, or even continuation. A case study can serve as a good source of initial information that may prove sufficient for decision making about the program itself. It also may provide the basis for the design of a monitoring system or for survey research, either of which may in the long run produce the evaluations of interest. A case study can even be the first step in setting up an experimental design to answer questions about the relevance, effectiveness, progress, adequacy, impact, or sustainability of a program.

A case study does not necessarily need to be purely exploratory, however. The extensive, although often subjective, knowledge that a case study produces can be quite effective in providing an initial appraisal of the extent to which the program conforms to planning design and of its overall impact and effectiveness. Also, a number of cases on the same topic permits the examination of process and outcomes across cases. This lattter situation provides an opportunity to examine how and why events occur under different conditions (Miles and Huberman 1994). What must be remembered, however, is that most of the information derived from a case study will be subjective, and decisions will be based on information collected in the absence of any control group.

Limitations of Case Studies

The case study approach has several problems that limit its use in a number of settings: lack of clear categories, selective perception, and interactiveness.

- *Lack of clear categories.* This problem can be remedied fairly well by clear thought prior to the study about the issues that require decisions and the specific information that must be obtained to allow these decisions to be made. After a series of questions is established, the categories for information should follow.
- *Selective perception.* This is not only a problem of how the answers to questions are perceived and recorded, but also one of initial formulation of questions. To avoid the problem at the formulation stage, the questions can be pretested, along with the reasons for asking them, on a few people who can react to the appropriateness of the questions for producing the information desired. In the actual study situation, selective perception of answers can be avoided somewhat by the chance to ask for clarification, and sometimes by restating the response in terms that the evaluator understands so that misperceptions may be corrected. Although this approach still leaves room for problems of perceptions, this is an effective data-collection procedure.
- *Interactiveness.* This is clearly a problem in the case study setting. Although observation is a means of obtaining data about program activity in a more or less natural setting, the observation itself immediately creates an unnatural setting. Because the case study creates an unnatural setting, evaluators must be very careful interpreting their observations. If so, knowledge gained in the case study approach may not differ markedly from the true situation. A major problem of interactiveness is the difficulty in actually measuring its effect on study results. Except in highly controlled situations, most effects of interactiveness cannot be assessed. To tell how much of an answer is real and how much was produced simply because the question was asked is impossible.

In a way, the appropriate setting for case studies as being inappropriate settings for other types of evaluation may be easiest to discuss. Case studies are often carried out where no initial planning was conducted for evaluation before implementation of the program. No comparison groups were set up, or no criteria for inputs, process, or outputs were established by which to evaluate the program. The case study thus frequently becomes the only strategy available for conducting an evaluation of a program.

Appropriate Data for Case Studies

Almost any type of data is appropriate for case studies. The data collected in the course of a case study may include observation of program activity, reports prepared by the program, unstructured conversations with program personnel, statistical summaries of program activities, structured or unstructured interview data, or information collected through formalized questionnaires. Because the case study as an evaluation strategy is most effective when its purpose is to provide information for decisions best made in the light of a general overall view of a program, any data source can be used. Data collected through the case study approach are apt to be submitted ultimately to a subjective and impressionistic type of analysis, and so any type can be successfully incorporated.

A broad distinction in types of data that may be collected through the case study approach would be the classifications of subjective and objective data. *Subjective data* can include such information as may be collected through participant or nonparticipant observation and unstructured interviews. *Objective data* may include information collected from organization or program documents and records, or structured or closed-ended questionnaires and interviews. This distinction is not perfect. A subjective component to questionnaire data exists, no matter how rigorously collected, as well as an objective character to nonparticipant observation at its best. Nevertheless, the general distinction is useful. Specific treatment of interview and questionnaire data, particularly of the structured and closed-ended type, is described in Chapters 7 and 8 on survey research, for this approach depends almost entirely on these two forms of data collection even though they are applicable to the case study. Discussion of the use of organization documents and records, including organization statistical reports or program reports, appears in Chapters 9 and 10 on time-series analysis. This section and the material immediately following deals primarily with the subjective data of case studies (i.e., the informal and unstructured sources of data, such as participant observation, informal discussion, and open-ended questionnaires).

Participant and Nonparticipant Observation

Observation, whether participant or nonparticipant, may be thought of as the primary source of information. Participant observation is a strategy that received wide usage among anthropologists in the latter part of the nineteenth century and the early part of the twentieth century. Participant observation is essentially a strategy by which the researcher becomes a member of, and lives within, a given society. Such a strategy can be used for program evaluation when the evaluator assumes a working role within the program or organization being evaluated and collects data about it while working in the group.

Nonparticipant observation is a strategy seldom used in research per se but frequently used in evaluation. In this approach, a team of experts reviews and examines the workings of an organization or program for a period of time.

Although nonparticipant observation is more effective in serious evaluation work, both participant and nonparticipant observation have problems—some common to both and some greater for one or the other. These problems parallel the limitations of case studies mentioned earlier and are loosely characterized as three types. The first is the problem of cataloging and categorizing observations. The second is the problem of selective perception. The third is the problem of interactiveness. Selective perception is a clear problem in participant observation. Interactiveness is a clear problem in nonparticipant observation. The lack of ways to catalog and categorize observations is a general problem in both approaches.

Lack of Clear Categories

If an evaluator comes to a particular problem on an exploratory basis without much information about the program, early observation probably will be largely unstructured and resulting data may not be easily classified in ways that will be useful to the evaluation. To avoid this situation, it is critical to have a clear understanding of what the evaluation is to accomplish, what decisions are to be made as a result of the evaluation, and what information must be obtained to make them, even in exploratory stages. If not thought out in detail at the outset, the result is likely to be a random set of observations, all seemingly unrelated to one another or to the evaluation issue of concern.

Selective Perception

The problem of selective perception is in many ways a mirror image of the problem of a lack of clear means for cataloging and categorizing observed activities. Under the best circumstances, a set of selective categories to define needed data and classify observations is extremely useful to any evaluation study. What is natural is for observers to automatically note actions or occurrences to which they have been sensitized by cultural values or learning and classify them in preexisting categories. To a certain extent, this situation is desirable. It greatly limits the number of phenomena that need to be observed and permits rapid and fairly effective handling of those that do. Although selective perception permits conscious preselection of phenomena for observation, it has clear problems. Selective perception is often responsible for missing important aspects of program operation that do not fit predetermined categories. It may also contribute to interpreting program activities incorrectly. Possibly the most undesirable aspect of selective perception is that the preconception that a program may work in a certain way or be relatively successful or unsuccessful may produce what is known as the *self-fulfilling prophecy*.

Consider a program evaluation concerned with a training program for health managers. The evaluator may believe—perhaps subconsciously—that a problem of such training programs is that they lack practical content. Here, the evaluator is likely to look for evidence of lack of practical content and to find it. The evaluator's initial perception becomes one of the findings of the evaluation, even though the perception may not have been accurate.

The self-fulfilling prophecy is an important source of invalidity in experimental evaluations and surveys, observations, and structured interviews. However, because the process of collecting data through observation and unstructured interviews is highly subjective, avoiding the problems of selective perception and self-fulfilling prophecy is extremely difficult when data collection consists of observation or unstructured interviews.

Interactiveness

Interactiveness occurs because an observer, whether participant or nonparticipant, is rarely anonymous. While researchers or evaluators are observing and recording what is going on in the program, they are also, by their presence, affecting and shaping those activities. The results of an evaluation involving observational methods, especially over a long period of time, may be influenced as much by the observation technique as by the program.

This is not to suggest that other evaluation techniques do not also have some interactive characteristics. Both surveys and experiments can be interactive and will be discussed in subsequent chapters. The distinction, however, between interactiveness in case studies and other approaches is that it can be protected against in the case study or expert evaluation less easily than in other evaluation approaches. Surveys and experiments provide the quantitative basis for assessing interactiveness. Such a basis is not present for case studies; thus the evaluator using case studies must be particularly careful.

Unstructured Interviews

Observations and interviews can be used effectively together to obtain a great deal of information about a program. What is unlikely is that a case study would be carried out that did not combine both observations and interviews, at least in practice if not by design. The same types of problems that occur with observation occur with unstructured interviews.

Even though this approach to data collection is referred to as unstructured, every effort should be made to determine, before the interviews begin, precisely what information is to be obtained. This may take the form of a checklist of specified items about which to ask or a series of roughly worded questions that can be paraphrased. At the very least, several leading questions to direct the conversation to the important issues should be determined ahead of time. Having a brief checklist of points to cover and questions to raise arranged in a logical sequence, and then trying to adhere to this sequence is probably best. Such a sequence may somewhat reduce spontaneity, but will help to guarantee that at least most major points are covered. In an interview, getting away from the main subject or forgetting or skipping points of importance is easy to do, particularly for persons who are not highly experienced in the technique.

Data for Case Studies from Two Different Settings

To give additional specificity to the data appropriate to case studies, consider again the community clinical oncology program and the primary healthcare program discussed in Chapter 3.

Illustration: Community Clinical Oncology Program (CCOP)

While the CCOP evaluation was designed to monitor the ability of new organizational forms to accrue patients and to change physician practice patterns, an equally important function of the evaluation was to explain the dynamics of these organizations and their relationships with research bases and with the National Cancer Institute (NCI)—in effect, the why and how of what is happening (Kaluzny, Warnecke, and Associates 1996).

The case study was a preferred strategy to meet this objective. Twenty CCOPs were selected along with five research bases for in-depth site visits. Each site represented a specific case study in which specific individuals were interviewed. A template outlining required data items was developed that provided guidelines for interviewing the principal investigator, data managers, participating community physicians, administrators from participating hospitals, and representatives from relevant community organizations. Substantive areas that provided the organizational framework for each case study included:

- CCOP goals
- CCOP organizational structure
- clinical trials
- management procedures
- physician relationships
- component/affiliate relationships
- organization of cancer control research
- research base relationships
- NCI/DCPC relations
- relationships with community groups
- relationships with community physicians
- environmental factors
- emerging issues and other significant factors.

The exhibit in Appendix 5.1 indicates the topical area covered by each type of interviewee. The appendix also presents an illustrative template used to interview one of the designated key informants, the project principal investigator (PI).

Based on site visits, 20 CCOP cases and 5 research bases cases were prepared. For each group (CCOPs and research bases), the identified cases were reviewed comparatively. They were used to develop a series of hypotheses for testing based on data from the larger study and provided the basis for a dialogue with National Cancer Institute (NCI) and National Institutes of Health (NIH) program administrators about the various managerial actions to enhance program performance.

Case studies provided the initial observation of the actual structure and operations of the individual community-based CCOPs and their relationship to the research bases and the NCI. These observations were used to identify the critical variables thought to be predictive of accrual to protocols, and design the subsequent survey collection instruments. The case studies also provided knowledge of the actual operations and structure of the CCOP sufficient to use this information to influence initial funding decisions at the national level. The case studies clearly demonstrated the ability of the CCOPs to accrue patients within local communities, but they were embryonic organizations that were fragile. To succeed, they needed a great deal of support. The PI was clearly a major factor in the success of the program at this point. The commitment of the PI and a small but dedicated staff made the difference between success and failure.

What was learned?

Illustration: Early Detection in Primary Care

While the primary purpose of the evaluation was to help community-based primary care practices increase the utilization of prevention and early detection services, an equally important purpose was to focus on the problems and challenges associated with implementation and the identifying factors that facilitate or inhibit the implementation process. Four case studies were conducted to complement the quantitative data and provide insight into the dynamics involved in the implementation process (Jackson et al. 1994).

In each site visit, three types of data were collected: interviews, participant and nonparticipant observations, and records and documents. These are data beyond that collected in the regular overall study. For example, in the case study practices, in-depth interviews were conducted with all physicians, nurses, and clerical-support personnel. These interviews collected information on such areas as the structure of the practice; how capital investment decisions are made within the practice; and specific deliberations regarding actions around clinic policy versus managerial policy with the practice.

The case study provided important supplemental information. While quantitative data provided important practice-pattern data suggesting that the intervention had a modest effect (Kinsinger et al. 1998), the case studies suggested some conditions that enhanced or inhibited the ability of the practice to implement screening activities. Six factors were identified as critical to the implementation process:

What was learned?

1. *Professional autonomy.* Primary care providers develop a set of expectations about what is appropriate practice, and these expectations constitute the operating culture of the practice. Any change presents a level of uncertainty and the attendant problems of untried work rules.

2. *Team-based communications.* Communications is a critical component of any change initiative. Unfortunately, the hierarchical structure of professional roles is clearly evident in a primary care setting and may present considerable barriers to any change initiative.

3. *Data availability.* The saying goes, "If you can't measure it, you can't manage it," and within a primary care setting, many of the providers just don't have the skill and time to provide quick and reliable information upon which to base clinical decisions.

4. *Service effectiveness.* Primary care physicians either implicitly or explicitly are interested in whether an activity can make a difference. While many of the activities involved in prevention have not been evaluated, an inherent skepticism of many of the screening and CQI initiatives inhibits implementation.

5. *Cost/efficiency.* To practice successfully in a primary care setting requires more than a commitment to service; it requires an ability to manage unpredictable demands and conflicting expectations. Because many preventive services are not compensated, limited time and energy are given to more acute activities that generate revenue for the practice, despite the recognition that various preventive services may have significant benefits for the patient.

6. *Patient expectations.* Increasingly, patients present with a set of expectations that influence the actual provision of care. Failure to meet these expectations may cause patients to seek care from other providers.

These factors provide the context within which any intervention activity must operate and contribute to the ability of the intervention to have an effect. Subsequent intervention efforts must be carried out in a manner that capitalizes on these factors and thereby assures the success of the intervention.

Application to Decision Making and Types of Evaluation

In the right circumstances, perhaps more can be learned through the case study method than through any other evaluation strategy. Because the evaluator is not bound by either a specific data collection methodology or a specific set of analytical techniques, the scope of a case study can range broadly across all aspects of program activity. The case study approach allows the evaluator to probe areas of specific interest and obtain a wealth of detail about the operation of specific programs.

The major limitation of a case study, in terms of producing knowledge, is the absence of any method for establishing the causal importance of a particular program. Because no comparison can be reached between settings in which a program does or does not exist, no formal way to assess the program's causal effect exists. Even when such evaluations are made in case studies, the number of factors that could be responsible for any apparent causal effect is quite large and uncontrollable. To provide in a case study a statistic mechanism for the elimination of possible causal variables is impossible. No way exists to ensure that no other factor except the actual program itself was responsible for changes that may have taken place.

However, the case study is a relatively inexpensive way of acquiring information about how well a particular program works, plus subjective knowledge about whether it is performing according to expectations. The extent to which decision makers can have confidence in the kinds of results that a case study produces, and can base decisions on such a case study, lies very much in the realm of the extent or degree of their confidence in the objectivity, ability, and competence of the evaluators. Certainly, however, many important program decisions have been made on the basis of case-study evaluations.

To consider the decisions that can be made on the basis of case studies, and with what degree of confidence, a return to the types of evaluation (i.e., relevance, adequacy, progress, efficiency and effectiveness, impact and sustainability) is useful.

Relevance

The major questions raised in regard to relevance are as follows:

- Is there a problem that a particular program should confront?
- How clear is the problem if it exists?
- How well defined is the problem?

Examining the nature of the problem, determining whether it is of sufficient magnitude to warrant a program, and delineating the nature of the program needed to solve the problem are all issues amenable to the case study method.

Suppose, for example, that the health status in certain communities is low. A case study may be undertaken in one community or an area of a community to determine which factors lead to low health status and which programs may be useful in attempting to improve health status. Such an exploratory effort is an appropriate use of the case study approach. The exploratory effort should provide information about health problems, and shortcomings in health systems and other systems that may lead to high rates of morbidity and mortality.

What is unlikely, however, is that such a case study would point clearly to any specific solution. In primary care, for instance, the primary care worker would solve general health problems. What is more likely is that a case study of this type would identify a broad range of factors leading to poor-health outcomes, many of which would be related, others unrelated, some working in opposite directions to one another, and many about which nothing can be done.

For any conclusion from a case study to be an appropriate strategy for solving the problem, it would need to be drawn from extensive information, including both the evaluator's initial subjective impressions and also perceptions grafted onto the study by the evaluator, community experts, or decision makers during the course of the work or afterward. In essence, a case study could identify a number of areas in which problems exist, but would only coincidentally lead to the conclusion that a primary healthcare program may be the appropriate mechanism for attacking them.

Adequacy

The case study can provide important information on the extent to which some activity or initiative is able to address the full scope of the problem. The abilities to observe, to query people involved with actual service activities, and to follow up and simply listen provide important information to the decision-making process. Perhaps its most important contribution is the ability to understand the ongoing processes and dynamics involved and thereby explain or at least provide a rationale for what actually happened.

Progress

The case study approach can also provide information on the question of progress in a health services program. Progress concerns whether inputs, process, and outputs meet some type of normative, predetermined standards for their level of operation or success. Very often, however, if a case study is to be used to address the progress of a health services program as an alternative to uninterrupted monitoring, the types of standards required for a good monitoring probably have not been thought through or determined at the outset. As a result, the case study generally becomes both an examination of the program and an effort to set reasonable performance standards for the program as the examination is going on. Much can be learned from such an activity, but standards set as a study progresses are likely to be influenced by the actual performance of the project, thus removing the basic objectivity that could exist in the study situation.

Efficiency

The chief concern in an evaluation of efficiency is whether the results obtained by the program could have been obtained less expensively. In the most rigorous sense, a case study cannot evaluate efficiency simply because no comparisons exist between what is produced under a given program and by a given process versus what the cost is to produce the same results by using another strategy. The fact is that a case study is the study of a single example of the program with no comparison group available. Still, a knowledgeable person involved in a case study situation can make judgments about the extent to which the program is operating efficiently. These judgments must be based strictly on the experience and knowledge of the evaluator or evaluation team and cannot be based on comparisons with other operating programs. Such results can be useful in suggesting whether a program is operating efficiently and whether it should be modified in more efficient ways.

Effectiveness, Impact, and Sustainability

Effectiveness determines whether the program has produced what it is expected to produce; *impact* determines the program's long-term consequences; and *sustainability* describes whether the program will continue after external resources are withdrawn. Using the case study approach, it is quite possible to determine whether the aims of the program in the short run—the effectiveness aspect—have been met. Examining the long-term consequences and sustainability may be more difficult unless the case study is conducted at a time that allows for retrospective analysis of the program. If this is the case, results accompanying the existence of the program can readily be perceived. The major problem, however, in evaluating effectiveness, impact, and sustainability from a case study is that it is impossible to tell if major results of interest would have been obtained whether the program of interest had existed or not and whether its continuation is a function of activities attributable to the program or just random events in the environment.

Discussion Questions

1. Why is a case study considered more an art than a science?
2. Under what conditions would the case study be an appropriate evaluation approach?
3. Under what conditions would the case study be an inappropriate evaluation format?
4. Why is interactiveness a particularly difficult problem in case studies? How may the problem be avoided or at least minimized?

Topical Areas by Type of CCOP Interviewee

	CCOP PI	CCOP MDs	CCOP Coor.	CCOP Data Managers	Non-CCOP Funded Staff	Hospital Admin.	Non-CCOP Physicians	Community/ Voluntary Agency Representative
CCOP Goals	X	X						
CCOP Organizational Structure	X	X	X	X				
Physician Relationships	X	X	X	X			X	
Interrelationships Between Components and Affiliates	X	X				X		
CCOP-Hospital Interaction						X		
Relationships with Non-CCOP Affiliated Hospitals	X		X			X		
Protocol Selection and Dissemination Process			X	X				
Clinical Trials Management				X				
Relationships with Hospital IRBs	X		X	X				
CCOP Participation in Clinical Trials	X	X						
Cancer Control Issues	X	X	X	X		X	X	X
Relationships with Research Bases	X	X	X	X	X			
Relationships with NCI/DCPC	X		X	X				
CCOP Operating Budget			X					
Financial and In-Kind Support for CCOP						X		
Community Awareness of CCOP					X			
Relationships with Community Groups	X	X						
Relationships with M.D. Community	X	X		X				
Roles and Responsibilities					X			
Board/Committee Relationships								X
Joint Activities with CCOP								X
CCOP Success Factors	X	X	X	X	X	X	X	X
Awareness of CCOP Program						X	X	X

CCOP Principle Investigator

(Questions also are applicable for co-principal investigator [co-PI] or associate principal investigator.)

A. CCOP Goals

1. What do you see as the main goals of this CCOP?
2. How do you think that these goals may differ from NCI goals for the CCOP program?
3. What strategies is this CCOP using to achieve each goal?

B. CCOP Organizational Structure

1. How adequate is the level of staffing in your CCOP for:
   a. Meeting cancer treatment accrual targets?
   b. Meeting cancer control accrual targets?
2. (If interview is a co-PI or associate PI) How are CCOP administrative responsibilities divided between you and (name of PI)?
3. Confirm that a board/executive committee with oversight responsibility exists for the CCOP. If not applicable, go to question 4.
   a. Who serves on this board/committee?
   b. How often does this board/committee meet?
   c. What kinds of policy and programmatic decisions are made by this board/committee? (Get copies of meeting minutes, if possible.)
4. For CCOPs without a board or executive committee: How are policy and programmatic decisions made in this CCOP?

C. CCOP Physician Participation

1. How many oncologists in the CCOP service area do not participate in the CCOP?
   a. Why don't they participate?
   b. Are any of these physicians enrolling patients on protocols through a cooperative group outreach program (CGOP)?

D. Competition

1. How much competition exists between CCOP oncologists and other oncologists in the CCOP service area?
2. How has competition among area oncologists affected the ability of the CCOP to accrue patients to research protocols?

E. Physician Departures

1. Have any physicians left this CCOP?
2. If so, why did they leave?

F. Communication

1. In general, how often do you communicate with participating physicians on CCOP matters?
2. What kinds of issues or problems do you discuss with them?

6

CASE STUDY TECHNIQUES AND INTERPRETATION

Because much of the data gathered through a case study approach is qualitative, analysis and interpretation tend to be highly subjective. Yet a few techniques are available to help the evaluator add structure to the data collection effort and analysis as well as guide the interpretation. Success depends on the evaluator's ability to fit many bits of information into an overall picture that has meaning, relevance, and clarity. Perhaps more than any other evaluation approach, case studies depend on a multi-method approach to data collection and analysis. The objective of this chapter is to consider techniques that help structure the analysis and interpretation of data collected in a case study format for the improvement of decision making.

Observational Techniques

When data from a case study are limited to unstructured observations or informal interviews, analysis also remains relatively informal. In general, analysis of data collected through observations and unstructured interviews requires careful sifting, cataloging, and recombining by the evaluator rather than application of specific analytical techniques. The evaluator must bring an objective eye and a creative mind to the interpretation of the data.

To increase objectivity and permit the application of simple quantitative techniques while maintaining the exploratory quality of the case study, it is possible and often advisable to use a variety of more structured forms of observation (Miles and Huberman 1994). One approach is *structured observations*, in which the evaluator develops categorical schemes during and after the observation. Using this technique, the evaluator is influenced in the coding process not by previous research or personal experience but by the events observed. The approach couples the flexibility of an open-ended or unstructured observation and the discipline of a structured evaluation. It provides an opportunity to understand things we may know nothing about. The approach is nicely illustrated by an ongoing study of health departments.

Illustration: The Organization and Operation of
Local Public Health Agencies

To examine trends, financing, and operations in local public health agency organization, researchers conducted detailed case studies of 15 local health departments (Mays, Miller, and Halverson 1998). Departments were selected to achieve diversity with respect to geographic location, population characteristics, and health resources availability. Data sources for the case studies included:

- structured and semi-structured interviews with departmental administrators;
- document reviews of contracts, public health ordinances, annual reports, and governing board meeting minutes;
- participatory observations of management team meetings; and
- passive observations of clinical service delivery sites.

Structured telephone interviews, which were designed to collect basic information on organizational structure, organizational performance, and relationships with other community organizations, were conducted with the director of each local health department. In-person interviews and observations were subsequently conducted to collect more detailed information about health department organization and operation.

Protocols for conducting in-person interviews and observations included concepts from existing models of organizational structure, management style, interorganizational relations, and health services delivery. For example, researchers used established models of organizational structure to record observed attributes of local health department organizations. Similarly, for observations of management team meetings, researchers used established models of management style to record and classify meeting attributes. Interviews and observational sessions also included unstructured, open-ended components designed to capture unanticipated attributes of public health agencies. For example, information about community participation in health department activities was collected through open-ended questioning, unstructured observations, and document reviews.

In examining health department relationships with other organizations, researchers used principles from *network analysis*. Health department interviews and observations were used to identify other organizations that were central to the department's public health activities. Interviews were subsequently conducted with these organizations—including hospitals, primary care centers, managed care plans, and other health and human service agencies.

Information collected through interviews, observations, and organizational documents were subjected to a systematic content review. A coding scheme was developed using concepts from existing theoretical and empirical work, as well as from trends noted during the data collection process. All information was coded based on content and organized into a database for further analysis. This approach enabled comparisons to be made across different public health jurisdictions and across the different types of organizations that maintain relationships with local health departments.

Use of Existing Information Systems

Programs routinely collect information about their operations. Much of this information is in aggregate form—number of clients served, number of visits made by different types of people, and so on. Many programs, however, collect information on patients' visits through the use of encounter forms. The specifics may vary, but information usually includes patient characteristics, diagnostic classification, treatment, and level of provider skill.

Because these data are collected routinely on all patients, they are generally available in standard form over a relatively long period of time. This availability permits a thorough and structured assessment of patterns and trends about a single program. The availability of this type of data, for example, permits the assessment of resource use and a detailed analysis of the types of patients served and their clinical problems. Consider the following use of existing data systems to facilitate evaluation efforts and enhance decision making.

Illustration: Patterns of Coordination and Clinical Outcomes— A Study of Surgical Services

Monitoring and evaluating selected patient care and support service activities using data routinely collected by an organization provides an opportunity to identify traceable variables that influence the quality of patient care. In 1991, the Department of Veterans Affairs initiated the National Veterans Affairs Surgical Risk Study (NVASRS) (Young et al. 1998). The purposes of this study were to develop and validate a methodology for adjusting patient outcomes to account for differences in preoperative risk of surgical patients and to identify best clinical and managerial practices for providing surgical care.

Intra-operative and outcome data are collected prospectively from patients undergoing a major surgical procedure as defined by the use of general, spinal, or epidermal anesthesia. All major surgical procedures are included, except cardiac surgery, and surgical outcomes consisting of both mortality and morbidity. Mortality is measured as the death of a patient as a result of any cause inside or outside the hospital within 30 days of the index procedure. Morbidity is measured as the occurrence of any one of 21 selected surgical complications (e.g., deep vein thrombophlebitis or wound infection) within 30 days of the index procedure.

The risk adjustment process uses patient-level preoperative clinical data including the complexity of the surgical procedure performed within a stepwise logistic regression model to calculate mortality and morbidity rates for each surgical service. Using this information, it is possible to compare observed rates with expected rates for morbidity and mortality. A ratio of 1 indicates that the surgical service's observed number of adverse outcomes (i.e., mortality or morbidity) is above the number expected based on the risk profile of the patients. A ratio below 1 indicates that the service's observed number of adverse outcomes is below the expected number.

An examination of these data by surgical service followed by site visit to selected hospitals suggested substantial differences in the patterns of staff coordination between those hospitals whose observed rates of adverse surgical outcomes (i.e., mortality or morbidity) were higher than expected and those hospitals whose observed rates of adverse outcomes were lower than expected.

The data collected from the existing information system provided the opportunity to examine different coordination patterns in use by the various hospitals. Analysis reveals that coordination is an important factor for reducing morbidity and mortality in surgical services.

Tracer Methodology

To provide focus to the case study format, particularly as it concerns program performance relating to the quality of care provided, evaluators may wish to structure the observation and data collection efforts around a particular disease entity. These particular disease entities are known as *tracers* and provide a framework for evaluating the interaction between providers and patients in their environment. The following criteria are considered appropriate for the selection of tracer conditions:

- A tracer should have a definite functional impact.
- A tracer should be relatively well defined and easy to diagnose.
- The prevalence rate should be high enough to permit the collection of adequate data from a limited population sample.
- The natural history of the condition should vary with the use and effectiveness of medical care.
- The technique of medical management of the conditions should be well defined for at least one of the following processes: prevention, diagnosis, treatment, or rehabilitation.
- Effects of nonmedical factors on the tracer should be understood. (Kessner, Snow, and Singer 1974)

Despite its intuitive appeal, the use of tracer methodology has had little application in the study of single programs or organizations. When it has been used, tracer methodology has provided an opportunity to thoroughly study the provision of services within a particular organization. The approach, however, is time consuming, requiring a systematic effort to select the tracer and to designate criteria associated with the evaluation, diagnosis, treatment, and follow-up of patients with the tracer problem, as well as developing consensus among relevant providers in the program to the developed criteria. After these criteria are developed and accepted, data are abstracted from the medical record to determine the extent to which actual care provided by the program matches that established by the criteria. Work to date indicates that use of tracer conditions is a feasible approach for the repeated assessments required in a thorough case study analysis of program performance.

A special application of the tracer methodology occurs in the selection of particular innovations for which managers require information for improved decision making. For example, managers of integrated delivery systems are investing unprecedented sums to develop and implement information technology and are very interested in the process through which these technologies are implemented and the factors that facilitate or inhibit their use. Using a tracer methodology, it is possible to identify innovations that are being implemented within the systems that meet a set of criteria and then proceed to assess the diffusion and implementation process and the factors that facilitate and/or inhibit that process at various levels within the system and across systems. Below are criteria used to select clinical process innovations. The innovations must:

- have a definite functional impact;
- be relatively well defined and easy to observe;
- have been developed in response to an organizational problem or opportunity;
- have impact on one or more operational dimension (e.g., quality, efficiency, cost);
- have been disseminated within the past 18 months;
- demonstrate organization breadth and depth;
- lend themselves to cross-case comparisons; and
- have value to the collaborating integrated delivery system. (Savitz and Kaluzny 1998)

The following illustration presents a more traditional application of the tracer methodology.

Illustration: Determining the Need for Medical Assessment at School Entry—Rural/Urban Differences

Bhrolchain and Schribman (1995) used three tracer conditions to examine characteristics of children likely to have a greater need for medical assessment at school entry. These tracer conditions were undescended testicles; speech and language delay, requiring referral; and asthma. For each condition, doctors within the school district were asked to record how many children had the condition, how many received adequate treatment before school entrance, and how many were identified for the first time at school entry or were receiving inadequate treatment despite the identification of the condition. Undertreated asthma was defined as those who missed school because of their asthma in the previous term, had sleep disturbance on two nights per week during the previous two weeks, and/or had exercise-induced wheezing but were on regular prophylactics.

The use of tracers requires the application to be a relatively common condition, relatively easily defined, amenable to medical intervention, serious enough to need treatment, and for which nonmedical influences on progress must be known. The three conditions chosen fulfilled the criteria. Participating physicians did not find data collection onerous, and the selection and use of tracers proved useful in assessing morbidity at school entry and in differentiating between urban and rural areas in terms of need for medical assessment at school entry.

Content Analysis

Case studies frequently use available memoranda, documents, and reports routinely generated by the program under study. Content analysis provides an unobtrusive and flexible method for studying and analyzing these types of communications in what can be a systematic, objective, and quantitative manner. However, the technique is difficult to master and is seen by some observers to be as much an art as a science (Marshall and Rossman 1989). While few evaluations have used content analysis (e.g., Kanouse et al. 1990; Wortman, Vinokur, and Sechrest 1982), it provides a useful technique for resolving the following types of evaluation questions:

- *To describe trends in communication content.* For instance, what are the major clinical or managerial issues receiving attention in the program?
- *To relate known characteristics of sources to communications they produce.* For instance, are individuals or programs with one set of characteristics likely to produce information with an orientation or content different from individuals or programs with a different set of characteristics?
- *To analyze forms or styles of persuasion used within a program context.* For instance, was the implementation of a program the result of a coercive versus a more conciliatory attempt to influence behavior? (Holsti 1968)

Perhaps the most critical problem in the use of content analysis concerns the selection and definition of categories, the pigeonholes into which content units are to be classified. Many possible schemes for classifying content exist. A list of possible schemes for classifying data frequently used in content analysis follows. Because there are as many schemes as possible questions, they are neither exhaustive nor do they define the limits of content analysis (Berelson 1952).

"What Is Said" Categories
- **Subject matter.** What is the communication about?
- **Direction.** How is the subject matter treated (e.g., favorable versus unfavorable; strong versus weak)?
- **Standard.** What is the basis on which the classification by direction is made?
- **Values.** What values, goals, or wants are revealed?
- **Methods.** What means are used to achieve goals?
- **Traits.** What are the characteristics used in describing people?
- **Actor.** Who is represented as undertaking certain acts?
- **Authority.** In whose name are statements made?
- **Origin.** Where does the communication originate?

- **Target.** To what persons or groups is the communication directed?
- **Location.** Where does the action take place?
- **Conflict.** What are the sources and levels of conflict?
- **Endings.** Are conflicts resolved happily, ambiguously, or tragically?
- **Time.** When does the action take place?

"How It Is Said" Categories

- **Form or type of communication.** What is the medium of communication (e.g., newspaper, radio, television, or speech)?
- **Form of statement.** What is the grammatical or syntactical form of the communication?
- **Device.** What is the rhetorical or propagandistic method used?

Discussing content analysis in the abstract is difficult, for the process is highly dependent on the particular problem under study.

The following illustrations show two different uses of content analysis. The first examines the manner in which music videos on four television networks portray tobacco and alcohol use. The second examines the variations in the content and style of a number of National Institutes of Health (NIH) consensus statements to determine what impact they have on subsequent dissemination among relevant clinicians.

Illustration: Content Analysis of Tobacco and Alcohol Use Behaviors Portrayed in Music Videos

Television is a powerful medium for influencing children and adolescents that will affect health behavior for a lifetime. In a study by DuRant et al. (1997), music videos ($N = 518$) were recorded during randomly selected days and times from four television networks. The content was analyzed to determine their portrayal of tobacco and alcohol use and for portrayals of such behavior in conjunction with sexuality. The videos were recorded during a block of time when adolescents would have the most opportunity to view televised videos (e.g., 3:00 p.m. to 9:00 p.m. Monday through Thursday, 3:00 p.m. to 1:00 a.m. Friday, and 10:00 a.m. to 12:00 a.m. on Saturday and Sunday).

Each program was judged using a pretested data collection instrument that measured individual occurrences of multiple types of smoking-related behaviors, smokeless tobacco use, alcohol use behaviors, violence and weapon-carrying behaviors, and alcohol and tobacco advertising. For example, smoking-related behaviors included lighting a cigarette; holding a cigar or pipe in the mouth or hand; and portraying the lighting of a cigarette, pipe, or cigar in an ashtray or any other location. Alcohol-use behaviors included holding a drink or bottle; drinking or pouring alcohol; offering or serving a drink or bottle; and portraying a bottle or glass on the table.

Analysis found significant differences among the networks in the percentage of videos that portrayed tobacco and alcohol use. For example, MTV had the highest percentage (25.7 percent) of the videos portraying smoking behavior, while CMT had the lowest (11.9 percent). MTV had the highest percentage (26.9 percent) of the videos with alcohol use, although the difference in this category was not statistically significant among the networks.

Illustration: Content Analysis of NIH Consensus Development Statements

As part of a much larger evaluation assessing the overall impact of the NIH consensus development program, an effort was taken to systematically examine the content and style of NIH consensus statements (Kanouse, Winkler, Kosecoff et al. 1990). The content analysis performed two functions:

1. Examining the variation in content and style of the actual statements provided an opportunity to select certain conferences for intensive study.
2. Examining how statements vary provided an opportunity to assess how this may bear on how the statements were received by the physician community.

Content analysis was performed on 24 of the 30 conferences held between the beginning of 1979 and the end of 1983. Conferences covered a wide range of topical areas including:

- antenatal diagnosis;
- estrogen use and postmenopausal women;
- cervical cancer screening;
- Pap smear;
- Reye's syndrome, both diagnosis and treatment; and
- liver transplantation.

Each of these areas was coded for selected attributes including the treatment setting in which they were used, their physical nature, their medical purpose, and their stage of development. Given this fairly broad classification, attention was then focused on the content of the statement itself. Here each sentence of a consensus statement, beginning after the introductory material, was separately coded. The coding was on a multi-hierarchical basis as follows:

A. Recommendations
   1. Medical Care
      a. Global (applying to all patients) versus differentiating
      b. Concrete versus abstract
   2. Research
   3. Nonmedical
B. Declarations about Topic
   1. Research references
   2. Assertions
C. Contextual Comments
D. Other

In addition, each item was separately coded and combined into a rating of consensus judgment. An agreement score was developed and assigned to each code item as follows:

1. **Unanimity.** All coders agreed on a coding category.
2. **Agreement about recommendations.** There was agreement that an item was a recommendation but there was disagreement over which subcategory it fit into. Alternatively, there was agreement that the item was not a recommendation but disagreement as to whether it was a contextual comment, an insertion, or reference to research.
3. **Partial agreement.** Two raters agreed on a specific item but the third disagreed.
4. **Disagreement.** All three disagreed.

Analysis revealed a great deal of variability in both the characteristics of the conferences and the content of the consensus statements. Consensus conferences varied evenly between hospital-based and office-based medical procedures despite the office of medical research application's mandate to evaluate emerging technologies that focused on new, expensive, hospital-based procedures.

Even more interesting was the analysis of the consensus statements' content, which varied across content areas. Using a factor analytic approach, analysis revealed that it was possible to characterize the various statements on three dimensions: discursive, didactic, and scholarly. *Discursive* statements tend to be long and abstract, containing few specific recommendations for clinicians. Consensus statements characterized as *didactic* offer clinicians practical and detailed guidance, while *scholarly* statements offer up-to-date descriptions of the scientific evidence bearing on a topic and develop more attention than most statements (Kahan, Kanouse, and Winkler 1984).

Nominal Group Techniques

Individuals within a program are the most knowledgeable source of information about what a program is trying to accomplish and what activities have transpired to accomplish them. The critical issue facing the evaluator is to obtain a true representation of these objectives and activities and to channel individual contributions. The problem is difficult, for individuals have varying degrees of status, and one or two tend to dominate the program. The nominal group technique may be used to generate data systematically within a case study format.

The nominal group technique was first developed by Delbecq, Van de Ven, and Gustafson (1975). The technique involves a structured group meeting in which individuals are given a specific task. This task usually requires a judgmental decision characterized by a lack of agreement or incomplete state of knowledge concerning the nature of the problem or the components to be included in the solution. Participants are asked to respond to this task not by speaking to one another but by writing their ideas on a pad of paper. At the end of five to ten minutes, all members of the panel present their ideas in a sequential process. These ideas are recorded so that the entire group can see them, but the ideas are not discussed as they are recorded. After all ideas are presented, a discussion follows in which the ideas are clarified and evaluated. After the discussion, a vote on the priority of areas is held, and the group decision is derived from the ranking of ideas on the basis of the vote.

The process provides a systematic basis whereby all individuals, regardless of their status, are able to present their ideas before the entire group. This ensures greater objectivity in the identification of issues or problems—but also increases the likelihood that individuals will identify with the process and thereby cooperate in and suggest evaluation activities.

The nominal group technique is particularly useful in initiating exploratory case study evaluation. The technique can be used to:

- identify and enrich the evaluators' understanding of a problem;
- arrive at a set of hypotheses concerning the meaning of the effects of aspects of the problem; and
- focus attention on the major areas or types of problems amenable to evaluation, defined by knowledgeable individuals in their own language.

These areas may later be pursued in greater detail by means of structured observations, interviews, or questionnaires. The following illustrate the use of nominal group technique in the evaluation of health services.

Illustration: Developing a Research Agenda

The configuration of health service organizations is undergoing unprecedented change. One major development has been that of alliances among existing organizations. In 1992, the Agency for Health Care Policy and Research (AHCPR) sponsored a conference at the University of North Carolina at Chapel Hill to develop a research agenda for the study of these new organizational forms. The conference was attended by invited executives and health service researchers. The conference involved a number of commissioned papers followed by a panel discussion (Kaluzny, Zuckerman, and Ricketts 1995).

To arrive at the research agenda, the participants were divided into four equal groups. The groups were formed following the formal paper presentations and panel discussion. Individuals were assigned to specific groups, and each group was diverse with respect to members' background in terms of policy, research, and management practice. Each group had a moderator who was trained in the nominal group technique. The group was given two hours to address this question: What are the most important issues for research on strategic alliances in healthcare?

The moderator requested each group to list in a round-robin fashion the issues that each individual felt to be important. These were listed without debate or discussion and the lists were collected from the four groups and summed into three general categories:

- overarching questions (i.e., questions about health services research and the future of alliances in healthcare);
- basic issues in the definition, formation, structure, operations, and performance of alliances; and
- specific questions that elaborate on these basic issues.

The questions that arose from this nominal group activity became the research questions that made up the decided on research agenda.

Illustration: Development and Implementation of a Performance Evaluation System for State and Local Health Departments — Problem Selection Stage

Development and implementation of a performance evaluation system is substantively difficult and politically challenging. The University of North Carolina School of Public Health, in cooperation with the Centers for Disease Control, the Association of Schools of Public Health, and the North Carolina Division of Health Services, expanded an existing performance evaluation system for state and local health departments (Kotch et al. 1991). This developmental effort occurred in a process consisting of five distinct stages:

Stage 1: selection of a single maternal and child health problem judged amenable to performance evaluation

Stage 2: determination of objectives for a maternal and child health program designed to combat the selected health problem

Stage 3: definition of all activities necessary for fulfillment of these objectives

Stage 4: delineation of standards for all activities

Stage 5: development of an assessment mechanism to note and correct any problems in the overall system

To develop a performance evaluation system with relevance to public health personnel, a current maternal and child health problem was selected for use throughout the project. To select the problem, Stage 1, a nominal group technique was used with public health personnel at the state, local, and regional levels. The selection involved the following steps:

1. Assemble the relevant providers and ask this question: What maternal and child health problems exist in this state today? Replies may include any condition proposed by any participant, such as:
   - maternal and child health conditions negatively influenced by poor timing and spacing of children;
   - postneonatal death rate due to accidents and poisoning;
   - high rate of teenage pregnancies and related health and social problems;
   - lead poisoning;
   - prematurity;
   - high incidence of genetically-determined disease; or
   - low birth weight.

2. Record each response in sequential fashion. Care should be taken to write down exactly the words used by the speaker. At this point, no discussion of ideas is allowed except for clarification. The sequence continues until the participants' ideas are all listed.
3. Eliminate overlapping items.
4. Determine ten problems participants consider most important. Individuals rank and list the problems using two criteria:
   - how much positive change can be expected if an effective performance system is implemented on an existing program designed to combat the problem; and
   - the financial and personal cost of implementing the performance system on the already existing program.
5. Arrive at consensus on the top ten problem areas based on consideration of individual rankings. Make nominations by sequential procedure. Reach consensus, by vote, on the top ten selections.
6. Discuss and clarify each of the selected ten problems. Participants consider agreements and disagreements within the group, analyzing the reasoning behind each selection and the appropriateness of each problem to development of the performance evaluation system.
7. Select one problem, from the top ten problems, for use in the project. Following discussion of the ten problems, each participant reconsiders his or her earlier vote in view of group analysis of the top ten selections. A final vote determines the single problem to be used in the project. (In the nominal group session, participants chose the prevention of prematurity and low birth weight as the problem most appropriate for development of the performance system for state and local health departments.)

Delphi Technique

The Delphi technique is usually associated with forecasting and large-survey strategies but has equal utility in providing structure to case study approaches. The primary objectives of the Delphi technique are to:

- determine, develop, or arrange the set of alternatives;
- explore or expose underlying assumptions or information leading to different judgments;
- seek out information that may generate consensus among the responding group;
- correlate informed judgments on a topic with a wide range of perspectives; and
- educate the responding group about the diverse and interrelated aspects of the phenomena under study.

The approach has many variations that involve a series of questionnaires and feedback reports to a designated panel of respondents. Researchers develop an initial questionnaire distributed by mail to the potential responding group. Respondents independently generate their ideas in answer to the first questionnaire. The researchers summarize the responses to the first questionnaire and develop a feedback report along with a second set of questionnaires for the responding group. Based on this feedback information, the respondent panel members evaluate their earlier responses. Based on the returns of the second questionnaire, the researchers develop a second summary and feedback report to the responding group.

This generic approach is being used increasingly in a number of health services settings. The following illustrate the use of the Delphi technique in two different health service settings.

Illustration: Meeting Changing Educational Needs of Healthcare Providers

The training of healthcare providers must keep pace with the changes occurring in the world of health services. For example, dentists in general practice have a continual need to upgrade their skills and knowledge because the practice of dentistry, its knowledge base, and the oral health needs of the population are changing and expanding. Moreover, the existing continuing education curriculum is often outdated or logistically inaccessible to busy practitioners in the community.

The University of Kentucky College of Dentistry is developing and testing a university-based extended educational program leading to a graduate certificate in advanced general dentistry (Smith et al. 1995). The program will allow general practitioners to continue to spend the majority of their time in practice but devote time to obtaining advanced education in general dentistry. A major challenge of the program was to design a curriculum that would be relevant to the practice community. The Delphi technique was used to identify the curriculum content.

Forty dentists were invited to participate. These dentists were selected for the study by three criteria: location, experience, and participation in continuing education. Dentists were sent an initial letter explaining the study and asking them to answer the following question: "In your opinion, what are the three or more important topics for general dental practice that should be included in an advanced-training program for general dentists? Please be specific—name clinical treatment techniques, clinical problems, or related topics."

Fifteen dentists returned answers to the first question that generated 100 initial topics, which, by eliminating duplication, yielded a 65-item questionnaire. In a second mailing the original 40 dentists were asked to rate the 65 items for inclusion in a curriculum for an advanced training program for general dentists. The rating was done on a ten-point Likert scale ranging from essential = 10 to desirable = 8, and somewhat desirable = 5 to unnecessary = 1. At this mailing, 32 of the 40 responded; a clear majority of respondents rated 53 of the topics as desirable or essential for an advanced general dentistry training program. One topic, the use of general anesthetic in hospital dentistry, was rated by 66 percent of the respondents as undesirable or unnecessary. Respondents were divided on the remaining 11 topics.

Those dentists with strong, definite positions on each topic (i.e., rated the topic essential or unnecessary) were then contacted by mail and asked to state the reasons for their rating. The reasons were then compiled into pro and con statements on each of the 11 topics; these statements were sent to the 32 dentists who had returned the original questionnaire and asked to review and vote yes or no on the inclusion of each topic in the curriculum.

The process produced 59 topics judged to be essential or desirable for the curriculum, 40 topics by a two-thirds majority. These topics were included in the advanced-training curriculum, in which 20 dentists enrolled; six of these dentists participated in the Delphi panel. Interestingly, the curriculum generated by the panel did not agree completely with the topics identified for advanced general-dentistry training in a national survey of 265 directors of postgraduate general-dentistry programs. These results suggest the importance of generating information from the potential participants of a program, if the program is to be relevant to their needs. The Delphi technique provided a convenient and inexpensive method of generating this information.

Illustration: Assessing Attributes of Clinical Protocols

The use of *clinical protocols* within a community setting may be viewed as an organizational innovation (i.e., an idea, practice, or material artifact perceived to be new to a relevant unit of adoption [Rogers 1995]). These protocols as innovations are characterized by a series of attributes that interact with the characteristics of the adopting agent (i.e., the physicians and the organization). Three are considered to be particularly relevant to the study of clinical protocols: relative advantage, compatibility, and complexity. *Relative advantage* is the degree to which the protocols are perceived as being better than the previous practice. *Compatibility* is the degree to which the innovation is perceived as being consistent with the existing values, past experience, and needs of potential adopters. *Complexity* is the degree to which the protocols are perceived as relatively difficult to understand and use.

As part of a larger evaluation of the NCI Community Clinical Oncology Program (Kaluzny, Warnecke, and Associates 1996) designed to assess CCOP's ability as a working group of community-based hospitals, physicians, and support staff to accrue patients to treatment and prevention and control protocols, assessing the attributes of the protocols became important. Using a modified Delphi approach, a panel of expert physicians was convened to identify relevant measures of the protocol attributes (Veney et al. 1991).

Two attribute indicator rating forms were constructed (one for the attributes of treatment protocols and one for the attributes of cancer control protocols), each with approximately 130 indices (or measures) of the three attributes: relative advantage, complexity, and compatibility. The indices include structure, process, and outcome measures with varying levels of specificity. The attribute indicator rating forms were derived from a review of:

- data from the larger CCOP evaluation;
- detailed content analysis of approximately 40 cancer protocols;

- information concerning cancer control and treatment research from 20 CCOP site visits and 6 research base visits;
- information from a survey of key informants in the 52 participating CCOPs;
- literature on clinical trials design and management; and
- innovation literature concerning attributes and their operationalization.

The expert panel consisted of 13 cancer specialists who were knowledgeable about both community-based treatment and cancer control clinical trials. This group of oncologists participated in a modified Delphi technique comparable to that described by Park et al. (1986, 30). The members of the panel were mailed the two attribute indicator rating scales (AIRFs), one containing a list of cancer treatment (CT) protocol attributes and the other a list of measures of cancer control (CC) protocol attributes. Panel members were asked to score these initial lists of protocol attribute indices on a ten-point scale. The anchor points were 10 = crucial to the patient enrollment decision and 1 = not relevant to the patient enrollment decision. Panel members were encouraged to list additional attribute measures that they considered important.

The initial ratings of attribute measures by the expert panel were analyzed within the framework of the three core attributes: relative advantage (RA), compatibility, and complexity. In preparation for the second round of panel ratings, each rating form was reduced to the approximately 50 attribute measures with the highest mean scores, derived from the initial expert panel ratings, within the various attribute categories. At least five indicators for the five subdimensions of RA and five indicators for compatibility and complexity were retained in the lists of measures. AIRFs containing these measures, along with any added to the initial lists by panelists, were mailed to the panel members for a final round of scoring on the same ten-point scale. The 40 measures with the highest mean scores within their attribute categories or subcategories were selected for the final rating instruments. Appendix 6.1 presents illustrative attributes for assessing treatment protocols. Appendix 6.2 presents a corresponding list of attributes for cancer control protocols.

An important task was to assure the validity of the AIRF instruments. The operational indices chosen to represent an attribute are proxies for the attribute, which are defined by theory. The construct validity of the proxy measures chosen to specify the attributes of interest is an unresolved problem within this type of study. However, the criterion or predictive validity of clusters of operational measures generally is much stronger than any single indicator because the validity derives from the amount of variance each indicator can explain in the outcome variable. In our study, the outcome measure—physicians' accrual to protocols—is of specific interest to NCI policymakers, research-based personnel, and CCOP participants.

Focus Groups

Focus groups have been used extensively in health service planning and program evaluation, as well as curriculum planning, health communications, and survey instrument design. This qualitative method of data capture provides an invaluable source of in-depth information about the attitudes, perceptions, knowledge, beliefs, and opinions of participants. Commonly, focus groups allow the researcher to:

- identify service or information needs of special populations;
- target development of specialized programs and messages for relevant subpopulations;
- generate relevant performance and outcomes measures for program evaluation;
- examine group attributes that may serve as facilitating or inhibiting factors to program use; and
- provide information to explain the successful or unsuccessful use of newly developed services or products.

Qualitative data generated from focus groups is particularly useful for the design and monitoring phases of an evaluation project. Focus groups are basically small (6- to 8-person groups), homogeneous groups brought together to informally discuss a series of open-ended questions (Krueger 1994). Depending on the particular application, several focus groups may be indicated for the evaluation of any particular program to fully encompass the sociodemographic, ethnic, organizational level, and/or professional perspectives for the particular program or protocol under evaluation.

Focus group discussions are normally audiotaped with the consent of participants, and these audio tapes are augmented with personal notes and observations made by the focus group leader or facilitator. Transcripts can be coded to detect general themes and provide a basis for cross-group comparison when multiple focus groups are involved. Sophisticated data analysis programs are now available to analyze resulting narrative transcripts (e.g., NUDIST, Ethnography), but simple word-processing software with key word search capabilities often suffices. While focus groups can be validly used as a singular evaluation tool, they are often used in combination with other quantitative and qualitative methods (Frasier et al. 1997; Miles and Huberman 1994).

Illustration: Focus Groups as Part of a Process for Outcome Evaluation of the Practice Environment Project

The Practice Environment Project (PEP) was created to provide a framework for current and ongoing evaluation of the effectiveness of major healthcare delivery changes affecting nursing care services in a 750-bed, tertiary-care facility in the northeastern United States (Grindel et al. 1996). In this dynamic environment, the quality of patient care provided by nursing staff in the practice environment was being evaluated from the perspective of patients, nurses, and physicians using a core set of variables intended to measure quality, cost, and satisfaction.

The first phase of this evaluative effort consisted of a series of surveys with nurses, patients, and physicians from each of the 44 identified patient care units.

The nursing-staff survey included questions related to job satisfaction, autonomy, and nurse-physician collaboration. The patient survey measured the patients' opinions of nursing care, and the physician survey measured the physicians' perceptions of the quality of nursing care.

While quantitative data resulting from these survey efforts provided useful information about the respondents' perceptions of the practice environment, these data lacked specific information concerning facilitators and barriers to providing quality nursing services that were suggested by the qualitative data. This latter aspect of the evaluation was gleaned from focus groups with nursing staff at three levels, the goal of which was to identify key factors affecting the nurses' ability to provide quality services. Content analysis of these data suggested a series of four problem categories: process or interactive issues; clinical issues; administrative issues; and interdepartmental issues. Common themes within these four categories were further specified. These results were used to develop unit-based action plans to manage barriers to service delivery, and support by administration for ongoing evaluation has been reported as a result of the success of the input provided through the formative evaluation of the PEP project.

Discussion Questions

1. How does the use of structured observation or an a priori classification scheme assist in gathering information?
2. What are the limitations of using existing information systems in case study evaluations?
3. Develop and analyze questions that are appropriate to the use of content analysis. What are the major advantages and limitations in using content analysis?
4. How does the nominal group technique differ from the Delphi technique as a case study methodology?

Part 1: Benefits and Costs

APPENDIX 6.1
Attributes for Assessing Treatment Protocols

	Not Important								Crucial to Decision	
1.1 Adequacy of the patient's health insurance coverage for the care required by the protocol	1	2	3	4	5	6	7	8	9	10
1.2 Staff time required per test or other treatment activity	1	2	3	4	5	6	7	8	9	10
1.3 Clinical relevance of the pre-treatment evaluation	1	2	3	4	5	6	7	8	9	10
1.4 Potential for improved patient survival	1	2	3	4	5	6	7	8	9	10

APPENDIX 6.1

Attributes for Assessing Treatment Protocols

Part 1: Benefits and Costs *(Continued)*

	Not Important									Crucial to Decision
1.5 Severity of potential side effects	1	2	3	4	5	6	7	8	9	10
1.6 Definition of protocol endpoints	1	2	3	4	5	6	7	8	9	10

Part 2: Protocol Compatibility with Physician Practice Style

	Not Important									Crucial to Decision
2.1 Patient understanding of the treatment choices available in the protocol	1	2	3	4	5	6	7	8	9	10
2.2 Existence of an observational (i.e., no treatment) arm	1	2	3	4	5	6	7	8	9	10

Part 3: Protocol Complexity

	Not Important									Crucial to Decision
3.1 New skills required by the physician to perform the cancer control protocol	1	2	3	4	5	6	7	8	9	10
3.2 Number of data collection forms to be completed per patient	1	2	3	4	5	6	7	8	9	10
3.3 Number of tests required to determine patient eligibility	1	2	3	4	5	6	7	8	9	10
3.4 Difficulty of data management	1	2	3	4	5	6	7	8	9	10

Part 1: Benefits and Costs

	Not Important								Crucial to Decision	
1.1 Adequacy of patient's health insurance coverage for the care required by the protocol	1	2	3	4	5	6	7	8	9	10
1.2 Potential for increased referrals for participating physicians	1	2	3	4	5	6	7	8	9	10
1.3 Adequate financial support for ancillary staff needed for protocol	1	2	3	4	5	6	7	8	9	10
1.4 Incidence/prevalence of the problem in the protocol target population	1	2	3	4	5	6	7	8	9	10
1.5 Potential for improved survival or decreased mortality for patients in general	1	2	3	4	5	6	7	8	9	10
1.6 Overall feasibility of participating in the project in a community setting	1	2	3	4	5	6	7	8	9	10

Part 2: Compatibility with Physician Practice Style

	Not Important								Crucial to Decision	
2.1 Number of different departments/units in the participating organization needed for the project (e.g., nutrition, pain clinic)	1	2	3	4	5	6	7	8	9	10
2.2 Nurse participation in protocol development	1	2	3	4	5	6	7	8	9	10

APPENDIX 6.2
Attributes for Assessing Cancer Control Protocols

7

SURVEY RESEARCH AS AN EVALUATION STRATEGY

Survey research has long been the province of social scientists. As the need for evaluation has become more widely recognized and as social scientists have taken on the role of evaluator, survey research has become a common evaluation strategy. As such, survey research has been used primarily for summative evaluation of programs and for formative evaluation. Survey research may also overlap or be used in conjunction with monitoring, case studies, time series analysis, or even experimental strategies. The objective of this chapter is to define survey research, describe the context within which it occurs and the types of data collected, and illustrate its application in various healthcare settings.

What Is Survey Research?

Survey research is an approach to knowledge that uses information collected through questionnaires or interviews directed to a sample of persons drawn from a population of interest. In program evaluation, a survey may be directed at any or all of the following groups: the recipients or potential recipients of services provided by a program; the service providers; or the program planners and managers. The purpose of these interviews or questionnaires is to obtain information about the perceptions and feelings of the recipients or providers of services on such issues as the adequacy, effectiveness, or continuity of a program's services.

Survey research may be either mainly descriptive or mainly analytic. Although it need not be overstressed, this distinction should be understood because different types of evaluation questions are best considered by one or the other. Descriptive components of analytic research and vice versa may not exist in any particular survey; in general, however, the research will have primary features of one or the other.

Descriptive surveys are chiefly concerned with producing as accurate a picture as possible of a real-world situation. Specifically in the context of evaluation, a descriptive survey may be concerned with describing a problem that requires a type of program activity, describing the program itself from the perspective of providers or service recipients, or describing results of the program or project from the perspective of providers or recipients.

The following example illustrates a descriptive survey conducted to obtain a better understanding of the specific types and forms of physician-hospital organizations.

Illustration: Managed Care and Physician-Hospital Integration

While much attention is given to the reconfiguration of health service organizations and particularly to the development of integrated delivery systems that involve hospitals and physicians, in reality limited data exists that describe these arrangements. Such data may include the following:

- What is the extent of these relationships among existing service delivery organizations?
- What are the types of organizational arrangements that exist?
- What is the relationship of these types of arrangements to managed care activity in the service area?

Data from a nationally representative sample of 1,495 U.S. community hospitals responding to a 1993 survey about different organizational structures answer these questions (Morrissey et al. 1996). The results indicate that only 23.3 percent of the hospitals participated in any physician-hospital arrangements nationwide, but 47 percent did so in the Northeast and 31 percent did in the Pacific region. In contrast, fewer than 14 percent participated in such arrangements in the central part of the country.

The survey also revealed that the vast majority of organizational arrangements were relatively simple. As described in the study, "In these structures neither physicians nor hospitals give up much autonomy or freedom of action . . . the arrangements are little more than contracting vehicles with little organizational infrastructure" (Morrissey et al. 1996, 71).

The study also revealed that participation in physician organizational arrangements is associated with the portion of hospital revenue obtained from managed care sources. There appears to be a threshold of 15 percent of patient care revenues above which the hospital is two and one-third times more likely to participate than hospitals below the threshold.

As with most descriptive surveys, the analysis leads to subsequent questions that are critical to improved decision making. For example, to what extent has the local marketwide growth of managed care led to the adoption of the various forms of managed care, and what factors have led physicians and hospitals to engage in such arrangements? Answers to these more analytic questions will help managers design improved arrangements that will facilitate the integration of healthcare services within the community.

Analytic surveys are concerned chiefly with describing relationships among real-world phenomena. An analytic type of evaluation survey may be concerned with whether program recipients having different types of characteristics viewed a program more or less favorably, or whether there is a differential effect of the program on recipients having certain characteristics.

An analytic survey must have a relationship to reality; that is, the survey must be concerned with issues that exist in the real world. Although these surveys need not provide a true description of a given population, they must focus on the relationship between attributes of a person, a group, or a set of organizations in the study population. Consider the following example.

Illustration: Study of Physician-Organization Arrangements

Two objectives of this evaluation by Zuckerman et al. (1998) were primarily descriptive, focused on documenting physician-organization arrangements (POA) and on integration activities and their effects on physicians and organizations participating in the Center for Healthcare Management Research entitled "Evaluating Physician-Organization Arrangements." A more analytic objective involved the analysis of environmental and organizational conditions, under which physician-organization arrangements occur, along with the assessment of factors influencing that relationship. To meet these objectives, the evaluation included three surveys:

- A survey administered to 105 hospitals and system CEOs (response rate of 80 percent) was designed to categorize the number and types of POAs being used by participating organizations; define market and environmental conditions under which these arrangements were developed; and describe their structures, governance and management, financing, operation, locus of control, level of physician participation, and relationship to organizational strategy.
- A telephone follow-up survey of 75 hospitals (response rate of 81 percent) explored specific issues of interest such as the appropriate size of physician panels, physician compensations, and physician leadership development.
- A survey of 4,200 physicians involved with institutions owned by the participating systems (response rate of 43 percent) examined physician attitudes and perceptions regarding alignment with their respective institutions.

Analysis revealed that strategic intent of physicians and hospitals in aligning interests was important. From the organizational perspective, strategies for alignment centered on protecting existing markets, expanding into new markets, and integrating and coordinating delivery of care. From the physician perspective, physicians seek to align their interests with those of the organization, gain the expertise and resources of the organization, achieve a degree of security, build a buffer against external threats, maintain autonomy in clinical decision making, assert physician leadership, become involved in governance, and influence the mix of providers.

The effects of integration vary by degree of economic alignment, primary versus specialist, gender, and age group. General analysis revealed that the most highly integrated physicians:

- report higher levels of trust in the organization;
- see more physician involvement in decision making;

- display greater commitment to the origination;
- are more willing to invest in network development;
- show a preference for group practice;
- have lower anxiety over practice costs;
- have less desire for control and independence; and
- perceive they have greater clinical autonomy.

Three factors were identified as critical in bringing management and physicians together: building trust among physicians, placing physicians in management and governance positions, and developing physician leadership capabilities.

Appropriate Settings for Survey Research

Survey research can be a powerful tool in various evaluations. Descriptive survey research can be particularly useful for assessing program relevance, progress, and effectiveness. Analytical surveys can be used as a formative evaluation tool to compare the views of different stakeholders to a program. Consider the use of descriptive and analytic survey research in these types of settings.

Descriptive Surveys and Program Relevance

Descriptive survey research can be used prior to the establishment of any program to examine the nature of a particular problem that appears to warrant a program—in essence, to consider the relevance of a program. From this standpoint, survey research can be used to define a problem as seen by potential program recipients and relevant personnel. In a rural community, for example, a descriptive survey of the general population and relevant provider personnel to determine their perceptions of primary health problems improves the effectiveness of any subsequent primary healthcare program developed. A comparison of survey results may reveal considerable discrepancy about perceived problems between provider and recipient groups. Designing the program to recipients' rather than providers' expectations could enhance both its use and its efficiency.

Descriptive Surveys and Program Progress

A well-designed descriptive study can also provide information about how a program is actually progressing. This is the major function of monitoring, but survey research, particularly descriptive survey research, can shed substantial light on program progress. An example of survey research in this sense can be taken from the experience of an international agency that set out to identify personnel training needs in developing countries. The initial assumption of the program designers was that many developing countries needed continuing education for their national health service program managers. In one country that had agreed to participate in the effort to upgrade the health services program, the suggestion was made that perhaps training per se may not be the primary problem. Instead, an effort may be undertaken to determine the types of problems involved in the national health services administration and management, whether these problems involved training or lack thereof, and what other steps, if any, may be taken to improve the system's management and administration. A survey of all health service managers at various governmental levels was then initiated to determine the extent to which problems existed and were attributable to limited training.

The actual survey was never carried out, but the pilot study and pretest indicated that the lack of adequate training was a clear problem in the management and administration of the health services system. However, it was far outweighed by few resources, poor distribution of facilities, and simple lack of personnel—trained or untrained. This potential survey, directed at an ongoing national health services system, not only revealed how the system was working, but even in its formative stages also indicated that problems in its operation were not primarily those that introduction of a training program could solve. This survey, therefore, had the potential to define a problem to be addressed by one program and to evaluate the progress of another, much larger program.

Descriptive Surveys and Program Effectiveness

Descriptive survey evaluations are generally employed in a summative type of evaluation. In this type of evaluation, the survey will be directed toward determining how the program worked, whether it was perceived as successful by personnel and clients, and what aspects of the program were perceived as making the program more or less effective. Emphasis is on perception, for individual actions rest on this basis rather than on an objective accounting of program activity.

Analytic Surveys and Formative Evaluations

When an analytic evaluation is used, the objective is to compare the views of various groups about a program or health service activity and account for differing views rather than to describe the program or its operation per se. The descriptive survey can be used to define a problem as seen by various audiences, including the potential program recipients and providers. The analytic survey compares views of a problem among different types of potential recipients and tries to account for these differing views as a first step in launching a useful program. Similarly, analytic surveys provide comparative information about how programs are currently operating or how a program has worked in the past.

Analytic surveys often provide insight into problems of program operation. Suppose that a survey of program administrators and service providers indicates that, in general, recipients were satisfied with a primary healthcare program. Analysis reveals that even though administrators are satisfied with the program, many of the actual service providers are not. This result may be due to a number of factors, which a survey may indicate. Managers, for example, may be satisfied because they perceive the program to be operating according to plan. Further questioning may reveal, however, that they have little knowledge of actual day-to-day program operations. However, service providers' first-hand knowledge of day-to-day operations leads them to perceive the program as not working as well.

Illustration of analytic surveys

In essence, one variable that may be identified as contributing to a view that the program is or is not successful would be knowledge of actual program operations at the local level. The same survey, however, may show that recipients are satisfied with the program because they are getting services that had never been available before, whereas providers are unhappy with the program because they realize that recipients (possibly because of lack of resources or time) are not receiving all the services that should be available to them. This analysis would indicate that satisfaction with the program is partly the result of the difference between expectations and reality.

Appropriate Data for Survey Research

Except for the limited cases in which survey data are acquired from various physical measurements, such as height or weight (aspects of monitoring), data appropriate to survey research are almost exclusively collected from people using a type of formalized questionnaire or interview schedule. As such, the data actually applied to evaluation via the survey research format are an amalgam of personal opinions, knowledge, and perceptions of people involved in the program or affected by it. When such information is used to describe a program, the data sample must represent the population of interest.

Questionnaires versus Interviews

Because survey data are collected through either formal questionnaires or interviews, these two techniques deserve discussion. The basic distinction is how each is used to acquire evaluation information. A *questionnaire*, in general, is an instrument or a schedule for collecting data that the respondent essentially self-administers. An *interview* generally is an instrument or schedule for collecting data that an interviewer administers. This difference between questionnaire and interview is quite important for the design and structure of the two formats. Because an interviewer will administer the interview and usually will record answers in appropriate categories, an interview schedule can be substantially less formal and less carefully designed than the questionnaire.

This does not mean that the interview schedule should not be well-designed. In fact, when the purpose of the interview schedule is to collect survey data for a systematic analysis, clear categories for recording responses to questions should be available for the interviewer ahead of time. What this does mean, however, is that the interviewer knows the structure of the interview schedule and is able to move through it with the interviewee without difficulty. A questionnaire must be simple and have clear and straightforward instructions so that respondents can follow and complete it without assistance from the study directors.

Another difference between the questionnaire and interview schedule is that interviewers can deal with and record responses that do not fit predetermined categories. In the development of a questionnaire, particularly, ensuring a possible response from everyone to whom the questionnaire is addressed is necessary. Consequently, both interviews and questionnaires are usually subjected to a fairly extensive pretest. The purpose of the pretest is to see that the interview or questionnaire schedule can be answered and that it provides the types of answers that the evaluator considers important to understand the situation.

Measurement

Whether a questionnaire or an interview is used to acquire data for survey research, an important aspect of that data collection is the problem of measurement. Measurement is discussed in substantial detail in Chapter 13, but several important points are presented in the following paragraphs.

In survey research, measurement generally refers to the problem of acquiring data that will give both valid and reliable measures of personal opinions and knowledge of perceptions. One purpose of an evaluation activity, for instance, may be to determine the perceptions of program recipients about a primary care program. A strategy may be to ask the respondents directly whether they were satisfied or dissatisfied with the primary care program. But, in general, the survey researcher would assume that this question was attempting to tap too many dimensions of satisfaction or acceptability of the program. Instead, the researcher would try to get an evaluation of the program through questions concerning satisfaction with the program, or acceptance of it, in more specific areas. Questions may be asked about satisfaction with information obtained from the primary care program, treatment of clients by the personnel, acceptability of hours of operation or physical facilities, acceptability of advice given, and other aspects of satisfaction with the program.

The evaluator would have predetermined, specific aspects of satisfaction that the various questions would raise. Several questions, for example, may refer to adequacy of physical plant and other physical facilities. Others may consider satisfaction with staff, treatment by them, and staff-client relationships in the agency. Yet another series of questions may concern the ease of scheduling access and hours of operation. After the data has been collected, the evaluator would construct measures of satisfaction in various areas, using a number of questions to tap each area or dimension. For example, five questions about physical facilities would be combined in a manner to form a single measure of acceptability of physical facilities.

How Data Are Acquired

As noted, survey data are acquired through questionnaires or interviews. Certain problems occur, however, in the acquisition of either type of data, particularly identification of respondents, access to them, and their willingness to cooperate.

Identification

Whether the strategy for collecting information is the interview approach or the questionnaire approach, legitimate respondents for the data collection instrument must be identified. If, for example, the survey was to determine client opinion about treatment received in a primary care clinic, identifying people who had used the clinic's services would be necessary. If the clinic maintains good records of consultations and has, in addition, a record of addresses, identifying potential respondents through clinic records may be possible.

If, on the other hand, the clinic does not maintain names or addresses in its records, the only possible way to identify people who have used its services may be to ask respondents who have been selected on some basis from the general service area of the clinic. Under these circumstances interviewing five to ten times as many people as ultimately desired may be necessary to find a large enough group of clinic users for purposes of analysis. In general, such an approach to acquiring a specific sample is so costly that it would not be used. In the conduct of any survey it is necessary to identify the population about which inferences are to be drawn either with a global statement, such as all people living in a given community, or by a limiting statement, such as all people who say on questioning that they have used the services of a particular primary care clinic.

Access

For data collection to proceed in survey research, access to people who are to serve as respondents must be possible. This aspect may not be too difficult for program personnel. In most instances, personnel can be reached through the program because the program must be able to contact them to pay them or give instructions, for example.

Clients may be much more difficult to reach. If a questionnaire is used, information about clients' addresses or another strategy for ensuring that they receive the questionnaires must be devised. If an interview is used, the interviewer must be able to find the respondents and gain their cooperation. The difficulty of gaining access to respondents is illustrated with the evaluation of a five-year health plan in a developing nation.

Illustration of access to survey data in Nepal

The original study was conceived as a six-month effort beginning in December 1990. As such, data collection in the field was planned for March and April 1991. Various delays, including a ten-week wait for the Health Ministry to process a request for funds to pay interviewers (though the funds were available from donor agencies), postponed the start of data collection to late June. Late June is when the monsoon starts—a season during which roads in many parts of the country are completely unpassable. Data collection in most areas then became extremely difficult, and a number of areas had to be abandoned completely.

The weather problems were exacerbated in many areas by inaccurate information on the location of health post facilities and incomplete lists of households. A number of interviewers indicated that they would not agree again to undertake a task of this type during the monsoon season.

There were numerous difficulties, some unavoidable, in interviewing at the household level. In two villages where murders had recently occurred, interviewers were mistaken for police and generally found people quite reluctant to talk with them. In one village they were mistaken for criminals who had raided the village earlier. In another area, they were thought to be leprosy workers who, according to rumor, inject people with poisonous black serum and spread leprosy as a means of population control.

Even after gaining access to households, difficulties remained, including problems of awkward questions or those that were a source of embarrassment in the questionnaire, particularly in the family planning topic. Some concepts, such as time (e.g., how long it takes to walk to the health clinic), also were difficult for respondents to understand (e.g., there is little conceptual difference in rural areas of the country between one hour and three hours).

Nonresponse

Nonresponse refers to the unwillingness or the inability of people selected for the sample to cooperate in answering either the questionnaires or interviews. The problem of nonresponse is most acute in the questionnaire situation. Unless prior groundwork has been done to impress on potential respondents the importance of the questionnaire and the critical need for its completion, nonresponse to a questionnaire may run as high as 50 to 60 percent. If the questionnaire is addressed to busy professionals, such as physicians, nonresponse may run even higher. If questionnaires are simply received in the mail with a request to fill them out, they may be ignored. Numerous ways to deter nonresponse in questionnaire settings, including the use of personally signed cover letters, follow-up letters and calls, self-addressed return envelopes, and partial payment for time spent completing the questionnaire.

Nonresponse is less of a problem in interviews than in questionnaires. Fewer people are willing to decline to be interviewed than are willing to throw a questionnaire away. Nonetheless, nonresponse remains a problem because it is not reasonable to assume that those who fail to respond to a questionnaire or interview are essentially no different from those who do respond in regard to the subject of the survey. If, for example, a survey was used to try to elicit opinions about a primary care program as an evaluation of that program, people may be unwilling to respond to the questionnaire because they perceive the program to be irrelevant, undesirable, and unacceptable. People willing to respond may do so because they perceive the program to be useful or valuable. Analysis of the information supplied by respondents would thus substantially mislead the evaluators.

Guarding against all nonresponse is usually impossible. Generally, however, it is better to accept a smaller sample with a lower proportion of nonresponse than a larger sample with a larger proportion of nonresponse. If evaluators set out to interview or obtain questionnaires from 400 respondents because they believe only 100 will respond and they desire 100 responses for the analysis, the results of that study are much less reliable than if they set out to collect data only from 100 people and make every possible effort to get those 100 people to respond.

Data for Survey Research from Two Different Settings

To discuss appropriate data for survey research on a somewhat more practical level, consider again the community clinical oncology program and the primary care program initially described in Chapters 3 and 5.

Illustration: Community Clinical Oncology Program (CCOP)

The evaluation was designed to monitor the implementation and impact of the program and to determine the characteristics of CCOPs and research bases, and how their interaction affects implementation and impact. As part of the effort to explain variation in implementation and impact, as well as to map activity within CCOPs and between CCOPs and research bases, a key informant survey was designed and implemented (Kaluzny, Warnecke, and Associates 1996).

Key informants were selected from all 52 CCOPs and 17 research bases, and were selected from three strata: CCOP principal investigator/co-principal investigator; physicians within the community who enter patients on NCI-approved protocols; and CCOP administrative staff. Prestudy telephone calls to each CCOP principal investigator requested his or her assistance in identifying one physician respondent from each of five specialty areas: medical oncology/ hematology; radiation therapy; surgical oncology/general surgery; gynecologic oncology/gynecology; and pediatric oncology/pediatrics. The principal investigators also identified the two administrative respondents, a coordinator and a data manager. In the case of the research base survey, the research base principal investigators and chairpersons of the cancer control committee served as the informants.

These informants were mailed a survey instrument in which questions were specifically designed to address nine areas corresponding with the information gathered in the 20 in-depth site visits. Key informant questions included these topics:

- goals for the CCOP program;
- CCOP internal structure;
- CCOP principal investigator and physician attributes;
- physician and staff relationships;
- CCOP-hospital relationships;
- cancer control issues;
- CCOP-research base relationships;
- CCOP and research base relationships with NCI Division of Cancer Prevention and Control; and
- CCOP relationships with community group.

The analysis plan for the CCOP survey included both a descriptive and an analytic component. Many of the same questions were asked of respondents in the three strata. This provided rich descriptive data and allowed comparison of responses from the three respondent strata on such topics as the relative importance of various goals (relevance); CCOP success in attaining these goals (effectiveness); and policy changes that may enhance goal attainment (program progress).

The analysis component of the evaluation included an investigation of the association between both the individual respondent strata and the combined respondent strata (responses and measures of effectiveness such as the number of cancer patients enrolled in clinical trials). The data also allowed the development of consensus variables that measured the extent of agreement or disagreement among the respondent groups in each CCOP on the topics addressed in the questionnaire. This made possible the examination of the relationship between the level of consensus among staff and CCOP effectiveness.

Illustration: Early Detection in Primary Care

The evaluation was designed to assess the implementation and impact of an office system for preventive care among primary care physicians to increase the number of eligible patients receiving early detection activities recommended by the NCI for cervical, breast, colo-rectal, and prostate cancer. The evaluation involved a randomized control trial with the intervention group receiving an intensive "office system for preventive care" program of academic detailing, meetings with physicians and staff, consultation about office systems, and educational modules about proper techniques of early detection activities. As part of that objective, a survey was conducted among a sample of practice physicians and staff, as well as patients.

Questionnaires to physicians and staff were hand-delivered by study research assistants in an attempt to personalize the process as much as possible and thereby increase the response rate with follow-up questionnaires and physician telephone calls to nonrespondents. Respondents included all primary care physicians in the practice, one nurse per physician, and the office manager for the practice. Practices were paid $100 per physician (to be distributed at the discretion of the practice) for completing the questionnaire. Survey questions focused on perceptions of efficacy of the screening activities, screening impact on the patient, screening impact on the practice, existence of a practice policy concerning cancer screening, and existence of a system to implement the policy. Nursing personnel were asked especially about their current time involved with screening and their interest in screening activities. Administrative personnel were asked their perception of the cost effectiveness of screening for the practice and the perceptions of the patient demand for screening.

Patients completed a patient exit questionnaire. The questionnaire was quite brief, asking whether the patient has had a screening activity within the previous 12 months and whether the patient had any interest in screening. Patients were selected as they were visiting the practice on one of 20 randomly chosen index days in months 9–12 of the intervention period, again in months 15–18, and finally in months 1–6 after the intervention. To assure patient completion of the questionnaire, the patient receptionist was paid to take charge of this activity, receiving $5 for each patient who met the criteria who completed the questionnaire before leaving the office, and $10 for every patient requiring assistance in completing the questionnaire.

A critical challenge in the project was recruitment and retention of the practices in the project. While evaluations are increasingly focused on how effective clinical strategies (therapeutic or preventive) can be integrated into routine practice, the practice setting is by definition not designed for such activity. Thus, special attention must be given to the recruitment and retention of clinicians and their staff to such evaluation activities (Carey et al. 1996).

In addition to the survey phase previously described, the project involved extensive chart audits (described in Chapter 9) requiring significant commitment of the participating physicians, thus requiring an intensive recruiting strategy. Eligible practitioners received lead letters from the appropriate medical organization (i.e., the North Carolina chapter of the American College of Physicians, North Carolina Academy of Family Physicians, or the Old North State Medical Society, an organization of African-American physicians). The initial telephone contact was made from a physician for the project or from a physician from the regional Area Health Education Center's office.

Physicians for the project visited eligible physicians at their practice at a time of their convenience. These efforts proved very successful with 90 percent of the randomly selected eligible practices agreeing to participate (62 out of 69). Retention was equally strong, with 58 of the initial 62 practices (93.5 percent) remaining active in the project at the end of four years. One solo physician retired, another moved, and two practices declined follow-up data collection.

Application to Decision Making and Types of Evaluation

Many insights can be gained about decision making as a result of survey research. These insights correspond to the various types of evaluation: relevance, progress, efficiency, effectiveness, impact, and sustainability.

Relevance

Survey research provides descriptive information about the perceived state of the system or the perceived nature of the problem with which a program is to deal. Although this is valuable information, it may not always be as accurate as desired. For example, increasing recognition of the importance of providing medical care services to the poor and near poor in the United States exists. A survey of the relevant population likely would indicate that these people recognize a need for more medical care services.

A close examination of the kinds of problems that these people deal with in regard to their health, however, would probably show that their major problems are problems of low income, poor housing (including lead-painted walls), malnutrition, poor sanitation, and lack of basic immunizations. Very few of these primary health problems would be affected appreciably by an increase in medical care services, although a survey of that population may reveal medical care services as the biggest perceived problem. In a sense, the major difficulty with survey research is that it invariably provides perceptions or beliefs.

Adequacy

In terms of adequacy, survey research provides a valuable approach to measuring perception of whether a particular programmatic initiative is able to address the full scope of the problem. The ability to gather perceptions in a reliable and valid manner is critical for improved decision making because much of what happens in organizations is determined by perception.

Progress

Survey research can also provide information about how well a program is operating. When addressed specifically to managers and other program workers, survey research can offer insight into the progress and efficiency of a program. This kind of information can also be derived from client responses.

Survey research can also provide analytic information on how program effects occur; how different parts of a system work; whether certain strategies provide for more efficiency and effectiveness than others; and what the perceived impact of a program is among different groups of people.

Two additional points about the knowledge produced by survey research should be understood. First, survey research provides information about perceptions or beliefs of respondents. Other strategies provide more objective data, but information derived from survey research emphasizes subjectivity—what informants perceive are the problems to which a program is directed, or what percentage of respondents perceives the program to have an impact. This is often considered a limitation of survey research; yet decisions are made on subjective judgments rather than objective reality. Robert Sigmond, an early pioneer in health planning, says of hospital planning, "planning decisions are not made over 'hard facts,' they are made over 'hard liquor.'" This is equally applicable to the world of program evaluation.

Second, in the analytical framework where cause-effect relationships are to be examined, survey research depends heavily on theory for the establishment of these relationships. Specifically, theory must be able to establish time ordering between various aspects of the program being measured and specify in enough detail those variables that need to be accounted for at the same time, or ruled out to ensure that all variables are measured as part of the survey and can be examined simultaneously with the relationships of interest.

Serious evaluation problems result in regard to the evaluation of efficiency, effectiveness, and impact. Overviews of these problems are in the following sections.

Efficiency

A survey can be addressed to personnel or service recipients to gain their impressions about the efficiency of the program or about alternative ways to operate that may be more efficient. Comparisons can be made between those who think the program is efficient and those who do not; causal statements can be drawn about the characteristics of personnel that are led to believe the program is more or less efficient. All that is available from such a survey is perceptions about efficiency. Yet, these perceptions are generally gained in the absence of any comparison between alternative strategies and are formed only in the context of the existing program.

Effectiveness, Impact, and Sustainability

Effectiveness is the extent to which a program realizes its short-term or immediate goals, whereas *impact* and *sustainability* are the extent to which the program changes the state of the world in a desired direction and is maintained in the long-run.

Again, questions can be addressed to respondents about the extent to which they perceive the program to be effective or, at a later stage, about the impact of the program. The questionnaire can also provide information for a causal analysis of the characteristics of program operation or of respondents that are perceived to lead to greater effectiveness or impact. This analysis will be made largely in the absence of any comparison. The absence of a comparison group is particularly important with regard to assessments of effectiveness and impact. It is generally impossible to tell whether an alternative program may have been effective, unless a specific strategy for examining alternative programs is set out in the beginning of the evaluation. This leads to the experimental model. An alternative to the experimental model is examination of time series data from before the program was put into place and after the program was implemented.

Given the problems in survey research, the question of why survey research is used for evaluation is likely to arise. There are two important reasons that survey research has been used as an evaluation format. First, despite the arguments against it, much information for program evaluation, particularly about the state of the system and of the program, can be acquired from survey research at any given time. Causal relationships can be inferred from survey research, particularly in the presence of a fairly good conceptual framework or theoretical perspective.

Second, survey research is an approach to evaluation that is relatively well-known to social and behavioral scientists who are often charged with responsibility for evaluation. The skills and strategies involved in evaluation through the use of survey research (i.e., questionnaire design, sampling, questionnaire administration, and data analysis) can be passed on fairly effectively through didactic settings.

Discussion Questions

1. What is the difference between descriptive and analytic survey research?
2. What types of basic evaluation questions are appropriate for each approach?

3. What are the limitations of using survey research in program evaluation?
4. What precautionary steps are possible to increase the use of survey research as an evaluation format?
5. Consider a primary care program operating in a rural community. How may survey research help resolve problems associated with program relevance, adequacy, progress, efficiency, effectiveness, impact, and sustainability?

SURVEY RESEARCH TECHNIQUES AND INTERPRETATION

Because the purpose of surveys may be either descriptive or analytic, the analysis of survey data must be appropriate to the survey's purpose. The objective of this chapter is to present some basic descriptive and analytic techniques and to demonstrate their use in various types of evaluation.

Descriptive Techniques

Analysis techniques appropriate to descriptive surveys are concerned with assessing the parameters of a problem in a given area or population or with describing how a program operates as a means of assessing the effect of experimental changes prior to the initiation of full-scale programs. Frequency distributions and contingency analysis are two useful techniques. Their use requires little mathematical ability, yet provides important insights into evaluation questions.

Frequency Distributions

A major analytical tool appropriate for descriptive purposes is the frequency distribution. A frequency distribution is a table format that displays data in discrete categories (e.g., male and female; five-year age groups from age 0 to age 85 or over; insurance coverage in the categories of Medicare, Medicaid, private, or group). A frequency distribution will typically provide the number and percentage of individuals from a total population who fall into each category. Frequency distributions, depending on their subject matter, can provide significant information for evaluation purposes.

Table 8.1 provides a simple, typical example of a frequency distribution. This table shows the distribution of preferred provider organizations (PPOs) and PPO enrollees by type of owner in 1994. The column Type of Owner, on the left of the table, provides a category for every type of PPO ownership, including an Other category to enumerate 150 PPOs that cannot be classified in the specific ownership categories given, and a Multi-Ownership category to classify 35 PPOs that are owned by a combination of the named types. Both the number of individual PPOs in each category and the percentage of the total in that category are shown in Table 8.1. The number of enrollees and percentage of enrollees also are shown for each type of ownership.

The primary purpose of the frequency distribution is to provide easy access to overall information about a specific topic. As shown in Table 8.1, there were

TABLE 8.1
Number and
Percentage of PPOs
and PPO Enrollees
by Type of Owner,
1994

	Operational PPOs		Eligible Enrollees	
Type of Owner	Number (in 1,000s)	Percentage	Number (in 1,000s)	Percentage
Insurance Company	371	46.3%	18,489	23.4%
Independent Investor	164	20.4	43,677	55.3
Physician/Hospital Joint Venture	43	5.4	N/A	N/A
Hospital Alliance	39	4.9	2,573	3.3
Other	150	18.7	10,155	12.8
Multi-Ownership	35	4.4	4,148	5.2
Total, All Types	802	100.0	78,042	100.0

Source: From Corrigan et al., 1997, reprinted with permission of authors.

802 PPOs of all types of ownership in the United States in 1994. Nearly half of the PPOs were owned by insurance companies. The largest number of enrollees in PPOs, more than 43 million, were enrolled through independent investor-owned PPOs. Additional information available from the table includes the relative ranking of each type of ownership in terms of numbers of PPOs and enrollees. The frequency distribution gives a broad overview of PPO status in the United States as of 1994.

Limitations   Frequency distributions may leave many questions unanswered. The fact that most enrollees in PPOs are enrolled through independent investor-owned entities may mean:

- that these organizations provide more attractive options than other types of PPOs;
- that the independent investor-owned PPOs have been most aggressive in seeking new enrollees; or
- a combination of these two or other reasons.

The frequency distribution in Table 8.1 will not provide this information; it will also not provide information about where PPOs are available geographically, or whether they are available to selected groups or individuals as explanations for the differential numbers and enrollments. Table 8.1 does not give us any information about the contrasting nature of benefits or restrictions associated with the PPO ownership types. They may all provide basically the same benefits. We cannot learn this from Table 8.1, although we may be able to from a different frequency table.

An important aspect of Table 8.1 is that the categories of ownership are mutually exclusive (if a PPO is owned jointly by an insurance company and independent investors, it appears under Multi-Ownership but not under either Insurance Company or under Independent Investor). The categories are also exhaustive, which is ensured by the inclusion of the Other category of ownership.

Contingency Tables

A simple extension of the frequency distribution, also useful for analysis in the descriptive mode, is the contingency table. While the frequency distribution shows the distribution of categorical data on a single dimension, such as type of PPO, a contingency table shows the distribution of categorical data on two or more dimensions as a means of comparing the dimensions.

Table 8.2 shows a typical contingency table taken from a study of risk management and quality management for ambulatory care cases (Macnee and Penchansky 1994). It is concerned with whether medical management was the cause of an untoward event in the case of 203 untoward events (123 appendicitis cases and 80 birth injury cases) reviewed in the article. Untoward events were rated in three categories: those that were judged to have no causation in medical management by two independent reviewers; those judged to have some causation in medical management by one of two reviewers; and those judged to have some causation in medical management by two reviewers. This three-level dimension forms the left column of the table. The second dimension, forming the row headings, is whether the untoward event was appendicitis or a birth injury. The table gives numbers and percents in the six categories defined by the two dimensions of the table. The percentages sum to 100 in the two columns.

The table shows the distribution of causation by type of problem. One of the important characteristics of contingency tables is that they are always, at a minimum, presentations of one variable classified by another—a two-variable analysis. In certain presentations, a contingency table may include three variables, but rarely would a contingency table involve more than three variables. The complexity of multi-variable tables makes them very difficult to interpret.

The two variables in Table 8.2 are type of causation assessed by reviewers (either medical management or not medical management) and type of problem. In a two-variable contingency table a causal direction is often assumed. In Table 8.2, the causal direction is assumed to be from the type of problem (appendicitis or birth defect) to assessment of cause. It is not assumed that the assessment by the reviewers (the row categories) was the cause of the type of problem.

TABLE 8.2
Ratings on Medical Management Causation for Appendicitis and Birth Injury Cases

	Appendicitis ($n = 123$)		Birth Injury ($n = 80$)	
	Number	Percentage	Number	Percentage
Cases reviewed as no causation by two reviewers	80	65%	60	75%
Cases reviewed as some causation by one reviewer	20	16	14	17
Cases reviewed as some causation by two reviewers	23	19	6	8

Source: From Macnee and Penchansky, 1994, reprinted with permission of authors.

Contingency tables generally are designed so that the independent or causal variable is shown on the top of the table, and the dependent variable is shown on the left. Percentages are calculated by column, so that each column sums to 100. Percentages are compared across rows.

The main purpose of a contingency table is to show the relationship between two variables. If a relationship exists, then the percentages in each of the rows will be different from one another. In particular in Table 8.2, 65 percent of appendicitis case problems are judged by two reviewers not to have been caused by medical management, compared to 75 percent of birth injury case problems. Nineteen percent of appendicitis case problems are judged by two reviewers to have been caused by medical management, compared to 8 percent of birth injury case problems.

The conclusion is that appendicitis case problems are more likely to be judged to have had medical management causation than are birth injury case problems. The conclusion is not that appendicitis case problems actually are more likely to have medical management sources, but only that the reviewers were more likely to judge them this way. Thus, another conclusion is that a relationship exists between type of case problem and assessment of whether medical management was the source of the problem.

A test of whether the number of observations in the various cells of the table are different from what would be expected by chance if no relationship existed between the variables examined can be made using the chi-square statistic. The chi-square statistic is applied to the actual number of observations in each cell. As shown in Table 8.2, a chi-square can be calculated to determine whether there was a statistically significant difference between type of case problem and assessed source of the problem. The calculation of the chi-square is given later in the chapter as Equation 8.1. On the basis of the chi-square for Table 8.2, which turns out to be approximately 5.0 with two degrees of freedom, there is no statistically significant difference between appendicitis and birth injury in the assessment of medical management versus non-medical management causation.

Continuous data   Often data that are essentially continuous are collapsed into a relatively small number of categories for presentation in a frequency distribution or contingency table format. One example of this is shown in Table 8.3, where the major column headings are age categories. Creating a contingency table in which years were given in one-year intervals would be possible, if unwieldy. This would be very difficult to interpret, however, and would take up a very large amount of tabular space. As an alternative, Swartz (1997) has elected to categorize the nonelderly population into five age groups. Each age category represents a different number of years. The longest category, 25 to 54 years old, spans 30 years, while the shortest, 15 to 17 years old, spans only three.

While the collapse of data within categories makes the table substantially easier to display, interpret, and use, how categories are chosen can make a considerable difference in how the data appear when arrayed in a table. Equal age intervals would have given a different picture of the distribution of health insurance by

	Age									
	<15		15–17		18–24		25–54		55–64	
	N	%	N	%	N	%	N	%	N	%
Medicare	185	.3%	43	.4%	89	.4%	1,862	1.6%	1,544	7.4%
Medicaid	14,457	24.4	1,674	15.0	3,176	12.7	8,137	7.2	1,295	6.2
CHAMPUS	2,268	3.8	440	4.0	1,047	4.2	3,529	3.1	1,464	7.1
Private	38,359	64.6	7,903	71.0	15,468	61.9	85,287	75.0	15,729	75.8
Group	36,100	60.8	6,866	61.7	12,851	51.4	78,991	69.5	13,490	65.0
No Insurance	8,255	13.9	1,748	15.7	6,700	26.8	19,822	17.4	2,877	13.9
Total	59,372		11,132		24,999		113,655		20,743	

Source: Adapted from Swartz, 1997, with permission of author.

TABLE 8.3

Estimates of Numbers and Percentages of Nonelderly People with Different Types of Health Insurance by Age, 1995

type across ages than the one that is given. Ultimately, the evaluator's decision determines how a continuous distribution is categorized for presentation and analysis, but the categories should make logical sense in terms of the subject under assessment.

A contingency table, of which Table 8.3 is an example, normally will be constructed in such a way that both horizontal and vertical categories are mutually exclusive and all-inclusive. While the age categories as the horizontal categories are mutually exclusive, the vertical categories (insurance type) are not. This can easily be seen by virtue of the fact that the columns labeled N add to more than the total, and the columns labeled Percent sum to more than 100. Presumably the category No Insurance is mutually exclusive with respect to the other categories, but a large number of people must have two or more types of insurance. Those with group insurance are also likely have a form of private insurance.

Including categories that would ensure that each category is mutually exclusive is often desirable. One strategy, for example, is to include a Private and Group category and perhaps an Other Combinations category. Such categorization makes a contingency table much easier to understand and interpret.

Analytic Techniques

Survey data can also be examined from the standpoint of analytic studies, and analysis of such data can bear on analytic questions. Analytic surveys are concerned mainly with attempting to answer questions about why a situation exists, how it occurred, where it occurs (e.g., if it does not exist among one group of people but may exist among another), and what has caused this situation to arise.

The ultimate purpose of an analytic study is to look for cause-effect relationships: if X occurs, Y will follow. If a program is structured in a certain way, certain results in terms of success or failure will occur. If a program is structured in a certain way under certain circumstances (e.g., in a rural area) the program may not be successful, whereas if it is structured differently and set in a different environment (e.g., an urban area), a different success or failure outcome will result. Although the ultimate test of cause and effect lies only in well-designed experiments, and even then only through the accumulation of a number of such well-designed experiments, survey research can help to provide insights about cause-and-effect relationships. The analysis of survey research data from the standpoint of analytic evaluations is concerned almost totally with the question of cause and effect.

Three criteria, originally suggested by John Stuart Mill (Cook and Campbell 1979) and generally accepted by the scientific community and by the rules of logic, must be satisfied if a cause-and-effect relationship is to be established. These are:

1. time order of the events;
2. association; and
3. elimination of other variables.

The following sections provide overviews of each criterion.

Time Ordering of Events

By definition, cause must always precede effect. But in a survey setting where data are collected on the basis of interviews at one point in time, it is frequently difficult to establish convincingly the time ordering of perceptions, attitudes, or knowledge of respondents about a particular program.

For example, suppose a survey shows that respondents who have a negative attitude toward primary healthcare personnel also fail to visit primary healthcare personnel. On the basis of the single survey, determining whether the negative attitude preceded the decision not to use the health workers' services or whether not using the services produced a negative attitude toward these people would be impossible.

Certain personal characteristics can be enumerated for which the question of time order is irrelevant. It would be reasonable to hypothesize that as people grow older they become more set in their ways and less likely to use new forms of services, thus making them less likely to use primary healthcare services. However, it would be unlikely for anyone to suggest that people who are less likely to use primary healthcare services will grow older. Clearly, age, along with a limited number of other variables (e.g., gender), can never be considered a dependent variable.

Apart from variables such as age and gender, it is impossible to establish the time ordering of events in survey data on the basis of empirical evidence alone. What is required is the existence, availability, or development of a plausible theory or conceptual perspective that indicates the time ordering. A very simple model of human behavior, for instance, would suggest that behavior follows attitudes. Thus, those people whose attitude is not to accept the primary healthcare worker would also be less likely to use the services. This is not the only possible theory. An alternative plausible theory of human behavior may suggest that people take on attitudes compatible with behaviors in which they engage. Thus, behavior would lead to a certain attitude.

In time series analysis, including panel surveys (those addressed to the same people regarding the same questions at more than one point in time), and in true experiments, time ordering of events is established by the evaluation format itself. In survey research, time ordering must be assumed on the basis of a reasonable theory or conceptual perspective.

Association

Association refers to the notion that as one measure, phenomenon, or attribute changes, another measure, phenomenon, or attribute changes. As temperature increases from a low level, for example, ice will first melt and become water, and then water will eventually boil and turn into vapor. A change in the state of the water is associated with a change in the temperature.

With association, both phenomena of interest must show variation. There can be no association and hence no causal relation between one phenomenon that changes and one that remains constant. If, for example, temperature remains constant at 100°F but the water under consideration is gradually subjected to less and less atmospheric pressure, at some point before reaching a total vacuum, the water will begin to boil and change to water vapor. Now there is no association between the change in the state of the water and the temperature because the temperature is constant. Here temperature cannot be seen as the cause of the change in the state of the water. A variable cannot be causally related to a constant.

In certain evaluation settings—especially in monitoring, time series analysis, and experiments—observing change occurring over time may be possible. In survey research, on the other hand, it is generally only possible to observe different levels of two phenomena that are assumed to be related to one another. If the question is attitudes toward a primary healthcare program and the use of services provided by primary healthcare workers, association can be established only if both the attitudes toward the program vary from person to person and use of primary healthcare services vary from person to person. But if no differences exist between the people in the survey either in feelings or behavior, there can be no association and hence no causal relationship between the two. What may be argued is that measures of either attitudes or behavior in regard to this particular question of interest may be so insensitive as to obscure real differences among respondents (see Chapter 13 for more on measurement). The evaluator's task in this setting is to devise instruments for measuring both attitudes and behavior that are sensitive enough to detect variation in each.

Lack of variation in one or both measures under observation (e.g., behavior and attitudes) is not the most important reason that the two measures may not be associated. Even if both measures show substantial variation, the variation in one may be random with respect to the variation in the other. In such circumstances, association still may not be shown. Several analytical techniques— contingency analysis, correlation, regression, and analysis of covariance, all discussed later in this chapter—are capable of establishing the existence or absence of an association.

Elimination of Other Variables

If the time sequence is correct or can be established from a plausible theory or conceptual framework, and if association can be shown, the final task in establishing cause is to eliminate other variables as logical candidates for having caused the observed result, output, or effect.

In a survey situation, other variables can be ruled out on the basis of a theoretical framework or conceptual perspective that makes them irrelevant to the process. For example, if the concern is the relationship between attitudes toward primary healthcare and use of primary healthcare services, it is unlikely that an evaluator would consider the height of interviewees as a cause of use of services. Height would be considered irrelevant to the use of primary healthcare facilities in most conceptual models. It may be quite reasonable to assume, however, that a person's perception of personal health status may be quite important to the use of primary healthcare facilities. Perception of health status must be considered, and its effect controlled or eliminated, through the analysis.

Illustration: Attitudes and Behavior in a Primary Care Program

To clarify the issues of establishing cause, consider two hypotheses often examined in the evaluation of primary care programs:

- H_1 = Attitudes of respondents toward the program are the cause of their utilization behavior.
- H_2 = Any apparent relationship between attitudes and respondents' utilization behavior is a function of perception of personal needs for services.

In terms of time ordering it is assumed, on the basis of our conceptual framework, that both attitudes and perception of need precede utilization behavior, and that the differential perceptions about services produce different use of services or that differential perception of need for services produce different use of services. What has been ruled out, a priori, is the possibility that use of services can create either attitudes about services or need for services. The alternative possibility that use causes attitudes or needs will not be examined. The conceptual framework has thus ruled out the problem of time ordering.

Analysis of Contingency Tables

The problem of association can be resolved, as indicated above, through a number of mechanisms. To keep this example as simple as possible, this section deals only with analysis of contingency tables. Regression and analysis of covariance, as other possible analytic techniques, are presented in later sections of the chapter.

Assume that a sample has been drawn from people who would normally use primary healthcare services in a particular organizational setting. Perhaps the initial sample is 200 people drawn on a random basis. The evaluator has gone out to interview these 200 people and managed to get usable interviews from 190. Ten people who were not interviewed, representing a non-response of 5 percent, may have an effect on the results obtained from the evaluation, but this non-response rate is very low, even for an interview. Consequently, we will not be concerned about non-response in this example.

The evaluator, with a usable sample of 190 people who have answered a series of questions, is able to construct three scales:

- attitude toward the primary healthcare program;
- number of symptoms of ill health perceived by respondents that would be likely to require primary healthcare services; and
- use of primary care services.

Assume that the evaluator has decided that the scales are so gross that they should be divided into two categories only for each scale. For attitude toward the program, the scale is divided into the two categories "favorable to the program" (containing 90 people who give the most favorable responses) and "unfavorable to the program" (containing the remaining 100 people). Use of services is divided into "high use of services" (containing 80 people who use the most services) and "low use of services" (containing the remaining 110 people). The first question to be examined is whether attitudes toward the program are associated with use of services, association being the second of the three criteria by which to judge the existence of a causal relationship.

Assume further that the evaluator has now examined a simultaneous occurrence of attitudes toward the program and use of services. The result of that examination may be as shown in Table 8.4—another example of a contingency table. This table shows that 38 of the 90 respondents who were favorable toward the primary healthcare program had high use of services and 52 had low use. At the same time, 42 of the people unfavorable to the program had high use of services and 58 had low use. The table indicates no relationship between attitudes toward the program, at least as measured on this two-dimensional scale, and use of services as measured on the two-dimensional use scale. Of those favorable to the program, 42 percent had high use of services; of those unfavorable to the program, 42 percent also had high use. Essentially no difference exists between the two groups of people in their use of services. On the basis of Table 8.4, if the evaluator were examining the question of whether attitudes toward the program resulted in subsequent use of services, he or she would conclude that they did not.

Furthermore, from the standpoint of decision making about strategies for increasing the acceptance of services from the primary healthcare program, the evaluator would probably recommend that program managers not try to change the attitudes of people toward the program. If they wish to increase use, they should find an alternative strategy. This recommendation may not lead to any productive behavior for increasing use of services, but it can restrain the administrators from wasting time and other resources in education or attitude adjustment.

TABLE 8.4
Relationship
Between Feelings
About the Primary
Healthcare Program
and Use of Services:
Alternative 1

	Favorable to Program		Unfavorable to Program		
	N	Percentage	N	Percentage	Total N
High Use of Services	38	42%	42	42%	80
Low Use of Services	52	58	58	58	110
Total N	90		100		190

Table 8.5 presents an association between attitudes toward a program and use of services leading to a different conclusion. The categories remain the same, but the numbers have been changed within the cells for demonstration purposes. In this case, of the 90 people favorable to the primary healthcare program, 50 had high use of services. Among the 100 people unfavorable to the program, only 30 had high use of services. The difference in these two categories is 56 percent as compared to 30 percent.

Table 8.5 represents a probable relationship between attitudes toward the program and use of services. A higher proportion of people favorable to the program had higher use of services. Those unfavorable to the program had lower use of services. If Table 8.5 had resulted from an examination of actual interviews with 190 respondents, the conclusion would be that the second criterion for cause (association) has been satisfied. A statistical test of significance of the data in Table 8.5 would also show that the relationship was not likely to have occurred by chance. The statistic used in this case would be the chi-square, which is discussed in the next section of this chapter.

The final step in the analysis is to eliminate other variables as possible causes of high use of services. The assumption is that this is a very simple theory. Either attitudes toward the program or perceptions of number of symptoms appropriate for treatment result in use of services. No other factors are assumed to cause use of services. This assumption would likely be too simple for a realistic explanation of use of services, but this is simply a demonstration.

To determine whether the number of symptoms perceived can be eliminated as an alternative causal explanation for use of services, examining all three variables simultaneously is possible. One possible result of such an examination is

TABLE 8.5
Relationship
Between Feelings
About the Primary
Healthcare Program
and Use of Services:
Alternative 2

	Favorable to Program		Unfavorable to Program		
	N	Percentage	N	Percentage	Total N
High Use of Services	50	56%	30	30%	80
Low Use of Services	40	44	70	70	110
Total N	90		100		190

shown in Table 8.6. For this analysis, the 190 respondents are grouped into eight categories, representing those with many or few symptoms, favorable or unfavorable attitudes toward the program, and high or low use of services.

Two points about Table 8.6 should be noted. First, 80 people are classified as having high use of services and 110 people are classified as having low use of services. Second, the four cells in Table 8.5 can be reconstructed from the data in Table 8.6. Those people with favorable attitudes toward the program and high use of services, for instance, are divided into those with many symptoms (45) and those with few (5). The total is 50 people, just as with that category in Table 8.5. Those people with unfavorable attitudes toward the program and high use of services are divided, again, into those with many symptoms (15) and those with few (also 15), making a total of 30 people in the category of unfavorable attitude and high use as shown in Table 8.5. The reader can verify that the same relationships hold between Tables 8.6 and 8.5 for people who have low use of services.

The importance of Table 8.6 is that no relationship exists between attitudes toward the program and use of services when this relationship is controlled for numbers of symptoms. For those people with many symptoms, attitudes toward the program had little effect on use of services. Of those with favorable attitudes, 64 percent had high use of services while 75 percent of those with unfavorable attitudes had high use of services. An opposite result is shown for those with few symptoms: 75 percent of those favorable to the program and 81 percent unfavorable to the program had low use of services.

The conclusion from Table 8.6 is that the relationship between attitudes toward the program and use of services as shown in Table 8.5 is not a direct causal relationship between favorableness to the program and use of services. Rather, the relationship is called a *spurious relationship*; that is, the relationship exists because both use of services and attitudes toward the program are related to numbers of symptoms.

Table 8.7 presents the same categories but demonstrates a situation in which attitudes toward the program do have an effect on use of services. In the category of people with many symptoms, 60 percent of those with favorable attitudes toward the program use services extensively, whereas only 20 percent of those with unfavorable attitudes had similar patterns of use. In the category of few symptoms, 54 percent of those favorable toward the program also had a high use of services, and 33 percent of people with unfavorable attitudes had a high use of services. In this case, attitudes about services cannot be ruled out as a cause of service use.

Tables 8.6 and 8.7 lead to substantially different conclusions and thus different action strategies on the part of program managers. Table 8.6 leads to the conclusion that the relationship between attitudes toward the program and use of services found in Table 8.5 was a function of the relationship of number of symptoms to both attitudes and use. These data lead to the conclusion that efforts toward education or other activities to improve attitudes toward the program will have relatively little effect in terms of increasing use of services. On the other hand, Table 8.7 has essentially ruled out numbers of symptoms as an alternative cause of the relationship between attitudes and use of services and confirms the

TABLE 8.6
Relationship Between Feelings About the Primary Healthcare Program and Use of Services Controlling for Reported Symptoms: Alternative 2a

| | Many Symptoms | | | | Few Symptoms | | | | |
| | Favorable to Program | | Unfavorable to Program | | Favorable to Program | | Unfavorable to Program | | |
	N	%	N	%	N	%	N	%	Total N
High Use of Services	45	64%	15	75%	5	25%	15	19%	80
Low Use of Services	25	36	5	25	15	75	65	81	110
Total N	70		20		20		80		190

TABLE 8.7
Relationship Between Feelings About the Primary Healthcare Program and Use of Services Controlling for Reported Symptoms: Alternative 2b

| | Many Symptoms | | | | Few Symptoms | | | | |
| | Favorable to Program | | Unfavorable to Program | | Favorable to Program | | Unfavorable to Program | | |
	N	%	N	%	N	%	N	%	Total N
High Use of Services	15	60%	5	20%	35	54%	25	33%	80
Low Use of Services	10	40	20	80	30	46	50	67	110
Total N	25		25		65		75		190

information of Table 8.5. In consequence, Table 8.7 suggests that if use of services is to be increased, people should be given information that will improve their attitudes toward the program.

The interpretations of the two 3-way tables can also be discovered if the tables are arrayed with attitude toward the program as the first classification and number of symptoms as the second. Table 8.8 shows the data from Table 8.6 rearranged so that attitude toward the program becomes the main column classification. Now what is shown is that people with many symptoms tend to have higher use of services whether they are favorable to the program or not (64 percent for those favorable with many symptoms and 75 percent of those unfavorable with many symptoms). What is also clear is that those with few symptoms are likely to be lower users of services (75 percent of those favorable with few symptoms and 81 percent of those unfavorable with few symptoms).

The values in the cells in three-way tables may be distributed in other possible ways. Only one other way will be mentioned: this is the possibility that a relationship between two variables, such as in Table 8.5, will be neither eliminated by a three-variable analysis (as in Table 8.6) nor strictly confirmed by a three-variable analysis (as in Table 8.7). This is the possibility of a relationship between two variables that is *contingent* on the level of a third variable. Such a possibility is shown in Table 8.9. This table shows that for those who have many symptoms, being favorable or unfavorable to the program is irrelevant. Fifty percent in each group are high users of services. For people who have few symptoms, however, attitude toward the program is a significant factor in use.

Among those who have few symptoms, 60 percent of those who are favorable to the program are high users of services, while 90 percent of those unfavorable to the program are low users of services. This is known as a *contingent relationship*. A contingent relationship is one in which the effect of one variable on another is contingent on the level of a third variable. Contingent relationships are also frequently called *interaction effects*. In this case, the effect of attitude on use of services is contingent on the possessor of the attitude having few symptoms. The data in Table 8.9 is the same as the data in Table 8.5 when symptom level is removed from the table.

Statistical Techniques for Data Analysis

Several statistical techniques are appropriate and useful when survey research is the format for program evaluation. These techniques are presented under two headings, contingency analysis and regression-type analysis. This division may imply some distinctions in techniques that in other formulations are only artificial, but it is a useful division for a discussion of statistical techniques applied to program evaluation.

Statistical Technique for Contingency Analysis

Contingency analysis involves techniques that may be used when important variables in the evaluation setting are measured on nominal or ordinal scales, or

TABLE 8.8 Relationship Between Feelings About the Primary Healthcare Program and Use of Services Controlling for Reported Symptoms: Alternative 2c

	Favorable to Program				Unfavorable to Program				
	Many Symptoms		Few Symptoms		Many Symptoms		Few Symptoms		Total N
	N	%	N	%	N	%	N	%	
High Use of Services	45	64%	5	25%	15	75%	15	19%	80
Low Use of Services	25	36	15	75	5	25	65	81	110
Total N	70		20		20		80		190

TABLE 8.9 Relationship Between Feelings About the Primary Healthcare Program and Use of Services Controlling for Reported Symptoms: Alternative 3

	Many Symptoms				Few Symptoms				
	Favorable to Program		Unfavorable to Program		Favorable to Program		Unfavorable to Program		Total N
	N	%	N	%	N	%	N	%	
High Use of Services	20	50%	25	50%	30	60%	5	10%	80
Low Use of Services	20	50	25	50	20	40	45	90	110
Total N	40		50		50		50		190

where it makes sense to collapse continuous variables into nominal or ordinal categories. (For a discussion of levels of measurement, see Chapter 13.) Further, the contingency statistical techniques are relatively easy to understand, to communicate to decision makers, and to carry out.

Every statistical analysis technique, whether using a contingency approach or a regression-type approach, is basically a comparison between measurements taken on a set of objects that constitute the units of analysis. The objects may be people, geographic areas, political entities, organizations, or other units that may be subject to change because of the effects of a program under evaluation. The purpose of such a comparison is to determine whether the two phenomena being measured are associated with one another across the units of analysis to a degree that cannot be explained by chance alone. One measure generally will be assumed to apply to an independent or causal variable, while the other measure will be of a dependent or caused variable. This distinction, however, has no influence on the statistical or mathematical aspects of the analysis. To look at a statistical tool appropriate for analysis of contingency tables, review the data in Tables 8.4 and 8.5.

Statistical analysis becomes relevant when asking, for example, whether the difference between those who are favorable to the program and were high users of services when compared to those who were unfavorable to the program and were high users of services could be considered a chance occurrence. Put another way, would the observed data in Tables 8.4 or 8.5 cause us to reject hypothesis 1, that there is no relationship between attitudes toward the program and use of service? This question can be answered statistically using the chi-square statistic.

The statistical test used with contingency data presented in the tabular form of Tables 8.4 and 8.5 is known as the *chi-square*. The chi-square statistic is an appropriate statistic for categorical data, particularly when a relatively few variables are to be considered. A chi-square statistic is calculated as: **Calculating a chi-square**

$$X^2 = \sum \frac{(O - E)^2}{E} \qquad (8.1)$$

Here O represents the actual observed number in each cell and E the expected number in each cell. The expected number in each cell is simply the number that would appear in any cell if the values in the cells were distributed strictly proportionately to row and column totals. For example, in Table 8.4, 58 percent of the respondents had low use of services. The expected number of respondents in the category "favorable to the program and low use of services" should be 58 percent of the 90 respondents who were favorable to the program. This is the case in Table 8.4. In Table 8.5, however, only 44 percent of respondents favorable to the program had low use of service. The easiest way to obtain the expected values is to multiply the appropriate column total by the appropriate row total and divide by the overall total. The expected value for the first cell of either Table 8.4 or 8.5, then, would be (90 * 80)/190 = 37.89. The expected values for the other three cells are obtained in the same manner.

Calculation of the actual chi-square value for Table 8.4 is

$$X^2 = \frac{(38 - 37.89)^2}{37.89} + \frac{(42 - 42.11)^2}{42.11} + \frac{(52 - 52.11)^2}{52.11} + \frac{(58 - 57.89)^2}{57.89}$$

$$= .001 \tag{8.2}$$

The reader can verify that the chi-square for the data in Table 8.5 is 12.69.

Interpretation
The resulting chi-square value of .001 for the data in Table 8.4 or 12.69 for the data in Table 8.5 can be assessed on the basis of a table of the distribution of chi-square that appears in most elementary statistics books. Two things must be known to assess the chi-square: the actual value of the chi-square (in this case .001 for Table 8.4, or 12.69 for Table 8.5) and the number of degrees of freedom in the contingency table under analysis. The number of degrees of freedom in a contingency table is equal to the number of rows minus 1 multiplied by the number of columns minus 1. On this basis, both Tables 8.4 and 8.5 have one degree of freedom. If .05 is accepted as a reasonable level of statistical significance, a chi-square table will show that, with one degree of freedom, a chi-square value as large as 3.8 has less than a 5 percent (.05) probability of occurring by chance when there is no relationship between attitudes and use of services.

Consequently, a chi-square with a value as small as that for Table 8.4 would be considered to have occurred by chance, while the result in Table 8.5 would not be considered to have occurred by chance. The null hypothesis of no relationship between attitude and use would be accepted in the first instance and rejected in the second instance.

Three-Variable Analysis

Tables 8.6 through 8.9 show three-variable analyses for examining the question of whether people who are favorable to the program will be high users of services when numbers of symptoms are taken into consideration. Chi-square values can be calculated for any of these tables using Equation 8.1 where the summation is now over eight cells in any table. For both Tables 8.6 and 8.8, the chi-square value is 43.31, for Table 8.7 it is 14.34, and for Table 8.9 it is 30.01. All four tables have three degrees of freedom because rows minus 1 times columns minus 1 equals 1 times 3. If a table of chi-square distributions is consulted for three degrees of freedom, it will be found that any chi-square value exceeding 7.81 has less than a 5 percent (.05) chance of occurring if no relationship between the variables exists. Consequently, the evaluator is justified in concluding that the distributions seen in any one of the four tables did not occur by chance.

However, that the distributions did not occur by chance is as far as the chi-square statistic can take the analysis. The evaluator must interpret what the statistically significant result means in terms of program decision making. After inspecting Table 8.6, the evaluator will conclude that the statistically significant result was a function of the relationship between symptoms and use of services. Any earlier relationship found between favorableness to the program and use of services was a spurious relationship that was determined by the relationship of favorableness toward the program and number of symptoms.

After inspecting Table 8.7, the evaluator will conclude that the statistically significant result was not a function of a spurious relationship created by number of symptoms, but was a function of a true relationship between attitude and use. Table 8.8 will be interpreted essentially the same as Table 8.6. Table 8.9 will cause the evaluator to conclude that the relationship found in Table 8.5 was a function of a contingent relationship between the three variables under consideration, in which it was only for people with few symptoms that attitudes toward services affected use.

If important variables can be specified in advance, analysis of contingency tables is a valuable technique for evaluating certain types of programs in survey situations. But this analysis has two distinct methodological difficulties. The first difficulty is the complexity of analysis when more than three variables are considered simultaneously. A table that involves four or more variables at one time may be too complicated to interpret readily. Moreover, in real applications the results of an analysis involving more than two variables will rarely be as straightforward as shown in the tables above. These tables are ideal cases that will almost never occur in real life. When the distribution of data is quite complex in tables, interpreting the results adequately may be difficult.

Limitations of contingency analysis

The second difficulty of contingency analysis is loss of observations. The preceding example includes 190 respondents—a reasonable sample size. However, if sample size is so small that the expected values in cells begins to go below about five, which could easily happen with small samples and several levels of variables, the calculation of the chi-square statistic is no longer strictly appropriate. Except for two-by-two tables, no appropriate alternative exists. When expected frequencies in any cell approach zero, which is possible with small sample sizes and a large number of cells, the chi-square statistic may give a badly inflated view of the true relationship. Consequently, analysis of contingency tables using the chi-square generally must be limited to categorical data that take on relatively few different values, and to examination of no more than three or four variables at a time.

Continuous Data Analysis

This section provides an introduction to certain regression techniques and analysis of covariance useful to program evaluation. These types of analyses are particularly useful to program evaluation when multiple causal variables exist and the dependent variable is an interval or ratio measure.

Regression is the primary analytical form for survey data in which the dependent variable can be expressed either as a proportion or probability or as a true continuous variable of the interval or ratio type. In general, independent variables in regression can be either categorical or continuous. To present regression in the simplest form, we consider the continuous independent variable first, even

Regression

though for evaluation purposes it is often necessary to consider categorical data as well.

In its simplest form, regression is a technique for describing the relationship between two continuous variables related to one another in a linear fashion. This relationship between two variables is expressed in the form of Equation 8.3.

$$Y_i = b_1 X_1 + b_0 + e_i \qquad (8.3)$$

Here Y_i represents the continuous dependent variable or caused variable, X_1 is the continuous independent or causal variable, b_1 is the coefficient of the relationship between X and Y (often referred to as the *slope* of the equation), b_0 is an additive constant (often referred to as the *intercept*), and e_i is an error term that represents the difference between the actual and predicted value of Y.

In this simple two-variable case, X and Y are known values, and the problem is to estimate the values of b_1 and b_0. Estimates of b_1 and b_0 will then lead to estimates of the error, e_i. Ignoring the error term, Equation 8.3 is the equation for a straight line. If the joint distribution of X and Y is graphed with X on the horizontal axis and Y on the vertical axis, Equation 8.3 represents an attempt to put a best-fitting straight line through the joint distribution.

Illustration To understand what these statements mean in more concrete terms, consider the graph of a relationship between a variable X and a variable Y as shown in Figure 8.1. The oblong, shaded area represents a randomly generated set of 100 points

FIGURE 8.1

Illustrative Graph of Relationship Between a Variable X and a Variable Y

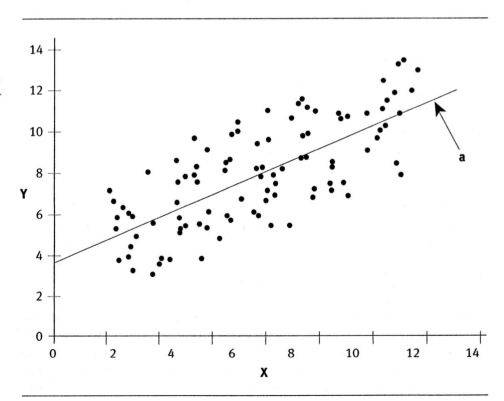

of the coincidence of the X and Y variables. When X is around 8, for example, there are several values that Y takes on as shown by the black dots above the value of 8 on the X-axis. When $X = 2$ there is no specific value of $Y = 10$, for this point falls outside the area represented by the 100 dots.

Regression is a technique for putting a best-fitting straight line through that set of points as indicated by line a. Best fitting, in this case, is understood to be the line that minimizes the sum of the squared differences between each of the actual values of Y and the predicted values of Y, based on X. It is from this concept of the best-fitting straight line that the term *ordinary least squares*, often used to characterize regression, is derived.

In Figure 8.1, line a crosses the Y-axis at approximately 3.60 on the Y scale and slopes upward so that, as the line moves one unit on the X scale, it moves about .56 units on the Y scale. Here, the value of b_0, the coefficient that represents the intercept, would be 3.60, and the value of b_1, representing the slope of the line, would be the distance traveled on Y as X moves one unit, or 0.56. In consequence, a formula for the relationship between X and Y based on the example of Figure 8.1 would be

$$\hat{Y}_i = .56X_i + 3.60 \tag{8.4}$$

where $\hat{Y}_i$ represents the predicted value of $Y (\hat{Y}_i + e_i = Y_i)$.

Calculating *b* values

In the simple two-variable case, the actual calculation of b_1 and b_0 are shown in Equations 8.5a and 8.5b. Because both values of X_i and Y_i are known and values of $\overline{X}$ and $\overline{Y}$ can be calculated from them, the value of b_1 can be computed from any set of variables X and Y to represent the slope of the relationship between those variables. The intercept term can then be calculated by using Equation 8.5b so that any set of variables X and Y will allow the calculation of predicted values of Y.

$$b_1 = \frac{\sum_{i=1}^{n}(X_i - \overline{X})(Y_i - \overline{Y})}{\sum_{i=1}^{n}(X_i - \overline{X})^2} \tag{8.5a}$$

$$b_0 = \overline{Y} - b_1\overline{X} \tag{8.5b}$$

Coefficients b_1 and b_0 calculated from Equations 8.5a and 8.5b are the coefficients that will produce the best-fitting straight-line relationship between X and Y as described by Equation 8.4. The question, however, is whether this best-fitting line actually represents a relationship between X and Y. The answer is based on whether knowledge of X is more useful in predicting values of Y than simple knowledge of the mean of Y itself. It is tantamount to the question of whether coefficient b_1 can be considered different from zero. There are various ways of testing whether coefficient b_1 is different from zero. A test of whether the coefficient is different from zero can be made by dividing the coefficient by its standard error. The standard error of the coefficient b_1 can be found using Equation 8.5c.

$$S.E.b_1 = \sqrt{\frac{\sum_{i=1}^{n}(Y_i - \hat{Y}_i)/(n-2)}{\sum_{i=1}^{n}(X_i - \overline{X})^2}} \qquad (8.5c)$$

The result of the division of the coefficient b_1 by its standard error is a t statistic with degrees of freedom equal to $n - 2$.

A second test of the likelihood that the coefficient of b_1 is different from zero is an F-test, which is carried out by dividing the average squared variance in Y that can be accounted for by X

$$SS_{Regression} = \sum_{i=1}^{n}(\hat{Y}_i - \overline{Y})^2 \qquad (8.6a)$$

by the average squared variance that cannot be accounted for by X

$$SS_{Error} = \sum_{i=1}^{n}(Y_i - \hat{Y}_i)^2 \qquad (8.6b)$$

divided by appropriate degrees of freedom. If the value of either the t-test or the F-test is large enough so that the probability of its occurrence would be less than a small value, such as .05 or .01, where no relationship actually exists in the population from which the sample of Xs and Ys was drawn, the assumption is made that a true relationship must exist between X and Y.

If the X_i represent a level of a continuous causal variable that can be directly manipulated by a type of service program, and the Y_i represent a hoped-for outcome as a result of the manipulation of the X variable, evaluation of the program to change the values of Y by affecting the values of X can be assessed at least for effectiveness.

Illustration: healthcare reform and professionalism

To illustrate regression as applied to a specific evaluation problem, consider an example taken from a recent article discussing changes in the practice of medicine that are likely to take place as the traditional relationship between the patient and the physician is being redefined (Wennberg 1994). As part of this article, Wennberg presents a graph that shows the relationship between patient days of hospital care per 1,000 Medicare enrollees in approximately 158 New England Hospital Service areas and the proportion of Medicare deaths that occur while the patient is hospitalized. While the actual data are not available in the article, the data are reconstructed in their essential details in Figure 8.2.

As shown in Figure 8.2, as the number of patient days per 1,000 Medicaid enrollees increases, the number of Medicaid deaths occurring in the hospital also increases. While this is not necessarily unexpected, it does provide the opportunity to look at the application of regression analysis in detail. What this does mean, however, is that the dependent or Y variable in this analysis is the number

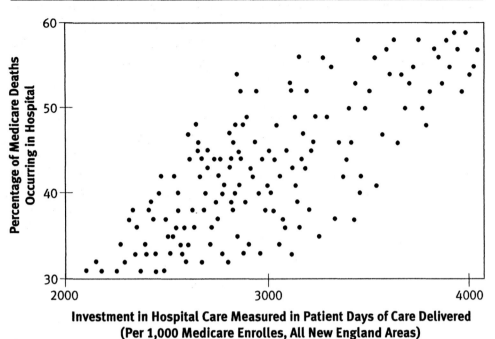

FIGURE 8.2
The Relationship
Between the Level
of Investment in
Hospital Care
Measured in Patient
Days of Care Per
1,000 Medicare
Enrollees and the
Proportion of
Medicare Deaths
That Occur While
the Patient Is
Hospitalized:
Hypothetical Data
Generated
Following Graph
from Wennberg,
1994

of Medicaid deaths occurring in the hospital, while the independent or X variable is the number of patient days per 1,000 Medicaid enrollees. If regression analysis is applied to the data as shown in Figure 8.2 (using a regression package or Equations 8.5a, 8.5b, and 8.5c), the results are:

$$\hat{Y}_i = 0.013X_i + 5.16$$
$$(0.009)$$
\hfill (8.7)

where $\hat{Y}_i$ is the number of Medicaid deaths occurring in the hospital, X_i is the number of patient days per 1,000 Medicaid enrollees, and the number in parentheses is the standard error for the number 0.013.

Significance test

The values 0.013 and 5.16 are often referred to as *regression coefficients*. The coefficient 0.013 indicates that as the number of patient days per 1,000 Medicaid enrollees increases by one unit, the number of Medicaid deaths occurring in the hospital increases by 0.013 units. The point at which the straight line defined by the regression equation in Equation 8.6 crosses the Y-axis (i.e., the number of Medicaid deaths occurring in the hospital when the number of patient days per 1,000 Medicaid enrollees is actually zero) is equal to 5.16.

One question often posed in regard to regression analysis is whether the regression coefficient b_1 (0.013) is significantly different from zero. A test of the significance of this coefficient can be made by dividing it by its standard error. In the case of the coefficient b_1, the t-test produces a resulting value of 14.56 (0.013/.0009). The t-test has 156 degrees of freedom (158 observations minus two) and is significant well beyond the .01 probability level. This means that the slope of the best-fitting ordinary least squares line through the 158 points shown in Figure 8.2 has a very small probability of not being different from zero. The evaluator will thus conclude that the slope is different from zero.

Proportion of variance accounted for by R²   The extent to which knowledge of the relationship between X and Y can account for the variation in Y is also of interest. There are, as previously noted, two forms of variation in Y: variation that is a function of X or is predicted by X (see Equation 8.6a), and variation that is not predicted by X, which is essentially error variance (see Equation 8.6b). Their sum is the total variance in Y. If the predicted portion of the variance is divided by the total variance, a statement of the proportion of variance in Y that is a function of X is produced. This is the same as the square of the correlation between X and Y and is often referred to as R^2. For the data in Figure 8.2, $R^2 = .58$. In other words, 58 percent of the variation in Y, the number of Medicaid deaths occurring in the hospital, is attributable to X, the number of patient days per 1,000 Medicaid enrollees.

Analysis of covariance   Analysis of covariance is an extension of regression that is particularly appropriate to program evaluation. It is especially relevant to those types of evaluations in which the people receiving the benefits of a particular program, or the areas in which a particular program has been implemented, have not been chosen on a random or probability basis so that the evaluation cannot take the form of an experiment. In this case, contrasting the group of people or the areas that receive the benefits of the program with groups of people or areas that do not receive program benefits is still desirable.

Given such a situation, evaluation is often likely to be based on the survey approach. Still, the aim is to compare people receiving the program, or areas in which it is implemented, to people not receiving the program, or the areas where it is not implemented. Doing so is difficult because it is unclear whether the people or areas where the program is implemented were comparable at the outset to the people or areas where the program was not implemented. Analysis of covariance is a mechanism for comparing two groups or two areas, or sets of groups or areas, when the effects of differences in other characteristics of the groups or areas are held constant.

Multiple regression   To understand analysis of covariance, exposure to multiple regression is first necessary. The discussion thus far has considered only a single dependent variable regressed on a single independent variable. The formulas for finding the coefficients of the regression equation were given in Equations 8.5a and 8.5b. *Multiple regression* is a technique for regressing a single dependent variable simultaneously on two or more independent variables where the equation is of this general type:

$$\hat{Y}_i = b_1 X_{1i} + b_2 X_{2i} + \cdots + b_j X_{ji} + b_0 \qquad (8.8)$$

In Equation 8.8 j different independent variables are designated X_1 through X_j. There will be j different coefficients to be estimated for each of variables X_{ji}, plus a single coefficient b_0 for the intercept. It can be shown that the values of coefficients b_1 through b_j and b_0 can be found by solving a set of simultaneous linear equations involving the dependent variable and each of the independent variables. There will be $j + 1$ of these simultaneous equations.

In Equation 8.8 the variables X_{ji} may be continuous variables representing characteristics of the populations under study that are to be controlled, or they may be one or more dummy variables representing either control for the population or actual program characteristics. To illustrate its application to an evaluation problem, consider the following example.

Consider a supplementary feeding program for newborn children administered through a local public health department. The purpose of this program is to ensure better nutrition to newborns who otherwise would be in danger of inadequate nutrition. Assume that the program operates through the child's first year of life. One clear goal would be to increase the child's weight throughout its first year of life—and obviously at the end of its first year of life—over what may prevail if the child were not given nutritional supplementation. Comparing the child at any point in the first year of life with the situation that would have prevailed had the child not had the nutritional supplement will be impossible; the child either has the supplement or does not. Comparing the children who received the supplement to a similar population of children who did not makes it possible to determine if weight at any particular point is different (particularly, greater) for the group receiving the nutritional supplement.

Illustration: evaluating a supplementary feeding program

From an experimental standpoint, what may be conceivable is to begin with the population of all children born within a certain time period and randomly assign them to the group that receives a nutritional supplement and to a group that does not. In practical terms, however, such a strategy is all but impossible for program evaluation. A program of nutritional supplementation would probably provide the supplement to anyone who was eligible and could be reached on a continuing basis. A great deal of negative publicity, if not actual legal action, could arise, attendant on a program so callous as to assign children randomly to receive or not receive nutritional supplementation just so evaluators could determine whether that nutritional supplementation made a difference in weight.

For any program of this type, some children will receive the benefits (in this case, the nutritional supplementation) because their parents are interested, concerned, willing to follow up and obtain the supplement; because they are in an area where the supplement is readily obtainable; or for other legitimate reasons. Other children, for equally legitimate reasons—and particularly for reasons not related to an experimental design propounded by the evaluator—will not receive these nutritional supplements.

Can a difference be detected between the children who received the nutritional supplement, even though not a random group, and another group of children that can serve as a control? The immediate reaction would be that the comparison is difficult because a number of factors associated with a child's weight cannot be controlled or taken account of in a non-experimental setting. This is precisely where analysis of covariance is useful.

The objective of the evaluation is to measure the effect of the program among children who have reached the age of one year. The evaluators realize that several factors could have influenced a child's weight in addition to having been in the program for a year—original birth weight, height, and some family predisposition to weight gain, for example. Birth weight can be taken from the original birth record. Height can be recorded at the time of the one-year physical examination, and a family propensity to weight gain may be taken by measuring the mother's weight. An evaluation of the program based on analysis of covariance could be constructed as

$$\hat{Y}_i = b_1 X_{1i} + b_2 X_{2i} + b_3 X_{3i} + b_0 \tag{8.9}$$

in which:

- Y_i = estimated weight at one year/height;
- X_1 = birth weight/birth length;
- X_2 = mother's weight; and
- X_3 = program participation (1 if in program, 0 if not in program).

X_3 is a *dummy variable*. Unlike mother's weight or birth weight divided by birth length, X_3 (program participation) takes on only two values: 1 if the child participated in the program; and 0 if the child did not.

Table 8.10 shows constructed data of the type to be analyzed for 20 children, 12 who have participated in the program, and 8 who have not. Table 8.11 shows the actual result for a regression analysis on the data in Table 8.10, in which:

- Y is the weight at one year in grams divided by height in inches;
- X_1 is birth weight in grams divided by birth length in inches;
- X_2 is mother's weight in pounds; and
- X_3 is a representation of program participation.

These may not be all the variables that can influence weight at one year. The variables have been restricted to two continuous variables and a single variable for program participation to keep the example simple.

Calculating sums of squares Table 8.11 is in three parts. The first shows the sum of squares that can be attributed to regression and the sum of squares attributed to error (the column marked SS). The sum of squares that can be attributed to regression can be calculated from Equation 8.6a, where

$$\hat{Y}_i = 0.35 X_{1i} - 0.06 X_{2i} + 11.44 X_{3i} + 232.19. \tag{8.10}$$

Child	Y	X_1	X_2	X_3
1	304	212	131	1
2	311	205	111	1
3	305	202	115	1
4	292	178	102	0
5	290	183	94	0
6	301	183	128	1
7	305	205	185	1
8	292	184	136	0
9	311	197	122	1
10	296	197	127	0
11	310	202	108	1
12	293	192	127	0
13	294	192	120	0
14	300	186	119	0
15	299	208	149	1
16	295	180	112	1
17	307	196	98	1
18	313	216	123	1
19	285	189	119	0
20	305	198	93	1

TABLE 8.10

Example of Data for Analysis of Covariance of Effect of Supplementary Nutrition Program

	SS	MS	df	F
Regression	1121.53	373.84	3	17.58
Residual	340.27	21.27	16	
Total	1461.80		19	
Multiple R	0.88			
R^2	0.77			

TABLE 8.11

Example of Results of Regression Analysis on Constructed Data Shown in Table 8.10

	Coefficients	Standard Error	t Stat	P-value
Intercept	232.19	19.08	12.17	0.00
X_1	0.35	0.11	3.16	0.01
X_2	−0.06	0.06	−0.90	0.38
X_3	11.44	2.48	4.62	0.00

The *sums of squares due to regression* is the proportion of variance in the observed values of Y (the proportion of variance in the child's weight to height at one year) that can be attributed to the three variables: birth weight to birth length; mother's weight (because the coefficient on X_2 is not statistically significant, it can be eliminated from Equation 8.10); and program participation.

The *error sums of squares* (designated Residual) is also provided in Table 8.11 and is calculated by Equation 8.6b. The error sums of squares represents the difference between each observed value of the ratio between child's weight and height at one year minus the predicted value for the same child. The total *sums of squares* is also given in Table 8.11. This is the addition of the sums of squares due to regression and the error sums of squares.

The *mean sums of squares* (designated MS) is shown in the second column in the first part of Table 8.11. The mean sums of squares takes into account the degrees of freedom. To predict a regression line, four degrees of freedom, representing three variables and an intercept, are accounted for out of the total degrees of freedom associated with 20 observations. The mean square for regression is regression sums of squares divided by three degrees of freedom, excluding the coefficient for the intercept. The mean square for the error is found by taking the remaining degrees of freedom minus the one degree of freedom for the intercept, or 16, and dividing the total sums of squares due to error. These two calculations result in a mean square due to regression of 373.84 and for error of 21.27.

Significance tests
The final column in the first section of Table 8.11 represents a test of significance of the overall regression equation. This is an *F*-test, as the column is labeled, with degrees of freedom 3 and 16. This *F*-test is the mean square due to regression divided by the mean square due to error. If the value of *F* exceeds a certain level (the level can be read from a table of the *F* distribution, which can be found in the appendix of most statistics books), the overall regression is said to be significant in the sense that it represents something other than random chance. What it represents is a non-chance relationship between a set of the independent variables and the dependent variable. With 3 and 16 degrees of freedom, an *F* of 17.58 would be significant beyond the .01 level (i.e., the probability that such a value would occur by chance when the predictor or independent variables have no real effect on the dependent variable is smaller than .01).

Multiple R and R^2
The second section of Table 8.11 has two designations, multiple *R* and R^2 (R square). The R^2 may be slightly easier to understand than multiple *R*. The R^2 represents the sums of squares due to regression divided by the total sums of squares, which in this case produces the value .77. In other words, 77 percent of the variance in the ratio of weight at one year in grams to height at one year in inches for this constructed data can be attributed to the independent variables under consideration. Multiple *R* represents a multiple correlation between the dependent variable set and the independent variable set, and is simply the square root of R^2. The multiple *R* is equivalent to a correlation coefficient.

Coefficients
The last section of Table 8.11 shows the actual coefficients for the independent variables, the intercept term, and statistical analyses of those coefficients. There, the coefficient for X_1, the ratio of birth weight to birth length, is .35 (i.e., as the ratio of birth weight to birth length changes by one unit, the ratio of weight at one year to height at one year changes by .35 units). The standard error of this coefficient is given as 0.11. A *t*-test for the significance of the individual coefficient is given by dividing the coefficient by its standard error, as shown in the column

labeled t. Whether this ratio is significant is shown in the column labeled P-value. In this column the coefficient of X_1, the coefficient of X_3, and the intercept term are all statistically significant (i.e., they are all different from zero at some level of probability). The coefficient of X_2, -0.06, is not large enough relative to its standard error to show statistical significance. The probability of finding the t value shown is about 38 percent.

The coefficient of X_2 (the coefficient of mother's weight) is not statistically significant when considered along with birth weight and participation in the program. So mother's weight can be excluded from the predictor variables and the coefficients for the other two variables—weight to height at one year, and program participation—reestimated. If this is done, a slight change in the coefficients of the two remaining variables and in the intercept will occur. The result is shown in Equation 8.11, where the coefficients of the two predictor variables remain statistically significant at the .05 level:

$$\hat{Y}_i = 0.30X_{1i} + 12.57X_{3i} + 233.41 \qquad (8.11)$$

Here, a significant coefficient is found for the continuous variable X_1, and for the dummy variable X_3. These two coefficients mean substantially different things in interpretation, as can be seen when the two possible values for X_3 (0 and 1) are substituted into Equation 8.11.

$$(\hat{Y}_i | X_3 = 1) = 0.30X_{1i} + 245.98$$
$$(8.12)$$
$$(\hat{Y}_i | X_3 = 0) = 0.30X_{1i} + 233.41$$

In Equation 8.12 there are actually two regression lines. One regression line represents the relationship between birth weight and weight at one year for those who participated in the program. The second, parallel regression line is for nonparticipants, and these lines are exactly 12.57 units apart along their length. This 12.57 represents the increase in the ratio of weight to height at one year that can be attributed directly to the program itself, the program effect.

This example has considered only two continuous variables as controls that can be taken into account prior to examining the effect of the program (which, in this case, is a difference in weight of 12.57 grams per inch). The technique that it represents, however, can be used for any number of continuous or categorical variables that may be considered important to differences that must be taken into account before program effects can be measured. This approach to analysis of covariance represents a powerful technique for program evaluation when the basic data that must be relied on are essentially survey-type.

The preceding section was based on the assumption that the program was provided to any who took advantage of it, and those who did not were excluded for reasons unrelated to the program. It is often the case that programs are implemented to benefit those most in need. With regard to a supplemental feeding

Regression discontinuity

program, those most in need may be considered to be those who had the lowest weight to length ratio at birth. In such a situation, where random assignment is again not possible because those most in need will receive the intervention, a technique known as *regression discontinuity*, which is a similar application to that described above, can be employed.

After analyzing the preceding example of an infant feeding program, the expectation may be that in the absence of a feeding program a positive and linear relationship exists between the ratio of birth weight to birth length and the ratio of weight at year 1 to height at year 1. When the feeding program is provided for those who are at the lower end of the birth weight to birth length scale, and if the feeding program is effective, the evaluator would expect to see a regression discontinuity occurring at the cut-off point for the feeding program. To see what this means, consider the two charts, Figure 8.3a and Figure 8.3b. Figure 8.3a was constructed from the data in Table 8.10. The two lines represent the two regression equations in 8.12: the solid line represents the first of the two equations (i.e., those who received the feeding program); and the broken line represents the second. This figure demonstrates the effect of the feeding program when the ratio of birth weight to birth length is taken into account and when the feeding program is assigned to all children who are able to take advantage of it.

Figure 8.3b is a similar analysis, but represents regression discontinuity. Here the feeding program was assumed to be given to the 12 infants with the lowest ratio of birth weight to birth length as can be seen on the horizontal axis. The resulting regression line is discontinuous at the point on the horizontal axis scale where the infants no longer received the feeding program. This analysis, which is carried out precisely as the preceding analysis, can be a powerful test of a program effect where the program is designated specifically for the most needy

FIGURE 8.3a

Effect of Haphazardly Assigned Program

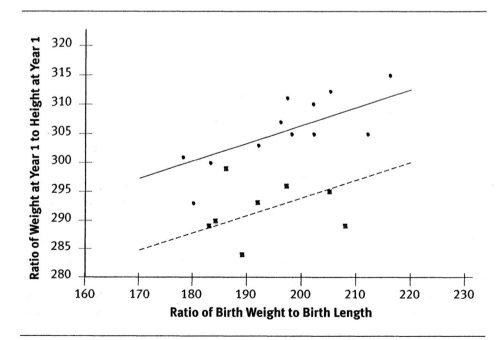

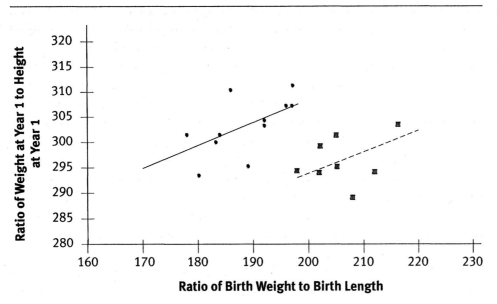

FIGURE 8.3b
Effect of Program
Regression
Discontinuity

members of the target population. However, it requires a prior measure (in this case, ratio of birth weight to birth length) that is expected to be associated with the final program outcome. The effect of the program is the difference between the two regression lines at the point of discontinuity, in this case, about 15 points on the vertical axis. The test of whether the coefficient representing the program dummy was statistically significant is the test of whether the program has been effective.

Dichotomous Evaluation Outcomes

The outcome of interest in an evaluation frequently may be assessed only as the presence or absence of some condition. For example, in terms of infant weight, it is common to assess birth weight as normal (2,500 grams or more) or low (less than 2,500 grams). For a program teaching a skill, participants may be classified as having acquired or not acquired the skill. Organizations may be classified as having a desired attribute after an intervention or as not having the attribute after the intervention.

When the outcome of interest takes on a dichotomous result that may be interpreted as indicating success or lack of success with a program intervention, an analysis of the result using multiple regression and ordinary least squares is not, strictly speaking, statistically appropriate. The reason for this is that statistical tests with ordinary least squares (OLS) assumes homogeneity of variance in the error terms (i.e., the deviation of predicted values of the dependent variable from actual values of the dependent variable). However, when the dependent variable is dichotomous, the error terms can be only two values for any given value of an independent variable. Hence, the resulting errors are not only not homogeneous, they are dependent on the values of the independent variables, and statistical tests are inefficient. (Excellent discussions of the problems associated with dichotomous dependent variables can be found in Aldrich and Nelson 1984, or Gujurati 1988.)

One way to circumvent this problem of inefficient statistical tests is to use weighted least square (WLS). WLS can be performed in a two-step process. The first step is to run OLS to obtain the estimated value of the dependent variable. From this estimate, a set of weights is obtained by multiplying the predicted value of the dependent variable by 1 minus the predicted value of the dependent variable.

The second step is to divide all values of the original data (both dependent and independent variables) by the square root of the weights and run OLS on the resulting values. When this procedure is used, it is necessary to include a constant term for each observation, which is also divided by the appropriate weight. OLS is then carried out with the transformed constant term serving as the estimator of the intercept (in doing this, forcing the regression program to estimate without an intercept is necessary).

The use of WLS produces a solution for which the statistical tests are appropriate and the coefficients and standard errors can be used as an estimate of the effect of the independent variable set on the dichotomous dependent variable. One problem that may arise in the use of weighted least squares is that in the first stage there may be predicted values of the dependent variable that are greater than 1 or less than 0. When this happens, the predicted value of the dependent variable multiplied by 1 minus the predicted value will always be negative. Because the square root of a negative number is undefined, this will result in a nonexistent weight.

A practical solution to this problem is to:

1. assign a large value less than 1 (such as .999) to those observations for which the OLS estimate is greater than 1;
2. assign a very small value greater than 0 (such as .001) to those less than 0; and
3. proceed with the analysis.

If there are many such cases, this may affect the resulting estimates, but they will still be unbiased and at a minimum variance. Another problem of WLS, particularly when sample size is small, is the likelihood of high correlation between the adjusted variables and the adjusted constant term. This can lead to large standard errors and inefficient estimates in small samples.

The major problem with WLS, however, is that it can result in estimates that are greater than 1 or less than 0, which tends to offend the sensibilities of serious statisticians. They see the use of regression to predict a dichotomous dependent variable as essentially an attempt to predict the *probability* that the dependent variable will be either 1 or 0 (hence the use of the term *linear probability model* to describe this type of analysis). A predicted probability should never be larger than 1 or smaller than 0. Further, if a variable (in this case, the probability of being either 1 or 0) can vary only between 1 and 0, logic may suggest that a nonlinear relation exists between the probability and any predictor variable.

To see what a nonlinear relation means, examine Figure 8.4. The horizontal axis in Figure 8.4 is the level of a single independent variable that ranges from 0 to 100. The vertical axis is the probability that the dependent variable is actually 1 or 0. If the straight line represents a linear relationship between the independent and the dependent variable, when the independent variable goes below 0, the probability must either go below 0 also—which makes no sense—or must truncate at 0, which is a nonlinear relationship in itself. The same problem arises if the value of the independent variable goes above 100.

The curved line in Figure 8.4 represents a different view of what happens as the independent variable goes from 0 to 100. In this case, the probability of the dependent variable being 0 or 1 approaches 0 and 1 but never crosses those two limits. The probability changes more rapidly near the mid-point and changes more slowly as the probability approaches the limits of 0 and 1. This type of model (called a *logit model*) is much more attractive to statisticians than the linear model and is the present model of choice to estimate relationships of independent variables to dichotomous dependent variables.

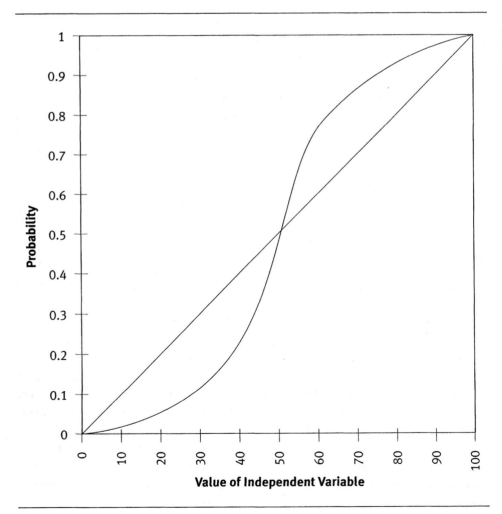

FIGURE 8.4

Two Views of the Probability of a Particular Outcome

In the ordinary least squares linear model, or in the weighted least squares linear model, the equation for the probability P that the dependent variable is either 1 or 0 (in the case of one predictor variable) is:

$$P_i = b_i X_{1i} + b_0 \qquad (8.13)$$

where the b values represent the coefficients and the X values represent the independent variables (or transformed independent variables in weighted least squares).

In the logit model, the equation for the probability P that the dependent variable is either 1 or 0 (in the case of one predictor variable) is:

$$P_i = \frac{1}{1 + e^{-(b_1 X_{1i} + b_0)}} \qquad (8.14)$$

where e is the natural logarithm (approximately 2.71828) and the other symbols are as given in equation 8.13.

While the linear model can be solved directly as a set of simultaneous equations, the logit model cannot be solved this way. The only solution to the logit model is the method known as maximum likelihood estimation (MLE). In MLE, a likelihood function, dependent on an initial estimate of the values of the b coefficients, is constructed from the data and then is maximized using an iterative process that will eventually converge to the values of b coefficients that maximize the likelihood of finding the observed results. This is the solution to the logit model.

It is perhaps desirable to show a comparison of the logit model with the OLS linear model and the WLS linear model from an example to see what the respective results look like. Review Table 8.10 again. Assume that any child with a weight to height ratio at year 1 (variable Y) less than 295 represents a child that is malnourished, and that any child with a weight to height ratio at year 1 of 295 or more represents a child that is adequately nourished. Fourteen children are considered adequately nourished (coded 1 on the dependent variable P) and six children are considered malnourished (coded 0 on the dependent variable P). Because the variable X_2 was not statistically significant in the earlier analysis (see Equation 8.10), that variable will be dropped from the analysis and only variables X_1 and X_3 will be retained. If OLS, WLS, and MLE are carried out with the dichotomous dependent variable representing adequately nourished or malnourished, and with variables X_1 and X_3 as predictors, the estimates of the b values, their standard errors, and a t-test for each b for each model is shown in Table 8.12.

While the OLS and WLS coefficients are directly comparable in Table 8.12, the MLE coefficients are not comparable to the OLS or WLS. Consequently, the only reasonable way to compare the coefficients for X_1 and X_3 for MLE with OLS and WLS is to look at the t-tests. For the data in Table 8.12, the t-test for X_1 would not be considered statistically significant at the .05 level for any of the three models. The t-test for X_3 would be considered statistically significant for all three models. Consequently, the decision made on the basis of the three distinct models would not be very different for these data.

		OLS	WLS	Logit
Coefficients	Constant	−1.880	−0.025	−21.020
	X_1	0.012	0.002	0.106
	X_3	0.500	0.604	3.163
Standard Errors	X_1	0.008	0.003	0.073
	X_3	0.177	0.154	1.471
t-test	X_1	1.433	0.711	1.453
	X_3	2.807	3.916	2.150

TABLE 8.12
Comparison of Results from OLS, WLS, and Logit for Data in Table 8.10 when the Dependent Variable Y Is Dichotomized at 295+ and <295

While the result shown in Table 8.12 will not always occur for every comparison of OLS, WLS, or MLE, it is not uncommon for the three analyses to produce highly comparable results. MLE has become an important analytical method for dichotomous dependent variables, essentially replacing the linear probability model as estimated by WLS. MLE does so by virtue of two facts: that it does not produce probabilities that are above 1 or below 0; and the ease with which it can be done with modern statistical packages such as SPSS, SAS, STATA, and others. In many cases the actual decision of whether a program had an effect (e.g., participation by infants in a nutritional supplement program, variable X_3) can be determined with an acceptable level of statistical credibility using WLS, or even in many cases using the relatively inefficient (but unbiased) OLS alone. An evaluator who is faced with a dichotomous dependent variable should probably use MLE as the analytical model if a computer program for doing MLE analysis is readily available, but if not, WLS or even OLS can be used to obtain some idea of whether the program made a difference. It is almost certainly true that if either of these techniques does not show a statistically significant result for a program variable, such a result is not likely to be found by MLE either.

Dichotomous dependent variables are not the only types of results that may be of interest but that are not, strictly speaking, quantitative. Program outcomes that are categorical, either ordered or unordered, can be analyzed using such techniques as multinomial logit, ordered probit, or tobit. These techniques, however, are beyond the scope of this text. Those looking for a good introductory treatment of the subject should see Aldrich and Nelson (1984).

Discussion Questions

1. What is the distinction between descriptive and analytic techniques? What is their relative utility in program evaluation?
2. What three conditions must be present in order to infer a causal relationship? How difficult or easy is it to achieve these conditions in program evaluation? Name factors that contribute to the ease or difficulty.

3. What are the distinguishing features of categorical versus continuous data? How does the evaluator handle the problem of spurious relationships in each situation?

4. Describe in plain language how a program effect can be determined within the context of analysis of covariance or regression discontinuity.

5. What are two ways to deal with assessing program effects when the outcome of interest is dichotomous? What are the advantages and disadvantages of these two?

V

TREND ANALYSIS

TREND ANALYSIS AS AN EVALUATION STRATEGY

Trend analysis, sometimes called *time series analysis*, is a general evaluation strategy that combines aspects of monitoring with an effort to determine whether the introduction of a particular program can actually be viewed as having a causal connection to changes in the condition that the program was established to influence. Trend analysis provides an evaluation strategy for assessing such changes over time. The implicit assumption in the establishment of any program is that it will produce or cause desirable changes. The objective of this chapter is to show how trend analysis can be used to assess such changes, to consider the settings in which it is an appropriate evaluation strategy and the types of data needed to use trend analysis effectively, and to present a health-related application.

What Is Trend Analysis?

Trend analysis is an evaluation strategy for examining the trends in performance indicators over a period of time. The strategy provides an opportunity to ascertain:

- whether changes have occurred in a measure of performance;
- whether such changes have occurred in association with a particular intervention program;
- whether such changes are outside the normal expected range of variation in the performance indicator(s); and
- whether possible explanations of the observed changes in performance other than a particular intervention program can account for changes observed.

The following illustration provides an example of trend analysis applied to the issue of whether the closure of rural hospitals is a function of market competition, or whether rural hospitals can reduce competitive pressures by differentiating services and thereby reduce the risk of closure.

Illustration: Effects of Market Position and Competition on Rural Hospital Closures

Increasing competition among health service organizations has resulted in cost reduction among many healthcare providers; for others it has threatened their basic viability. Rural hospitals are most vulnerable to competitive pressures; over the years, the number of rural hospital closures has been increasing.

Succi and colleagues (1997) use longitudinal data collected from the populations of U.S. rural community hospitals ($N = 2,780$) from 1984 through 1991 to examine the effects of competition and market position on rural hospital closures. Using time series analysis they found that rural hospitals operating in markets with higher density had a higher risk of closure. Rural hospitals, however, that were differentiated from others in the market had a lower risk of closure. Effects of market density on closure disappeared when market position was considered, indicating that differentials in markets must be considered when evaluating the effects of competition on rural hospital closure.

The use of trend analysis has important implications for managers of small rural hospitals. As described by Succi et al., "These findings render support for programs such as EACH/RPCH and rural hospital networks that encourage differentiation among rural hospitals. These findings may also encourage individual rural hospitals to depart from the 'follow the leader' strategies and to establish distinct market niches that can alleviate direct competition with other hospitals in the same market."

Appropriate Settings for Trend Analysis

Trend analysis depends for its application on information collected at more than one point in time and, in that sense, is quite similar to many monitoring strategies (discussed in Chapters 3 and 4). Because it is similar in character to monitoring, trend analysis evaluations may be conducted by using data collected either primarily for monitoring purposes or in conjunction with monitoring effects. But trend analysis also tends to be concerned with a program's impact, which makes it even more similar to experimental design (discussed in Chapters 11 and 12).

One of the major benefits of trend analysis is its ability to clarify observations from what might be considered "naturally occurring experiments where the observations are of the "before-and-after" type. Consider the following hypothetical illustration.

Illustration: The Case of High Perinatal Mortality Rates

A reporter for *The Elmtown News* writes an article on the perinatal mortality rate in Greene County. He indicates that the perinatal mortality rate is high relative to other counties in the same area of the state. The mayor of Elmtown reads the article, as do the director of the local health department and several local physicians. These people regularly communicate with one another on an informal basis, and they now agree among themselves that something should be done to try to reduce the county's perinatal mortality rate.

The health department director feels strongly that the high rate is primarily because of the lack of good and regular prenatal care for expectant mothers among the low-income population in Greene County. He points out to his colleagues that while the county health department has for some time provided prenatal care and consultation to low-income expectant mothers, reception of the services has not been overwhelming.

The mayor suggests that Elmtown allocate funds to launch an intensive and widespread publicity campaign to inform expectant mothers about the prenatal services available in the health department. This program is instituted, and Greene County leaders eagerly await the publication of the next year's state statistics for perinatal mortality.

When these data become available, they see that the county's perinatal mortality rate has declined and is now slightly lower than any other county in their immediate area of the state. The county leaders congratulate themselves on their wise use of resources in publicizing the availability of the prenatal counseling and treatment provided by the health department.

The illustration provides a classic example of the pretest–posttest–no control group design. A state of the system—that is, the perinatal mortality rate—was observed at one point in time. Subsequently a stimulus—publicizing the prenatal clinic in the local health department—was introduced into the system and, finally, a second measurement of the system was taken. On the basis of this design, the decision makers, who also play the role of evaluators, decided that their program had been a success.

Sources of Error

Although it appears from the one-year decline in perinatal mortality that the publicity campaign has had an effect, there are several possible reasons that such a conclusion could be in error. Four possible sources of error—discussed in some detail in Campbell (1969), Campbell and Stanley (1963), and Suchman (1967)—in the interpretation of these data are particularly worth noting.

Regression to the mean

Regression to the mean refers to the tendency for any time-related data to regress, or come back, to the long-term trend line. The perinatal mortality rate in Greene County became a matter of interest because the rate was higher than those in surrounding counties in the year in which it was observed and in which the newspaper article was published. This particular year may have represented an aberration in the rate that was on the high side of the long-term trend.

Figure 9.1 represents the two years in which Greene County was aware of the perinatal mortality rate as viewed in the long-term context. The figure shows a hypothetical set of perinatal mortality data for Green County for six time periods. The time period prior to the health department publicity campaign, designated t_0, and the period immediately following that campaign, designated t_1, are the observed rates, and four time periods, t_{-1}, t_{-2}, t_{-3}, and t_{-4}, are prior unobserved rates. The solid line in Figure 9.1 represents the long-term trend line for the perinatal mortality rate. The broken lines represent the expected limits that the perinatal mortality rate for any given year will fall within with some probability—for example, 95 percent.

In particular, the observed rates for the time periods t_0 and t_1 are both within the range that would be expected for perinatal mortality by chance alone.

FIGURE 9.1

Trend of Infant Mortality Over Time Showing Regression to the Mean

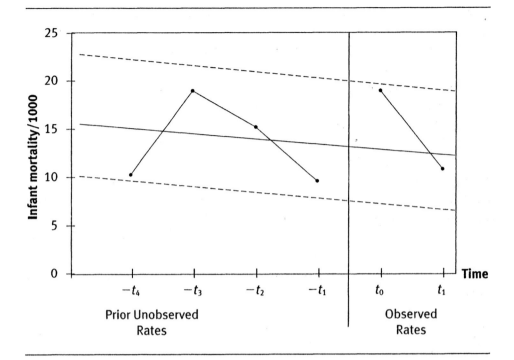

Further, it is possible to observe that the rate at t_0 was higher than the trend line and that at t_1 the rate has regressed to a level below, but closer to, the long-term trend. Thus, showing that the publicity campaign was effective in reducing the perinatal mortality rate is not possible because the change can be adequately explained by regression to the mean.

Reactiveness A second possible source of error in the simple before-and-after comparison of Greene County's perinatal mortality rate is the effect of *reactiveness*—the effect of the first observation of perinatal mortality rates on the level of the perinatal mortality in the second time period without regard to the program. In essence, reactiveness is the effect of knowledge of a situation on subsequent measures of the situation.

For example, concern about the perinatal mortality rate associated with the original newspaper article, independent of the publicity campaign launched by the public health department, could have accounted for the decline in perinatal mortality. The concern of community leaders could have been manifested in many ways that could produce a decline in rates. Various kinds of community resources could be diverted from other applications and be brought to bear on medical services for expectant mothers. The concern of community leaders could be reflected in different treatment of expectant mothers or newborn babies in county medical facilities. The concern could conceivably result in actual modification of the rates themselves through better or more selective counting.

Reactiveness, the effect of knowledge about a situation on subsequent conditions of the situation, is closely related to the self-fulfilling prophecy—the effect of expectations about how a situation will change on subsequent conditions of the situation. If community leaders expect the publicity program to influence perinatal mortality rates, they may be even more likely to make other changes in how expectant mothers are treated that will result in the reduction of rates, independent of the actual program. The power of reactiveness and the self-fulfilling prophecy should not be underestimated.

Consider the following classic example. Teachers in a selected group of classes were told that certain of their students, on the basis of IQ tests taken in the prior year, were likely to show significant improvements in school performance during the coming year. In fact, these students were simply selected at random by the researchers. At the end of the school year, these randomly selected students for whom the teachers expected better performance actually performed better than their nonselected classmates on a series of standardized IQ tests given to all students. The researchers ascribed the improvement in the selected students' performance to the expectation of the teacher about those children's performance (Rosenthal and Jacobson 1968).

This example clearly indicates the importance and effectiveness of reactiveness in producing outcomes of a desired type. Similarly, the expectation that the health department publicity program will make a difference in infant mortality rates produces a difference quite apart from the campaign's true effect because community leaders believe it will make a difference.

The difficult aspect of reactiveness or of the self-fulfilling prophecy is that we cannot successfully protect against it. In many research or evaluation settings the double-blind random clinical trial is the only research design that can successfully eliminate possible effects of reactiveness. This approach to evaluation is discussed in some detail in the chapter on experiments. Basically, the double blind random clinical trial is an evaluation in which two comparable groups are each given a treatment, one known to be ineffective or essentially a placebo, the other a new drug or technique to be evaluated. The person giving the drug or treatment and the person evaluating the outcome are unaware of which group received the treatment and which received the placebo. Although this is a powerful evaluation design and effective for eliminating reactiveness or the self-fulfilling prophecy, it is seldom, if ever, possible to apply this design to the problems of program evaluation. Unfortunately, for program evaluation, a double-blind random clinic trial stands as a good but unobtainable model.

Cohort changes refer to systematic changes associated with one particular age group of the population. A cohort change, for example, could be thought of as occurring if a large proportion of mothers with a potentially high risk for delivering children who would die in the first 28 days of life had moved from the county during the year. Although an unlikely occurrence, it could happen if, for example, a large group of migrant farm workers had left the area during that time period. Having data available for an extended period of time on population change would provide a means of evaluating this possibility.

Social structural change, in general, requires an extended series of observations for a successful evaluation. Such change can best be evaluated through some type of trend analysis. To consider how social structural change may have

Cohort and social structural change

impact on the change in infant mortality rates in the county, consider Figure 9.2. Figure 9.2 again shows the mortality rates for the six time periods of Figure 9.1, but it also plots on the same scale the percentage of population in Greene County with incomes below the poverty level. Figure 9.2 shows that it is quite plausible to infer that the decline in infant mortality rates experienced in the county between t_0 and t_1 was in some way a function of the decline in the percentage of families with incomes below the poverty level.

Figure 9.2 shows that the two variables move through time quite closely to one another; a correlation calculated between these two variables would probably be close to .9. This information, which would not be nearly as obvious if viewed only at time t_0 and t_1, serves as an alternative to the publicity program itself to explain the decline in neonatal mortality rates for t_0 to t_1. This situation is much more easily demonstrated and perceived on the basis of a trend analysis than it would be on the basis of a simple before-and-after view.

Miscounting as measurement error

A last possible source of error in the conclusion that the Greene County education program was effective may come from the way in which mortality rates for the first and second time period were measured. What has often been observed is that when a particular phenomenon begins to attract attention, the identification of incidents of the phenomenon are likely to increase simply because it is a current issue. After the first appearance of Legionnaires' disease, many new cases of the disease appeared that may have been diagnosed as something else had not Legionnaires' disease received publicity. The prevalence of AIDS, drug use,

FIGURE 9.2

Trend of Infant Mortality Over Time Showing Relationship to Percentage of Families Below Poverty Level

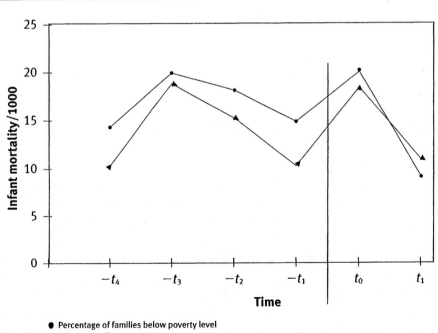

● Percentage of families below poverty level
► Infant mortality per 1,000

homicides, child abuse, and many other phenomena increase as attention is directed to them because they are better recognized and recorded.

It is not clear how miscounting could affect perinatal mortality in any given setting, but it is possible to imagine a situation in which the attention given to perinatal mortality could lower the rates through what is counted. For example, suppose that Greene County was the site of a large university hospital that provided relatively inexpensive care to low-income mothers. Mothers with limited resources, little or no prenatal care, and high-risk pregnancies come from several surrounding counties to deliver at the university hospital. In the first time period, when the perinatal mortality rate was high, all deaths in the university hospital may have been ascribed to Greene County. With the attention given to perinatal mortality in the county, a much more accurate count of deaths may have been taken that would have the effect of lowering the rate because fewer high-risk births from other counties would be included.

This, of course, is only one possibility. A careful review of how perinatal mortality was determined in the first time period could rule this possibility out, but it is not always possible to be certain how data have been counted, after the fact. Time series analysis itself, however, would be of little value in detecting this particular source of error.

In summary, trend analysis can be an effective tool separating either regression effects or cohort or structural change effects from the effect of a program designed to influence some problem. Trend analysis is not an effective tool for eliminating the possibility that reactiveness or measurement error may have been responsible for the changes that may be observed either before and after, or over an extended period of time.

Appropriate Data for Trend Analysis

The single most important characteristic of data appropriate for trend analysis is that they be collected or maintained over a period of time. Frequently, data on which trend analysis or time series analysis is based must be collected or maintained for substantially long periods of time. Such information as population change, change in average income, mortality rates by selected causes, and agricultural productivity has been maintained in the United States for many years. Information like infant mortality rates may be available for a selected community for a long period of time. Availability of this information makes it a possible candidate for output measure status in determining the effect of a type of program or the effect of increasing or decreasing resources to a particular type of program.

The clear requirement that trend analysis or time series analysis be based on data collected and maintained over extended periods of time serves to require that data used in time series or trend analysis is collected on a routine basis. When a particular program is implemented, ensuring that various pieces of information about inputs and process are maintained routinely for the program may be relatively easy. Monthly data on budget allocations, amount of space, number of people available to provide services under the program, specific quantities of services provided, or other program-specific information can be maintained routinely within a monitoring format, as reviewed in Chapter 4.

Much information that may be of interest to the evaluators of the program may not be available on a continuing basis, however. This makes necessary the consideration of an evaluation of program effectiveness or impact—concerns associated with the outputs of the program itself—only on the basis of data routinely maintained and collected by existing government or quasi-government agencies. This requirement usually excludes from consideration within the time-series framework of possible program results or expected results such entities as:

- improvements in general perceptions of lifestyle;
- improvements in knowledge to carry out particular program tasks; or
- declines or changes in morbidity status, to the extent that such morbidity data may not be routinely collected.

Instead, the evaluation or assessment of a program in the time series-trend analysis framework will much more likely depend on such output measures as changes in:

- mortality rates;
- number of households with water-sealed latrines;
- number of immunizations given;
- number of houses sprayed for malaria;
- number of hospital beds available; or
- other data of an easily collected and quantifiable type.

To provide concreteness to the notion of data for trend analysis, consider again the CCOP and early detection in primary care discussed in this same context in previous chapters.

Illustration: Community Clinical Oncology Program (CCOP)

One major objective of the evaluation is to monitor over time any change in physician practice patterns with respect to their treatment of breast cancer and colon and rectum cancer. The evaluation design requires a three-year data collection strategy based on determining whether there are any meaningful changes in the patterns of treatment of cancer patients (Kaluzny, Warnecke, and Associates 1996).

The changes are measured in terms of the proportion of patients treated according to protocol standards. This requires that patients be clustered by date of initial diagnosis and proportions drawn. To compare proportions between samples and determine if there is a change from one proportion to another, certain numerical requirements must be met. Because the impacts of the project on treatment patterns are to be measured over a three-year period, the comparison periods should be as far apart as possible. However, they should cover a time period that is sufficient enough to produce cancer cases, ensuring that any differences in the proportions observed are not due to chance.

To meet these requirements, three annual aggregations of patients are proposed for the fundamental analysis of proportional differences. Proportional change will be tested for significance for year 3 minus year 1, year 3 minus year 2, and year 2 minus year 1. The addition of year 2 permits the determination of whether there is a steady pattern of change. Figure 9.3 presents the potential patterns in the trend analysis.

The use of trend analysis can also be seen in the following assessment of preventive services within the context of primary care.

Illustration: Early Detection in Primary Care

The evaluation was designed to assess whether the implementation of an intensive "office system for preventive care" would increase the proportion of eligible patients receiving early detection activities in 68 randomly chosen primary care practices in North Carolina. The preventive care activities were composed of academic detailing, meeting with physicians and staff, consultation about office systems, and educational modules about proper technique of early detection activities. Cancer screening included mammography, clinical breast exam, smoking cessation counseling, Pap tests, sigmoidoscopy, and skin exam.

Chart audits were used as the primary measure of practice performance. Medical records were assessed for whether the six cancer detection activities were (1) recommended; (2) completed; and (3) recorded for the 12 months prior to the index visit (for the Pap test, 36 months; for the sigmoidoscopy test, 60 months). The criteria for selection of patients for chart audit were:

- age 50 years or above;
- no known terminal illness, such as metastatic cancer or end stage organ disease;
- no known dementia; and
- had visit on an index day with a practice primary care physician whom he or she saw for the first time more than 12 months ago, and whom he or she has seen at least one other time in the previous 12 months.

Twenty index days were randomly chosen from office days in the three months before the intervention began, and in months 9–12 of the intervention. Three patients fulfilling the criteria were chosen at random from among those listed in the practice log as having been seen that day. Random selection continued until at least two patients selected on each day were women. The proportion of eligible patients who had a screening procedure within the given time period was used to estimate the practice performance level. The proportion of patients

Year 3–Year 1	Year 3–Year 2	Year 2–Year 1	Characterization
Significant positive	Not significant	Not significant	Steady, low rate
Significant positive	Significant positive	Not significant	Late
Significant positive	Not significant	Significant positive	Early
Significant positive	Significant positive	Significant positive	Steady, high rate

FIGURE 9.3
Potential Practice Patterns Over Time

who also had the test result recorded in the chart was used as an indicator of quality of screening tests.

For example, in assessing mammography and clinical breast exam (CBE), information collected from the medical record included patient age, race, insurance status, number of visits to the practice, physician of record, receipt of mammography and CBE. Records were reviewed for a three-year time period (1989–1991 at base line and 1992–1994 at follow-up) (Kinsinger et al. 1998). Because the evaluation had a specific intervention that was evaluated between baseline and follow-up data, comparing practice patterns at the various points in time and assessing the effects of the intervention were both possible.

Application to Decision Making and Types of Evaluation

As previously stated, the appropriate realm of evaluation is the realm of cybernetic decision making, the use of feedback of information about the state of a system to make decisions that can improve the state of the system in the future. In many situations, decision makers likely will want information on which to base decisions on a short-term basis. For example, managers of small rural hospitals probably would like to have known the importance of service differential, taken appropriate action within a changing environment at the earliest possible time, and planned an appropriate strategy to reduce the risk of closure.

As previously discussed, however, determining with any degree of certainty whether short-term changes are a result of the intervention or simply the result of random variation or regression to the long-term trend may not be possible. It is often necessary to wait several time periods (e.g., weeks, months, or years) to be confident that observed changes following a program change are actually part of a new trend that may be ascribed to the program.

In many health areas (e.g., primary healthcare), the effect of changes may be detected only over a long period of time. Program managers may wish to know soon after the implementation of a new primary healthcare program whether it has been effective in increasing the use of early detection services for eligible patients. The effect of a new program in primary healthcare probably will not have an obvious, immediate effect but will only appear in a cumulative manner over a period of time.

The consequence of this is that trend analysis does not lend itself well to rapid day-to-day decision making. Nevertheless, it remains within the evaluation-based decision-making mode to the extent that system outputs are quantified and measurable, and information about these system outputs are used to make decisions about the nature of program inputs for the future.

Trend analysis provides important information for decision makers that corresponds to various types of evaluations. In terms of relevance, trend analysis gives important background information about the situation for which the program was designed to have an effect. Because trend analysis is usually based on an existing data system, it makes available a continuous source for defining the very nature of the problem.

More importantly, trend analysis gives information about program progress and adequacy. Because data are available over a period of time, it is possible to assess the changes outside the normal expected range variation. This point is particularly critical to decision makers, for it offers an opportunity to initiate corrective action during the life of the program.

Finally, trend analysis, like experimental design (see Chapters 11 and 12), gives managers the opportunity to assess effectiveness, impact, and sustainability of a program. Because data are collected over time, observing changes before and after the implementation of the program is possible, as well as hypothesizing other explanations for the change and thereby clearly deciding whether a specific program has had the desired effect.

Discussion Questions

1. Distinguish between monitoring and trend analysis. What are the similarities and differences between these two evaluation strategies?
2. Why is trend analysis so difficult to conduct and yet so important to health service programs?
3. Why is trend analysis appropriate to both summative-type and formative-type evaluations?

TREND ANALYSIS TECHNIQUES AND INTERPRETATION

In general, the approach to analyzing trend data for evaluation purposes is to examine the trends or series over time. At the simplest level it may be done graphically, making inferences about the effectiveness or impact of the program on this basis alone. At a somewhat more complex level, however, data from trends can be examined in two primary ways: bivariate and multivariate regression. *Bivariate regression* involves time as the independent variable, and *multivariate regression* involves time plus a number of possible causes of change in program activity measures as independent variables. The objective of this chapter is to examine these methodologies and illustrate their use in a health services setting.

Simple Graphic Approach

Figure 10.1 shows a trend line for an output measure of a health services program under three alternative program conditions. The output measure, undesignated in this case and strictly hypothetical, is measured on the left of the scale from 8 to 20. What must be realized is that the output measure being examined over time must be quantifiable in terms of either an interval or ratio scale (scales of measurement are discussed in Chapter 14).

The trend data available for analysis (Figure 10.1) represent 15 years of the output measure in question. In year 10, as the figure indicates, a program was initiated and remained in operation for a five-year period. The fifth year of the program is the year when an assessment on the output measure in question is being made.

Figure 10.1a shows that the program has had an effect on the output measure. The ten-year trend of the program output measure has been steadily upward from the beginning of the recording period to the time when the program was initiated (year 10). From year 10 to year 11, the program output measure continued at the same level as year 10, but in year 11 and subsequent years the trend line of the program output measure is a decreasing line. A reasonable conclusion to be drawn from this type of chart is that the program has been effective in reducing the program output measure.

The fact that the output measure has begun a fairly clear decline at the onset of the program can be taken as evidence of the effect of the program. It should be understood, however, that other activities may have been occurring at the same time as the program, which could alternatively account for the decline. Unfortunately, this simple graphic approach does not provide any information to

FIGURE 10.1

Effect of Program
on an Output
Measure, Three
Alternatives:
(a) Program Causes
Change,
(b) Program Does
Not Cause Change,
(c) No Change Has
Occurred

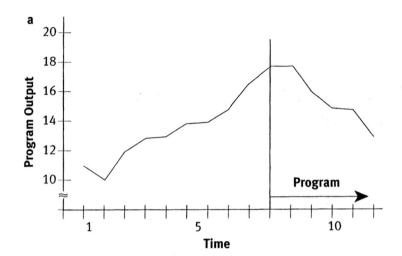

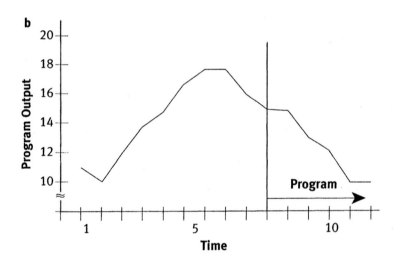

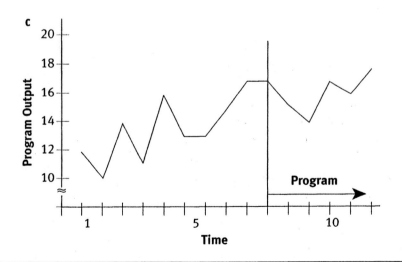

conclude that some other factors occurring simultaneously with the program may have produced the change in program output measures—but only that their decline occurred simultaneously with or were associated with the introduction of the program. Multivariate regression analysis of trend data can, to a certain extent, rule out these other possible causes. This strategy is discussed further in the next section.

Figure 10.1a shows that the change in output occurred simultaneously with the beginning of the program so that the program itself can be considered a possible cause of the change. The trend line in Figure 10.1b, however, indicates that the program should not be considered a cause of the change that has occurred in the output measures. In Figure 10.1b the trend line is increasing from year 1 through year 8, but at year 8, two years before the initiation of the program itself, the trend line begins its downward slope. The program, introduced at year 10, is probably associated with this downward trend, but the fact that the downward trend started at a point prior to the initiation of the program would clearly rule out the program as the likely cause of the change.

Figure 10.1c is another alternative trend line related to the program output measures and introduction to the program. In Figure 10.1c there is a steep decline in the output measure from year 10 to year 12. Given the general nature of the trend line in Figure 10.1c, however, including the large degree of variation in program output measures from one year to the next, and the fact that the output measure increases from year 12 to year 13 and again from year 14 to year 15, a reasonable conclusion is that the program has no discernible effect on the output measures.

This figure particularly shows the importance of long-term trend data in any type of serious trend analysis effort. If data had been available only for the five years from year 7 to year 12, a logical conclusion is that the steep increases in the output measures over the three years prior to the program were reversed by the program, and the desired decline in the output measure was realized. Only when data are available for a longer period is it clear that no real effect in the output measures has been produced.

The examples in Figure 10.1 are fairly clear because the hypothesized or illustrated effect of the program on the output measures is quite substantial. What is often the case, however, is that the shift in trend line that the evaluator is trying to detect or assess is not nearly as visually apparent as it is in Figures 10.1a and 10.1b. Under those circumstances using regression analysis to examine the possibility that the program in question has had an effect on the output measure of interest is possible.

Figure 10.2 shows two different possible effects of a particular program. The first (Figure 10.2a) is a change in intercept. What this means is that while the program may not have changed the rate at which a particular output measure is actually increasing, the program's introduction at a particular point has served to shift the general trend line of the increase in output measures downward. The trend line thus continues to increase from an essentially lower starting point. This

FIGURE 10.2

Effect of Program on an Output Measure, Regression Discontinuity: (a) Change in Intercept, (b) Change in Slope

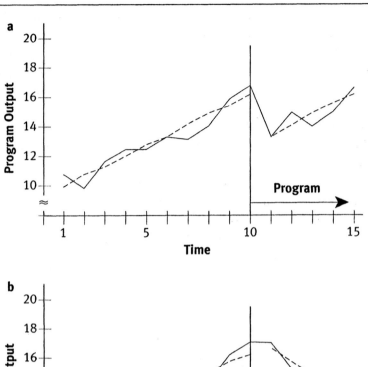

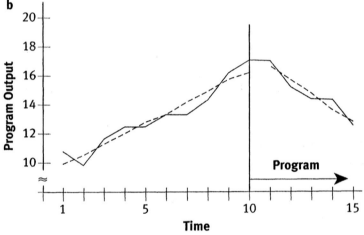

notion is shown in Figure 10.2a, in which a discontinuity exists at year 10, when the program was introduced, in the broken line that represents the long-term trend of the output measure.

Another possible way that a program may affect the general trend line and some output measure is through a change in the slope of the long-term trend line. Figure 10.2b shows this possibility. The long-term trend line for program output prior to program introduction is basically an increasing one, whereas after program introduction (year 10), the slope of the trend line is downward. Regression analysis can test whether this change in slope is one that could have been considered to occur by chance or one that is of too great a magnitude for this assumption to be made. If the downward shift in the slope was great enough to be assumed not to have occurred by chance, it would represent an effect of the program that could be revealed by regression analysis.

In regard to Figure 10.2b, the change in the trend line is qualitatively different from the change in the trend line in Figure 10.2a. In the case of

Figure 10.2b, however, clearly the trend line was increasing before introduction of the program and decreased after its introduction. In most real-life settings the effect of a program will probably not be as marked as it is in Figures 10.2a or 10.2b. The program, if it is effective at all, likely will be successful only in shifting long-term trend lines rather than completely reversing their direction. In circumstances where visual examination of the data does not reveal a shift as obvious as those in Figure 10.2, regression analysis can be extremely useful in determining whether slight modifications can be seen as real effects of the program or only as chance occurrences. The actual techniques involved in the application of regression analysis will be described later in the chapter.

Multivariate Applications of Trend Analysis

Thus far, this discussion of trend analysis as an evaluation technique has dealt only with the examination of the output measure itself and the assessment of whether that measure has shown a change with the introduction of the program. Now a somewhat more sophisticated analysis of trend data is presented, including an examination of input factors other than the program itself, as these may change over time, and an examination of changes in the actual level of program inputs.

Output measures selected to assess the impact of a program may be influenced by factors other than introduction of the program itself. Consider child mortality as an example of an output indicator to represent the effect of a primary healthcare program in a developing nation. The World Health Organization (WHO) indicates that the child mortality rate (the number of deaths per 1,000 children between ages one and four) is a valid indicator of child health for a nation and reflects the level of nutrition, sanitation, control of communicable diseases, and accidents.

A reasonable assumption is that the child mortality rate in any society will be influenced over time by a number of variables. Let us assume that only the gross national product (GNP) and average caloric intake for persons in a country are under consideration—perhaps because they are the only two variables measured. The important point here, however, is the general analytical principles rather than specific variables. The assumption may be that the child mortality rate will be influenced in a substantial way by both the financial resources available to persons in the country and their nutritional status. As a measure of financial status, it may be acceptable to use the country's GNP as measured over time, and to use the number of calories consumed per person per day as a measure of nutritional status. In explaining the method, only these two variables are considered as independent or causal variables in relationship to changes in child mortality over time.

A second set of factors making it desirable to carry out a sophisticated analysis using trend data concerns information about the program itself. In examining the trend data relative to time in the preceding discussion, only the point when the program was initiated and subsequent time periods were considered. It is possible that all program activities will not be put in place or begin operating at the immediate point when the program is initiated. For example, the funds going to a primary healthcare program may begin at a relatively low level at the onset of the program and increase over a period of time. Certainly, the number of personnel trained or in place to provide services is likely to increase over time as a function of program development.

Figure 10.3 is a composite of a number of different trend data measures. The child mortality rate is the heavy solid line in the figure; child mortality declines from 16 per 1,000 to approximately 10 per 1,000 in 15 years. Over the 15 years for which the rest of the data are recorded, GNP for the country in question increases from $10 billion to $14 billion. Daily caloric intake per capita increases from 1,800 to 2,000 calories. All represent hypothetical trend data for the entire 15-year period.

The vertical line at year 10 represents the initiation of a primary healthcare program. The dotted line beginning in year 10 shows the funding for the primary healthcare program in thousands of dollars from its onset in year 10 through year 15. As the line shows, a sharp increase in the amount of money occurs over this time period. The thin solid line beginning in year 10 shows the number of primary healthcare workers actually in place in the country over the five years of the program. Again, a sharp increase from a low of 50 primary workers to 500 over the five-year period occurs.

Visual examination of the data in Figure 10.3 may suggest several possible conclusions. First, the upward trend lines in GNP and calories consumed are generally matched by a downward trend line in child mortality. If GNP and caloric

FIGURE 10.3

Trends in Child Mortality, Caloric Intake, Gross National Product, Money to Primary Care, and Primary Care Workers in Place

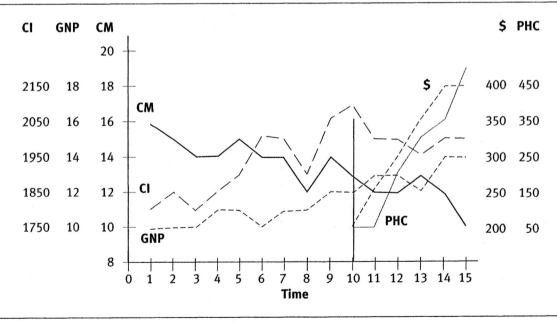

CI	GNP	CM		$	PHC
		20			
2150	18	18		400	450
2050	16	16		350	350
1950	14	14		300	250
1850	12	12		250	150
1750	10	10		200	50
		8			

Time

CI	Caloric intake	$	Money to primary care
GNP	Gross national product	PHC	Primary healthcare workers in place
CM	Child mortality		

intake can be thought of as causally related to child mortality, a portion of the decline in child mortality is a function of the increases in the measure of financial status and nutrition. The primary healthcare program is being introduced in a situation of declining child mortality as a function of improving living conditions within the country. The result is that any effect of the program itself is likely to be more difficult to detect than if conditions in the country had remained static.

The introduction or onset of the program in year 10 is not clearly or immediately associated with a greater or more obvious decline in child mortality. As shown in Figure 10.3, however, the substantial gains in program funding and workers in years 14 and 15 are associated with a fairly steep decline in child mortality for those two years. This situation may be evidence that the program itself has begun to have an effect on child mortality rates.

Nonlinear Trend Lines

The examples of trend line data discussed so far are all trends that are primarily linear. Trend line data does not always follow a linear pattern. The trend line in Figure 10.4 can be considered an example of a nonlinear trend. Through year 10 the data appear to follow a more or less linear pattern of very slight increase. In year 10 the pattern seems to change to a much sharper rate of increase and by years 14 and 15 the trend appears to be growing at an increasing rate. Such trends may be difficult to analyze visually unless program effects are of a high order of magnitude. If the nonlinear aspect of the trend is not too great, analysis can adhere to the basic linear assumptions of regression.

If the nonlinear trend is substantial, however, analysis should not proceed directly with regression techniques because the regression approach automatically assumes that the relationships under examination are linear. In Figure 10.4 the relationship between time and the level of program output or the measure being considered is not linear. Rescaling such data is possible, however, to make it

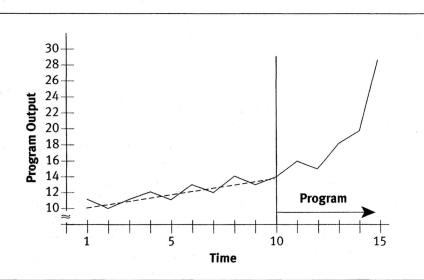

FIGURE 10.4
Effect of Program on an Output Measure, Nonlinear Increase

compatible with the regression requirement for linearity in the relationships under examination. *Rescaling* refers to the use of a non-interval scale to measure a variable that is not linearly related to another variable of interest. For example, in the relationship shown in Figure 10.4, Program Output increases at an increasing rate (not a constant rate) after the program is implemented. Using a non-interval scale, such as the square root of program output or the logarithm of program output, will tend to put the increase in program output back into a linear relationship with time. A general discussion is beyond the scope of this particular section, but extensive discussions of rescaling appear in most econometrics books—for example, Gujarati (1988).

A common rescaling technique, as indicated above, is to convert the dimension on which a particular trend is changing most rapidly to its logarithmic value. If a trend like the one in Figure 10.4 is developing, the transformation of the program output to its log will substantially flatten the trend line and make it more adherent to the basic linear assumptions of the regression model. An alternative strategy is to model the curvilinear nature of the output measure using a square term in regression. This and other regression modeling techniques for time series data are discussed in the rest of this chapter.

The Application of Regression to Time Series

Regression analysis was introduced in Chapter 8. In this section, the application of regression analysis is examined to determine whether a program intervention can be seen as having a statistically significant relationship to observed program changes over time. To do this, the concentration primarily is on the constructed data shown in Figures 10.2a and 10.2b. Figure 10.2a was described as showing a change in intercept of the program output as a consequence of the program (i.e., the program had a one-time effect of lowering the overall level of program output). Figure 10.2b was described as showing a change in slope in the program output (i.e., the program actually reversed the direction of the program output). How can this be analyzed using regression?

To address that question, we will proceed first to look at a simple regression analysis for the data in both Figures 10.2a and 10.2b with time as the independent variable and the level of program output as the dependent variable. Then we will look at the level of program output as the dependent variable with time and a variable representing the implementation of the program as independent variables, and finally we will look at time, the program implementation variable, and an interaction between the two as independent variables.

The data to be examined in this section is shown in Table 10.1. The first column is the independent variable, time. The second column represents a rescaling of time so that the starting year of the program is coded as time 1, with time being measured backward and forward from the program start. The third column is a variable that is coded 0 prior to program initiation and 1 after program initiation. This is known as a *dummy variable* and is commonly employed in time

1	2	3	4	5	6
Time	Time Rescaled	Program	Time/ Program	Figure 10.2a	Figure 10.2b
1	−9	0	0	11	11
2	−8	0	0	10	10
3	−7	0	0	12	12
4	−6	0	0	13	13
5	−5	0	0	13	13
6	−4	0	0	14	14
7	−3	0	0	14	14
8	−2	0	0	15	15
9	−1	0	0	17	17
10	0	0	0	18	18
11	1	1	1	14	18
12	2	1	2	16	16
13	3	1	3	15	15
14	4	1	4	16	15
15	5	1	5	18	13

TABLE 10.1
Constructed Data for Figure 10.2

series analysis. Column 4 is an "interaction" between time and the program variable. It is constructed by multiplying column 3 and 4. Columns 5 and 6 represent the program output for Figures 10.2a and 10.2b, respectively.

To begin the analysis of the program output in Table 10.1, first consider time alone as an independent variable to determine if there is a trend over time that is detectable whether the program is considered or not. In this analysis program output is the dependent variable and time is the independent variable. The equation to be estimated using regression is:

$$Y_t = b_1 X_t + b_0 + e_t \qquad (10.1)$$

where Y_t is the program output measure at time t, X_t is time at time t, b_1 is the regression coefficient on time, b_0 is the constant term, and e_t is the error at time t. Looking first at the data from Figure 10.2a, the results are:

$$b_1 = .450 \ (.079)$$
$$b_0 = 15.300 \ (.378) \qquad (10.2)$$
$$t(b_1) = 5.70$$

The standard error of each coefficient is shown in parentheses. Because the coefficient of time (b_1) divided by its standard error (a normal t-test) is greater than 2, the general conclusion is that a statistically significant increase exists in program output over the 15-year period. This regression has an R^2 of .69, which means that time accounts for 69 percent of the variance in the program output measure.

Examining the data for program output shown in Figure 10.2b, the results are:

$$b_1 = .346 \ (.112)$$
$$b_0 = 14.960 \ (.531) \tag{10.3}$$
$$t(b_1) = 3.09$$

Again the standard error is shown in parentheses and, again, the coefficient of time divided by its standard error (the t-test) produces a value larger than 2, indicating that the coefficient for time is statistically significant. The R^2 for these data is .38, indicating that only 38 percent of the variance is accounted for by time in this case.

FIGURE 10.5

Actual and Predicted Lines for Figures 10.2a and 10.2b with Time as the Single Independent Variable

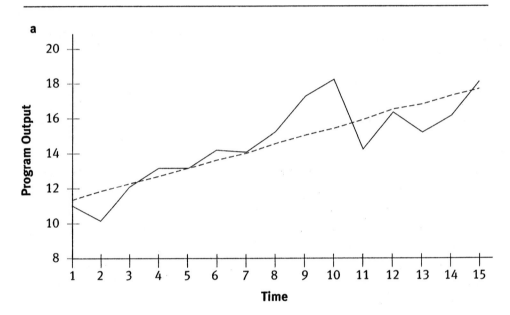

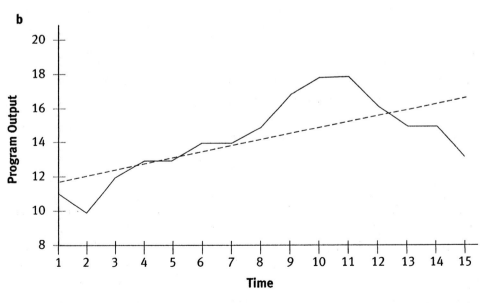

The results of these two analyses, including the predicted lines for each, are shown in Figures 10.5a and 10.5b. The analysis thus far, in looking only at time as an independent variable, can say nothing about the effect of the program intervention that began in time 10. Each figure, however, indicates that there has been a general upward trend in both Figure 10.5a and Figure 10.5b, as indicated by the two regression coefficients for b_1 in Equation 10.2 and Equation 10.3.

When examining time series data such as this using regression, however, one particular assumption of significance testing in regression must be considered: the error terms e_t are uncorrelated over time. If the error terms are correlated, the standard error of the coefficients will be underestimated and statistical significance may be detected where it does not exist. While a number of different types of serial autocorrelation may exist (e.g., error terms for monthly data is likely to be correlated with error terms for data from the same month in preceding years), the most common type of serial autocorrelation is the correlation of each successive error with the one immediately preceding it.

An example of what this means is shown in Figure 10.6. The values of the error from Equation 10.3 are:

1. negative for the first three time periods;
2. positive for one time period;
3. negative for the next time period;
4. positive for seven time periods; and
5. negative for the last three time periods.

This tendency for error values to be negative or positive in fairly long strings is evidence of autocorrelation in the errors.

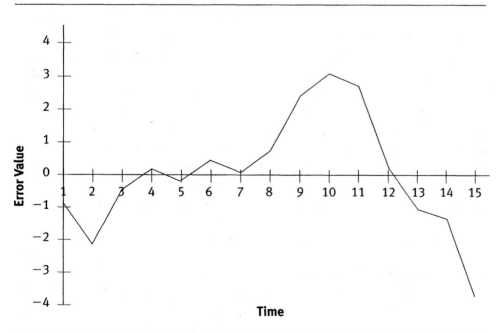

FIGURE 10.6

Distribution of Errors (Actual Values Minus Predicted Values) for Data from Figure 10.2b Analyzed with the Model in Equation 10.3

Even though the coefficient estimates found using ordinary least squares (OLS) on autocorrelated data are unbiased, they tend to be inefficient because they are likely to have large variances—while appearing to have small variances—so that tests of significance applied to the coefficients will generally overestimate the extent of the effect. In regard to Equation 10.3, the indicated increase in program output of .346 per time period possibly may not be a statistically significant increase at all, relative to its standard deviation. This would indicate that the apparent increase in program output is not actually occurring over time but rather only appears to be as a result of correlated errors. A test to determine whether the data are subject to autocorrelated error is known as the Durbin-Watson test. This test is discussed in the following section.

Autocorrelation in Time Series

The Durbin-Watson statistic provides a test for serial autocorrelation in the error terms shown in Equation 10.1. The Durbin-Watson test is calculated as

$$d = \frac{\sum_{t=2}^{T}(e_t - e_{t-1})^2}{\sum_{t=1}^{T}e_t^2} \tag{10.4}$$

where e_t is the error term at time t from Equation 10.1 (i.e., the difference between the actual and predicted values of program output) and e_{t-1} is the value of the error at time $t-1$. The Durbin-Watson d statistics calculated for the coefficients in Equation 10.2 and Equation 10.3 are 1.55 and .49, respectively. In general and for large samples, values of d near or exceeding 2 are evidence of no serial autocorrelation in the errors. Most econometric texts will include a table of critical values of d. For example, for 15 observations, Gujarati (1988) gives the value of d below which there will be a suspected autocorrelation at the .05 level of significance as 1.36, and the value below which there will be certain autocorrelation as 1.08. Given these limits, the data in Figure 10.2a appears to not show autocorrelation serious enough to warrant concern about the t-test of significance of the coefficient on time. The data in Figure 10.2b do show autocorrelation serious enough to invalidate the significance test of the coefficient on time for those data. Consequently, the conclusion that a statistically significant increase over time exists in the program output in Figure 10.2b would have to be subjected to further analysis before it could be maintained. This further analysis would normally involve one of two strategies: adjustment for the autocorrelation; or respecification of the model to eliminate the autocorrelation. The following section addresses adjustment for autocorrelation.

Adjustment for Autocorrelation

One way to deal with serial autocorrelation in the error terms is to attempt to remove the autocorrelation by adjusting the values of the dependent variable for that correlation. The adjustment most frequently used is

$$X_t^* = X_t - \rho X_{t-1}$$
$$Y_t^* = Y_t - \rho Y_{t-1} \tag{10.5}$$

where X_t^* is the adjusted value for X_t, Y_t^* is the adjusted value for Y_t, and ρ is the coefficient of autocorrelation. If more than one independent variable (X_t) exists, each is adjusted in the same manner as shown in Equation 10.5. An examination of Equation 10.5 reveals that the adjustment works for every value of the independent (X_t) and dependent (Y_t) variables, except the first in the series (X_1 and Y_1). These are adjusted using Equation 10.6:

$$X_1^* = \sqrt{1 - \rho^2}\, X_1$$
$$Y_1^* = \sqrt{1 - \rho^2}\, Y_1 \tag{10.6}$$

Finally, the value of the constant, which will produce the equivalent of b_0 in the adjusted computation, is calculated as shown in Equation 10.7:

$$X_{0,1}^* = \sqrt{1 - \rho^2}$$
$$X_{0,t}^* = 1 - \rho \tag{10.7}$$

where $X_{0,1}^*$ is the adjusted value of the constant for the first observation, and $X_{0,t}^*$ is the adjusted value of the constant for all other observations.

These adjustments for the values of X_t and Y_t can be made quite easily once the value of ρ is known. However, as is true in most statistical analyses, the true value of ρ is never known, but can only be estimated. An estimate of ρ can be found a number of ways, but the estimate most effective for data from most time series is the Theil-Nagar d (henceforth called d' to distinguish it from the Durbin-Watson d), which produces an estimate of ρ appropriate for small samples (Gujurati 1988, 382). The value of using a small sample estimate represented by d' is that in most cases time-series data available to decision makers will be small samples, often representing data for fewer than 20, commonly no more than 10 or 12 time periods. The d' estimate of ρ is found using the value of the Durbin-Watson d as shown in Equation 10.8:

$$d' = \frac{n^2(1 - d/2) + (k + 1)^2}{n^2 - (k + 1)^2} \tag{10.8}$$

where n is the number of observations and k is the number of independent variables not including the constant term.

Table 10.2 shows the calculations involved in adjusting the data from Figure 10.2b for autocorrelation. Columns 1 and 2 show the original independent variables, time and the data from Figure 10.2b, respectively. Column 3 represents the predicted values for the data in column 2 based on the regression coefficients in Equation 10.3. Column 4 is the set of error terms, e_t, for each time period. It is on the basis of this column of error terms that the Durbin-Watson d of .49 was calculated, using Equation 10.4. The Theil-Nagar d' as an estimate of ρ was then calculated from d using Equation 10.8 as .786. Column 5 represents

TABLE 10.2

Data from Figure 10.2b Adjusted for Autocorrelation

1	2	3	4	5	6	7
Time	Data from Figure 10.2a	Predicted Data from Figure 10.2b	Error (Col 2– Col 3)	Adjusted Constant	Adjusted Time	Adjusted Data from Figure 10.2b
−9	11	11.84	−0.84	0.62	−5.57	6.80
−8	10	12.19	−2.19	0.21	−0.93	1.36
−7	12	12.53	−0.53	0.21	−0.71	4.14
−6	13	12.88	0.12	0.21	−0.50	3.57
−5	13	13.23	−0.23	0.21	−0.28	2.78
−4	14	13.57	0.43	0.21	−0.07	3.78
−3	14	13.92	0.08	0.21	0.14	3.00
−2	15	14.27	0.73	0.21	0.36	4.00
−1	17	14.61	2.39	0.21	0.57	5.21
0	18	14.96	3.04	0.21	0.79	4.64
1	18	15.31	2.69	0.21	1.00	3.85
2	16	15.65	0.35	0.21	1.21	1.85
3	15	16.00	−1.00	0.21	1.43	2.43
4	15	16.35	−1.35	0.21	1.64	3.21
5	13	16.69	−3.69	0.21	1.86	1.21

the adjusted constant term calculated from Equation 10.7. As shown, the constant term is actually no longer a constant when adjustment for autocorrelation is performed. Columns 6 and 7 represent the time variable and the data from figure 10.2b adjusted for autocorrelation using Equations 10.5 for all values after time 1 and 10.6 for time 1.

With the adjusted data in table 10.2, OLS regression can now be used to estimate the effect of time on the program output with autocorrelation in the errors removed. In general, most regression analysis packages do not require the independent specification of the constant term when regression is carried out. The computer program that does the analysis, whatever it may be, will independently supply the constant term, which is always 1. In doing regression with adjusted data, the constant term is treated in the analysis as is any other variable (i.e., it must be specified as one of the variables). Further, it is necessary to specify in the regression analysis that the normally supplied constant should be considered as zero. If this is not done, the results of the analysis will be incorrect.

Using the adjusted data in Table 10.2, the regression coefficients for time (b_1) and for the constant (b_0) are as shown in Equation 10.9.

$$b_1 = .208 \ (.199)$$
$$b_0 = 13.937 \ (1.307) \qquad\qquad (10.9)$$
$$t(b_1) = 1.05$$

Using the data adjusted for autocorrelation, the t-test for the statistical significance of the coefficient on time is no longer large enough—it would have to be about 2—to consider the coefficient b_1 to be different from zero. Hence, when autocorrelation is adjusted, no statistically discernible effect of time on the program level is shown in Figure 10.2b, if time is the only independent variable considered. Interestingly, the Durbin-Watson d for the residuals from the adjusted data is 1.12, which, for a sample of 15 data points and one independent variable, would be large enough to be evidence of no autocorrelation in the errors for the analysis using the adjusted data.

Model Specification to Remove Autocorrelated Error

One interpretation of the presence of autocorrelated error is that an important variable has been left out of the regression analysis. Hence, a second way—and perhaps the best way—of dealing with autocorrelated error is to try to respecify the model so as to remove the autocorrelation in the error in the first analysis. In regard to the data from Figure 10.2b, it is not difficult to imagine that the model is misspecified.

Regression is a tool for examining linear relationships between independent and dependent variables, and the general relationship shown in Figure 10.2b is a curvilinear one in which program output first increases and then declines over the 15 time periods. While the relationship of time to the data in Figure 10.2a did not show autocorrelated errors over time, a reasonable argument is that the real relationship of program output to time in that figure is also probably not a simple linear relationship. The sharp drop in the program output score between time 10 and 11 suggests that something other than a simple linear relationship is at work. One way to examine this is to try alternative specifications of the models to better characterize what is happening over time in regard to program output.

To proceed with this strategy, first review the data in Figure 10.2a. Even though it did not show evidence of serial autocorrelation among the errors, time alone is probably not an adequate explanatory variable due to the dip in program output from time 10 to time 11. One way to model the dip in program output is to include in the analysis a second independent variable (a dummy variable) that is coded 0 prior to the initiation of the program intervention and is coded 1 afterward. The independent variable data for this analysis are shown in Table 10.1 as columns 2 and 3. The dependent variable is represented by the data in column 5. Using time and the program dummy as independent variables, the results are as given in Equation 10.10:

$$b_1 = .795\ (.077)$$
$$b_2 = -3.859\ (.701)$$
$$b_0 = 17.276\ (.416) \qquad\qquad (10.10)$$
$$t(b_1) = 10.38$$
$$t(b_2) = -5.50$$

where b_1 is the coefficient for time, b_2 is the program dummy coefficient, and $t(b_1)$ and $t(b_2)$ are the t-tests for b_1 and b_2, respectively.

The results in Equation 10.10 indicate that the program output in Figure 10.2a can be predicted by both time and the program dummy, and that both coefficients are statistically significant. Because there was no autocorrelation of errors in the analysis of these data with time alone as an independent variable, there is no expectation that such autocorrelation should exist with the addition of the dummy variable. However, when the Durbin-Watson d statistic is calculated for this analysis, it is 2.25, which is large enough to show no autocorrelation in the error terms; hence, there is no need to be concerned that the t-tests overstate true statistical significance.

The effect of including a dummy variable for the program intervention in the prediction of program output is shown in Figure 10.2a, where the dotted line is actually constructed by the predicted values of program output. The program output measure is increasing both before and after the program intervention and predicted to be increasing at the same rate both before and after. The program intervention, however, was associated with, and thus reasonably assumed to have caused, a one-time decline in the program output of 3.859 units (the coefficient b_2).

A similar use of model respecification can be applied to the data in Figure 10.2b, except that in this case, a dummy variable representing the initiation of the program alone will be insufficient to adequately describe what is going on in Figure 10.2b. The dummy variable alone can detect the presence of a one-time change in the level of the overall process, with the process proceeding after the intervention in the same manner as it proceeded prior to the intervention. This is a fairly adequate description of what is happening in Figure 10.2a. Clearly, the process in Figure 10.2b actually changes direction, from an increase to a decrease, after the program intervention. To adequately model this type of process, a dummy variable representing the program intervention must be included, as well as an interaction between the program intervention and time.

The construction of the interaction term is shown in Table 10.1, column 4. The interaction term is the multiplication of time (column 2) by the program variable (column 3). The interaction term is constant at zero before the program intervention and then increases as time increases after the intervention. Following is an examination of the effect of this modeling strategy on the prediction of the data in column 6 of Table 10.1.

The data analysis now actually includes three independent variables: time, the program dummy, and the time/program interaction. The result predicting the data from Figure 10.2b is shown in Equation 10.11:

$$b_1 = .794 \ (.076)$$
$$b_2 = 1.427 \ (.826)$$
$$b_3 = -1.894 \ (.701)$$
$$b_0 = 17.273 \ (.404)$$
$$t(b_1) = 10.49$$
$$t(b_2) = 1.72$$
$$t(b_3) = -8.23$$

(10.11)

where all terms are as given in Equation 10.10 and b_3 is the coefficient for the time/program interaction.

To adequately interpret the results shown in Equation 10.11, it is necessary to do a little simple algebra. The regression equation being estimated in Equation 10.11 is shown in Equation 10.12:

$$Y_t = b_1 X_{1t} + b_2 X_{2t} + b_{3t} X_{1t} X_{2t} + b_0 + e_t \qquad (10.12)$$

where Y_t is the program output measure at time t, X_{1t} is time at time t, X_{2t} is the program intervention at time t, X_{3t} is the time/program interaction at time t, and all other terms are as defined previously. With this in mind, it is possible to indicate what happens before and after the program intervention as:

$$
\begin{aligned}
(Y_t \mid X_{2t} = 0) &= b_1 X_{1t} + 0 b_2 + 0 b_{3t} + b_0 \\
(Y_t \mid X_{2t} = 0) &= b_1 X_{1t} + b_0 \\
(Y_t \mid X_{2t} = 1) &= b_1 X_{1t} + 1 b_2 + 1 b_3 X_{1t} + b_0 \\
(Y_t \mid X_{2t} = 1) &= (b_1 + b_3) X_{1t} + b_2 + b_0
\end{aligned}
\qquad (10.13)
$$

What should be apparent from 10.13 is that the coefficient b_3 is an assessment of the degree of change in the relationship of time to program output before and after the program intervention. If b_3 is statistically significant, this indicates that a change of the magnitude of b_3 in the relationship between time and the program output has occurred as a result of the program intervention. In the data shown in Figure 10.2b, the two regression lines (before and after the program intervention) are predicted as:

$$
\begin{aligned}
(Y_t \mid X_{2t} = 0) &= .794 X_{1t} + 17.273 \\
(Y_t \mid X_{2t} = 1) &= -1.100 X_{1t} + 18.700
\end{aligned}
\qquad (10.14)
$$

Prior to the program intervention, the program output was increasing at a rate of .794 units per year. After the program intervention, the program output was decreasing at a rate of 1.100 units per year. Predictably, in respecifying the model for the data in Figure 10.2b, the Durbin-Watson statistic is 2.02, which shows no serial autocorrelation in the errors. The dotted line in Figure 10.2b is actually constructed by the predicted values of program output based on Equation 10.14.

Alternative model specification in time series

The previous section discussed the inclusion of a dummy variable representing the program intervention and an interaction term between time and the program intervention dummy along with time as predictors of program output. This model is particularly useful in assessing the possible effect of a program intervention. But suppose the concern was not simply about a program intervention that was initiated at a particular point in time, but was also about the possible effect of some program input that may have varied over the entire time period for which the program output is measured. For example, suppose that the program input stream was as shown in Figure 10.6 (which also shows the program output as given in Figure 10.2b). The program output stream as shown in Equation 10.15 is characterized as:

$$Y_t = b_1 X_t + b_0 + e_t \qquad (10.15)$$

where X_t is now the value of the program input at each time period. If this model is applied to the data in Figure 10.7 (Table 10.3), the result is:

$$b_1 = .633 \; (.171)$$
$$b_0 = 2.063 \; (3.327) \qquad (10.16)$$
$$t(b_1) = 3.700$$

The result in Equation 10.16 indicates that the coefficient on the program input (b_1) is statistically significant ($t = 3.700$). The Durbin-Watson statistic for this analysis is 1.86, which is evidence of no serial autocorrelation in the error terms, and thus the statistical test is assumed valid. The result is an alternative explanation, other than the program intervention, for the changes seen in program output.

FIGURE 10.7
Program Output
and Program Input
Streams

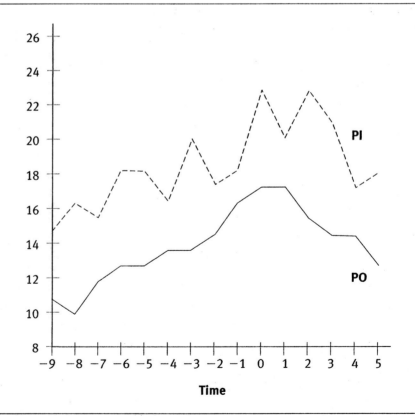

Time

PI   Program Input
PO   Program Output (Figure 11.2b)

1	2	3
Time	Program Input	Figure 10.2b
1	15	11
2	17	10
3	16	12
4	19	13
5	19	13
6	17	14
7	21	14
8	18	15
9	19	17
10	24	18
11	21	18
12	24	16
13	22	15
14	18	15
15	19	13

TABLE 10.3
Constructed Data
for Figure 10.7

Combining information such as a program input variable with information about a program intervention that occurs at a specific point in time is also possible. For example, it is possible to include both the program intervention information of Table 10.1 and the program input data of Table 10.3 in the same regression equation, which may be as shown in Equation 10.17:

$$Y_t = b_1 X_{1t} + b_2 X_{2t} + b_{3t} X_{1t} X_{2t} + b_4 X_{3t} + b_0 + e_t \qquad (10.17)$$

where all the variables are as given in Equation 10.12, except that X_{3t} is the program input variable in column 2 of Table 10.3. This formulation results in the following:

$$
\begin{aligned}
b_1 &= .854\,(.108) \\
b_2 &= 1.638\,(.882) \\
b_3 &= -2.044\,(0.302) \\
b_4 &= -.090\,(.404) \\
b_0 &= 19.213\,(.115) \qquad (10.18) \\
t(b_1) &= 7.91 \\
t(b_2) &= 1.86 \\
t(b_3) &= -6.775 \\
t(b_4) &= -.789
\end{aligned}
$$

As shown in Equation 10.18, the coefficients for time and the time/program intervention remain statistically significant (as they were in 10.12), indicating a change in the program output at the time of the program intervention. The effect of the program input is canceled out, largely because it also is closely associated with the program intervention. While the Durbin-Watson statistic was not calculated for this analysis, it probably would show no serially autocorrelated error because both the formulation in Equation 10.12 and the formulation in 10.15 showed no serial autocorrelation.

There is no particular reason to expect that the effect of some program input necessarily would be canceled out by the inclusion of the program intervention dummy and an interaction term with time. It occurred in this case because the program input measure was highly correlated with the program intervention. In another case, it may be the effect of a program intervention that is canceled out by a program input variable, or both may be simultaneously statistically significant.

Examples of the Application of Time Series Analysis to Actual Data

This chapter concludes with two examples of the application of time series analysis to actual data. The first of these is an application of the analysis of the effect of speed limit changes on highway deaths in the state of North Carolina from 1970 to 1995. The second is an analysis of 15 years' data on neonatal tetanus deaths in Sri Lanka, from 1967 to 1981, a time during which a major program to eradicate neonatal tetanus was initiated.

Highway Deaths in North Carolina

In 1974, the federal government mandated a 55-mph speed limit throughout the United States. This speed limit remained in effect until early 1987, when the government made it possible for the states to raise speed limits to 65 mph on limited access highways. A question of interest in regard to the original reduction in speed limits is whether there was an associated reduction in automobile deaths. A question of interest in regard to the subsequent potential increase in speed limit is whether it was associated with an increase in automobile deaths.

Before going directly to the examination of the effect (if any) of the change in speed limit, however, it would be useful to examine highway deaths in relation to two other variables that would be expected to influence highway deaths strongly, miles traveled and accidents. Table 10.4 shows the data from 1970 to 1995 for accidents, miles traveled in 100 millions of miles, and highway deaths for the state of North Carolina. Our first analysis is of the effect of accidents and miles traveled on highway deaths.

Equation 10.19 is the equation estimated using accidents and miles traveled to predict highway deaths. Because there is also a clear downward trend in highway deaths between 1970 and 1995, the year has also been included as an

Year	Accident	Miles Traveled	Fatalities
1970	124,784	314.18	1,772
1971	132,987	326.15	1,846
1972	127,872	370.65	1,983
1973	125,825	390.10	1,892
1974	121,552	360.23	1,585
1975	128,683	364.11	1,522
1976	138,444	385.64	1,531
1977	145,672	402.79	1,442
1978	155,704	424.37	1,515
1979	153,844	419.83	1,524
1980	145,881	411.41	1,514
1981	143,327	420.51	1,497
1982	144.543	431.37	1,320
1983	145,619	450.00	1,242
1984	147,425	481.06	1,448
1985	150,417	498.99	1,482
1986	162,216	528.94	1,645
1987	172,339	546.08	1,600
1988	173,279	577.09	1,587
1989	182,159	609.13	1,468
1990	165,962	626.24	1,384
1991	161,020	647.39	1,366
1992	172,868	667.72	1,262
1993	184,489	695.48	1,384
1994	199,209	718.09	1,429
1995	214,824	743.81	1,443

TABLE 10.4
Accidents, Miles Traveled (100 Million Miles), and Fatalities, North Carolina, 1970 to 1995

independent variable to pick up those factors other than accidents and miles traveled that are effecting deaths over time. The equation is

$$D_t = b_1 Y_t + b_2 A_t + b_3 M_t + b_0 + e_t \qquad (10.19)$$

where D_t = deaths in year t, Y_t = year t, A_t = accidents in year t, and M_t = miles traveled in year t. The results of this analysis, using ordinary least squares, is as shown in Equation 10.20.

$$
\begin{aligned}
b_1 &= -57.868\ (12.545) \\
b_2 &= .002\ (.003) \\
b_3 &= -2.210\ (.833) \\
b_0 &= 114{,}838.7\ (24{,}499.524) \\
t(b_1) &= -4.613 \\
t(b_2) &= .784 \\
t(b_3) &= 2.653
\end{aligned}
\qquad (10.20)
$$

where the standard errors of the coefficients are given in parentheses. As Equation 10.20 shows, the coefficients of year and of miles traveled are statistically significant at .05, while the coefficient of accidents is not. Examining the possibility of autocorrelated error, however, is necessary before concluding that the t-tests give unbiased results. When the Durbin-Watson statistic is calculated for Equation 10.19, it is .71. According to any standard table of the Durbin-Watson statistic, a value this low is evidence of positive first-order autocorrelation, which means that the standard errors given above are underestimated. The Theil-Nagar value of ρ as an estimate of the autocorrelation in the errors is calculated for these data as .714. Using that value, the data in Table 10.4 can be adjusted for autocorrelation using Equations 10.5 through 10.7. When this is done, the regression results are as shown in Equation 10.21:

$$b_1 = -76.275 \ (19.196)$$
$$b_2 = .001 \ (.003)$$
$$b_3 = -3.496 \ (1.185)$$
$$b_0 = 594.036 \ (367.038) \tag{10.21}$$
$$t(b_1) = -3.973$$
$$t(b_2) = .391$$
$$t(b_3) = 2.951$$

In Equation 10.21, the t values for b_1 (time) and b_3 (miles traveled) remain statistically significant at .05. The t values for b_1 and b_2 have declined as a result of the adjustment for autocorrelation, as is expected. The t value for b_3 has increased as a result of the adjustment—uncommon, but not impossible. The Durbin-Watson statistic for the adjusted data is 1.43, which is large enough so that serial autocorrelation in the errors can be said not to exist at the .01 level and is unlikely at the .05 level. Some confidence can thus be placed in the results for the adjusted data given in Equation 10.21.

Now look at the possibility of respecifying the model in such a way as to include the possibility of an effect of the federally mandated drop in speed limit in 1974 and the federally mandated state option to increase speed limits on limited access highways in 1987. Note the model shown in Equation 10.22:

$$D_t = b_1 Y_t + b_2 S_{1t} + b_3 S_{1t} Y_t + b_4 S_{2t} + b_5 S_{2t} Y_t + b_6 M_t + b_0 + e_t \tag{10.22}$$

where D_t, Y_t, and M_t are as given in Equation 10.18, S_{1t} is a dummy variable that is 0 from 1970 to 1974 and 1 for years thereafter representing the reduction in the speed limit in 1974, S_{2t} is a dummy variable that is 0 from 1970 to 1987 and 1 for years thereafter representing the possible increased speeds beginning in that year, and both terms $S_{it}Y_t$ are interaction terms between the speed dummy variables and year. Miles traveled has been retained in Equation 10.22 because it was statistically significant in Equation 10.19. The variable Accidents was dropped from Equation 10.22 because it was not statistically significant in Equation 10.19. The results for this model are as shown in Equation 10.23.

$$b_1 = -54.195 \ (58.159)$$
$$b_2 = -241.787 \ (101.759)$$
$$b_3 = 1.018 \ (46.428)$$
$$b_4 = 982.030 \ (353.765)$$
$$b_5 = -60.853 \ (22.418)$$
$$b_6 = -3.816 \ (1.568)$$
$$b_0 = 617.901 \ (490.895) \qquad\qquad (10.23)$$
$$t(b_1) = -.932$$
$$t(b_2) = -2.376$$
$$t(b_3) = .022,$$
$$t(b_4) = 2.776$$
$$t(b_5) = -2.715$$
$$t(b_6) = 2.433$$

Essentially, the four coefficients for which the absolute value of the t-tests (division of the coefficient by its standard error) are greater than 2 are those that are statistically significant in the model as given in Equation 10.22. Thus, the coefficient for the dummy representing the change in speed limit in 1974 (b_2) is statistically significant and indicates a one-time drop of 241 deaths per year after the speed limit reduction. The coefficient for the speed limit change in 1987 (b_4) is also statistically significant and indicates a one-time increase in deaths of 61 per year following the ability of states to raise speed limits on limited access highways. The coefficient for the interaction between the speed limit change in 1987 and the year (b_5) is also statistically significant, which means that after 1987 the secular downward trend in highway deaths over time (represented by the nonsignificant coefficient of b_1) actually declines each year by 2.7 additional deaths. Finally, the coefficient of miles traveled (b_6) remains statistically significant in this model, indicating that there are 2.4 additional deaths for each 100 million miles traveled.

The Durbin-Watson statistic for Equation 10.22 is 1.13, which for 25 observations and 6 independent variables is not large enough to *guarantee* no autocorrelation in the errors but is large enough so that it could be *assumed* that there is no autocorrelation in the errors. However, when the results from Equation 10.22 are used to adjust the values of the data for autocorrelated error, only the coefficient for miles traveled remains statistically significant at the .05 level. Thus, there is reason to suspect that the changes in highway speed limits, at least as reflected in the data from 1970 to 1995 for North Carolina, did not have statistically significant effects on highway deaths. An examination of a time series of automobile deaths by month in North Carolina from 1964 to 1980 (Veney and Luckey 1983) showed that a reduction in deaths of as much as 30 to 40 deaths per month occurred following the introduction of the 55-mph speed limit. The data examined above included only data from 1970 on, which may account for the difference in results.

Neonatal Tetanus Deaths and Immunization in Sri Lanka

What is the effect of a program championed by WHO and UNICEF, the Expanded Program on Immunization, on the neonatal tetanus deaths in Sri Lanka as an example of the use of time series analysis using regression? (Veney 1993) This analysis was based on data on neonatal tetanus deaths occurring from 1967 through 1980, a 15-year time period that included the introduction of the Expanded Program on Immunization.

The data on neonatal tetanus deaths for Sri Lanka are shown in Table 10.5. Column 1 of Table 10.5 is the year beginning with 1967. Column 2 of Table 10.5 is the year rescaled so that the first year of the program is assigned a value of 1 and previous and subsequent years are numbered consecutively forward and backward from that point.

The purpose of this is to force the intercept term in the regression model to be measured at the point in time at which the Expanded Program on Immunization actually began and makes the intercept term somewhat more meaningful than it may be otherwise. The point of scaling time to improve the interpretability of the intercept term is treated in somewhat more detail in the section below on the meaning of the intercept.

The third column in Table 10.5 shows the dummy variable representing the Expanded Program on Immunization begun in 1978. That dummy is coded 0 prior to 1978 and 1 from 1978 on. The fourth column in the table is the interaction between the rescaled time variable (column 2) and the program dummy (column 3). Finally, the last column represents neonatal tetanus deaths per 10,000 live births in each year (World Health Statistics Annual 1984).

TABLE 10.5

Neonatal Tetanus Deaths in Sri Lanka, 1967 to 1981 and Expanded Program on Immunization

1	2	3	4	5
Year	Year Rescaled	Expanded Program on Immunization	Interaction	Neonatal Tetanus Deaths
1967	−10	0	0	14.0
1968	−9	0	0	21.0
1969	−8	0	0	16.0
1970	−7	0	0	22.5
1971	−6	0	0	16.5
1972	−5	0	0	20.5
1973	−4	0	0	28.0
1974	−3	0	0	21.0
1975	−2	0	0	20.7
1976	−1	0	0	17.5
1977	0	0	0	20.5
1978	1	1	1	20.5
1979	2	1	2	11.0
1980	3	1	3	8.5
1981	4	1	4	4.8

The model that is estimated to assess the effect of the Expanded Program on Immunization on neonatal tetanus deaths is one that regresses column 5 in Table 10.5 on columns 2, 3, and 4. It is shown in Equation 10.24:

$$N_t = b_1 Y_t + b_2 E_t + b_3 Y_t E_t + b \qquad (10.24)$$

where Y_t is the coded year score (-10 to 4), E_t is the Expanded Program on Immunization dummy variable, and $Y_t E_t$ is the interaction term. In estimating this model using OLS, the results are as shown in Equation 10.25.

$$
\begin{aligned}
b_1 &= .374 \ (.340) \\
b_2 &= 1.895 \ (4.808) \\
b_3 &= -5.334 \ (1.630) \\
b_0 &= 21.705 \ (2.011) \\
t(b_1) &= 1.099 \\
t(b_2) &= .394 \\
t(b_3) &= -3.271
\end{aligned}
\qquad (10.25)
$$

The Durbin-Watson statistic for Equation 10.24 is 2.34, which is strong evidence of no autocorrelation in the errors.

Consider what Equation 10.25 indicates. Prior to the initiation of the Expanded Program on Immunization, there was very little change in the neonatal tetanus death rate in Sri Lanka (nonsignificant coefficient on time of .374). After the initiation of the program, neonatal tetanus deaths declined by 5.334 deaths per 10,000 live births each year. This indicates a powerful effect of the Expanded Program on Immunization.

Meaning of the Intercept Term

Some confusion in interpretation of results of regression analysis with time as an independent variable can occur due to the scaling of time. Take the data that make up the neonatal tetanus example from Sri Lanka. If time is scaled not from -10 to 4 as shown in column 2 of Table 10.5, but from 1967 to 1981 as shown in column 1, the same exact analysis can be done as is shown in Equations 10.24 and 10.25 above. In that case, however, the interaction term in Table 10.5, rather than having 1, 2, 3, and 4 as the series of values for the years 1978 through 1981, will actually have the values 1978 through 1981. The results of the analysis using the actual year date are as shown in Equation 10.26:

$$
\begin{aligned}
b_1 &= .374 \ (.340) \\
b_2 &= 10546.495 \ (3227.035) \\
b_3 &= -5.334 \ (1.630) \\
b_0 &= -716.975 \ (670.445) \\
t(b_1) &= 1.099 \\
t(b_2) &= 3.268 \\
t(b_3) &= -3.271
\end{aligned}
\qquad (10.26)
$$

Now the coefficients for the intercept (b_0) and the coefficient for the change in intercept at the initiation of the program (b_2) are measured not at the time of the program intervention but 1967 time periods before.

A consequence of measuring time in its actual year values is that the intercept becomes a large negative value (because of the b_1 value of .374), which means nothing as a rate. Another consequence is that the coefficient for the change in intercept at the initiation of the program becomes a very large positive value (because of the negative b_3 value of -5.334), which also means nothing in terms of mortality rates. This is not a problem in prediction but only a problem in interpretation. If the reviewer does not know that time was measured from year 0 with the first time period being 1967, the regression results would seem quite anomalous. Knowing the scaling of time, however, the reviewer can understand why the coefficients of b_2 and b_0 are outside the normal limits for a rate (0 to 100).

Measuring time beginning with the first time period in the series (1967) being coded 1 and the last time period being coded 15 would also be possible. This would produce another set of values for b_2 and b_0 (the reader may confirm this), but these values would still be right if the scaling of time is known.

Discussion Questions

1. What is the difference between bivariate and multivariate regression in the analysis of time series data? Give an example of each type.
2. What is autocorrelation? How may it be avoided, or at least handled, in the analysis of trend data?
3. Define the term *model specification*.
4. What does it mean when a model is misspecified?
5. How may misspecification lead to inappropriate decision making?

VI

EXPERIMENTAL DESIGN

11

EXPERIMENTAL DESIGN AS AN EVALUATION STRATEGY

Experimental studies have long been viewed as the pinnacle of evaluation research efforts. This view is not without justification. Under the proper circumstances, an experimental study can provide an unequivocal answer to the ultimate evaluation question: Did the program make any difference? No other evaluation strategy can do so. This chapter describes various types of experimental designs and the settings in which they are appropriate, and illustrates their use in different health services settings.

What Is an Experiment?

In its simplest form, an experiment can be characterized by the following sequence of events:

1. An indicator of a system state is observed.
2. Following this observation, an experiment is attempted on the system.
3. A second observation of the indicator of the system state is made.

The difference between the first and second observation determines whether the modification had an effect.

The following is an example of a simple experiment that introduces some of the benefits and difficulties of this evaluation strategy.

Illustration: A Training Event

Does a training event make a difference? The answer must be yes, because training events are held by the thousands. But the question could be treated in an experimental manner. If we remain with the very simple characterization of an experiment given above, viewing a training event as an experiment is possible.

In this experiment, the state of a system (i.e., the level of knowledge or ability of a group of potential trainees) is assumed or measured at one point in time. Then an intervention, the training event, is introduced (i.e., the trainees attend the training event). Finally, the state of the system (i.e., the level of knowledge or ability of the group of trainees) is measured at some point after the training event.

While assuming the level of knowledge or ability before the intervention may be enough, measuring the level of knowledge or ability after the training for the activity to constitute an experiment is critical. The basic sine qua non of an experiment are that an outside agent introduces an intervention into a system and the expected results of that intervention are measured after the event. Without these two components, an experiment has not been carried out.

To remain with the simplest possible example in the training context, suppose that a group of family planning personnel from a national family planning program attend a two-week training session on management of family planning programs. At the end of the training event they are given a four-page, multiple choice examination on material covered during the course. The ability of the participants to answer the questions then becomes an assessment of the effectiveness of the course. If the participants can answer the questions at a satisfactory level, the conclusion may then be that the training event made a difference in knowledge. Further, while it would be a stretch to make the leap of logic to the conclusion that training events in general are effective, that inference may be drawn by many.

The training event is an experiment in the most rudimentary sense, but there are some significant, and generally obvious, problems with conclusions either about the actual training event itself, or about training events in general. First, it is not clear that the ability of the participants to answer the questions on the final examination (i.e., the assessment) was a function of the course or something they already knew, because they were not assessed before the event. This illustrates the importance of prior assessment. Prior assessment also carries the risk of sensitizing the participants to the materials on which they will be tested, which adds to the difficulty of showing that the course per se, rather than sensitization to specific material to be contained in the assessment, made a difference.

Failure to measure knowledge levels at the outset is only one problem associated with assessment of the training event. A second problem, which is really two problems, has to do with measurement of any type, whether measurement is prior to the training event or after the event. This is the dual problem of measuring the right element and of measuring it well. If the assessment of the training event is to be a test of knowledge, devising some type of assessment tool that will effectively measure the knowledge that is to be gained from the training is critical. Frequently, however, the knowledge that may be gained is not easily assessed, especially if it is knowledge designed to improve decisions and actions, rather than simple rote learning of facts. This leads to the dual nature of the measurement problem. In this event, the ultimate aim may be to improve management skills.

Carrying out an assessment that will test management skills may be a long-term, high-cost endeavor. Thus, knowledge may be used as a proxy. However, a clear relation may not exist between the ability to parrot expected answers in a written test and the ability to manage well in a real-world situation. The results of the training event may be too subtle and complex to be measured by a test, and the ability to answer test questions may be trivial compared to the skills that are expected to be gained.

This last point is, in fact, a major problem of evaluation. Often, what can be assessed objectively tends to be only trivial or minor aspects of the program. This can be seen for example, in regard to the World Health Organization

(WHO) definition of health: "complete social, mental, and physical well-being, and not simply the absence of disease." WHO acknowledges, however, that some of the only useful measures of health as an outcome are such relatively insensitive measures as mortality rates.

The problems of measurement are only one set of problems that plague the attempt to use experiments to assess programs, and they are actually problems for all types of assessment. Measurement issues are discussed in detail in Chapter 13. Other issues are important to the success or failure of an experiment. These include design issues, study site and sample selection issues, adequate observations for effective decision making, and economic and political realities.

Experimental Design

In program evaluation, the conduct of an experiment is a complex undertaking, but the basic pattern is relatively simple. The state of a system at a given time is observed, an experimental variable or stimulus is introduced, and the state of the system is again observed after the fact. This straightforward statement does not do justice either to the complexity of launching a good experiment in a program evaluation setting or to the number of different alternative strategies that may be used to structure such experiments. While a range of experimental designs exist, for the most part many of the designs are too complex for reasonable application in health program evaluation. Following are descriptions of several experimental designs feasible and appropriate to healthcare settings. (The designs are based on material in Campbell and Stanley 1963.)

Pretest-Posttest Design

The pretest-posttest design may be characterized in the following manner.

$$
\begin{array}{ccccc}
 & & t_1 & & t_2 \\
E & & O_1 & X & O_2
\end{array}
$$

In the pretest-posttest design the only group considered is the experimental group (represented by E in the illustration). At time 1 a first observation (O_1) is made. From the standpoint of evaluation this may be an observation of a number of characteristics of a particular delivery system. In the case of a national health system, it may include:

- information about current infant, child, and maternal mortality;
- population;
- number of cases of malaria;
- families without a safe source of drinking water; or
- whatever other important classes of information may characterize the system.

Between time 1 and time 2 an experimental intervention is introduced, or an event of interest occurs, and is indicated by X. The intervention may be an entire program, such as providing primary healthcare services. It may also be a more limited activity, like exposing personnel to a particular type of training program, or a restructuring or cost containment initiative. Finally, at time 2 a second observation (O_2) of the system is made, and the effect of the program is considered to be the difference between the measure of the system state at time 2 and time 1.

The following is an illustration of a pretest-posttest design used to assess the effects of downsizing and cost containment initiatives on job satisfaction and nursing turnover.

Illustration: the effects of healthcare reform on job satisfaction and voluntary turnover among hospital-based nurses

Among the consequences of downsizing and cost containment in hospitals are major changes in the work life of nursing personnel. This study examines the effects of system changes on job satisfaction and turnover of hospital-based nurses—specifically how changes occurring from 1993 to 1994 affected the job satisfaction of hospital-based nurses, and what the impact is of these changes on voluntary turnover among hospital nurses (Davidson et al. 1997).

This is a longitudinal study based on the self-administered survey distributed twice from 1993 to 1994 to the total population of nurses actively practicing more than 20 hours a week at Beth Israel Hospital in Boston, Massachusetts. During this time period, the hospital has undergone major reforms affecting the work life of nurses participating in the study. Changes in reimbursement forced the hospital to cut its operating budget approximately 7.5 percent. Two patient care units closed, requiring nurses to leave familiar work groups and managers, and to transfer to other units where vacancies existed. In addition, all the employees, including nurses, experienced changes in pay and benefit structures.

The study group baseline initially consisted of the entire population of staff nurses and nurse managers, a total of 1,002 nurses. Of these, 736 responded to the survey yielding their response rate of 73.5 percent. At time 2, all nurses who were still working at the hospital, regardless of whether they changed their unit work site or not, participated in the survey.

The major source of data was the nursing survey at both time 1 and time 2, with additional items gathered from the human resource data file. These data included variables such as wage and clinical advancement level. The principal use of these secondary data, however, was to develop the termination variable and obtain information on nonrespondents.

The survey instrument consisted of:

- personnel demographics;
- objective work conditions such as number of work days per week, the unit size, years of work, and so on; and
- the three major existing instruments: the Hinshaw and Attwood Nurse Job Satisfaction Scale, the Price and Mueller Model on Turnover, and the Perlinn and Schoolers Personal Mastery Scale.

Analysis revealed that significant declines existed in most aspects of job satisfaction. Multivariate analysis indicated that the most important determinants of low satisfaction were poor communications within the organization and too great of a work load. Intent to leave was predicted by the perception of little promotional opportunity, high routinization, low decision latitude and poor communications. Predictors of turnover were few years on the job, expressed intent to leave, and not enough time to do the job well.

This study can be considered to be a *natural experiment* because it capitalizes on unfolding events that are occurring within an organization. The purpose of the evaluation is to assess the extent to which these changes affect the quality of work life of nursing personnel. Without taking any stand with regard to the efficacy of these changes, this study can be used to demonstrate the several design problems inherent in a pretest-posttest design with no control group, and to show how these design problems may affect the value of the evaluation.

Design problems

Because the experimental group itself is the only group under examination, eliminating any real effect of the changes (the experimental variable) from other simultaneously occurring factors is impossible. During a major program, such as restructuring or making changes in programmatic initiatives to improve quality, a number of factors other than the program itself probably are influencing the observation at time 2 and producing a difference between the two observations. Generally available resources may change, attitudes of relevant populations about a particular problem may shift, and so on. The design described here cannot eliminate the effect of these other possible factors.

Extraneous variables

The possibility of cohort change that is unrelated to the study intervention must be considered, particularly in any situation where the study compares different subjects over time and where a great deal of fundamental change is occurring within the larger community. In the job satisfaction study, the comparison is of nurses over a two-year period. While that is not necessarily a long period of time, the changes may in fact be due to a fundamental change of the personnel within the organization. Possibly, the cohorts of personnel may have been different at time 1 and at time 2. Without a control group a cohort change must always be suspected, and this is always a possibility in a study that extends over a number of years.

If the first observation was off the trend line relative to the system state under observation, the second observation can be expected to shift back toward the trend line, either a higher or lower value, without regard to any effect by the program that was introduced. With the pretest-posttest design, there is no way to assess whether the original observation was on the trend line, above it, or below it. Consequently, this effect cannot be separated from any apparent program effects.

Regression to the mean

While no reason exists to suspect that participants in the initial survey had unusually high levels of job satisfaction, it is nonetheless a source of error that cannot be accounted for in the pretest-posttest design with no control group.

Sensitization   Recognition that one is participating in an evaluation may by itself have an effect on assessment outcomes. This recognition of the experimental situation, including a natural experiment or *sensitization* to it, may result in a change between two observations that is not a function of the program or event at all, but simply is a function of being in the evaluation. This phenomenon is referred to as the *Hawthorne effect*, first recognized in conjunction with studies by Roethlisberger and Diskson (1939) at the Western Electric plants in Hawthorne, Illinois. Essentially, what they observed was that when workers in the plant knew they were the subject of experiments, they acted differently than they would otherwise, and this difference was substantial enough to obscure the expected effects of the interventions.

It may be difficult to imagine how the Hawthorne effect could have an influence on personnel attitudes and turnover. But for example the decline in job satisfaction may have nothing to do with the restructuring initiatives or changes in benefit packages but rather the endless series of meeting and data collection efforts associated with the evaluation. The effect therefore is not a function of the substantive change but rather the manner in which the evaluation was conducted. The design used cannot control for the possibility of this sensitization.

Reactiveness   The expectation of the observer or the one measuring the system state may also have an effect. Actually, this effect may not be the evaluator's expectation but may also be bound up with the expectations of those people involved with providing the program. This problem of expectations is sometimes referred to as the *self-fulfilling prophecy*, described in more detail in Chapter 5.

The importance of the self-fulfilling prophecy in an evaluation of program effectiveness or impact may be reasonably doubtful. If fairly objective measures are taken of the system state at the two time periods, the evaluators' expectations are not likely to have an effect if the evaluators are honest in their assessment.

However, if the expectation of the people introducing the program was high, this is likely to be a legitimate aspect of program implementation rather than a confounding factor to protect against. Consequently, the self-fulfilling prophecy may be of less concern here than in other settings. Suppose, however, that a program change is introduced on an experimental basis, and that desirable results actually occur because of the program implementers' expectations rather than because of the program. If this is the case, the results may be quite misleading for the establishment of the same type of program on a routine basis by people less committed to it than those involved in the initial experimental situation.

Relative efficiency of   Because the pretest-posttest design involves a single experimental variable (i.e., a
program inputs   single program structure), assessing the efficiency of alternative strategies for providing the same services or of alternative ways of organizing those same services within this design is impossible.

Pretest-Posttest with a Control Group Design

The pretest-posttest design with a control group can be characterized in the following manner.

$$
\begin{array}{ccccc}
 & t_1 & & t_2 \\
E & O_{E1} & X & O_{E2} \\
C & O_{C1} & & O_{C2}
\end{array}
$$

This design includes both the experimental group E and the control group C. At time 1, observations are made on both groups. Between time 1 and time 2, an intervention is introduced to the experimental group. At time 2, second observations are made on both the experimental group and the control group. The comparison of interest in such an experimental design is:

$$
(O_{E2} - O_{E1}) - (O_{C2} - O_{C1})
$$

Consider the following illustrations involving the evaluation of several different types of interventions. Interventions may be a priori designed or may capitalize on ongoing events within the field, such as the implementation of fluoridation and the subsequent use of restorative services and the impact of community based nursing services. All use a pretest-posttest with control group design.

Water fluoridation is a major U.S. public health program; approximately 54 percent of all Americans drink fluoridated water. This program is estimated to reduce dental carries by 20 to 40 percent in children and adults. Relatively little is known about fluoridation influences on use of restorative dental services among adults.

Illustration: post-fluoridation reduced the use of dental services among adults

Three hypotheses are evaluated regarding the indirect relationship between consumption of fluoridated water and the use of restorative services among adults.

- Because fluoridation reduces dental carries, adults who continuously drink fluoridated water at optimal levels receive lesser restorative services than those who do not.
- Fluoridation is unrelated to the use of restorative services because the majority of fillings and crowns in adult populations are replacements of failed restorations.
- Dental demand is determined primarily by several factors, such as the individual's age and education as well as dentists' treatment decisions. (Grembowski et al. 1997)

The study population consisted of 10,628 Washington state employees and spouse dependents aged 20–34 who lived in three communities in August of 1989: Olympia, Seattle, and Pullman/Moscow, Idaho. Sites were chosen to satisfy sample size requirements and to obtain equal numbers of subjects in fluoridated and nonfluoridated communities.

Over half of all state employees lived in Olympia, Seattle, or the Pullman/Moscow area, providing an adequate population of adults aged 20–34 in fluoridated and nonfluoridated communities. Olympia, the state capitol of Washington, had nonfluoridated water. Pullman, the location of Washington State

University, fluoridated its water supply in 1956. Neighboring Moscow, Idaho, has naturally fluoridated water. Seattle fluoridated its water supply in 1970.

Baseline adults were interviewed by telephone, and oral assessments were conducted to measure personal characteristics, lifetime exposure to fluoridated water, oral disease, and the quality of restorations. Adults were followed for two years to measure dental demand from dental claims.

Analyses reveal that relative to adults with no lifetime exposure to fluoridated water, adults drinking fluoridated water for half or more of their lives had less disease at baseline and a lower nonsignificant probability of receiving restorations. Among adults aged 20–34 with private dental insurance, fluoridation reduces oral disease but may or may not reduce the use of restorative services depending on dentists' clinical decisions.

Illustration: impact of integrated community nursing services on hospital utilization and cost in a Medicare risk plan

Service integration is viewed as an important method for improving quality and effective use of healthcare resources. Specifically, the integration of services requires particular attention to the needs of high-risk populations and their transition between acute care and community services. The purpose of this evaluation is to assess the impact of an integrated set of community services on hospital utilization and costs among older adults enrolled in a Medicare Risk plan (Burns, Lamb, and Wholey 1996). Hospital use and costs are compared for plan members who receive one or more of a capitated set of community services following hospitalization, versus members who were hospitalized or used one or more hospital-based services but did not receive any of the capitated community services.

The study compared hospital-based service use and costs incurred by elderly patients who were enrolled in the integrated community nursing service program versus those that were not enrolled. All patients were members of a Medicare Risk HMO, which contracted with a two-member hospital system for inpatient/outpatient services. All patients used at least one hospital service, including an inpatient stay, emergency room visit, ambulatory surgical visit, or outpatient visit during one of the three study periods. The study tracked these patients in terms of the use and costs for inpatient/outpatient emergency and outpatient services. Data for the dependent variable were taken from the hospital system's cost accounting and cost-mixed databases.

Analysis reveals that patients receiving integrated services had significantly higher utilization and cost during the period of enrollment and significantly lower utilization and cost during the period following enrollment compared to nonprogram patients. These results suggest that integration of nursing services at the community level can reduce the use of expensive hospital services.

Design problems

How does this new design deal with the confounding effects in the pretest-posttest design? Consider the evaluation of a primary healthcare program.

Extraneous variables

Can the addition of a control/comparison group eliminate the effect of other factors occurring simultaneously? If the assumption is that the experimental group and the control/comparison group will be subjected to the same type of other factors, this design will essentially control for their effect.

For example, suppose that a primary healthcare program is being implemented in a rural community and there is some desire to determine its effectiveness by using an experimental design. The pretest-posttest design with a control/comparison group will control for any other forces active in the community at the same time as the program if the assumption is that these factors affect all areas of the community in the same way. If the control/comparison and experimental groups have the same basic health problems, social structure, and geographic characteristics, probably any other simultaneously occurring factors that could confound the results of the experiment will be effectively controlled by the comparison between the two groups.

If, however, the experimental group is influenced by different factors from the control group, if it is in a different geographical region or has different surface characteristics such as being in the mountains as opposed to a control group in the lowlands, if it has a different social structure, or if the government is treating the experimental area differently in terms of other resources apart from the program, the comparison between the experimental and control groups will probably not be effective in eliminating these other factors and in demonstrating the true results of the program.

One factor that may create difficulties in separating the program effect from confounding factors is how the two areas are chosen to act as the experimental or the control group. For example, if the experimental area is selected because the type of problems that primary healthcare would be expected to address are particularly acute there, the comparison between experimental and control groups is questionable at best, and apparent program effects would be debatable.

For the pretest-posttest with a control/comparison group design to be truly effective in controlling for factors occurring simultaneously outside the actual experimental variable, two areas or groups that are matched as nearly as possible on relevant characteristics such as geography, region of a country, language style, and social characteristics must be selected. Then one of the two groups must be randomly selected to be the experimental group. This is the only truly effective way of deciding which group should serve as the control and which should serve as the experimental.

Regression effects

Will the pretest-posttest with a control/comparison group design solve the problem of regression effects? Again, if the assumption is that the experimental group and the control group are both essentially identical with regard to the problem or factors affecting the problem, then it can be assumed that regression effects will be essentially equal for both groups or areas between time 1 and time 2. This may be a relatively weak assumption, but without time series data to measure the trend line for the two areas or groups over time, no other assessment of regression effects can be made. In any case, the control group design provides a better assessment of the program effect than the pretest-posttest design does without a control group.

Sensitization   The control group design is not entirely effective in controlling for the problems of sensitization—the Hawthorne effect. Both the experimental and the control group are observed at time 1 so any difference occurring between them cannot be attributed to the observation or the measurement because the groups are equal on this aspect of the experiment.

Sensitization to a particular characteristic such as mortality rates, or another impact measure being evaluated, however, may result in a different effect when an experiment follows immediately (e.g., the provision of a program) than a similar observation would produce if a program did not follow. In a sense, it may be called an interaction effect between the observation and the experiment or experimental variable. There is relatively little information on the magnitude of this effect, but its possibility should be recognized.

Reactiveness   The pretest-posttest design with a control group will not control the possible effect of expectations on the part of program evaluators or program personnel. As noted, the self-fulfilling prophecy is that the expectations of committed program providers may produce a result under experimental conditions that would not be produced on a routine basis by the same type of program provided by people less committed to the program.

A second problem of expectations is that evaluators, if they have some stake in the program's outcome, may unconsciously, and with the best intentions, observe the results of the program differently. This situation would be rather unlikely when before-and-after measurement is taken in a fairly objective manner, such as comparing morbidity or mortality rates. A substantial problem could exist, however, if before-and-after observations were more subjective.

Controlling expectations: double-blind experiments   One approach devised in clinical research to attempt to control the effect of expectations on the part of service providers and subjects of the experiment themselves is known as the *double-blind random clinical trial.* In such a study, a group of people to be included in an experiment—for example, on a new drug—is divided equally into an experimental group and a control group. The experimental group receives the drug under test, while the control group receives a placebo, a drug that appears the same as the experimental drug but is known to have no effect. Subsequently, the two groups are observed by an evaluator to assess their status on the condition that the drug was expected to affect. The important characteristic of the double-blind test in this case is that neither the physician administering the drug nor the subjects receiving the drug or placebo nor the evaluators are aware of which specific individuals received the drug or which received the placebo.

This experimental approach is quite powerful for establishing the true effects of a treatment such as a drug. Cochrane (1972), for example, sees it as the only true test of drug efficacy. Clearly, such a test cannot reasonably be applied to all medical procedures. For example, doing a double-blind test on the efficacy of tonsillectomies or the value of acupuncture in controlling pain during surgery would be quite difficult. Designing a double-blind experiment that could assess the effectiveness of some type of complex program in producing results in some problem area would be even more difficult.

In a program setting a placebo for the program very likely would not be conceived of or provided in any reasonable manner. It would be extremely difficult to conceal from persons involved as members of either the control or the experimental group, and any external evaluators very likely could know where the program was being operated or who was being influenced by it. Despite the value of the double-blind approach in clinical experiments, it is probably not possible to apply this approach effectively in any program evaluation setting. This limitation will affect, in part, all the experimental approaches that may be taken to program evaluation.

Multiple Group Pretest-Posttest Design

The multiple group pretest-posttest design can be characterized in the following manner.

$$
\begin{array}{cccc}
 & t_1 & & t_2 \\
E_1 & O_{E11} & X_1 & O_{E12} \\
E_2 & O_{E21} & X_2 & O_{E22} \\
E_3 & O_{E31} & X_3 & O_{E32} \\
\cdot & \cdot & \cdot & \cdot \\
\cdot & \cdot & \cdot & \cdot \\
E_n & O_{En1} & X_n & O_{En2} \\
C_1 & O_{C11} & & O_{C12} \\
\cdot & \cdot & & \cdot \\
\cdot & \cdot & & \cdot \\
C_m & O_{Cm11} & & O_{Cm12}
\end{array}
$$

In this design are multiple experimental groups, each with an observation at time 1, an experimental variable introduced between time 1 and time 2, and an observation at time 2. Control groups may or may not be used in this design, depending on circumstances and purpose. If used, they act as a control against any experimental effects. The major interest, however, is often in comparing the various experiments, or various programs, or various ways programs are structured, rather than comparing a program to no program.

In the late 1980s, the Health Care Financing Administration (HCFA) funded a number of demonstration projects to test the implications of covering prevention/health promotion services under Medicare. This evaluation examining a demonstration project carried out by the University of Pittsburgh was designed to determine whether community-dwelling rural Medicare beneficiaries would use health promotion and disease prevention services if they were covered, and to

Illustration: evaluation of a health promotion demonstration program for rural elderly

determine whether local physicians and hospitals would be willing to provide such services if they were paid by Medicare (Lave et al. 1996).

Community-dwelling Medicare beneficiaries who lived in five rural counties in northwest Pennsylvania were recruited between May and December 1989. The demonstration lasted 18 months and beneficiaries were followed for an additional 18 months. Data for the evaluation came from initial health risk assessment, Medicare administrator records, follow-up surveys, and redeemed vouchers for waived services. The waived services included health screening, influenza immunization, nutritional counseling, smoking and alcohol cessation, and depression dementia evaluations.

Beneficiaries were randomized to one of two experimental groups and a control group. The one experimental group received the newly waived services from hospitals that received the capitated fee; the other received services from providers who were paid a fee for service. Eligibility for most waived services was based on risk.

Analysis revealed the participation rates in the new program varied by program and experimental group, and ranged from 16.8 percent for smoking cessation programs to 58 percent for influenza immunization. The demonstration led to an increase in influenza immunization rates relative to the control group. There were no differences in the use of medical care services or health outcomes between the experimental and control groups.

Analysis reveals that older, rural Americans will modestly increase their use of disease prevention and health promotion services if Medicare covers them. Use will be higher among those with more education; however, like most evaluations, further research is needed to assess the long-term benefits of such a program.

Illustration: using academic detailing techniques in continuous quality improvement teams to increase compliance with national guidelines for primary care, hypertension, and depression

The availability of clinical guidelines has generally failed to promote voluntary change in practice patterns. However, the development of continuous quality improvement and academic detailing as two intervention modalities to theoretically increase compliance with clinical guidelines provides an opportunity to evaluate the effectiveness of these techniques for increasing compliance with national guidelines for primary care of hypertension and depression.

Fifteen small-group practices at four Seattle primary care clinics were assigned to one of three study arms: academic detailing alone; academic detailing plus continuous quality improvement (CQI); or usual care (Goldberg et al. 1998). The evaluation monitored the activity of 95 providers and 4,995 patients during a year-long baseline and studied periods to examine changes in hypertension, prescribing blood-pressure control, depression recognition, and scores on the Hopkins System Checklist for depression.

Clinics varied considerably in their implementation of both academic detailing and CQI interventions. Across all sites, academic detailing was associated with changes in single-process measures and a decline in the percentage of depressives prescribed. No intervention effects were demonstrated for CQI across all sites for either disease condition. Within the clinic independently judged most successful as implementing both change strategies, the use of CQI teams and academic detailing did, in combination, increase the percentage of hypertension controlled. On balance, however, this randomized trial of two popular change strategies proved relatively ineffective in improving guideline compliance and clinical outcomes regarding the primary care of hypertension and depression.

The characteristics of this design, in terms of its ability to control for effects of other factors, regression, and sensitization by observation or treatment and expectations of the people involved, are all quite similar to those of the single experimental group and control group design. The multiple experimental group design, however, has the additional advantage of being able to assess from the standpoints of effectiveness and impact, and particularly from the standpoint of efficient alternative strategies by which a program can be conducted or by which an experimental variable is introduced.

Design problems

Posttest Only Design

The posttest only with a control group design can be characterized as follows:

$$
\begin{array}{cccc}
 & t_1 & & t_2 \\
E & - & X & O_{E1} \\
C & - & & O_{C1}
\end{array}
$$

As this design indicates, no observation is made at time 1. An experimental variable, such as a program, is introduced and observations on both the experimental and control group are made at time 2.

Significant reduction in cancer morbidity and mortality is not evenly distributed across the population. Minorities have consistently experienced higher morbidity and mortality and, as a result, reduced survival for all major cancer categories. In September 1990 the National Cancer Institute instituted the Minority Based Community Clinic Oncology Program (MBCCOP) to expand the clinical trials network to minority populations (Kaluzny et al. 1993). This network involves academic and community physicians in the development and evaluation of clinical trials of chemotherapeutic agents and techniques for prevention and control, including such activities as early detection, pain control, and rehabilitation.

Illustration: assuring access to state-of-the-art cancer care for U.S. minority populations

While accessing practice patterns and outcomes is not possible, accessing the extent to which this program was able to accrue patients to both the cancer treatment and prevention control protocols was possible. Data for this analysis were taken from primary and secondary sources generated as part of the larger CCOP evaluation (Kaluzny, Warnecke, and Associates 1996). Sources included site visits to nine of the participating minority-based CCOPs and accrual data obtained from National Cancer Institute (NCI) records and patient log data available from the NCI.

Although the study did not have access to a control group, its findings were compared with accrual to the ongoing Community Clinical Oncology Program. Table 11.1 presents accrual data from patient logs for the first two years of the minority-based program and clearly documents its ability to accrue patients to both treatment and cancer prevention and control protocols. A total of 344 patients were accrued on an annualized basis from June 1, 1990 through May 31, 1991, and this number increased to 470 during the second accrual year. Similarly, annualized patient accrual to cancer prevention control studies increased from 256 in 1990–91 to 423 in 1991–92.

Table 11.2 shows comparisons of minority-based CCOP with previous findings in the 50 CCOPs, which demonstrates clearly that the proportion of eligible minority-based CCOPs who entered treatment in 1992 are similar to the yearly proportion of eligible patients who enter trials in the overall CCOP from 1985–89. The study interprets this finding to indicate that a major factor influencing participation in clinical treatment research by minority patients is access; it also refutes the widely held belief that minority patients are not willing to participate in clinical trials.

Design problems Critical elements in this design are the ability to assign individuals randomly to either experimental or control groups and the ability to control statistically for equivalency between the control and experimental groups. Obviously, random assignment is an extremely powerful tool for eliminating the effect of simultaneously occurring events, regression, and sensitization by prior measures. It may reduce the importance of the expectations of the observer by reducing the number of observations made and by expanding the number of experimental cat-

TABLE 11.1
MBCCOP
Treatment and
Cancer Control
Accrual,
1990–1992

	Cancer Treatment Patients (Accrual Credits)	Cancer Control Patients (Accrual Credits)
Annualized 1990–1991*	344 (414)	256 (81)
Actual 1991–1992[†]	470 (534)	423 (82)

*Actual dates: June 1, 1990 to May 31, 1991. MBCCOP funding began in September 1990; therefore, accrual patients and credits were annualized to a 12-month period.
[†]Actual dates: June 1, 1991 to May 31, 1992.

TABLE 11.2
Proportion of
Eligible Patients
Entering Treatment
Protocols:
Comparison of
MBCCOP and
CCOP

	MBCCOP	CCOP
Total	3,536	44,156
Trial Available	805 (22.7%)	17,773 (40.2%)
Eligible for Trial	668 (82.9%)	9,508 (53.5%)
Entered into Trial	234 (35.0%)	3,242 (34.1%)

egories that can be used to assess alternative strategies. Unfortunately, randomization is often difficult to achieve in field situations.

In the posttest only design, it is possible when there are sufficient subjects to control statistically for equivalence between groups. Additional experimental designs have been detailed and discussed by other authors. For the most part, these designs are too complex for health program evaluation of reasonable type or magnitude. In fact, it should be relatively clear at this point that even the preceding designs would be difficult to apply in many program evaluation situations. The next section considers the issues of when a program setting is appropriate for an experimental evaluation and what these specific settings may be.

Appropriate Settings for Experimental Design

Experimental design is appropriately applied to evaluation when the major concern is either the effectiveness of the program or the efficiency of alternative programs. Properly designed experimental studies, even in the realm of program evaluation, can provide a substantial amount of information on effectiveness, efficiency, impact, and sustainability.

An experimental approach generally is not appropriate for assessing program relevance, adequacy, and progress. It is probable that the evaluator conducting an experimental evaluation of a program will be primarily external to the program itself and will not be concerned with its daily, weekly, or monthly internal working. From an experimental point of view, progress is irrelevant if the program can be shown either to reduce a problem or to modify a situation in the long run.

In assessing the results of an evaluation experiment, however, having information about progress may be quite useful—particularly if a program is designed and put in place on an experimental basis. It is one thing to design a program on paper, to plan for its implementation, to budget and allocate resources, hire staff, find quarters, and begin the program. To say that the program operated as it was expected to operate is something else—that the resources were available in the right places at the right times, that the staff was in place, that people received the services to be provided, and so on.

Such questions of progress are best answered by a monitoring approach. When a program cannot be proven to be more effective or more efficient than another program through an experimental design, it is extremely important to know whether the program was operating as it was expected to operate if it were to affect the state of the system. If such information is not available in an experimental evaluation of a program that appeared to have no effect, it will be impossible to separate the program as ideally operated from the program as actually operated. If information is available on progress and it indicates that the program was not implemented and carried out as projected, this fact will not, of course, mean that the program would have been effective in producing the desired results had it progressed as planned. It will show, however, that the lack of expected results cannot simply be attributed to the program strategy itself but may also be a function of poor management at any one of many different levels. Superficially an experimental evaluation seemingly should be appropriate to an assessment or evaluation of program impact—the long-term consequences of providing a particular program. For decision-making purposes, however, issues of impact will probably be resolved too late to affect program strategy or tactics. Experimental evaluations may be relatively expensive. Decisions about continuing with the experiment, or the program that the experiment aims to test, probably cannot be put off long enough to assess the actual impact of a program on the health characteristics of a population.

Evaluation is concerned primarily with effectiveness or efficiency in the experimental or quasi-experimental setting. This concern should also be a real one for the effect of the program and should not be a political issue. Many evaluations, particularly quasi-experiments, are undertaken with the expressed purpose of assessing a particular type of program or programs, when their hidden agenda may be primarily political or may become part of a larger political process. This phenomenon is clearly evident in recent evaluations of managed care plans.

The United States has experienced rapid growth in managed care enrollment during the decade of the 1990s. This growth has given rise to many concerns about the cost and quality of care within these health services delivery models. A large number of evaluations have been conducted on these plans; however, variations in plan design, evaluation methods, and target populations have led to a diversity of findings regarding efficiency and quality. As a result, both proponents and opponents of the managed care industry can find support for their political agendas in the evaluation literature. A recent meta-analysis of 68 managed care evaluations conducted during the 1990s documents this phenomenon (Miller and Luft 1997). Managed care opponents are using the evaluation literature to call for more stringent government regulations on the managed care industry. At the same time, managed care supporters are using the literature to lobby for the further expansion of managed care programs within government-financed health insurance programs.

Despite the difficulties of trying to evaluate within a politically sensitive environment, organizations or political bodies likely will be unwilling to support the cost of an experiment that does not involve an issue of substantial concern to them. If the issues to be resolved do not have major financial or political ramifications, organizations will be unwilling to expend the resources necessary to undertake a realistic experiment. In such cases, separating the political overtones from a concern for the true results of the experiment will always be difficult. Nevertheless, such a separation must be attempted and, to the extent possible, ensured if useful results are desired.

Short-Term versus Long-Term Designs

Experiments or experimental programs as evaluation efforts—especially evaluations involving either complex programs or alternative ways of providing or generating the same types of services through a given program—will have a greater chance of success if the programs will provide an evaluation result relatively quickly. In the best case, initiation of a program on an experimental basis in any area probably will be costly in terms of resources required, including planning and implementation expertise. Program managers and health service providers likely will be unwilling to wait long for results before making critical decisions about program strategies and modifications.

For example, if an experimental program does not seem to be producing expected results in a fairly short period of time, managers or health providers may terminate or modify the program in ways that would essentially invalidate the results of the evaluation. If an experimental program appears to be producing desired results in a relatively short time, however, policymakers (who are always under pressure to provide at least a semblance of equity) may be tempted to expand the program to a much wider population before it has been adequately shown to be useful. The best way to avoid both possibilities, either of which could result in tremendous wastes of resources in the long run, is to limit the types of evaluation questions to settings in which definitive information can be gained fairly quickly—in perhaps six months to a year.

A second problem is that the resolution of evaluation issues takes considerable time through the experimental approach. This problem actually is common to all evaluation formats but may be most acute in the experimental setting because of the relatively high cost of implementing and maintaining a well-designed experimental program evaluation. It stems from the fact that questions that can be resolved only in the long run through experimental evaluation may be no longer current or interesting issues by the time they have been resolved.

A final problem associated with long-term designs is in maintaining an adequate population base. Over time, individuals initially involved in a program on which impact or effectiveness is measured may selectively drop out, reducing the size of the population on which change is to be measured. Because the dropouts are not likely to be random, there is a high probability that they will influence study results in consistent but unexpected ways. The problem of dropout is known as attrition and limits the validity of the evaluation.

Evaluation versus Political Rationality

Because of the weakness of the pretest-posttest design with no control as an experimental approach, an experimental strategy for program evaluation probably should be avoided in a setting where no opportunity exists to identify reasonable control groups or areas, or multiple or alternative experimental groups or areas. On the basis of evaluation rationality, many major federal and private initiatives could have been implemented, and their effects evaluated, by comparing program and control areas. Such programs include the major efforts of the Joint Commission on Accreditation of Healthcare Organizations' "Agenda for Change," the Health Care Financing Administration's hospital and physician mortality listing program, and the National Cancer Institute's Physician Data Query (PDQ) as classic examples. Evaluation rationality is not always the same as political rationality, however. From a politically rational standpoint, implementing such programs on a basis that called for extensive experimental efforts in the experimental areas of the country may have been impossible, but possible in other areas. One political and major reason for the difficulty of designating experimental areas is the fact that all four programs have clear implications for the number of federal dollars that flow into areas where they are located. In such circumstances a well-designed experiment is difficult to carry out.

Randomization

Closely related to the problem of ensuring reasonable control groups or areas—or at least multiple or alternative experimental groups or areas—is making certain that assignment to the experimental or control group is based on purely experimental or evaluation factors rather than political or other considerations.

For an experimental design to be useful in program assessment, the results of the evaluation or experiment must not be confounded with any factors whose effect cannot be assessed within the experiment. One clear factor, the consequences of which could not be assessed within a program or experimental program setting, is the outcome of assigning a new program to be evaluated to certain groups or areas because their problems, which the experimental program is to alleviate or reduce, are the most acute.

Assigning an experiment program to such areas subjects the ultimate evaluation to several problems and criticisms. First, when programs are implemented in areas where certain problems are more acute than elsewhere, it is reasonable to expect a reduction in the level of the problems simply by virtue of the regression to the mean phenomenon. Second, when experimental programs are assigned to acute problem areas, improvements may be misinterpreted even if regression is not a realistic possibility. The results may be misinterpreted because it may be considerably easier for a program to produce desired results in an extreme or acute problem area than to produce even modest results in an area where the problem is less obvious.

Even if an experimental program is assigned to a particular area on the basis of other factors—such as the political importance of local citizenry, the program's ability to serve as a showcase in a particular locality or set of institutions, or for any other reason not basically dictated by the experimental design—problems may still arise in interpretation. What is naive and perhaps misleading is to assume that such areas are sufficiently similar to other areas or institutions so that they would provide reasonable controls for the experiment or evaluation.

Appropriate Data for Experimental Design

The data necessary to evaluate experimental programs can be seen as more limited than those necessary for evaluations under almost any other strategy. Essentially, a realistic experimental evaluation can be based on only a single indicator of program effectiveness. A program to reduce infant mortality within a given area, for example, may require no more information for a useful evaluation, when based on an appropriate experimental design, than the infant mortality level in the experimental area after the program has run for a predetermined period and the level in the control area for comparison.

In addition to data on effects, monitoring information to assess program progress relative to expectations can be quite useful. In a setting where the experimental program cannot be shown to be significantly more effective or useful than no program (i.e., where the experimental group turns out to be no different from a control group) this is particularly important. However, monitoring-type information can be equally important in a situation where there is clear evidence of a program effect when compared to a control group. It can be determined whether the results may have been improved had more attention been paid to ensuring that the program progressed as expected. Quite possibly, the effectiveness of a program in producing changes in important population characteristics may be substantially enhanced if efforts were made to ensure that it was on schedule, received the resources expected, and generally had the type of management necessary for a successful program.

Whether progress data are maintained for monitoring purposes or not, two types of information should be obtained to measure the results of the experiment or the program as an experiment. The first type of information is measures of impact to assess effectiveness. Regardless of whether the experimental program is a single program design to be compared to a control group or whether it is represented by a whole series of different program strategies all compared to one another or to a control group, the absolute minimum data requirement is a relatively objective measure to assess program impact.

If the program is designed to improve the effectiveness of a local health department, an objective measure of the effectiveness of the health department must be available. This may be a composite measure of a number of different aspects of health department operation, a number of individual measures of health department effectiveness in several different areas, or a single measure that taps only one aspect of health department functioning. Clearly, it is necessary in any experimental evaluation to have some objective measure to be assessed as part of the evaluation. In a family planning program, for example, the objective criterion may be number of births. If the program is for malaria eradication or control, the objective criterion may be prevalence of mosquito larvae. The objective criterion in a program to reduce traffic accidents may be number of accidents per thousand miles driven.

Whatever the objective criterion to be assessed as part of the experiment, it must be measured for both the experimental and control groups and both before and after the introduction of the program. The only exception is a situation with enough potential experimental and control units that a control in the study for possible differences between the experimental and control group at the outset of the study can be handled through random assignment. In such a case, measuring the objective criterion is necessary only after the study or program has been introduced and a sufficient time has elapsed for an effect to take place.

The second type of information for assessing programs via the experimental approach is maintained if the assessment primarily is one of alternative strategies for reaching the same goals—an evaluation of efficiency. If measuring efficiency is a major aspect of an evaluation experiment, it is necessary to have a good measure of the differences between programs being assessed and, through some monitoring device, to ensure that the differences exist not only at the outset of the program but also continue throughout the course of the experiment.

This matter is not as simple as it may seem. Various programs may be designed as alternative ways of reaching the same goals, and these alternative programs may be set in motion under the assumption that the design differences will be maintained through the course of the programs. Through various management and administrative decisions and minor oversights, actual program operations in the different alternatives quite possibly may become similar. As in the case of comparing an experimental group to a control group, where it is important to have good monitoring and progress information to evaluate the extent to which the program actually worked as designed, so, too, in the case of several alternative programs, such information is critical to ensure that they maintained their differences throughout the course of the evaluation.

A final point on data for experiments must be made again in regard to information about controls: In many instances, experimental controls are often assumed to be areas or all other groups of people who do not receive a program introduced on an experimental basis in one particular area or group. Within a state, for example, several counties may be designated as experimental counties and a program, such as primary care or family planning services provided through a health department, may be introduced into these counties. Those charged with the conduct of the experimental programs and those concerned with their evaluation probably will maintain good records of the operation of the programs over the course of the evaluation. Because the control counties or areas often may be taken for granted, evaluators may be less likely to remember to take the necessary steps to maintain similar data for them. Without such data, however, making a reasonable comparison between the experimental and control counties will be impossible. In general, the same information collected about the experimental programs must be collected and maintained for areas with no program that are being treated as controls.

Data for Experimental Design from Two Different Programs

Consider again the CCOP and early detection program in primary care. Using an experimental design, what data are required to evaluate experimentally the effort of CCOP to affect physician practice patterns in local communities? What data are required to evaluate the implementation of an office system for preventive care designed to increase the proportion of eligible patients receiving screening for breast, cervical, colo-rectal, and skin cancer within a primary care setting? The following illustration addresses these questions.

Illustration: Community Clinical Oncology Program (CCOP)

The evaluation of CCOP implementation and impact is an experimental study or, more accurately, a study of quasi-experimental design. The ultimate objective is to determine whether this particular organizational mechanism is able to facilitate the transfer of state-of-the-art technology to local physicians and make a difference in physician practice patterns (Kaluzny, Warnecke, and Associates 1996).

Defining the Community Clinical Oncology Program as an intervention, the evaluation challenge is to determine whether any change in physician practice patterns is a function of the program or simply a function of larger secular trends. Randomly assigning CCOPs to communities is not possible. Establishing a series of matched control CCOPs is not considered feasible. However, assessing practice patterns for the identical disease sites in non-CCOP communities participating in the Surveillance, Epidemiology, and End Results Program of the NCI is possible. Identical data will be collected from this secondary data source and compared with the practice pattern data collected within the 20 CCOP communities.

It is also possible to have a set of natural experiments to examine comparisons for selected measures of implementation and impact among groups of CCOP categorized by predefined environmental structure and process variables aggregated across CCOPs. These comparisons will use both cross-sectional and longitudinal data for CCOP-specific data collected at baseline and at follow-up. For example, it may be postulated that a strong leadership style is essential for the success of the CCOP. Suppose there are ten CCOPs with strong leaders as defined in an accepted manner, and 15 CCOPs without persons characterized as strong leaders. The natural experiment is to compare the two sets of CCOPs on a measure of program impact, such as accrual of patients to treatment or control regimens.

Four or five important and appropriate hypotheses such as the preceding one can be identified and explored using CCOP natural experiments. Identifying the hypotheses and framework of the natural experiment prior to data analysis and post hoc searching of the data will be important. The natural experiments represent the best available comparisons to be made without the use of control programs or communities. They can isolate a CCOP effect by selecting conditions in the environments that vary, such as location (rural versus urban) and resources (high and low competition for cancer patients in the community), and by comparing the performance of CCOP physicians and non-CCOP physicians in their treatment of nonprotocol patients. The accrual levels of the CCOPs will also be entered into analyses of practice patterns to determine if there is an exposure effect based on the activity of the CCOPs. Proposed a priori comparison categories using all 52 CCOPs may include:

- high versus low competition;
- group practice dominated versus hospital dominated;
- centralized leadership style versus other patterns;
- old versus new CCOP; and
- centralized versus decentralized decision making.

Illustration: Early Detection in Primary Care

The evaluation involved a randomized controlled trial in which the unit of randomization was the primary care practice. Sixty-two randomly selected community family practice and internal medicine practices in North Carolina were allocated to control and intervention groups. Physician investigators and facilitators met with practice physicians and staff in the intervention group over a 12–18 month period to provide feedback on their use of early detection screening activities for breast, colo-rectal, cervical, and skin cancer. The objective was to assess the proportion of eligible patients receiving early detection activities (Kinsinger et al. 1998).

The first requirement for an experimental evaluation of the proposed intervention is to establish an objective measure that can be used to assess its effect. As described in Chapter 9, data collected from chart audits was obtained to determine whether the six cancer detection activities were recommended, completed, and recorded prior to, during, and after the intervention for both the control and intervention groups. The objective is to compare the intervention and control groups at baseline and follow-up to determine whether the proportion of eligible parties in the intervention group had a significant increase.

Table 11.3 presents a comparison of the proportion of women receiving a mammogram and clinical breast exam (CBE) in both the control and intervention groups at baseline and at follow-up. While no difference apparently exists in the proportion of women with mammogram reports in the chart for the intervention and control, a significant increase exists in the mention of mammograms and CBE in the chart over the period of time.

The ultimate payoff in an experimental evaluation is the demonstration of a difference between the experimental and control groups in terms of an objective output measure of the program under evaluation. To provide a basis for interpreting performance differences, however, it is useful to have other types of information (i.e., types that may be considered primarily monitoring data) to assess the extent to which a program has been executed in a manner consistent with implementation plans. Of particular interest to the evaluation of a primary healthcare program is the difference in service provision between the experimental and

TABLE 11.3

Performance of Breast Cancer Screening in Last Year for Women Age 50 or Older by Chart Review

	Baseline (1991)	Follow-up (1994)	Change *	Baseline (1991)	Follow-up (1994)	Change *	Difference in Change **	P	OR	95% CI
Mammogram Mention	38.7	51.4	12.7	40.5	44.0	3.5	9.2	.01	1.5	(1.1, 2.0)
Mammogram Report	28.0	32.7	4.7	30.6	34.0	3.4	1.3	.56	1.1	(0.8, 1.4)
Clinical Breast Exam (CBE) Mention	41.1	46.4	5.3	44.6	43.9	−0.7	6.0	.06	1.3	(1.0, 1.6)
Mammogram Mention and CBE	28.2	38.7	10.5	30.3	32.6	2.3	8.2	.01	1.4	(1.1, 1.9)

*Change from baseline to follow-up
**Difference in change in early intervention practices compared to late-intervention practices

control groups—particularly the ability to monitor the extent to which the experimental group received the healthcare services the program is designed to provide.

Physical accessibility to a health service may be a prime concern in the provision of primary healthcare and an important aspect of care to be measured. Of course, any particular community must define accessibility in its own terms, but this probably would be in terms of travel time to the target population. In any case keeping record of the average distance to a health facility from any part of a local jurisdictional area will be important.

Information may also be obtained on the economic accessibility of care. Comparisons between the cost of care in nonprimary care areas and primary care areas give important information on which to judge the overall efficiency and effectiveness of services. This latter type of information is critical to improved decision making.

A major area of concern in monitoring primary care will be use of services. The actual number of people who use services can be rather easily obtained through a well-designed recording system. The extent to which services are provided to populations at risk (e.g., the proportion of children immunized, or pregnant women who receive antenatal care or receive a mammogram) is a more difficult, but also more important, measure to obtain. Doing so requires information about the populations at risk and the delivery system itself.

Additional monitoring data useful in assessing the extent to which a primary healthcare program is reaching its goals can include information about the dissemination of health education, including the recommended screening procedures. Further monitoring information can include the level of endemic diseases, treatments for common diseases and injuries, provision of drugs, coverage by a referral system, and information about various categories and types of health personnel and personnel availability.

The indication of clear differences between experimental and control areas on the basis of monitoring information will not necessarily result in differences in the output measures, but differences in output measures are certainly unlikely to occur if differences in the input measures do not exist. Differences in output measures especially will not occur if the monitoring of input measures indicates that the program is not progressing according to a reasonable program plan.

Application to Decision Making and Types of Evaluation

When properly planned and executed, the experimental or quasi-experimental design approach is the most powerful evaluation technique available for assessing the actual effectiveness or impact of a given program. No other evaluation approach, with the possible exception of time series analysis, can give such a clear and definitive assessment of the true value of the efficiency, effectiveness, impact, and sustainability of a program.

One important decision that can be made on the basis of experimental design evaluation data is whether a program has produced more in terms of a desired output than the absence of such a program or, alternatively, that one program strategy has performed better in regard to the desired output than another strategy. From this standpoint the clear decision derived from experimental design evaluations is the decision to continue or discontinue a program. If this decision is to be based on the demonstrated effectiveness of the program, experimental design is the evaluation of choice.

A second type of data that can be derived directly from the experimental approach is specific information about the comparative efficiency of one program over another or of comparative efficiency among a number of alternative program strategies. Here, the decision is whether to adopt the program approach that produced the most output for the least amount of input—the most efficient program. The application of this approach to decision making is not without risk to the people most affected. Because of the disclosure that a control group of persons with syphilis in public health hospitals had never been provided penicillin treatment despite its obvious effectiveness, withholding program benefits—or hypothesized program benefits—from groups of people who would be considered to be helped by such a program has been impossible.

In fact, standard operating procedures now require that any evaluation closely monitor interventions and be terminated if it appears that the experimental treatment is clearly superior to that provided to the control group. However, given the increasing demand for the results of many evaluations in a variety of treatment and prevention areas, an uneasy balance always exists between the need to maintain the rigors of the evaluation and the need to make the program available at the earliest possible time.

Discussion Questions

1. Why is experimental or quasi-experimental design usually considered the ultimate evaluation strategy, while its actual field application is quite limited?
2. Discuss the relative advantages and disadvantages of the following designs: pretest-posttest design, pretest-posttest with control group design, multiple pretest-posttest with control group design, and posttest design.
3. What is the function of control groups in an experimental design?
4. List the various problems associated with the use of controls and the methods used to ensure comparability.
5. What are the advantages and disadvantages of experimental designs within a managed care environment?

EXPERIMENTAL ANALYSIS TECHNIQUES AND INTERPRETATION

The basis of data analysis for an experimental evaluation of a program is a comparison of output or outcome measures between a setting in which a program is not present and one in which it is. In a before-and-after study with no control, the comparison is between the pretest and the posttest. With a pretest-posttest design involving a control group, the comparison is the change between the pretest and the posttest for the experimental group compared to the change between the pretest and the posttest for the control group. For a posttest-only design, the comparison is simply between the posttest measures.

Change or difference must be in the direction expected, but showing that a difference exists is not sufficient in itself to indicate that a program has been effective in producing a true difference in results. Even assuming that no factors except the experimental program can reasonably be expected to affect the results, the identification of a simple difference in the direction expected may not be adequate to indicate a program effect. Showing that the difference is large enough that it may not be expected to appear by chance alone is also necessary. The objective of this chapter is to present analysis techniques to determine whether the differences found in various settings could be assumed to be the consequence of an experimental program.

The three basic study designs discussed in the last chapter—the pretest-posttest with no control, the pretest-posttest with a control, and the random posttest-only design with a control—can be examined through the analysis of difference scores, using relatively straightforward t-tests. This chapter reviews specific tests for each design mentioned, with an extension to regression analysis. It concludes with a review of type I and type II error, particularly as these relate to the evaluation effort.

Analysis of Pretest-Posttest Data (No Control Group)

Although the hazards inherent in relying on a pretest-posttest design with no control group for attempting to assess program effects have been described in some detail, such a design may frequently be the only one available to an evaluator. Despite the number of problems that arise in the pretest-posttest design without a control group for inferring a program effect where none exists, understanding how such an effect may be assessed statistically is still useful. To examine this situation, consider a hypothetical program to improve the public's knowledge of actions to be taken in emergency or first aid situations until competent medical attention can be obtained. The basic assumption of such a program would be that a better understanding of emergency procedures may lead to fewer deaths or more favorable prognosis from situations involving medical emergencies.

Illustration of the Analysis of Pretest-Posttest Data with No Control Group

Suppose that the program itself is a simple ten-minute film presentation of several aspects of emergency or first aid medical treatment, perceived to be important lifesaving or medical-crisis-averting procedures. The ultimate evaluation of the film strip would be to determine whether people who had viewed it would at a later time be able to take control of a medical emergency in a way that would avert death or improve the prognosis following the situation. A more measurable, and certainly more proximate, output at the level of effectiveness of the film strip would be a measure of the amount of knowledge that people who saw it had about activities to be performed or avoided in a medical emergency. Knowledge possessed by the viewers must be compared with an alternative setting if any statement about the effect of the film strip is to be made. The alternative setting in the case of a pretest-posttest with no control group design would be knowledge of the subject possessed by people before they viewed the film strip.

Assume that ten people are selected to view the film strip as a means of assessing its effectiveness in imparting knowledge of emergency medical procedures. Before the viewing, each of the ten people is tested on his or her knowledge of emergency medical procedures; they may score from 0 to 20 points. After viewing the film strip, they are retested, and again the possibility is a score from 0 to 20 points. The effectiveness of the program for imparting knowledge can be assessed by using a simple t-test of the difference between means for correlated data.

Table 12.1 shows an example of constructed data that may be used to test the effectiveness of the film strip in imparting knowledge about emergency medical procedures. The data are shown for only ten people; in general, most evaluations of a film strip of this type would involve more people. A reasonable minimum number to include in such an evaluation would be about thirty people, although it is possible to use fewer, as shown later.

Table 12.1 has five columns. The first column is the personal identification numbers. The second column represents the scores received on the 20-point test prior to seeing the film strip. The third column represents the scores received on the same test by the same people after seeing the film strip. The assumption is that these two testings will have occurred relatively close in time, because the film strip lasts 20 minutes. Both administrations of the test and viewing the film strip may involve no more than a total of one hour. The fourth column is the difference between the first and second scores, and the fifth column is the square of that difference. With this information, the mean difference, designated $\bar{d}$, and the standard error of the mean difference, designated $s_{\bar{d}}$, can be calculated as shown at the bottom of Table 12.1.

Person	Score 1 (Pretest)	Score 2 (Posttest)	d	d^2
1	2	9	7	49
2	9	8	−1	1
3	8	15	7	49
4	5	19	14	196
5	10	18	8	64
6	17	19	2	4
7	6	17	11	121
8	11	19	8	64
9	5	10	5	25
10	12	12	0	0

TABLE 12.1

Example of a Test of the Effectiveness of a Film Strip on Emergency Medical Procedures: Pretest-Posttest (No Control)

$$\bar{d} = \frac{\sum d}{n} = 6.1$$

$$s_{\bar{d}} = \sqrt{\left[\sum d^2 - \frac{\left(\sum d\right)^2}{n}\right]\left(\frac{1}{n(n-1)}\right)} = 1.49$$

Significance Tests

On the basis of these data, a test of the significance of the difference between the first and second observation is a t-test:

$$t = \frac{\bar{d}}{s_{\bar{d}}} = \frac{6.10}{1.49} = 4.09 \tag{12.1}$$

With a t-test of this type, a value exceeding 2.23 (with an n of 10) is assumed to occur fewer than 5 times out of 100. Thus a value of 4.09 could be assumed to be significant at the .05 level. The probability distribution of t generally is given as an appendix to most statistical texts.

Interpretation and Limitations

Based on this example, the assumption is that a statistically significant difference exists between the scores of the first and second testing. The implication is that the film strip has made the viewers more knowledgeable about emergency medical procedures. Remember, however, that this conclusion is based on a pretest-posttest with no control group experiment and is subject to several types of errors or threats to validity, including:

- sensitization to the test itself;
- measurement decay;
- history, in terms of other things occurring at the same time the film strip was being viewed (e.g., the viewers may discuss the film strip or

emergency medical procedures in general, increasing the overall level of knowledge available to the group); and

- time lapse; the short period of time between the test and retest decreases the possibility that other factors will have accounted for or produced the change in the scores, but it increases the possibility that instrument decay (or the ability to improve on the second testing by virtue of having seen or taken the test the first time) will have produced the improvements in scores.

The pretest-posttest with no control group format generally does not allow for the ruling out of the effects of other factors that may be occurring at the same time the program is in operation (i.e., factors that may reasonably account for changes observed between the first and second testing). With regard to the simple example of viewing the film strip, a reasonable assumption is that few other important causal forces are operating at the same time. If the program were an experimental family planning effort, introduced nationwide in a developing country, that ran for three years, the incidence of births occurring as a measure of program effectiveness before and after the program is in operation may be substantially influenced by factors other than the program.

Analysis of Pretest-Posttest Data (with Control Group)

A design useful in assessing or controlling for external factors is the pretest-posttest with a control group. To demonstrate the calculation of the appropriate statistics for this design, the data on measuring the effectiveness of a film strip is again used.

Illustration of Pretest-Posttest Data (with Control Group)

Table 12.2 contains constructed data to assess the effectiveness of the film strip. In this case, we will use exactly the same data as Table 12.1 shows for ten people who viewed the film strip, but Table 12.2 also shows data for ten others who did not see the film strip. The data are constructed to have the same mean score and variance on the first test but a different mean score with the same variance on the second test.

Analysis of variance for an experiment with repeated measures on one variable and two groups can be used to obtain a great deal of information about the differences in scores for the two groups on the first and second test. The primary question of concern, however, is whether the difference in the before-and-after scores for the experimental group is greater, on average, than the difference of the before-and-after scores for the control group (Winer 1991). This question can be answered by a simple t-test of the difference between two means. The computations needed for this test are the average difference for the experimental group, the average difference for the control group, and the pooled standard error for these two means. The formulas for the calculation of these values are shown at the bottom of Table 12.2. The experimental and control groups need not necessarily be the same size for this t-test to be acceptable. A general assumption, however, is that the variance for the two groups being compared is essentially the same. An

Person	Score 1 (Pretest)	Score 2 (Posttest)	d	d^2
Experimental				
1	2	9	7	49
2	9	8	−1	1
3	8	15	7	49
4	5	19	14	196
5	10	18	8	64
6	17	19	2	4
7	6	17	11	121
8	11	19	8	64
9	5	10	5	25
10	12	12	0	0
Control				
11	9	11	2	4
12	5	14	9	81
13	6	9	3	9
14	11	6	−5	25
15	12	12	0	0
16	5	8	3	9
17	17	14	−3	9
18	10	16	6	36
19	2	4	2	4
20	8	2	−6	36

TABLE 12.2

An Example of a Test of the Effectiveness of a Film Strip on Emergency Medical Procedures: Pretest-Posttest (with Control)

$$\bar{d}_E = \frac{\sum d_E}{n} = 6.1$$

$$\bar{d}_C = \frac{\sum d_C}{n} = 1.1$$

$$S_{\bar{d}\,pooled} = \sqrt{\left[\sum d_E^2 - \frac{\left(\sum d_E\right)^2}{n_E} + \sum d_C^2 - \frac{\left(\sum d_C\right)^2}{n_C}\right]\left(\frac{1}{n_E + n_C - 2}\right)\left(\frac{1}{n_E} + \frac{1}{n_C}\right)} = 2.11$$

F-test is available to determine whether the variance of the two sets of difference scores can be considered comparable, which is

$$F = \frac{s_1^2}{s_2^2} \qquad (12.2)$$

where s_1^2 is the larger variance and s_2^2 is the smaller variance. The degrees of freedom of this F-test are equal to the number of cases less 1 for both numerator and denominator. In Table 12.2, for example, the degrees of freedom for that F-test would be 9 and 9. The variance for either the control or the experimental group is calculated according to the following standard variance formula:

$$S_d^2 = \frac{\sum d^2 - \frac{\left(\sum d^2\right)}{n}}{n-1} \tag{12.3}$$

In Table 12.2, the variance for both the control and the experimental groups is the same—approximately 22.3. Consequently, it is reasonable to pool the variance for the purposes of a test of the effectiveness of the film strip. The t-test used in this case is:

$$t = \frac{d_E - d_C}{s_{d\,pooled}} = \frac{6.1 - 1.1}{2.11} = 2.37 \tag{12.4}$$

The total degrees of freedom for this t-test are equal to the number of cases in the experimental group plus the number in the control group minus 2, or 18 degrees of freedom. A standard statistical table giving distributions of t probability for 18 degrees of freedom would show that a t of 2.1 or larger would occur by chance only 5 times in 100. Therefore, a t value of 2.37 would be considered evidence of a difference between the experimental and the control groups in the before-and-after scores. This would be interpreted as indicating that the film strip has been effective in improving knowledge of emergency first aid procedures for the experimental group.

Replication of the t-Test Using Regression

The test of difference between the experimental and the control group (a t-test, shown previously) can be replicated using regression analysis. In this analysis, the difference scores (the column marked d in Table 12.2) represents the dependent variable. The independent variable is represented by a single dummy variable, which is coded 1 for the experimental group and 0 for the control group. If the dummy variable is designated X (in this case designating the experimental variable, but in general representing the independent variable or variable set), the regression equation to be estimated is:

$$d = b_1 X + b_0 \tag{12.5}$$

Solving this using ordinary least squares will produce exactly the same results as the t-test. In this case, the coefficient of X (b_1) will be exactly 5 (the difference between the means of the two groups). The coefficient b_0 will be 1.1, the mean value for the control group. The standard error for the coefficient b_1 will be 2.11, the same as found for the t-test.

Interpretation and Limitations

Assuming that the experimental and control groups are basically subjected to the same external stimuli during the program period, the pretest-posttest control group design will be effective for controlling such extraneous sources of variation or external threats to validity as history, maturation, and other influences occurring at the same time of the study. This design will not control for the effect of having been sensitized to the posttest questions by having been initially subjected to these questions in the pretest. In a pretest-posttest control group design, both the experimental and the control subjects, as the data in Table 12.2 show, were administered a test on their knowledge of first aid procedures. The administration of this test in itself may have sensitized the experimental group to the important questions so that, as they viewed the film strip, they recognized and formulated answers to them. Thus, the film strip per se may not have been the cause of an improvement in their scores, but rather the combination of prior knowledge of the questions to be asked and the film strip.

Analysis of Multiple Group Pretest-Posttest Data (with Control Group)

The same type of analysis procedure demonstrated for one experimental and one control group can be extended to multiple experimental and control groups in the same format. It can be extended to a number of different groups that may be considered experimental in the sense that a type of program is introduced for the group, but that program is different for each group. The example given in Table 12.2 can be extended to include a second experimental group, perhaps one that received a lecture on emergency medical procedures rather than the film strip.

Suppose three groups of people were involved in the study, one group of ten would view the film strip, a second group of ten would receive a lecture, and the third group of ten acts as the control. A simple way to analyze data from such an experiment would be to treat the difference score as the dependent variable in the regression sense and to form two independent variables. The first independent variable, perhaps designated X_1, would be coded 1 for each person who saw the film strip and 0 for all others. The second independent variable (X_2) would be coded 1 for each person who received the lecture, and 0 otherwise. The regression equation corresponding to this model would be the following:

$$d = b_1X_1 + b_2X_2 + b_0 \qquad (12.6)$$

In this model, b_0 represents the mean for the control group, $b_0 + b_1$ represents the mean for the first experimental group, and $b_0 + b_2$ represents the mean for the second experimental group. One caveat must be made to this design: the t-test associated with each of the coefficients (i.e., the coefficient divided by its standard error) is a test of whether the group to which that coefficient corresponds is different from the omitted group (in this case, the control group). To determine if two experimental groups are different from one another, a second analysis would have to be run with one of the two experimental groups treated as the omitted group (i.e., the group for which no dummy variable is constructed), and the control group assigned a variable with a value 1 if the person was in the control group and a value 0 otherwise.

Analysis of Posttest-Only Data

A design that can solve all the problems presented by the pretest-posttest control group design but that avoids the difficulty of an interaction effect between the first stage of testing and the subsequent program itself is the posttest-only control group design. Again, consider efforts to evaluate the effectiveness of a film strip.

Illustration of the Analysis of Posttest-Only Data

Table 12.3 shows constructed data for a posttest-only control group experiment. Again, the data are the same as those under score 2 in Table 12.2 for the experimental and control groups. An important and necessary assumption of this design is that the 20 people under study were randomly assigned at the outset to either the experimental or the control group. In the case of the showing of the film strip, for example, 20 people may be selected to come to a meeting on a particular evening. After they have arrived, these 20 people could be assigned on a random basis either to the experimental or to the control group. This could be done, for example, by writing a 1 on ten slips of paper and a 2 on ten other slips of paper, mixing all these slips of paper in a container, and allowing each person to draw out one slip. This would be an acceptable method of randomly dividing the group for the purpose of having an experimental and a control group. The equations necessary for calculating a t-test for the significance of the difference

TABLE 12.3

Example of a Test of the Effectiveness of a Film Strip on Emergency First Aid Procedures: Posttest Only (with Control)

Program Group		Control Group	
Person	Score (Y_E)	Person	Score (Y_C)
1	9	11	11
2	8	12	14
3	15	13	9
4	19	14	6
5	18	15	12
6	19	16	8
7	17	17	14
8	19	18	16
9	10	19	4
10	12	20	2

$$\bar{Y}_E = \frac{\sum Y_E}{n_E} = 14.6$$

$$\bar{Y}_C = \frac{\sum Y_C}{n_C} = 9.6$$

$$S_{\bar{Y} \, pooled} = \sqrt{\left[\sum Y_E^2 - \frac{\left(\sum Y_E\right)^2}{n_E} + \sum Y_C^2 - \frac{\left(\sum Y_C\right)^2}{n_C}\right]\left(\frac{1}{n_E + n_C - 2}\right)\left(\frac{1}{n_E} + \frac{1}{n_C}\right)} = 2.03$$

between the experimental and control groups are shown at the bottom of Table 12.3. It should be noted that the formulas for $\overline{Y}_E$, $\overline{Y}_C$ and $s_{\bar{y}\text{pooled}}$ are the same formulas used in Table 12.2 to test the difference between the differences, the only change being the designation of Y as the score for the posttest rather than d for the difference between the pretest and posttest. A t-test for the significance of the difference between the scores is:

$$t = \frac{\overline{Y}_E - \overline{Y}_C}{s_{\bar{y}\text{pooled}}} = \frac{14.6 - 9.6}{2.03} = 2.46 \qquad (12.7)$$

Again, this is the same formula as given for the t-test for the difference between means of the two groups. This t-test has $n - 2$ degrees of freedom, where n is the total of both the experimental and control group. A t of 2.46 with 18 degrees of freedom is significant at the .05 level. The conclusion that would be drawn from these data is that, on the assumption of random assignment at the outset, the film strip was effective in producing a higher score, on the average, for the people who viewed it.

Replication of the t-Test Using Regression

The results of the preceding t-test can be replicated, as was the case with the pretest-posttest example, using regression. In a replication using regression, the posttest score for each person (Y) is the dependent variable. The independent variable is again represented by a single dummy variable coded 1 for the experimental group and coded 0 for the control group. Again designating the dummy variable X, the regression equation to be estimated is:

$$Y = b_1 X + b_0 \qquad (12.8)$$

Solving this using ordinary least squares will again produce the same results as the t-test. In this case, the coefficient of $X(b_1)$ will be 5—the difference between the means of the two groups. The coefficient b_0 will be 9.6, the mean value for the control group. The standard error for the coefficient b_1 will be 2.03, the same as found for the t-test.

Interpretation and Limitations

The posttest only control group design solves all the problems of extraneous sources of variation or external threats to validity such as history, maturation, and other influences occurring at the same time of the study as long as no other interventions are taking place at the same time. In addition, this design controls for the interaction between a pretest and the subsequent introduction of the experimental stimulus, because there is no pretest. When implemented as a double-blind study, this posttest-only design is the most powerful technique for controlling all sources of external invalidity. In addition, convincing evaluation subjects to participate in a study if the assessment is only one shot, as compared to a pretest and posttest design, is relatively easier.

Extension of the Experimental Model: Analysis of Covariance

Analysis of covariance was discussed in Chapter 8 as being relevant to the survey setting. This analysis is also relevant to the experimental setting.

The evaluator may have more information than simply the results of the test of interest. For example, in an assessment of a particular type of diet on weight loss, a researcher may have additional information about both the experimental and control subjects such as age, sex, height, and physical activity. All of these may affect the extent to which weight loss may occur given a particular type of diet. The evaluation in this case could be treated statistically as an analysis of covariance. Analysis of covariance can be carried out quite simply using regression. The regression model may be as follows:

$$W_2 = b_1X + b_2W_1 + b_3A + b_4S + b_5H + b_6PA + b_0 \qquad (12.9)$$

where:

- W_2 is weight at the end of the study;
- W_1 is weight at the beginning of the study;
- X is the experimental dummy variable;
- A is age;
- S is sex;
- H is height; and
- PA is physical activity.

This model will show the independent effect of the experimental variable while holding constant the other factors that may affect weight. The coefficient b_1 is the difference between the mean value of the control group and the mean value of the experimental group, net of the other factors. If this value is more than twice as large as its standard error, the effect of the experimental intervention is statistically significant at about .05.

Illustration of Analysis of Covariance

As a simple illustration, the data shown in Table 12.2 can also be treated in an analysis of covariance format. Instead of calculating a difference score between the first and second testings for the experimental group and two testings for the control group and then testing the difference between these difference scores, the analysis of covariance approach can be used directly to test the effect of the program. This can be done by treating the score received on the second testing as a dependent variable and regressing it on the score received on the first testing. In addition, the model tested would include a dummy variable coded 1 if the observation is for a person in the experimental group and 0 for a person in the control group.

If such an analysis is carried out, the format would be as shown in Equation 12.10, where S_2 is the estimate of the score in the second testing, S_1 is the actual first testing score, and *D* represents the experimental control dummy. The result of an analysis of covariance of this type is precisely the same as that of the differences in means test as shown in Equation 12.4. The coefficients from the analysis are shown in Equation 12.11. A test of the coefficient on the dummy variable in Equation 12.11 is essentially the same as the test of the difference in mean differences shown in Equation 12.4 and produces precisely the same conclusion.

$$S_2 = b_1 S_1 + b_2 D + b_0 \qquad (12.10)$$

$$S_2 = 0.45 S_1 + 5.00 D + 5.75 \qquad (12.11)$$

Standard errors for Equation 12.11 are equal to .23, 1.89, and 2.37 respectively.

The evaluator could select either the *t*-test of differences or the analysis of covariance strategy for the analysis of the type of data shown in Table 12.2 with exactly the same results.

Interaction and Non-Random Selection

Analysis of covariance can be extended to examine the possibility of interaction effects between the experimental variable and some or all of the covariates. If the researcher studying the effect of a particular diet program on weight felt that the relationship between, for example, age and weight may be different for the experimental group than for the control group, this could be modeled by including a variable that represents the multiplication of the experimental dummy by age. The resulting variable would be 0 for all people in the control group and the same as age for all people in the experimental group.

The addition of this variable to the model shown in the preceding prediction of weight would detect this possible interaction effect if it existed. Similarly, interaction effects can be included for any of the other control variables with the experimental variable if there is a reason to do so. The problem with this strategy is that each new interaction examined adds one variable and reduces the degrees of freedom in the analysis. Further, because a high degree of correlation is likely to exist between interaction terms and the original variables they represent, standard errors can become inflated when interaction terms are added, especially with small samples. Thus, examining interaction effects is probably not a good idea, unless a compelling theoretical reason exists to do so.

As was discussed in Chapter 8, analysis of covariance can also be used to ameliorate, to an extent, the undesirable effects of non-random selection. In general, it is assumed even with the pretest-posttest designs that the subjects are assigned to the experimental variable randomly. In many cases, however, this is simply not practical. In many settings, evaluators are forced to accept groups of people that were selected in a non-random manner. If the evaluation focuses on institutions or political areas such as counties, random selection may be totally out of the question. Frequently, evaluators are asked to assess naturally occurring experiments where no opportunity for assignment of the intervention exists. In such situations, analysis of covariance offers a possibility of rescuing what would otherwise be an impossible evaluation situation.

If analysis of covariance is to be used to try to rescue an evaluation where assignment is non-random, the most effective strategy would be to have measures on any of the potential covariates that may reasonably be expected to affect the outcome of the evaluation. In the example of the effect of diet on weight, previous weight, age, sex, height, and physical activity may be the entire list of important covariates; in other settings, the list may be substantially longer. If the number of observations is small, the adding of covariates will again present problems of degrees of freedom. However, if the evaluator cannot control assignment to the intervention, analysis of covariance is one of the few mechanisms available to solve the problem of assessing the effect of the experimental variable.

Application in Field Situations

The designs and data analysis presented above are quite simple compared to the number of complex experimental designs available. Moreover, the analysis of data from these designs has been given strictly in terms of tests of differences between means, or t-tests. Although this is the first level of analysis of variance, the data have not been subjected to true analysis of variance—even though they could be—because of the relatively straightforward and simple nature of the results sought.

Experimental designs can be, and often are, much more complicated than those shown here. Presenting more complicated designs seems unnecessary, however, because few evaluators are likely to find themselves in a position in a real-life situation to institute any experiment much more complicated than those presented here. In fact, many program evaluators are likely to be in a situation in which they must evaluate an entire program on the basis of a single output measure, rather than having data for a large number of people relative to the results of the program. Such a problem may preclude the use of any statistical analysis.

Illustration of Problems with a Single Output Measure

Suppose that, after the pretest or posttest, a person wishing to evaluate the effectiveness of the film strip received not an individual score for each of ten people but a total score for all ten people in the experimental group and all ten in a control group. With no more information than this, it would be impossible to determine whether the difference between the two groups was a significant one in any statistical sense. The evaluator would only be able to make statements such as that the difference between the two groups is large or small, or important for substantive reasons.

To further illustrate from an evaluation standpoint, consider again the data shown in Table 12.3. If no more were known about these data than the program group score of 146 points and the control group score of 96 points (or mean scores of 14.6 and 9.6, respectively), no statistical test of the difference between the two groups can be made. The ability to determine whether the groups are actually different from a statistical standpoint depends on knowledge of their variation.

Consider further the constructed data in Table 12.4. In Example 1 the program and control groups show the maximum amount of variation possible in a test where the mean scores remain 14.6 and 9.6, and where the individual scores may range from 0 to 20. Among those in the program group, seven scored a 20, one person scored a 6, and two people each scored 0. In the control group, four people scored 20, one person scored 16, and five people scored 0. The difference between the means of the two groups is still 5. (The program group has a total score of 146 and the control group has a total score of 96.) The pooled standard error for the two groups is 4.45, calculated by the formula at the bottom of Table 12.3. The t statistic for the comparison is 1.12. Such a t value is not statistically significant, so the conclusion is that no difference exists between the program and control groups on the basis of the statistical analysis.

The data in Example 2 of Table 12.4 show just the opposite picture. In this case, the minimum possible variance exists, for a total score of 146 for the program group and a total of 96 for the control group. Again, the difference between the means remains 5, but the pooled variance, as calculated by using the formula at the bottom of Table 12.3, is 0.23. This gives a t statistic of 21.65, which is significant at any level. Clearly it is necessary to know something about the variation in the group or groups to be compared if any statement about statistical significance is to be made.

Type I and Type II Error

In Table 12.4, Example 2, it was possible to conclude that a statistically significant difference existed between the control group and the group that viewed the film strip. The mean difference score between the two groups is 5, which when divided by the pooled standard error of .23 resulted in a t value that would appear much less often than 5 percent of the time by chance alone. If .05 is the significance level accepted, the conclusion is that viewing the film strip made a

TABLE 12.4
Two Possible Data Strings for Mean Scores of 14.6 and 9.6

| Example 1 | | | | Example 2 | | | |
| Program | | Control | | Program | | Control | |
Person	Score	Person	Score	Person	Score	Person	Score
1	20	11	20	1	15	11	10
2	20	12	20	2	15	12	10
3	20	13	20	3	15	13	10
4	20	14	20	4	15	14	10
5	20	15	16	5	15	15	10
6	20	16	0	6	15	16	10
7	20	17	0	7	14	17	9
8	6	18	0	8	14	18	9
9	0	19	0	9	14	19	9
10	0	20	0	10	14	20	9

difference in performance on the posttest, and thus probably increased the knowledge of the viewers about emergency first aid procedures.

In Example 1 in Table 12.4, however, to say that the people who viewed the film strip have more knowledge of emergency medical procedures than those who did not is not possible. This is not on the basis of the mean difference between the two groups (which remains 5), but rather on the basis of the greater variation within the two groups, and hence the much larger standard error. Would the conclusion that viewing the film strip did not make any difference in performance on the test (and, thus, did not make any difference in knowledge) be justifiable? Peculiarly, the answer is *not necessarily*. To try to understand why this is so, discussing type I and type II error is necessary.

Type I error is relatively familiar to most users of statistics. It is the probability of making the error that, for example, the program group is different from the control group when in fact it is not. To avoid this error, the confidence limit is set at .05 or .01, or another very low level. Doing this poses the risk that in .05 (1 chance in 20) or .01 (1 chance in 100) of the chances, the conclusion that two groups are different will be erroneous.

Then a single test is conducted: one group of ten people who have seen a film strip is compared to another group of ten people who have not. The result produces a *t*-test with a probability beyond, for example, the .05 limit, as in the case of Table 12.4, Example 2. In this case, this single test is assumed to *not* be the 1 in 20 that would give a *t* value this large when the groups were really not different. However, the nature of statistics is such that we will never be absolutely certain that the two groups are different regardless of the size of the *t* value calculated; there is always chance for a type I error.

Type II error is the obverse of type I error. (Many people who use statistics will have an understanding of type II error.) Type II error is the probability of making the error that the program group is *not* different from the control group when in fact it is. In Example 1 in Table 12.4, the *t*-test leads us to reject the conclusion that the two groups are different, and hence that the conclusion that the film strip made a difference. In drawing this conclusion, however, there is the risk of type II error, and in this case that risk is much larger than .05.

Figure 12.1 is a portrayal of the problem of type II error in regard to the comparison in Table 12.4, Example 1. Figure 12.1 shows two normal distributions, one with a mean at 9.6 (i.e., the mean score for the control group) and the other with a mean at 14.6 (i.e., the mean score for the group that viewed the film strip). The .05 level of statistical significance for the distribution with a mean of 9.6 is shown as line A. Line A is two standard deviations from the mean of 9.6 (i.e., the approximate number of standard errors that includes 95 percent of all possible sample means). To the right of line A is an arrow pointing in the direction of type I error. The .05 refers to that portion of the area under the curve centered at 9.6 that is to the right of line A. To the left of line A is an arrow pointing in the direction of type II error. The .75 refers to that portion of the area under the curve centered at 14.6 that is to the left of line A. Type I error is in

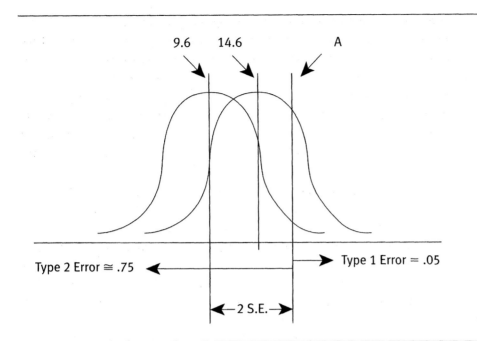

FIGURE 12.1

Type I and Type II Error for Data in Table 12.4, Example 1

regard to the distribution around 9.6, but type II error is with regard to the distribution around 14.6.

The distribution around 14.6 indicates that if a very large number of samples were drawn of a size equivalent to the sample that produced the original standard error value from a population in which the true population mean was 14.6, the distribution of the means for the samples would look like the distribution shown for 14.6 in Figure 12.1. If this were the case, however, about 75 percent of the time a value for the mean of the sample that did not exceed the .05 level for a mean of 9.6 would be derived, even when the true mean of the population from which the sample was drawn was 14.6. In this case, a .75 probability of making the type II error exists—assuming that the intervention had no effect when in fact it did.

In the realm of science, avoiding the type I error is most important. A scientist would be more likely to fear the possibility of mistakenly concluding that an experiment showed something new when in fact it had not over the alternative of assuming nothing had happened when it had. In the realm of evaluation, however, the choice is not necessarily so clear. Suppose a program intervention is tested against an earlier strategy and both of these interventions are equally costly. In such a case, it may be reasonable not to make a decision about the efficacy of the new program intervention on the basis of one—or several—negative results, but rather to wait for additional information before making a decision. In essence, in many evaluation settings avoiding the type II error would be better than avoiding the type I error.

A reasonable question, of course, is whether making both errors at the same time can be avoided. The answer is yes, but at a price. The price is the cost of carrying out the assessment on larger samples. The data in Table 12.4, discussed previously, is for a sample of 20 people, ten in the program group and ten in the control group. Decreasing type II error while maintaining the .05 type I error is possible by increasing the number of observations in the evaluation.

For example, if the number of people in both the program and control groups in Table 12.4, Example 1 were increased to 80, but the same proportion of responses were retained, the pooled standard error becomes 2.04, because of the increased sample size. The result is shown in Figure 12.2: much narrower distributions around the means of 9.6 and 14.6. This figure also shows line A (two standard errors from 9.6) between the mean of 9.6 and the mean of 14.6. Rather than concluding that the program has had no effect, because of the increased sample size, the conclusion is that the program did have an effect.

The chance of a type II error occurring has also been reduced. If the real effect of the film strip was to produce on average a score of 14.6 for those people who viewed it, the line A is now positioned relative to the distribution around 14.6 in such a way that about 35 percent of the distribution is in the area of type II error. By increasing the sample size, the likelihood of finding a statistically significant difference between the two groups has increased, and the possibility of falsely concluding that no difference exists has decreased. However, the possibility of a type II error occurring remains quite large in this case. To further reduce the possibility, the sample size would have to be increased even more. Increases in sample size have diminishing returns. Standard error generally decreases in proportion to the square root of the increase in the sample size.

A solution to the problem posed by type II error, when simply ignoring the type I error is not an option, is to increase the sample size. In the evaluation of a film strip, this may be feasible. If the units under evaluation were counties in

FIGURE 12.2

Type I and Type II Error for Data in Table 12.4, Example 1 with Sample Size of 80

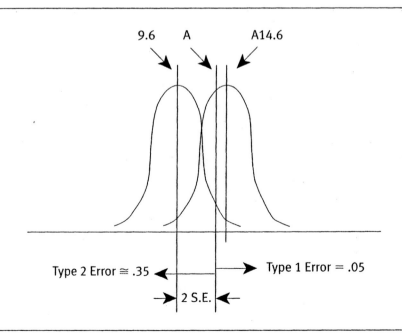

a state, however, this may be impossible. In such a case, and particularly if the program intervention is of low cost relative to the alternative, the evaluator must confront the question of whether the error to be avoided is type I or type II.

Analysis of Variance

The examples discussed here are likely to be as complex as most evaluators will see in program evaluation settings. As we have seen, evaluations of this degree of complexity can be adequately analyzed by using t-tests or regression to assess the significance of the differences between means. Evaluators should be aware, however, that much more sophisticated experimental designs exist and can be analyzed using a family of techniques referred to as analysis of variance. In an earlier version of this text analysis of variance was treated in some detail, but the present view of the authors is that analysis of variance is likely to be beyond the needs of most evaluation applications. To learn more about analysis of variance in assessing results of experiments, refer to Winer (1991).

Discussion Questions

1. What are the necessary and sufficient conditions to show program effect? Why are these conditions difficult to achieve in field situations?
2. In an experimental setting, what choice may an evaluator make between the use of the t-test as opposed to regression analysis in randomly assigned groups? in non-randomly assigned groups?
3. Discuss the difference between how a scientist and an evaluator may look at the issue of significance testing, especially in regard to type I and type II errors.
4. How well do the statistical tests of significance generally compensate for poorly designed experiments (e.g., ones in which random assignment has not occurred)?

VII

BASIC METHODS

13

GENERAL MEASUREMENT ISSUES

Our ability to evaluate, let alone manage, depends on our ability to measure accurately those items that are to be assessed—regardless of the particular type of evaluation strategy involved. In a monitoring strategy, for example, the evaluator is attempting to compare existing progress between the initiation and the implementation of a program with planned or projected criteria. The ability to accurately measure the extent to which progress toward these criteria is being achieved is precisely the problem in an evaluation of progress.

Similarly, a survey research effort to describe a problem or an analytical evaluation of the effect of different program strategies will succeed or fail on the basis of the ability to accurately measure those things that are to be assessed as part of the evaluation. If time series analysis or trend analysis is being used as the evaluation strategy, the ability to measure changes in important variables under assessment as time changes is again critical to the evaluation effort. If the measurement device used in such a situation is insensitive to changes over time, the evaluation cannot succeed.

In the experimental setting, any evaluation will only be as useful as the evaluator's ability to accurately measure program effects that may occur. If these effects cannot be measured, the evaluation will not indicate any program success. Even in the case study approach to evaluation, measurement remains an important component of the process. The objective of this chapter is to examine the subject of measurement and describe procedures used to develop measures of variables important to program evaluation and thus improved decision making. As often stated, "If you can't measure it you can't manage it."

What Is Measurement?

Measurement is the assignment of one set of entities—generally numerical values—to another set of entities—generally empirical facts or phenomena. In any measurement effort there is a set of rules by which the numerical values are assigned to the empirical entities. Measurement is the process of assigning the numerical values according to the established set of rules. Different sets of rules or methods for the assignment process have certain advantages or disadvantages. Consider something as simple as measuring the size of an organization.

Illustration: The Case of Organizational Size (Kaluzny and Veney 1980)

Suppose that an evaluation requires determining the relationship between organizational size and a measure of organizational design or performance. Focusing only on size, certain organizations are clearly larger than others, but the notion of larger is an abstract concept that the evaluator must translate into concrete terms. The total dollar value of the organization may be used as a measure for translating size from the abstract to the concrete, for instance. If that is the operational measure of size, the evaluator may be able to obtain the data from the records of the organization or from a regulatory agency. The operational definition of size may be the total area of the physical plant, however. Such data may be available from organization records.

Perhaps the most common definition of size used in organizational research is the number of employees. Assume that the evaluator has decided to put into operation the abstract notion of size as the number of employees in each organization. The question then becomes, What method does the researcher use to assign a numerical value to each organization to represent the empirical reality of the total number of organizational employees? At the most basic level, the evaluator will probably decide to treat each employee in each organization as adding equally to the organization's score for size and simply sum up the number of individuals who work for each organization. It is unlikely that the CEO, for example, will count more than one of the people in the mailroom in assessing size. An equally basic question, however, is how the evaluator will determine the number of workers in each organization.

Assume that the evaluator decides to apply the following method for assigning a score for each organization: The evaluator will stand outside the organization at quitting time and, as the people who work there come out, each one will be counted. On the basis of this process or this set of rules, the evaluator can assign a score to each organization, representing its size as determined by number of employees.

While this is a relatively unobtrusive mechanism for assigning a size to an organization, a consultant to the evaluator may legitimately point out that this measurement tool (i.e., this set of rules for assigning a score for organizational size) has inherent problems. All individuals employed in a given organization may not leave at the standard quitting time, for instance, and the people seen leaving the organization may not all be employees. Some employees may be ill or on vacation the day of the assessment. If the organization has more than one place to exit, counting all the people coming out would be difficult. The problems of measurement using this technique would be multiplied further if the organization happened to be in a major office building in a large city where employees from many organizations may leave work at the same time.

Based on these concerns, the evaluator may decide to employ a different measurement technique. The vice president for operations may be interviewed and asked for the total number of employees in the organization. The answer will serve as the evaluator's measure of size. This may be the least expensive mechanism for assigning a measure of size to each organization. The consultant, however, may again criticize the evaluator's choice of a measurement device. The consultant may say, for example, that the vice president for operations may not really know how many employees the organization has, or may know but may have rounded the answer. Possibly, an organization that has fewer employees may receive a score larger than another organization with more employees.

Finally, the consultant may suggest to the evaluator that the latter go to the personnel office and interview the personnel manager. At the personnel office the personnel manager would be asked if the evaluator could go through the files to determine how many active employees there are in the organization. This approach, although cumbersome and expensive, may provide the most nearly correct indication of the organization's size, as indicated by number of employees. There are problems inherent even in this approach. Possibly, on a particular day, personnel records—for example, of individuals recently hired—may not yet be in the files.

In this example, three methods are suggested for assigning a number to organization size: counting people as they leave work; interviewing the vice president for operations; and reviewing personnel records. Each measurement tool provides a way of assigning a number to an organization, but each rule has limitations relative to the others. Selecting a given measurement device is always a trade-off between the ease with which the rule can be applied and several important characteristics of any measurement, which are examined in the following section.

Characteristics of Measurement

All measurements have several characteristics that are of concern in any evaluation setting. These characteristics include quantification, scale, unidimensionality, reliability, validity, sensitivity, reproducibility, and transferability. The evaluator should be aware of the importance of each characteristic in the use of the measure and in its value for the evaluation task.

Quantification

The most important characteristic of measurement is its ability to quantify phenomena of interest. Certain phenomena are relatively easy to quantify, while others are much more difficult. What may be subject to measurement as part of an evaluation could be classified as:

- physical states and occurrences;
- performance, behavior, or practices; and
- attitudes, beliefs, perceptions, and knowledge.

Of these three categories, those phenomena that can be considered physical states or occurrences are probably most easily measured and quantified. Occurrences, such as births and deaths, accidents, the completion of a building, or the purchase of a quantity of drugs, are all relatively easily measured and quantified. Physical states, such as the existence of disease, numbers of facilities available, or mosquitoes in a given area, are also relatively easily measured and quantified.

Less easily quantified are performances, behaviors, or practices—such items as the amount of money budgeted and spent, numbers of houses sprayed for mosquitoes, the extent of the use of a particular type of contraceptive, or disease averted by a practice or activity.

Perhaps the most difficult phenomena to quantify are attitudes, beliefs, knowledge, and perceptions. Attitudes, beliefs, knowledge, or perceptions toward birth control, the use of primary care clinics, physician assistants, or toward any type of program that may be of interest will always be the most difficult phenomena to quantify. Much of the literature on measurement is devoted to quantification of attitudes, beliefs, knowledge, and perceptions.

Scale of Measurement

Measurement can occur along four basic dimensions or scales. In terms of quantification it is useful to discuss briefly the nature of these scales. The simplest scale of measurement—the *nominal scale*—does not represent quantification at all; it simply classifies. In a nominal scale only a distinction between similar or dissimilar items is made. Nominal scales provide such information as A equals B or A is not equal to B (Miller 1991). Nominal scales may include sex and racial classification, job title, marital status, hospital control, type of organization, or any of a number of other types of measures that simply name the members.

The first of the four scales actually to represent quantification is the ordinal scale. In the ordinal scale, the information A equals B or A does not equal B is available, as well as the information that A is greater than B or A is less than B. In the category of ordinal scales physical states or occurrences may be measured, such as a disease exists or does not exist, a birth has taken place or has not taken place, an accident has occurred or has not occurred, or a facility exists or does not exist. These are all ordinal categories in the sense that the occurrence of an accident or the existence of a facility shows more or less program success than would the opposite.

If the categories were irrelevant relative to program success, a measurement like disease exists or does not exist could be considered a nominal scale only. If disease status has a consequence for the program, however, it must be considered an ordinal measurement. In every instance it will be true that the absence of disease is preferable to the presence of disease, so that a measure that classifies persons on the basis of presence or absence of disease could be treated as an ordinal (ordered) scale. In terms of performance, acts, and practices, ordinal categories may, for example, be used to classify frequency of occurrence. The event (i.e., use of contraceptives, occurrence of an accident, or visits to a clinic) occurs never, sometimes, often, or always.

A common measure of attitudes, beliefs, or perceptions is the five- or seven-point scale. People for whom measures of attitudes, for instance, are desired will be asked whether they strongly disagree with a given statement, disagree with it, are undecided about it, agree with it, or strongly agree with it. This is an ordinal scale. Strongly disagreeing is different from, and in a sense is less than or greater than, disagreeing, which is less than or greater than being undecided, and so on.

With an *interval scale*, not only is there an order to the possible positions that a scale can take, but these positions also are equidistant from one another. For example, if four consecutive points on the scale were denoted A, B, C, and D, the distance from A to B is equal to the distance from B to C, which is equal to the distance from C to D.

The fourth and most sophisticated type of scale is the *ratio scale*. On a ratio scale, the points are ordered and spaced at equidistant intervals, and if A and B are two points on a scale and A times B equals C, then C divided by B equals A. A ratio scale is one on which multiplication and division, as well as all other mathematical operations, can be performed. This situation assumes a real zero point in the scale.

In general, quantifying a measurement on a ratio scale is better than doing so on an interval scale. Quantifying a measurement on an interval scale is better than on an ordinal scale, and an ordinal scale is generally preferred to a nominal scale. A ratio scale or interval scale is likely to be more precise than an ordinal scale in the ability to indicate the extent to which a quantified measure is greater or less than another quantified measure. The mathematical operations of addition and subtraction also have a real meaning with both interval and ratio scales, and both multiplication and division have a real meaning with quantification on a ratio scale. Further, most statistical techniques are simplified when measurement is at the interval or ratio level.

Looking again at the three types of attributes that may be measured as part of a program evaluation effort, certain aspects of these three categories may be measured on ratio scales, on interval scales, and on ordinal scales. Many occurrences of interest in program evaluation, for example, can be quite readily quantified on a true ratio scale.

If the interest is in evaluating a program in different areas, then number of births, deaths, accidents occurring, facilities available, or people with a specific disease state are all measures easily quantified on a ratio scale. In the area of performances, acts, and practices, quantifying activities on a ratio scale is also relatively easy. Numbers of dollars budgeted or spent, immunizations given, contraceptives dispensed or numbers of women using birth control pills, and cases of cholera identified are all items that can be quantified on a ratio scale.

In the area of attitudes, beliefs, and perceptions, it is less clear that ratio scales can be successfully developed. A common approach to measuring attitudes is the five-point scale or continuum ranging from strongly agree to strongly disagree that was mentioned above. This scale is nearly always translated to a numerical scale by scoring 1 for strongly disagree, 2 for disagree, and so on to 5 for strongly agree. In most practical applications the five-point scale is considered ratio (e.g., it is not uncommon to see means calculated for such responses), or at least interval, in measurement, but in reality such a scale may be only ordinal. The perceptual or attitudinal difference between strongly disagree and disagree is not necessarily the same as the perceptual or attitudinal difference between, for example, disagree and undecided.

In the United States, where attitude assessment has become very common, the accepted perception may be that the distances in a five-point attitude scale are equivalent, and that perception may be acted on in response to such items. In other cultures, however, that perception need not be true. In fact, it has been suggested that many languages exist in which the distinction between agree and strongly agree, for example, cannot even be made. Such scales may need to be treated as ordinal measures only in many settings.

Several strategies are available for attempting to raise the level of sophistication of five-point attitude scales from ordinal to interval. The most common approach is to combine a number of similar attitude statements or perceptual statements into a single composite score, using, for example, a technique like item-to-scale correlation or factor analysis. It can be claimed with some credibility that scores derived from the combination of a number of attitude or perceptual items will result in an interval scale. We will discuss the use of item-to-scale correlation and factor analysis for measurement in evaluation later in the chapter. Raising the quantification of attitude or perceptual items to the ratio level of measurement is generally not possible.

Unidimensionality

The characteristic of unidimensionality essentially assures that a numerical value assigned to any particular phenomenon to represent a point on a measurement scale will be assigned to one and only one real world state. Consider two statements that may be used to evaluate a particular service program:

1. The resources of this program have been used in an efficient manner.
2. This program has been effective in reaching its goals.

People involved in the program could be asked to respond to these two questions on a five-point scale from strongly agree to strongly disagree. Each measure could be used individually as an ordinal scale of perceptions about the program. Frequently, however, evaluators may wish to treat both responses in a single composite score. A simple, straightforward way of producing such a composite score would be to add together the responses of each person on each of these two questions. The resulting scale would range, for example, from two, which indicates a strongly disagree response on both questions, to ten, indicating a strongly agree response to both questions.

Problems of multidimensionality do not arise for those people who answer both questions in the same way. The person who believes that the program has been both inefficient and ineffective, for instance, can respond with a strongly disagree or disagree to both statements. If someone is undecided about both questions, that person may respond with an undecided for both, or those people who agree with both statements can respond accordingly. At this level there are no problems of multidimensionality. The scores for all people of this type will be basically unidimensional because the responses represent essentially the same perception by each person on both questions.

Problems of multidimensionality arise if a respondent believes that the program has been efficient in using resources in the best manner possible but has been ineffective in producing the results expected. A similar type of problem could arise, however, if the respondent felt the program had been effective but had used its resources inefficiently. In either case, a respondent may answer strongly disagree to one of the statements and strongly agree to the other, for a total summed score of 6. A score of 6 represents any of five substantially different response patterns: a strongly disagree to the statement on efficiency and a strongly agree to the one on effectiveness; an agree on efficiency and a disagree on effectiveness; the reverse of either of these first two; or no opinion on either. In short, scores in the midrange of the scale can be multidimensional.

Such problems of multidimensionality can be controlled to a great extent by using techniques like item-to-scale correlation or factor analysis when a number of measures are brought together in a summed or cumulative scale. The application of such techniques to measurement is presented in the sections on item to scale correlation and factor analysis.

It should be realized that it is not simply attitudes, beliefs, knowledge, or perceptions that may produce logically multidimensional scales. Many health programs have as their ultimate aim the improvement of health status. Measurement of health status is difficult because it is, in itself, a multidimensional concept. The best-known definition of health is that of the World Health Organization (WHO): "Health is not merely the absence of disease but rather a state of complete physical, mental, and social well-being." Suppose a composite measure were devised that attempted to quantify health according to physical, mental, and social well-being simultaneously. In this case, many people would probably be at substantially different points on the three different continua and in the midranges of the composite (where a number of different mixes of physical, mental, and social well-being would produce the same numerical result), and the scale clearly would be multidimensional.

A similar type of problem of multidimensionality can occur from an entirely different source. Such a seemingly straightforward measure as number of accidents occurring in an area or within a period of time is, for certain purposes (such as gross enumeration), unidimensional. However, that unidimensional scale carries within itself a completely different and quite multidimensional set of attributes related to the type and severity of the accidents. An occurrence that may be considered an accident for the purpose of accumulating gross numbers may be much less consequential in terms of disability, disablement, handicap, or death than another occurrence that would also be considered an accident for the purpose of gross numbers. However, the consequence of this difference for behavior, perceptions, activities, and particularly for program evaluation may be quite important.

The same type of statement can be made about the existence of disease: Certain types of diseases are more life threatening, more debilitating, or more handicapping than other types and yet may be counted together in a single measure of the incidence or prevalence of disease. A measure that shows only the number of facilities available may carry within it an inherent measure of their quality. A measure that indicates the number of women accepting a contraceptive practice may carry within it an inherent multidimensionality of the extent to which the women adhere to the appropriate contraceptive practices. Qualifications of this sort in regard to the unidimensionality of measurement can be seen in almost any area of measurement. Although impossible, even under the best circumstances, to specify precisely what is being measured in every instance, it is important to be aware of these types of multidimensionality problems in any evaluation effort.

Validity and Reliability

Validity refers to the extent to which the measurement device being used actually taps or represents reality. *Reliability* is the extent to which the measurement tool will produce the same result when used more than once to measure precisely the same phenomenon.

Though validity and reliability are always discussed together, they are quite different concepts. A measuring device may produce a result that is highly reliable in that every time it is used to measure the same thing it produces precisely the same result. This fact does not guarantee, however, that a measure is valid, that it actually taps reality, or that differences assigned to different observations on the measurement scale actually reflect true differences along the dimension the measuring scale is assumed to gauge. The extent to which a measure is either valid or reliable is not easily assessed. Certain guidelines and suggestions for the assessment of validity and reliability can be made, however.

Validity Validity can be evaluated on two grounds (Kerlinger 1973): *content validity* (also called *face validity*), and *criterion validity*. A third type of validity assessment, usually termed *construct validity*, is sometimes considered. Construct validity is simply a combination of content and criterion validity, so only the characteristics of the two pure types are discussed in this section.

Content validity is an assessment of whether the measure being used to describe a real-world phenomenon seems to be describing that phenomenon. A physical examination, including an electrocardiogram, would be a more valid measure of the clinical existence of heart disease than the self-report of the same person before the examination. The report of a woman about her use of oral contraceptives is likely to have greater validity than the report of her husband. The report of a patient about his or her attitude toward services received in a cancer clinic is likely to have more validity than the report of a third party.

Content validity actually has two aspects. The first aspect is that the measuring device is directed toward the item to be measured—in a sense, a relatively simple and straightforward problem. Agreeing that a measure of the incidence or prevalence of cardiovascular disease is a valid component of a measure of health status would be easy. A measure of the incidence or prevalence of cardiovascular disease as a valid component of a measure of quality of life may also be considered.

Content or face validity has a second aspect, which is concerned with the extent to which the measurement device actually assesses the entire content area of the phenomenon being measured. If, for example, health status is being measured and is perceived to be a multidimensional phenomenon, the prevalence or incidence of cardiovascular disease is only one single and perhaps relatively minor component of the phenomenon. Ways of assessing a much broader range of physical states and occurrences would be required before the claim could be made that a measure of health status that had content or face validity exists. In terms of unidimensionality of measures, several related but independent measures of health status should be developed.

Despite the difficulty of ensuring that a measure being applied to a particular real-world phenomenon as complex as health status has content validity, the content validity remains an important criterion for assessing the validity of various types of measurements. A measure of health that contains no assessment of disease processes will be immediately questioned on the basis of content validity, for example. A measure of the use of contraceptives based on a series of questions about attitudes or beliefs about contraceptives would be equally questionable from the standpoint of content validity. Content validity assessments should undoubtedly be made about any measure that is devised.

Criterion validity tackles the issue of whether the current measure of the phenomenon produces results that are closely related to other independent measures of the same phenomenon that are believed—generally on the basis of content validity—to be valid. Criterion validity is less concerned with whether the measuring device is logically a measure of the real-world phenomenon being described or whether the entire content of that phenomenon is assessed.

WHO, recognizing that the health status of a person, community, or country, for instance, is a difficult trait to measure with a great deal of content validity, has suggested that a useful measure of health status for communities or nations could be a combination of infant and child mortality, maternal mortality, and age-specific mortality.

If health is not the absence of disease but also the complete physical, mental, and social well-being that WHO suggests, several categories of mortality are not going to be valid measures of health when content validity is the criterion. However, these measures will be closely associated with what WHO perceives to be health from a broad systems standpoint and hence show criterion validity.

Criterion validity is generally assessed by using a technique such as correlation to determine the extent to which a measure that could be used for assessing a group of phenomena is correlated or related to another measure. The validity of a measure of health status based on a self-report of perceived health level on a ten-point scale, for instance, could be assessed by drawing a small random sample of those people who responded to the self-assessment and giving them an extensive physical examination. The physician's assessment of health after the examination could be compared to and correlated with the initial self-assessment to determine the extent to which the two assessments correlate. If the two were highly correlated, the self-assessment could serve as an inexpensive measure of health that had stood the test of criterion validity.

Reliability

Reliability refers to the extent to which a measuring device produces the same results on multiple applications to the same phenomenon. If, for example, we want to measure the number of health facilities available in different areas, the measuring device should include a definition of what a facility is. If this definition is loose enough or limited enough so that the person counting the facilities has substantial freedom in determining what is a health facility and what is not, different people trying to count the number of facilities in the same area realistically may come up with widely different results.

In the late 1960s, after the passage of Medicare, at least three different organizations actively maintained records of hospitals in the United States: the American Hospital Association, the Blue Cross Association, and the federal government. The American Hospital Association had an active list of about 6,000 hospitals. Because of a slight difference in how hospitals were defined, the Blue Cross Association maintained a list of about 7,000, but the federal government, because of still different definitional criteria, maintained a list of about 12,000 hospitals. It would be easy to see that if several individuals were told simply to count the hospitals in the United States, they may produce widely different results, based on how they decided to determine whether a particular facility was a hospital.

Determining reliability

An obvious way to assess the reliability of a measuring tool would be to take several measures of the same item and compare the results. In certain evaluation efforts this step would not be difficult. A death would be counted as a death no matter how many times it is counted. Total dollars budgeted would probably be counted the same every time. Dollars expended in specific categories, however, may change, depending on the accounting system used. Numbers of certain types of facilities in an area may be the same every time they were counted, assuming that the definition of a facility were relatively precise. A woman's self-report on her use of contraceptives may change from time to time, however, because she failed to remember the original report or for other reasons. In the area of attitudes, beliefs, and perceptions, answers to the same questions may differ as a result of the respondent's mood, state of mind, or relative interest in participating in the survey, even though underlying perceptions had not, in fact, changed.

Problems exist with measuring the same item on more than one occasion. If something is measured that is not likely to change, such as death or birth, multiple measures are not necessary. Reliability would seem evident. If the measuring instrument is a question or attitude item, however, an effort to measure the phenomenon more than once could lead to an overestimation of reliability when people remember their previous answers and without thought provide them again, or to an underestimation of reliability if people become exasperated with the questions. The use of multiple tests of the same thing has led to the idea of a reliability test known as *split halves.* In this case, a number of questions all generally describing the same area would be asked and composite scores calculated on half the questions would be correlated with or compared to composite scores calculated on the other half.

A logical extension of the split-half technique is the multiple correlation between a number of items purporting to measure the same thing. If, for example, a cancer clinic is being evaluated and one area of concern is the attitude of clients, there may be a series of eight to ten questions all focused on the overall attitude toward clinic services. A measure of the reliability of this group of questions or items would be the multiple correlation between all the items. For a detailed discussion of this approach to the measurement of reliability, see Kaluzny and Veney (1980).

Validity and reliability have the interesting property that increasing one generally leads to decreasing the other. It is particularly true that to increase the reliability of a test or measuring device, additional items can be added to the measuring tool. If, for example, the measure of reliability consisted of five statements on perceptions about a cancer clinic program, reliability can be increased through the correlation technique by adding more items. At the same time, however, if the original five items are perceived to be relatively valid measures of attitude toward the clinic, the addition of five new items will decrease the overall validity of the total measure because they will tap additional dimensions of people's attitude toward the clinic. These conclusions can be shown mathematically but are beyond the scope of this discussion.

Increasing reliability

Sensitivity

Sensitivity refers to the ability of a measure to reflect changes in the state of the real-world phenomenon under evaluation. If the measures being employed in an evaluation are not relatively sensitive to changes in the real-world states, a particular program effort that has a true effect on the real-world state may be seen as ineffective. This situation could occur only because the measurement tool is not sensitive to changes in the real world.

To illustrate, WHO, as noted, has suggested as measures to evaluate the impact of primary healthcare efforts several categories of mortality—infant and child, maternal, and age-specific. A major problem with mortality as a measure, whether age- and sex-specific or simply mortality in general, is that it tends to be highly insensitive to changes in health status other than the gross change of death itself. If health is a function of mental, physical, and social well-being, many changes can take place in these categories of well-being that are never reflected in mortality data. A program like primary healthcare designed to affect and influence a wide range of health concerns or a wide spectrum of the health concept may have profound consequences for mental and social well-being and for certain aspects of physical well-being and not be reflected at all in changes in mortality.

Sensitivity is not simply a problem that can be identified as associated with such gross and fairly obvious differences as the difference between health and mortality, however. Measures may be closely related to real-world phenomena and perhaps appear to measure these phenomena, yet still have the problem of sensitivity—particularly measurements or attempts at measurement of attitudes, beliefs, or perceptions. A scale may be constructed of six or eight items related to how a person feels about a particular mental health clinic, for example. The items in the scale may be statements about the clinic to which people can respond on a five-point scale, strongly disagree to strongly agree.

People, however, are often unwilling to select extreme points on a scale as answers even though these extreme points may best reflect their perception. If these questions were directed at a number of people who had used a particular mental health center, they may be inclined to provide responses that differed very little as their perceptions of the clinic changed, when their real feelings toward the clinic may be quite different. In situations where measures are not sensitive to changes in real-world phenomena, the result will underestimate the effect of the program effort.

Reproducibility and Transferability

Both reproducibility and transferability are critical in measurement techniques whose purpose is discovering scientific knowledge but may be less important in evaluation. Nevertheless, it is appropriate to include a brief mention of them under the general subject of measurement.

Both reproducibility and transferability are components of reliability. *Reproducibility* refers specifically to the extent to which a given researcher or evaluator can reproduce measures used in one setting to apply to the same phenomenon in other settings. For example, an index of perception about medical services developed in the United States for application to U.S. citizens may be of little value if a similar program is to be evaluated in a different setting, such as within a developing nation. The extent to which an evaluator can take a measure that has been developed to provide an assessment in one setting and reproduce similar results in another setting is a result of the reproducibility of the measure.

Transferability may be considered a similar characteristic. The distinction between reproducibility and transferability centers on the uses of the measuring device. The issue for reproducibility is whether a given evaluator can use the same measuring tools in differing settings, whereas in transferability the issue is whether other evaluators can use the measuring tool and use it in similar or other settings.

Transferability from one researcher to another or one evaluator to another is a characteristic often assumed to exist in measurement; in many cases, this assumption is accurate. The major categories of physical states or occurrences, performance, behavior, and practices particularly provide for a high degree of both reproducibility and transferability.

It is in the area of attitudes, beliefs, and perceptions that reproducibility and transferability present difficulty. A classic example of the lack of transferability would be the Rorschach test of personality characteristics. The interpretation of a Rorschach test is by its very nature subjective; the test itself is not highly transferable from one researcher or evaluator to another. Interview schedules that may be used for focus group data collection could also show problems of transferability. When used by a person particularly skilled at interpersonal relations, a particular schedule may produce results unobtainable by people less skilled in interpersonal relations trying to use the schedule in similar circumstances.

The Rationale for Measurement

Measurement provides a means for learning something about a program that can be used for evaluation purposes. Two specific points should be made about measurement and its relationship to program activities. The first is that measurement leads to the ability to make comparisons, for example, between settings in which a program is operative and settings in which it is not. The second is that in order to be of value in an evaluation setting, measurements must show variability between individual entities under observation.

Comparisons

Measures are taken for the purpose of comparison. A great deal of information may be collected about any given program—the number of dollars budgeted for the program, dollars spent, personnel involved, visits made by clientele, or the number of drugs dispensed by the program. The items measured may represent an extremely large set.

All this measurement, however, is meaningless for evaluation purposes unless it involves a comparison. The comparison may be between the measure produced by the program (e.g., number of clients served), and an ideal measure as specified or set up prior to the implementation of the program. In this case, the comparison is between actual productivity or progress and an ideal or established norm. The comparison can be between different programs providing basically the same types of services—for example, the cost of providing them through one program as opposed to providing the same services through another program. A comparison may be between different areas served by the same or similar programs, so that the numbers of immunizations given may be compared from one county to another. Comparison can be over time, such as comparing the proportion of dollars budgeted to dollars spent by a program in each of five succeeding years or comparing the number of outpatient visits per month from one month to the next.

All the comparisons previously mentioned are legitimate comparisons that can be made in a program evaluation context and certainly do not exhaust the number of such possible comparisons. Nevertheless, comparison between units over time or between actual performance and a standard or norm is critical to program evaluation and is an underlying assumption of the whole measurement effort. If no comparison is anticipated on the basis of measurements taken, then such measurements are relatively useless.

Variation

If comparisons between a standard or a norm and performance are to be carried out, if comparison between units of observation is to be successful, or if comparison over time is to have any meaning, a basic assumption of measurement goals is that they should provide evidence of variation. A measure that shows no variation across a range of observations is useless.

It is possible that a particular measure to assess certain characteristics of a program will not show substantial variation over time, from one unit of analysis to another, or between performance and a standard. On one level, this situation may be acceptable in the sense that if the standard is being met, or if all units of analysis are performing equally, or if no change occurs over time, no variation should be evident. In many circumstances, however, the lack of variation in a measure is not so much a consequence of the absence of true differences, divergence from a standard, difference between units of analysis, or change over time as of sensitivity of the measure. The measure being used may not be adequately sensitive to reflect the variation that exists. If a measure is so insensitive that it does not reflect true changes or differences in units of analysis, it is worthless as a measure for evaluation purposes.

Variation is also essential to explanation. A program of immunization that operates in several different geographic or political areas may have widely differing results in terms of numbers of people immunized. An evaluation of these programs that would attempt to explain this difference in numbers of people immunized may wish to examine the relation between numbers of people immunized and, for example, attitudes of local recipients of immunization to immunization. However, if the measurement tool to be used to assess attitudes is insensitive to differences that may exist among the various areas, or if no differences actually exist, attitudes cannot be used to account for differential immunization rates. This idea extends to program interventions. If the evaluator wishes to assess the effect of a program on a varying program outcome, it is necessary to have differential implementation of the program (either areas in which the program is implemented or not implemented, or different levels of program effortto use the program as an explanation of differential outcomes.

Types of Measures

The only limits on the types of measures used in program evaluation are those imposed by the creativeness and imagination of the evaluators. Nevertheless, several different types of measures that can be used in evaluation are reviewed, including some of their characteristics, certain settings in which they may be more or less appropriate, and how they may be constructed. Five types of measures are considered: (1) numbers; (2) rates; (3) attributes; (4) perception measures; and (5) composite measures.

Any type of measure used is a means of assessing an attribute of a specific unit of analysis. The unit of analysis may be a person, a program, or a program in a given year. It may be a geographic location, a political entity, or an organization, such as a hospital. All the measures to be discussed could be applied to an extent to any of these units of analysis, but several types of measures seem to adapt more readily to certain types of units of analysis than others. For example, rates are more useful in discussing geographic areas or programs than individuals.

Perception measures are often more useful when the individual is the unit of analysis. Nevertheless, all these measures could be used in a setting where any unit of analysis is assumed. The discussion of the various types of measures will be based on the unit of analysis to which the measure is most likely to be applied; for example, rates generally apply to some aggregate group of individuals, while perceptions generally apply to persons specifically. Where clearly substantial adjustments in the use of the measures would be required for other units of analysis, this point is made.

Numbers as Measures

Numbers are certainly the simplest form of measures that may be applied to program evaluation. If a certain type of health services or social services program is operating in a given geographic area, its characteristics and those of the area can be described in terms of numbers. For example, the size of the population, the numbers of births, deaths, hospital beds, or clinics available in the area, dollars budgeted to or expended by the program, or number of people served by the program can be described in terms of numbers. Numbers are appropriate in characterizing programs or the areas within which they are operating. It is quite common, for example, to compare program areas, operations, or populations served, or dollars budgeted to indicate the relative size of a program. Numbers can also be applied to measures of characteristics of people being served by programs. Height and weight, age, or expectation of life at birth all are numbers that can be readily applied to individuals who may be the clients or recipients of service from a particular program.

As with any type of measure, basically three different comparisons may be made. One comparison is between the actual number and an ideal number for the same measure. A second is between units of analysis (people, programs, geographic areas, and so on). The third is among the values of the measure on a specific unit of analysis at different times. In monitoring program progress, the number of dollars expended on services at the end of any given fiscal period could be compared to the number of dollars expected to be spent on services. If these two numbers coincide, an evaluation of progress would indicate that, at least for this measure, the program was on track. A measure representing the actual number of people provided services through a type of program could be compared at the end of a period of time to the number of people who should have received services based on a program plan. Again, this would serve as a valid measure of progress and, to a certain extent, of effectiveness.

Comparisons across units of analysis are also possible. The number of services provided by each of several programs operating under the same circumstances could provide information about their relative effectiveness. Alternatively, the number of services provided by a single program in each of several successive time periods could be used as a means of assessing or evaluating program progress over time, or program effectiveness or impact over time.

Numbers are useful as measures of program progress or effectiveness and are easily obtained for purposes of program evaluation. A major difficulty with numbers as such, however, is that of relative scale. Two programs providing different numbers of services may do so because they are comparatively more or less effective. They may also do so because they are serving different-sized populations and thus have different numbers of potential clients to draw from. They also may have different numbers of program personnel and hence more personnel to provide services, or they may have differing budgets with greater or fewer resources with which to provide the services. These problems lead to the use of rates as measures.

Rates as Measures

A *rate* is essentially a ratio of two measures. The ratio of the total number of physicians in an area to the total number of people living in that same area is a rate. A rate may be expressed as physicians per capita (in the United States, approximately .0018). It may be expressed as the percentage of people who are physicians (in the United States, approximately 0.183 percent of the population), or it may be expressed as physicians per 1,000 or 1 million population (approximately 1.829 physicians per 1,000 population in the United States). Whether the ratio or rate is expressed on a per capita basis, a percentage basis, or per 1,000 or per 100,000 basis, the result is the same.

A rate provides a means of standardizing a number measure of interest, such as number of clients served, by a measure of the size of the unit of analysis assumed important in determining number of clients served. For example, the number of clients served per $1,000 budgeted (the number of clients served divided by the total number of dollars available and multiplied by 1,000) is a rate or ratio measure that can be used in comparing organizations or programs.

Because rates are standardized measures that take into account important scale aspects of programs or areas served by programs, they become measures of program effectiveness and efficiency. The number of clients seen per program employee or the number of immunizations given per $1,000 of program expenditures allows direct comparisons of the effectiveness and efficiency of one program with other programs of a different size.

Rates can be based on almost any measure that has conceptual meaning—numbers of services, physicians, dollars expended, or clinics per person or per 100,000 people represent useful rates based on numbers of people served. The base also could be number of dollars expended or budgeted, or time, such as services provided per month or dollars expended per day. In many cases, dealing with what may be considered double rates may be reasonable (e.g., visits per clinic per day, visits per physician per day, or budgeted dollars available to a program per capita per service area).

Rates are particularly useful for making comparisons across a number of similar programs of substantially different size. Rates can provide a standardized means of evaluating progress, efficiency, effectiveness, and, in certain instances, impact.

When rates are used to describe disease or morbidity states, a distinction is made between onset and persistence, particularly between acute and chronic diseases. Acute diseases are defined as having relatively rapid onset and short duration, whereas chronic diseases are those of perhaps less rapid onset but longer duration.

To recognize this distinction, disease rates are frequently expressed in terms of prevalence versus incidence. *Prevalence* refers to the number of people at any time (scaled to a relevant base, such as percentage or per 100,000) who actually show evidence of a disease. *Incidence* refers to the number of people (again scaled to an appropriate base) who succumb to the condition or disease within a given time range.

Certain diseases may have frequent onset and long duration; they have both high incidence rates and high prevalence rates. Diseases like colds, flu, measles, and mumps may have high incidence but relatively low prevalence (although most childhood infectious diseases are declining markedly). They are of short duration, and the people who have them recover rapidly.

Other diseases that may have relatively low incidence, such as diabetes or arthritis, because they are long-term chronic conditions have a much higher prevalence than incidence. New people are added to the ranks of those with the condition, but relatively few leave these ranks except through death. In assessing or evaluating the effect of any type of health-related program, particularly as that program is expected to reduce the rate of disease, an important consideration is whether the rate reduction concerns incidence, prevalence, or both.

Attributes as Measures

Attribute measures generally refer to those taken on a strictly nominal scale (i.e., a scale that serves to differentiate, but not to order, categories). In general, attributes cannot be used as objective criteria by which programs are assessed or evaluated. Instead, attribute measures serve as a means of clarifying the nature of the program or ensuring that expected target populations are being reached. Attribute measures of importance in program evaluation may include such variables as sex, race, ethnicity of the country or region, and profit versus nonprofit status.

The purpose of a particular program may be to provide services to a mixed community of native-born Americans and recent Spanish-speaking immigrants. An important aspect of program evaluation may be to ensure that the proportion of people receiving services from the clinic would be approximately the same as the proportion distribution in the population between native-born Americans and Spanish or Spanish-surnamed immigrants. In such a case, the attribute variable, ethnicity or place of birth, would be an important attribute for defining categories within which the program is assessed.

Similarly, a program directed toward the control of hospital costs may have as one of its important aspects the control of hospital costs in both for-profit and not-for-profit hospitals. In this case, the nominal or attribute variable profit versus not-for-profit status would be important as a component measure for evaluation purposes.

Perception Measures

Perception measures represent a broad category of measures that are generally defined along ordinal or interval scales—or, in certain instances, along ratio scales—and that can be useful in many aspects of program evaluation. Perception measures refer to a broad range of attitudes, beliefs, knowledge, and even consensual agreement that can be used in program evaluation. This is an area that has received extensive attention from psychologists, social psychologists, and sociologists.

Historically, numerous and different types of efforts have been made to measure attitudes, beliefs, or perceptions in more or less consistent and scientific ways. These include the use of such techniques as Thurston scaling, the semantic differential, Guttman scales, and Likert scales. We will not attempt to discuss all these types of perception-measuring devices, but several are presented because of their relevance to evaluation. For a detailed discussion of perception measures see Kerlinger (1986) and Miller (1991).

Likert scale   In recent years the most common technique for measuring attitudes, perceptions, beliefs, and, to a certain extent, knowledge and consensus has been the *Likert scale*. It has the advantage over many other attitude or perception measurement techniques of being fairly simple, straightforward, and, for the most part, easy for people to respond to.

A Likert scale refers to a statement or series of statements made in either a positive or negative manner. Respondents are asked to check one category from among several categories of answers that best represents their feeling about or belief in the statement. In general, each statement has five response categories, which may be labeled strongly disagree, disagree, undecided, agree, and strongly agree. In rare instances, Likert scales are constructed with three categories (i.e., disagree, undecided, and agree) or seven categories providing a greater differentiation along the continuum from strongly disagree to strongly agree. Because it is relatively difficult for most people to successfully differentiate among more than five to seven categories, Likert scales using more than seven response categories are rare.

Exhibit 13.1 shows a set of statements used to evaluate the perceptions of Veterans Administration personnel about a program to support primary care residency training (PRIME) in Veterans Administration hospitals (Kilpatrick 1995). Each of the eight statements in Exhibit 13.1 represents a separate attitude or perception about the PRIME program. Five possible responses to these statements range from strongly disagree to strongly agree. While these statements represent only a sample sub-set of the 20 statements that were actually included in the complete instrument that was used to assess attitudes toward the program, the eight statements still represent a range of considerations about the program.

Please consider the following statements in relation to the PRIME project, circling the number representing the extent to which you are in agreement with the statement.

	Strongly Disagree	Disagree	Undecided	Agree	Strongly Agree
1. I would like to *develop* working relationships with staff inside our medical center and staff in other medical centers with PRIME project.	1	2	3	4	5
2. Prime is taking too much of my *time*.	1	2	3	4	5
3. Staff *attitudes* toward PRIME are positive.	1	2	3	4	5
4. I would like to determine how to supplement and/or *enhance* PRIME.	1	2	3	4	5
5. I would like to *increase* my involvement in PRIME.	1	2	3	4	5
6. I don't think that PRIME has *improved* upon the way we provided primary care training before PRIME.	1	2	3	4	5
7. I do not like the way we have *approached* the PRIME effort.	1	2	3	4	5
8. I am concerned that participation in PRIME will have a *negative* effect on my professional status.	1	2	3	4	5

EXHIBIT 13.1
Example of Likert Scale Items: Statements Designed to Assess Stakeholder Attitudes Toward a Primary Care Training Initiative in the Veterans Administration Residency Programs

Statement 1, for example, represents interest in expanding the involvement of staff in PRIME, statement 6 addresses the effectiveness of PRIME, and statement 8 expresses concern about personal professional status.

Although the items included in Exhibit 13.1 represent a diverse set of perceptions about the PRIME program, they may not include everything that an evaluator may wish to know about the perceptions that a group of people holds about the program. In any effort of this type to generate statements that can be used to assess attitudes, perceptions, or beliefs about a program or an aspect of it, these statements must cover all aspects that the evaluators hope to assess about the program.

With attitude or perception measures constructed by using the scale or item statements shown in Exhibit 13.1, the basic value of the statements lies in comparisons between programs, between areas in which a program is operating, among people affected by the program, or over time within a given program. Gross values of the results are relatively useless for evaluating a program, except to the extent that it would be important to hope that the respondents would be more inclined to answer at the end of the continuum that reflects more favorably on the program. When many people respond to a given item, the tendency will be for the mean for all people to be relatively close to the midpoint, or frequently to favor responses reflecting a positive attitude about a program. Sometimes no standard may exist by which to judge whether the response meets a norm for the program.

Trade-off or utility measures Utility measures have been used in management science to account for decision making under risk situations. In regard to program evaluation, the notion of utility or trade-offs derived from utility may be successfully used to construct unidimensional measures of such concepts as health status or other concepts similarly difficult to measure. Because utility measures have begun to assume an important role in measurement, particularly with regard to health status, Chapter 14 is devoted to this discussion.

Composite Measures

Composite measures may involve attributes, numbers, rates, perception measures, or combinations of these categories. A composite measure is derived by putting together other measures in a combination to produce one single measure from the composite.

Weighted and Unweighted Sums

The most common approach to generating composite measures is to produce the weighted sum of a given set of measures about an attribute of a program under evaluation. The composite measure is of the following form:

$$C_i = \sum_{j=1}^{m} w_j Z_{ij} \tag{13.1}$$

C_i represents the composite score, w_j the weight for the jth variable, and Z_{ij} the standardized score for the jth variable for person i. The summation is over all m variables. The variables to be made a composite or to be summed should be transformed to standard score form—that is, Z score—before the summation is done. For example, if average family income were to be made a composite with the portion of families below the poverty level as a measure of economic health, family income (which has a mean of perhaps \$30,000 to \$35,000) would completely overwhelm the proportion of families below the poverty level, which is perhaps .20 or .25.

This caution about transforming items to be summed to Z scores is essential in the case of composites that differ in magnitude but is unnecessary in the case of items from, for example, a set of Likert scaled statements similar to what is shown in Exhibit 13.1. Because each statement is scored on exactly the same scale, the items can be summed to make a composite. Direction of the scoring for some of the items (e.g., statements 2, 6, 7, and 8 or 1, 3, 4, and 5) would have to be reversed for a composite to make sense, however.

The simplest type of composite score is a score in which the weights w_j are all equal. If the weights are all equal, usually it is reasonable to assume that they would be simply one. Then the composite score is the sum of the Z scores. A more complex scaling system or system for putting together a composite score would be one in which the weights w_j differ from variable to variable.

Consider a constructed score for each Standard Metropolitan Statistical Area (SMSA) in the United States, which represents a quality of health and education component of an overall quality of life score (Lieu 1976). Seven rates were used to make up the health portion of the health and education score:

- infant mortality per 1,000 live births;
- death rate per 1,000 population;
- dentists per 100,000 population;
- hospital beds per 100,000 population;
- hospital occupancy rates;
- number of physicians per 100,000 population; and
- per capita local government expenditures on health.

In addition, six education factors provide a score for the education portion of the health and education component.

In the composite score, equal weights were assigned to the health and education portions. Equal weights also were assigned to the infant mortality and death rates. Table 13.1 shows the specific variables included in the measure of health and education for each community. The numbers in parentheses on the left side of the table represent the weights w_j for each of the thirteen variables.

In Table 13.1 the total composite score clearly will be weighted most heavily by the two death variables and the two educational attainment variables, all four of which receive weights of .125. The medical care availability and accessibility variables each receive a score of .05, which means that taken together they are all equal to the death measure. If the subject of an evaluation was a program or series of programs to improve health and education in a number of geographical areas, this composite score could serve for evaluation purposes as a measure of the extent to which the programs were successful.

The logic of Lieu's (1976) weighting factors in constructing a health and education component score is fairly straightforward. Equal weights were given to individual and community conditions within the health and the education portions. Beyond this logic, however, the weighting may be quite arbitrary. In certain situations, logic may dictate the assignments of weight. For the health and education component, there seems to be clear logic to the assignment of a one-fourth weight to each of the four separate categories. In other instances, differential weighting may be less easy to justify. As Lieu points out, one strategy for dif-

TABLE 13.1

Items in Health and Education Component (Lieu's Scale)

Item Effect and Weight	Item

Individual Conditions

Health

−(.125) 1. Infant mortality rate per 1,000 live births
−(.125) 2. Death rate per 1,000 population

Education

+(.063) 1. Median school year completed by people 25 years old and over
+(.063) 2. Percentage of people 25 years and over who completed four years of high school or more
−(.063) 3. Percentage of males ages 16 to 21 who are not high school graduates
+(.063) 4. Percentage of population ages 3 to 34 enrolled in schools

Community Conditions

Medical Care Availability and Accessibility

+(.05) 1. Number of dentists per 100,000 population
+(.05) 2. Number of hospital beds per 100,000 population
+(.05) 3. Hospital occupancy rate
+(.05) 4. Number of physicians per 100,000 population
+(.05) 5. Per capita local government expenditures on health

Educational Attainment

+(.125) 1. Per capita local government expenditures on education
+(.125) 2. Percentage of people 25 years old and over who completed four years of college or more

ferential weighting, however, could be a survey of people assumed to be knowledgeable about the importance of various factors in determining aspects of program performance or, in this specific instance, community life.

Guttman scales

The Guttman scaling technique is based on the assumption that dichotomous attributes can be ordered in such a way that, for the least common attribute to exist or have a positive value for a given respondent or organization, all other attributes will also exist or be positive responses for the same respondent or organization. For the next least common attribute to exist, all attributes except the least common are assumed to exist, and so on, through the second least common attribute, the third, and so on. Any organization having only one attribute will have the most common one. If this is the case, and a respondent or organization receives a particular score on the scale, this immediately indicates the position of the organization or respondent relative to the items that comprise the scale.

Illustration

To provide a simple illustration of the Guttman scaling technique, assume a set of responses from ten hospitals to the question of whether the hospital provides each of five services: rehabilitation, mental health, medical social work, family planning, and home care. Table 13.2 shows the constructed data for the

TABLE 13.2

Example of
Guttman Scale
Using Constructed
Data for Ten
Hospitals

Hospital	Rehab- ilitation Services	Mental Health Services	Medical Social Work Services	Family Planning Services	Home Care Services	Maximum Marginal	Scale Score
A	1	1	1	1	1	5	5
B	1	1	1	1	0	4	4
C	1	1	1	0	1	4	3
D	1	1	1	0	0	3	3
E	1	1	0	1	0	3	2
F	1	0	1	0	0	3	1
G	1	0	0	0	0	4	1
H	0	0	0	0	0	5	0
I	0	0	0	0	0	5	0
J	0	0	0	0	0	5	0
Total	7	5	5	3	2	41	

responses of the ten hospitals about whether they provide any one of the services. If the service is provided, a 1 appears in the column.

As the table shows, seven of the ten hospitals provide rehabilitation services. Five provide mental health services, five have medical social work services, three have family planning services, and two provide home care services. The programs are ordered by the number of hospitals providing the service.

If a scale is to exist in the data, a distinct pattern should exist in which the hospitals not providing rehabilitation services (i.e., hospitals H, I, and J) will also, in general, not provide any other services, which is the case. Furthermore, those hospitals not providing mental health services (i.e., hospitals F, G, H, I, and J) also should not provide medical social work, family planning, or home care. Only hospital F violates this requirement. Of the hospitals not providing medical social work services, only hospital E provides family planning or home care. Of those not providing family planning services, only hospital C provides home care. Despite these "errors," it is possible to test whether the data demonstrate the characteristics of a Guttman scale.

The criteria for the existence of a Guttman scale are actually a combination of three separate calculations. The first criterion is the coefficient of reproducibility (CR)

$$CR = 1 - \frac{E}{nm} = 1 - \frac{3}{50} = .94 \qquad (13.2)$$

where E is the number of errors. An error is counted for each entry (1 or 0 in the table) that must be changed for each hospital to be a scale type; n represents the number of observations (hospitals), and m the number of items (programs). The second criterion is known as the minimum marginal reproducibility (MMR), defined in Equation 13.3 as the sum of the most frequent response for each organization

$$MMR = \frac{MM}{nm} = \frac{41}{50} = .82 \qquad (13.3)$$

where *MM* is the maximum of ones or zeros for each organization (the maximum marginal). The third criterion is the coefficient of scalability (*CS*).

$$CS = \frac{CR - MMR}{1 - MMR} = \frac{.94 - .82}{.18} = .67 \qquad (13.4)$$

For a Guttman scale to be present, it is commonly accepted that the coefficient of reproducibility should be greater than .9. The minimum marginal reproducibility must be less than .9, and the coefficient of scalability should be greater than .6. These levels are rather arbitrary but have the weight of usage on their side. If these criteria are accepted, it is clear that the constructed example for the ten hospitals forms a Guttman scale. The coefficient of reproducibility is .94, the minimum marginal reproducibility is .82, and the coefficient of scalability is .67.

Furthermore, it can be seen in Table 13.2 that hospitals A, B, D, G, H, I, and J are all pure scale types. That is, they perfectly fit the perception of the underlying scale. Hospitals C, E, and F are nonscale types: they each contain one error.

A scale score of 5 can be assigned to A, 4 to B, and so on for the pure scale types with confidence that the result will be clear and unambiguous. A score of 3 for a pure scale type means that the hospital provides rehabilitation services, mental health services, and medical social work services. A decision must be made in order to assign a scale score to hospitals that contain errors. Hospital C, for example, has an error either in the negative response to family planning or the positive response to home care. If the decision is that the positive response to home care outweighs the negative response to family planning, the hospital would be assigned a score of 5. If the reverse were decided, the hospital would be assigned a score of 3.

Although this decision will not have a major influence on overall relationships between the Guttman scale variables and other variables, it is likely to have consequences for the interpretation of results for hospital C and is always a difficult decision to make. Nevertheless, such a decision must be made for every organization that includes an error (hospitals C, E, and F). If the decision is that the affirmative answers will be treated as errors, the figures shown in the scale score column in Table 13.2 would be assigned to the ten hospitals. Scales could then be used as independent or dependent variables for further analysis of the data.

Item-to-scale correlation

Guttman scaling is a mechanism for accumulating responses from a number of dichotomous response items in a way that assures unidimensionality of the scale, if a Guttman scale can be verified. Item-to-scale correlation is another mechanism that can be used for the same purpose and can be applied not only to dichotomous response items but also (and more frequently) to interval or ratio scale response items. Unlike Guttman scales, which are difficult to verify in reality, item-to-scale correlation will allow the detection of scales in most practical data applications.

Item-to-scale correlation can best be understood through an example. Consider again the eight attitude items shown in Exhibit 13.1. These eight statements were asked of stakeholders in the PRIME project and responses were received from 458 people. Issues that immediately come to mind are:

- whether these eight items can be summed to represent the overall attitude of each stakeholder toward the PRIME project;
- whether the items should be treated as more than one scale (representing perhaps two or three independent attitudes about the PRIME project); or
- whether they each should be treated as representing eight separate and different attitudes about the PRIME project (and thus best treated as eight individual statements).

One strategy for making these decisions is item-to-scale correlation.

Item-to-scale correlation proceeds by forming the sum of the items to be examined. As previously mentioned, if items to be summed differ in magnitude (e.g., family income and percent of income spent on food), it is necessary to convert items to be summed to standard scores (Z scores) before proceeding. Z scores are calculated as

$$Z = \frac{x_i - \mu}{\sigma} \tag{13.5}$$

where x_i is any single observation for a variable, μ is the mean of all the observations and σ is the standard deviation. For the data in Exhibit 13.1, standardizing is not essential because each item is measured on a scale of 1 to 5.

For the overall sum of the variables to make sense in a summed scale, it is also necessary to ensure that the items are all scored in the same way. In Exhibit 13.1, items 2, 6, 7, and 8 are worded in a negative manner. To make those comparable to the other four items, subtract each from 6 before summing. The result is that all items are scored in a positive manner (i.e., the more favorable one is toward the PRIME program, the higher will be that person's score on each of the eight items). A resulting summed score for all eight items will range from a possible low of 8 (scores of 1 on each of the eight items) to a possible high of 40 (scores of 5 on each of the eight items).

Having constructed the sum of all eight items for 458 respondents, the next step in item-to-scale correlation is to calculate the correlation between each item and the sum of all eight items. The correlation between the eight-item scale score and each individual scale score is shown as the 8-Item Scale row in Table 13.3. In that line, the highest correlation between the eight-item scale score and each individual item is with the Attitude variable, which correlates .707 with the eight-item scale. This means that Attitude shares almost half its variance with the overall scale. The variable Time, however, with a correlation of only .495, shares less than one-fourth of its variance with the eight-item scale; the square of the

TABLE 13.3

Correlation Between Individual Items and Overall Scale, Item-to-Scale Correlation

Items in Scale	Item Name (Presented in the order shown in Exhibit 13.1)							
	Develop	Time	Attitude	Enhance	Increase	Improve	Approach	Negative
8-Item Scale	0.586	0.495	0.707	0.586	0.647	0.603	0.631	0.505
6-Item Scale	0.626	*	0.702	0.625	0.681	0.605	0.623	*
5-Item Scale	0.677	*	0.694	0.670	0.753	*	0.583	*
4-Item Scale	0.731	*	0.630	0.726	0.819	*	*	*
3-Item Scale	0.771	*	*	0.735	0.859	*	*	*

*Designates items dropped from scale at each step

correlation represents the proportion of variance shared between two items, so .495 squared equals .245, less than one-quarter.

To proceed with item-to-scale correlation, those items that are least highly correlated with a scale are removed in a sequential manner in an attempt to improve the individual item-to-scale correlations. In general, any item with a correlation less than .5 would be removed. In the case of the eight-item scale, both the variables Time and Negative were removed because of their low correlations with the scale. The next step was to construct a six-item scale based on the six remaining variables and compute correlations between the six-item scale and each of the variables contained in it. The results of this step are shown in the 6-Item Scale row. As shown, little has changed in the correlation of the individual items to the six-item scale, except that correlations on three variables, Develop, Enhance, and Increase, have increased. None of the correlations now clearly show that more than 50 percent of the variation in the variables are shared with the overall six-item scale.

With the aim of producing a scale with which all items included will share at least 50 percent of their variation with the overall scale, the next variable least correlated with the overall scale (Improve) is removed and a five-item summed scale is constructed. The correlations between the five-item scale and each of the component items is shown in the 5-Item Scale row. Now the correlation between the scale and Approach is lowest, so that variable is dropped for the next step. After construction of a four-item scale, clearly Attitude should be dropped, and the final three-item scale consists of Develop, Enhance, and Increase. Each item correlates higher than .71 with the overall scale, which means each one shares at least 50 percent of its variation with the three-item scale (.71 squared is .50). Thus, the three-item scale would be considered to represent an underlying dimension that can be measured by the summation of responses to the three items included. Further, that dimension will be unidimensional as discussed at the beginning of the chapter.

The idea that an item must share at least 50 percent of its variation with a scale before it is considered part of that scale could be viewed as somewhat arbitrary. Why not 40 percent, or 70 percent as the criterion for including an item with a scale? The answer is that the 50 percent criterion is arbitrary, but it has the weight of considerable usage on its side.

Given that a scale has been identified with which Develop, Enhance, and Increase share more than 50 percent of their variation, what becomes of the other five items? The most common strategy is to form a new scale from those five items and repeat the item-to-scale correlation process again to determine if any additional scales (i.e., composites with which selected items share more than 50 percent of their variation) are identified. Of the remaining five items from Exhibit 13.1, two additional scales are identifiable given the criterion of 50 percent of the variation shared and the item-to-scale correlation process. These are a scale composed of Improve, Approach, and Attitude with item-to-scale correlations of .79, .81, and .75, respectively, and a scale comprised of Time and Negative with item-to-scale correlations of .84 and .77, respectively.

Eight Likert-type response items about the PRIME project have been shown to measure three separate dimensions of people's attitudes toward the project. One of these, measured as the sum of responses to Develop, Enhance, and Increase may assess, for example, an attitude favorable or unfavorable to expanding the role of PRIME. A second, measured as the sum of responses to Improve, Approach, and Attitude, assesses, for example, an attitude favorable or unfavorable to the way PRIME is currently implemented. The last, measured as the sum of responses to Time and Negative, may assess an attitude favorable or unfavorable to personal involvement in PRIME.

The correlations among these three scales are not high. The correlation between the scale including Develop, Enhance, and Increase and the scale including Improve, Approach, and Attitude is .32—about 9 percent of the variance shared. The correlation between the scale including Develop, Enhance, and Increase and the scale including Time and Negative is .24—about 5 percent of the variance shared. The correlation between the scale including Improve, Approach, and Attitude and the scale including Time and Negative is .44—about 18 percent of the variance shared. If a single scale were developed based on the sum of all eight items, the scale would be multidimensional in the sense that people at the mid-range of the individual items could be strongly positive on certain items while strongly negative on others. With the three individual scales developed here, it is highly unlikely that people highly positive on one item in the scale would be highly negative on another. The item-to-scale correlation technique thus has eliminated items from the three scales on which respondents differ markedly in the direction of their responses.

To demonstrate graphically what item-to-scale correlation does, consider a simple example of variables x and y, both measured on a five-level response set from 1 to 5. Assume that on each variable all five of the possible responses are represented. Further assume that the number of respondents is 200. Figures 13.1a and 13.1b show two different possible configurations of all the responses in the two dimensions; a very large, but finite number of different patterns are possible with two variables having five response categories. Figure 13.1a shows the response pattern for two variables that are correlated .83—about 65 percent of variance shared between the two responses. As Figure 13.1a demonstrates, many probably exist, for example, at point 1,1, at point 1,2, at point 2,1, and so on. No responses exist, however, at 1,5 or 5,1, for example.

What this means is that if a score is assigned based on the sum of these two items, a score of 6 represents individual item responses of 3,3, but, because no responses are at these points, cannot represent individual item responses of 2,4 or 4,2 or 1,5 or 5,1. A score of 5 represents individual item responses of 2,3 or 3,2. A score of 7 represents individual item responses of 4,3 or 3,4. Mid-range scores on the scale represents mid-range scores on the items.

If the items are uncorrelated, as shown in Figure 13.1b, responses such as 1,5 and 5,1 can exist. In this case, if a scale was formed as the sum of the two

FIGURE 13.1a

Scatter Plot for Correlated Responses on Two Five-Level Variables ($r = .83$)

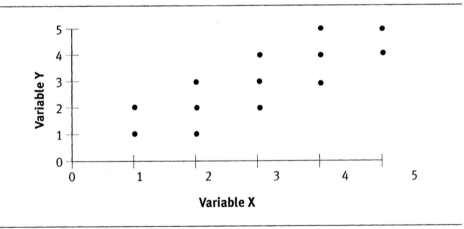

FIGURE 13.1b

Scatter Plot for Uncorrelated Responses on Two Five-Level Variables ($r = -.09$)

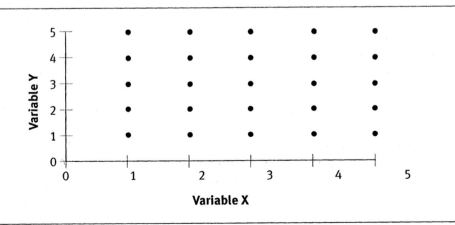

items, a score of 6 could represent individual item responses of 1,5; 2,4; 3,3; 4,2; and 5,1. A respondent could get a mid-range score by being at or near opposite extremes on each separate item. Having high item-to-scale correlations avoids this unattractive situation.

Factor analysis is a technique for finding composite weights that involves a certain empirical logic for determining the weights and at the same time ensures that the resulting scores will not be such that midpoint values are multidimensional. For a more detailed discussion of factor analysis, see Nie et al. (1975); for its application to health services, see Kaluzny and Veney (1980).

Factor analysis

To see how factor analysis works and to examine some of its results, consider certain select data for counties in North Carolina that correspond relatively closely to the measures included in Lieu's health section of the health and education score. These measures are the infant mortality rate for each county measured in terms of deaths per 1,000 live births; the death rate for each county measured in terms of total deaths per 100,000 population; and the number of active physicians, dentists, and hospital beds per 100,000 population. Hospital occupancy rates and per capita local government expenditures on health, two variables that Lieu uses, are not included in this set of data.

Illustration

Factor analysis begins with a matrix of correlations among the variables to be scaled. Table 13.4 shows the correlation matrix between the five variables taken from the North Carolina data for which we would like to produce a factor analysis result. In any set of data, such as that shown in the correlation matrix in Table 13.4, there is a variance shared with other variables in the data set and a variance unique to each independent variable. To a certain extent, the intercorrelations represent this shared variance. A correlation of 0.899 shown for the two variables physicians and dentists per 100,000 population indicates that there is more variance shared between those two variables than between, for example, physicians per 100,000 population and the infant mortality rate with a correlation of -0.129.

The approach of factor analysis in determining whether variables should be summed together and in determining the best empirical weights is to find a trans-

	Infant Mortality	Death Rate	Physicians/ 100,000	Dentists/ 100,000	Hospital Beds/ 100,000
Infant Mortaility	1.000	0.178	−0.129	−0.176	0.001
Death Rate	0.178	1.000	−0.141	−0.171	0.026
Physicians/100,000	−0.129	−0.141	1.000	0.899	0.247
Dentists/100,000	−0.176	−0.171	0.899	1.000	0.193
Hospital Beds/100,000	0.001	0.026	0.247	0.193	1.000

TABLE 13.4
Correlation Matrix for Data from North Carolina Counties

Source: Data taken from *North Carolina Health Statistics Pocket Guide*, Public Health Statistics Branch, Division of Health Services, Department of Human Resources, Raleigh, North Carolina.

formation of the original correlation matrix that will account for as much variance in the original correlation matrix as possible on the basis of a single vector. The vector that best reproduces the original correlation matrix is called the first principal component factor; its values are referred to as factor loadings. Table 13.5 shows the first principal component factor for the correlation matrix given in Table 13.4.

The factor loadings shown in factor 1 are the actual correlations between the five variables included in the factor and the factor itself. As Table 13.5 shows, physicians and dentists per 100,000 population are most highly correlated (at approximately 0.92) with the first principal component factor. This means that factor 1 is basically a measure of the physicians and dentists per capita or per 100,000 population. The low correlation between the variables infant mortality, death rate, and hospital beds per 100,000 population indicates that these variables are not closely associated with the underlying factor.

To further understand what a factor analysis means in this situation, consider the notions of communality and uniqueness. In any data set, such as is represented by the preceding five variables, there is the assumption that a certain variation in the data is common to several variables in the data set and that a certain variation in the data is unique to each single variable. Looking at the factor loadings in Table 13.5, determining what portion of the variance in each of the five variables is common (communality) and which part is unique (uniqueness) is possible. The square of each of the factor loadings represents the communality for each variable, as shown in the communality column in Table 13.5. Communality is the square of the factor loading.

As the communality column indicates, only about 3 percent of the variance in birth rate, death rate, or hospital beds per 1,000 population is shared with any of the other variables in the data set; therefore, 95 percent or more of the variance in those three variables is unique to each variable independently. This can be seen to a certain extent in the correlation matrix in Table 13.4, but it is much more apparent from the result of the factor analysis. The clear result of this information is that a summed score consisting of all five variables weighted equally is likely to produce a result in which intermediate range values are multidimensional or at least confused in pattern and meaning. If a summed score is to be created from these five variables, this should be done on the basis of weighting that reflects the correlations shown as factor loadings in Table 13.5.

Most factor analysis programs will produce the factor scores resulting from

TABLE 13.5

Factor Loadings and Communality: One Factor Solution of Data in Table 13.4

	Factor 1	Communality
Infant Mortality	−0.177	0.032
Death Rate	−0.177	0.031
Physicians/100,000	0.925	0.855
Dentists/100,000	0.925	0.856
Hospital Beds/100,000	0.229	0.052

a factor analysis of the data, weighting each of the variables proportionally to the factor loadings. Suppose the result is as clear as in Table 13.4, where physicians and dentists per 100,000 population are the only two variables that share a large proportion of the variance in common. In this case, simply ignoring the infant mortality, death, and hospital bed rates and producing a measure of physician and dentist services available (which would be the simple sum of the standardized scores for physicians and dentists for each of the counties under consideration) would be quite reasonable.

Discussion Questions

1. Distinguish between a nominal, ordinal, interval, and ratio scale.
2. Consider a primary care program and designate measures of impact that illustrate each type of scale.
3. What is the difference between content validity, criteria validity, and construct validity?
4. Why is validity more difficult to deal with, methodologically, than reliability?
5. Discuss the advantages and disadvantages of using composite scores.
6. In what ways does Guttman scaling and factor analysis resolve the problem of assigning weights when using composite measures?
7. Are the following response categories considered a unidimensional or multidimensional scale? Why?

14

MEASUREMENT: UTILITY MEASURES

C hapter 13 dealt with general issues of measurement. This chapter addresses additional issues of measurement that have recently begun to attract increasing attention (i.e., how values are assigned to health and well-being). It is widely recognized that commonly used measures of health have one of two major faults. The first fault is that they are measures so gross that they are of little value in assessing most changes in health states of populations (i.e., infant mortality rates, under-five mortality rates, life expectancy at birth or at various ages). The second is that they are measures of disease specific interest only (i.e., incidence of heart disease, prevalence of tuberculosis).

Many techniques have been developed to attempt to assess the full range of possible health states, from modest changes in feeling to death, as a means to providing a more sensitive measurement of health that can be applied to entire populations or subsets of populations. The value of these measures from the standpoint of evaluation is that they provide a mechanism for assessing the outcome of a particular program in a way that is more sensitive to changes in health state influenced by the program than could gross measures of health such as mortality or disease specific morbidity.

In speaking of measuring health states, however, this chapter addresses only one of two major streams of thought in the measurement of health states. The two streams of thought are the external, objective assessment of health state and the preference based, subjective assessment of health state. In the external assessment of health state, measures are devised based on objectively observable criteria, such as blood pressure, heart rate, serum cholesterol, and so on. A well known health state assessment is the Acute Physiology and Chronic Health Evaluation (APACHE) II and III system for assessing health state (Knaus et al. 1986; Bastos et al. 1996).

In the preference-based assessment of health state, measures are devised in a way that rates health states in a subjective manner based on the apparent utility that any given health state holds for a group of informants. These measures allow an external observer to assign a person or set of people to various levels of health or utilities. This is based on perception of informants about how desirable any given health state is relative to, for example, complete health at one end of a continuum and death, or possibly a health state even less desirable than death, at the other. Several strategies for creating utility measures of health states exist. This chapter particularly addresses standard gamble, time trade-off, rating scales, and paired comparisons.

Standard Gamble

Standard gamble is a classic method of measuring preferences originally described by von Neuman and Morganstern (1953) based on the indifference of informants to two alternatives. In regard to health status, the standard gamble has been elaborated by Torrance (1972; 1986) and Mehrez and Gafni (1991) and has been strongly criticized by Richardson (1994). An interesting discussion of the application of the standard gamble in a clinical setting is given in Rutten-van Molken (1995).

In its simplest form, the standard gamble proceeds by offering the informant two choices. The first choice is the chance of a relatively good health state (commonly given as complete health) or a relatively bad health state (commonly given as death). The second choice is the certainty of a health state intermediate between the two in choice number one. A diagram of the standard gamble given by this conceptualization is shown in Figure 14.1, where the relatively good health state is denoted the better state (h_1), the relatively bad health state is denoted the worse state (h_2), and the assessed state (h_3) is assumed to be intermediate between these two. In this conceptualization, the health value (h_3) of the assessed state is:

$$h_3 = ph_1 + (1 - p)h_2 \qquad (14.1)$$

Typically, when the better state is perceived to be complete health, the health value of that state (h_1), is given as 1. When the worse state is perceived as death, the health value of that state (h_2) is given as 0. Equation 14.1 is simply reduced to $h_3 = p$.

Assessment for a Chronic Condition

As an example of an assessment for a chronic condition, consider the assessment of diabetes. As a chronic condition, diabetes would typically be assessed against complete health, as the state better than diabetes, or death, as the state worse than diabetes. The diagram for this assessment is shown in Figure 14.2.

FIGURE 14.1

Standard Gamble
for Assessed State

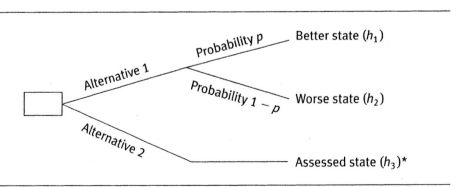

*the assessed state must lie between the better state and the worse state

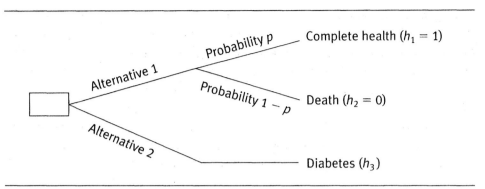

FIGURE 14.2

Standard Gamble
for Diabetes

In this standard gamble, the informant is typically told that he or she may accept diabetes, alternative 2, or may take a type of nonpainful treatment (e.g., a pill) as alternative 1. If the informant elects alternative 1, there will be a probability equal to p that the informant will be totally healthy as a result of the pill, and a probability $1 - p$ of death. The probability at which an informant is indifferent between alternative 1 and alternative 2 is the applicable probability for diabetes.

For example, an informant may decide that he or she is indifferent between alternative 1 and alternative 2 if the probability of becoming completely healthy is .75 (75 chances out of 100). This means that the informant would be willing to risk death to avoid diabetes if the probability of surviving the treatment is .75. The relative value assigned to diabetes, then, is as given by Equation 14.1: .75 × (health value of complete health) + (1 − .75) × (health value for death). Because the health value for complete health is typically assigned 1 and for death is 0, the value, h_3, for diabetes is .75.

In a real application, the informant would not be asked immediately to assign the probability p at which he or she would be indifferent to alternative 1 or alternative 2. Instead, the informant would be asked, for example, if he or she would be willing to take the gamble if the probability of success was high, such as .9. If the answer were yes, the informant would be asked the same question if the probability of success was very low, for example .1. The process moves up and down in that manner until the informant is indifferent between the treatment and diabetes. In the preceding example, the assumption is that the informant was willing to take alternative 1 when the probability of success was .8, but was not willing to take alternative 1 when the probability of success was .7. This leads to the decision that the informant was indifferent to the treatment or diabetes with a probability of treatment success of .75.

Assessment of a Temporary Condition

Diabetes as a permanent state would generally be compared to death. As shown in Figure 14.1, however, the standard gamble does not have to use either death or complete health as the two chance alternatives. In fact, Torrance (1989) has proposed that when a temporary state of ill health is being assessed, the worse state should be the worst temporary health state rather than death. The better state can remain complete health. If the worst possible temporary state of ill health were considered to be, for example, severe and persistent migraine and the comparison condition was radius fracture in a stiff cast (these two conditions are used because they match temporary conditions discussed as part of development of DALYs later in the chapter), the standard gamble would be as shown in Figure 14.3.

In Figure 14.3 the choice is between a probability p of complete health and a probability $1 - p$ of severe and persistent migraine or a radius fracture in a stiff cast. If an informant was asked to indicate the probability of complete health at which they would be indifferent between the two choices, they may accept .75 as the value of p for which they would be indifferent between taking the gamble and certainty of a radius fracture in a stiff cast. If the assumption was that the health value h of severe and persistent migraine was .25, the health value of a fractured femur, by Equation 14.1 is .75 + (1 − .75) × .25, which is .81.

In this formulation it is necessary to have a health value assigned to severe and persistent migraine. Torrance (1986) suggests that this be done by redefining the worst temporary condition (in this case, severe and persistent migraine) as a short-term chronic state that once entered will be followed by death and then assess it against immediate death as is done in Figure 14.2.

Assessment of States Worse Than Death

Torrance also provides direction on how to deal with a health state assessed by informants as being worse than death. In this case, the diagram is modified as shown in Figure 14.4. As shown, complete health, which has a health value of 1, and the state worse than death, which has a health value yet to be assessed, are the two chance points in choice number 1. Death, which has a health value of 0, is the alternative. The informant is then asked to choose either a treatment with probability p leading to complete health, or with probability $1 - p$ leading to the state worse than death against the alternative of certain death.

In this example, however, the problem of assigning a score to the state worse than death becomes a little complicated. In Equation 14.1, h_1 and h_2 are known and h_3 is the value sought. In the case of Figure 14.4, h_1, the value of complete health, is known, h_3, the value of death (the state intermediate between

FIGURE 14.3

Standard Gamble for Radius Fracture in Stiff Cast

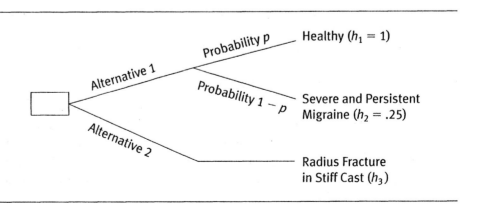

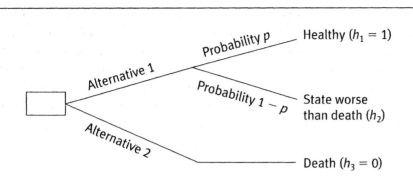

FIGURE 14.4

Standard Gamble
for State Worse
than Death

good health and a state worse than death), is known, and the desire is to find the value of h_2, the state worse than death. The solution proposed by Torrance and widely accepted by users of the standard gamble technique is to solve Equation 14.1 for h_2, which after some algebraic manipulation is:

$$h_2 = \frac{h_3 - ph_1}{1 - p} \qquad (14.2)$$

If h_3 is assumed to be 0 (the health value of death) and h_1 is assumed to be 1 (the health value of complete health), Equation 14.2 is reduced to $h_2 = -p/(1 - p)$.

While the result in Equation 14.2 is the algebraic solution to the problem of finding h_2 given Equation 14.1, problems of interpretation are created. As formulated in Equation 14.2, h_2 will be negative for all values of p when a state worse than death is assessed. This is reasonable if one assumes that the health value of death should be 0, which meets with fairly wide agreement. On the other hand, while the values of h_3 as calculated by 14.1 are linearly related to p (i.e., as the value of p increases, the value of h increase at a constant rate), the values of h_2 calculated by 14.2 are related to p in a geometric manner (i.e., as the values of p increase the values of h decrease at an increasing rate). Further, all values of h calculated by 14.1 will be in the range $0 \leq h \leq 1$. Values for h calculated using Equation 14.2 (i.e., when a state worse than death is being considered) have no lower bound. In fact, in a real application in a clinical setting, Rutten-van Molken et al. (1995) found that the value of h for states worse than death went as low as -19. This finding is the equivalent of the informant being indifferent to alternative 1 or 2 if the probability of complete health was .95.

There are two possible ways to deal with the difficulty of nonlinear negative health values, other than simply accepting the nonlinearity. Unfortunately, neither way produces a perfect result. One way is to always make the utility of the worst state worse than death equal to 0. Doing so allows all utilities, including the utility for death, to be developed as a value between 0 and 1. The problem with this alternative is that while death represents a fairly finite event that is relatively easily perceived by everyone, the worst state worse than death may be different for different informants, thus creating a situation in which the anchor (and hence the scale) is not universally applicable. Consensus and usage, therefore, are on the side of treating death as having a score of 0.

A second possibility is to ignore the algebraic equivalence between Equation 14.1 and 14.2 and make the health value (h) for any state worse than death equal to the negative of the probability, as assessed in Figure 14.4. Doing so automatically assures that the negative health values of states worse than death lie in the range of $-1 \leq h \leq 0$, and also assures that the relationship between p and h is linear. The obvious difficulty with this solution is that it ignores the algebra of expectations and for that reason is not likely to be widely accepted.

Time Trade-Off

A second method of assigning values to health states is the time trade-off method. Torrance (1989) says that this method gives results comparable to those offered by the standard gamble, but is easier for an informant to understand. While the standard gamble does not require a concept of time to be incorporated into the assessment, the time trade-off, as its name implies, depends on equating alternative health states on the basis of time.

The general form of the time trade-off is given by equating a specified amount of time in a less desirable state to a to-be-determined amount of time in a more desirable state. This equivalency is shown in Figure 14.5. In that figure, the amount of time spent in each state of health is given on the horizontal axis, and the health value of each state of health is given on the vertical axis. The time in the less desirable, assessed state is equal to t_1; the time in the more desirable, known state 2 is equal to t_2. The time t_1 of the less desirable state h_3 is specified for the informant (e.g., one year), after which the informant reverts to known state 1, which in this case is assumed to be less desirable than the assessed state. The informant is then asked how much time he or she would have to stay in known state 2 before reverting to known state 1 for that time to be equivalent to time t_1 in the assessed state. The value of the assessed state is then assumed to be the value for h_3 that makes the area under each of the two rectangles equal. The value of h_3 is:

$$h_3 = \frac{(h_2 - h_1)t_2 + t_1 h_1}{t_1} \tag{14.3}$$

FIGURE 14.5

General Model of the Time Trade-Off

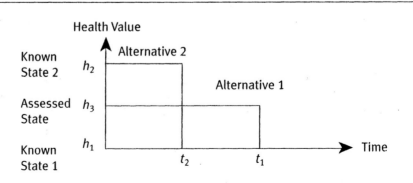

which is the solution for h_3 of:

$$(h_3 - h_1)t_1 = (h_2 - h_1)t_2$$

In a typical time trade-off assessment, known state 2 would be equated with complete health and, similar to the convention for the standard gamble, assigned a value h_2 of 1. Known state 1 would typically be equated with death and assigned a value h_1 of 0. Under these circumstances, Equation 14.3 is reduced to:

$$h_3 = \frac{t_2}{t_1}$$

Assessment for a Chronic Condition

Figure 14.6 shows the time trade-off used to assess diabetes, a chronic condition. As shown in this figure, the informant would be told that he or she could live for a time t_1 (e.g., ten years) as a diabetic, after which he or she would die. The alternative would be to live for a number of years less than ten in complete health, after which the informant would die. The informant would then be asked to specify the number of years he or she would be willing to accept in full health to make that time equivalent to ten years as a diabetic. If the informant agreed to 7.5 years, the health value of diabetes would be 7.5/10, which equals .75.

In the case of diabetes, a long-term, chronic condition that can be controlled with medication and diet, ten years of life as the value of t_1 probably is reasonable. In certain cases, the amount of time that a person may live in a chronic state may be substantially shorter. Progression to death with other chronic conditions (e.g., end-stage renal failure) may be much more rapid. In such a case, both t_1 and t_2 may be specified in terms of months rather than years.

Assessment of a Temporary Condition

The diagram in Figure 14.7 provides a model for the assessment of the temporary condition, radius fracture with stiff cast, against the worst temporary condition, severe and persistent migraine. In this assessment, the informant is asked to imagine

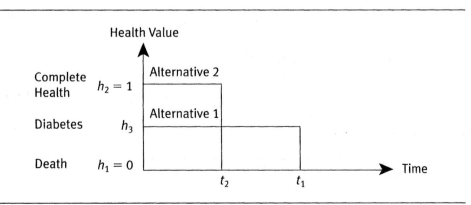

FIGURE 14.6

Time Trade-Off for Chronic Disease Diabetes

FIGURE 14.7
Time Trade-Off for
Temporary
Condition
Fractured Femur

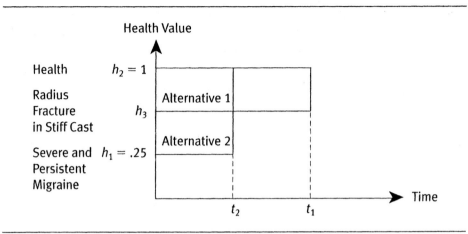

a trade-off between a certain amount of time with a radius fracture in a stiff cast, and then return to a better health state (usually complete health), or to imagine a lesser amount of time in the worst temporary state (severe and persistent migraine), and then return to the better health state. In this formulation, the objective is to equate the area represented by alternative 1, radius fracture (that is, $t_1 \times [h_2 - h_3]$) with the area represented by alternative 2, severe and persistent migraine ($t_2 \times [h_2 - h_1]$) and solve for h_3 given values for h_1, h_2, and t_1 set by the assessors and a value for t_2 established by the informant.

In general it would be expected that the value of t_1 would be set to a reasonable time for the complete healing of a radius fracture, for example, ten weeks. Then the informant would be asked how long he or she would be willing to be in a state of severe and persistent migraine before returning to the better health state, to be equivalent to ten weeks with a radius fracture before returning to the better health state. Using the approach of decreasing week intervals, the informant may indicate that he or she was unwilling to be in a state of severe and persistent migraine for a period of three weeks to avoid ten weeks with a radius fracture. The informant would be willing, however, to be in the same state for two weeks. In that case, 2.5 weeks would be assigned to t_2, and the value of h_3 is found by equating the area of alternative 1 with the area of alternative 2, or:

$$(h_2 - h_3)t_1 = (h_2 - h_1)t_2$$

Solved for h_3, the preceding equation is:

$$h_3 = \frac{t_1 h_2 - (h_2 - h_1)t_2}{t_1} \qquad (14.4)$$

Given that $h_2 = 1$ and $h_1 = .25$, 14.4 reduces to:

$$h_3 = 1 - \frac{.75 t_2}{t_1} \cong .81$$

Again, it is necessary a priori to have a health value assigned to severe and persistent migraine. This can be done within the context of the time trade-off by redefining the worst temporary condition as a short-term chronic state that, once entered, will be followed by death and assess it against immediate death, as is done with the diabetes example in Figure 14.6.

Assessment of States Worse Than Death

The time trade-off can also be used to assess states considered to be worse than death just as can the standard gamble. In the time trade-off, the diagram for states worse than death would be as shown in Figure 14.8. In this figure, however, the comparison is not living in one state or the other for a certain amount of time. Instead, the comparison is between immediate death as one alternative, or life for a certain amount of time in complete health, followed by life for another period of time in the state worse than death. In this formulation, the two areas to be equated are the area for the time lived in complete health ($[h_2 - h_1] \times t_2$) with the area for the time lived in the state worse than death ($[h_1 - h_3] \times [t_1 - t_2]$).

Typically, in the time trade-off, the informant would be told that he or she could die immediately or, alternatively, expect to live in a completely healthy state for a time period t_2, after which he or she would move to the state worse than death until time t_1, and then die. The informant would then be asked how much time he or she would have to spend in complete health (up to t_2) to be willing to spend the remainder of the time in the state worse than death (h_3). For example, if the total time was set at 12 months, they may be asked if he or she would be willing to have t_2 equal to 11 months. If the answer were yes, the question would be ten months. The number would decline until the informant would no longer be willing to make the trade. At that point, the value of t_2 would be given as the midpoint between the last month in which he or she would be willing to make the trade and the first month in which he or she would not.

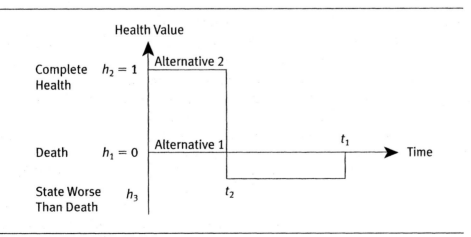

FIGURE 14.8
Time Trade-Off for State Worse than Death

When t_2 has been established, the value of h_3 can be found by the following equality:

$$(h_1 - h_3)(t_1 - t_2) = (h_2 - h_1)t_2$$

When solved for h_3, this becomes Equation 14.5:

$$h_3 = \frac{(h_2 - h_1)t_2 + t_2 h_1 - t_1 h_1}{t_2 - t_1} \qquad (14.5)$$

When $h_2 = 1$ (complete health) and $h_1 = 0$ (death), 14.5 reduces to:

$$h_3 = \frac{t_2}{t_2 - t_1}$$

For example, if an informant was willing to live 7.5 months in complete health in exchange for the remainder of 12 months in a state worse than death, rather than accepting the alternative of immediate death, the value of h_3 would be $7.5/(7.5 - 12)$, or -1.67.

As is the case with the standard gamble, values of health states more desirable than death are restricted to the range $0 \leq h \leq 1$, and the values of h are linear in respect to values of t_2. Also as with the standard gamble, however, no lower bound exists on the value of health states less desirable than death, and these values decrease at an increasing rate as t_2 increases relative to t_1. As with the standard gamble, no particularly satisfactory way exists to deal with this problem, although Torrance (1986) has suggested that the worst possible state worse than death may arbitrarily be given a value of -1 and other states be scaled accordingly. This can be done by dividing the health value of all states worse than death by the value of the worst state. While this would force the health value of states worse than death into the range $0 \geq h \geq -1$, it would not remove the nonlinear aspect of the measurement.

Rating Scales

In comparison to either the standard gamble or the time trade-off, the rating scale is both conceptually and, usually, computationally simple. In assessing the utility of health states with a rating scale, informants would typically be provided with a type of visual aid, such as a line on a page. An addition to this line may be clear reference points, as shown in Figure 14.9. Frequently, the end points of a figure like this would be death at one end and complete health at the other. Figure 14.9 is shown, however, with death not at the most extreme point on the scale to be consistent with the standard gamble technique and the time trade-off technique, because a possibility is that certain states may be worse than death.

Frequently, when the rating scale technique is used, informants are presented with the scale shown in Figure 14.9 and with a number of different named conditions (e.g., diabetes, radius fracture, severe and persistent migraine) or descriptions of conditions (e.g., trouble with hearing, remembering, or thinking

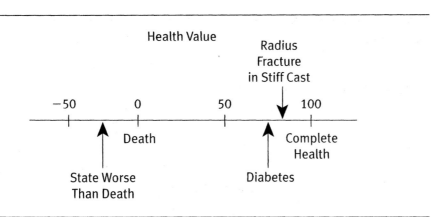

FIGURE 14.9
Rating Scale Model
for Health State
Assessment

clearly; headache or dizziness; ringing in the ears; hot spells; nervousness; or shakiness) that are recorded on small tags or slips of paper. The informants are then asked to place these tags in their relative position on the scale.

Authors who write on the use of rating scales make a point of saying that informants must be told that the conditions should not only be ordered according to their position on the scale, but that they should be placed at distances from one another that reflect the relative difference in how desirable or undesirable the conditions are. This is necessary to capture the underlying assumption that the rating scale is not only an ordinal scale, but also an interval scale. Most authors, including Torrance (1986), would argue that the inclusion of a 0 point for death does not raise the rating scale to the level of a ratio scale, just as the inclusion of a 0 point in a Fahrenheit thermometer does not raise the measurement of temperature to a ratio level.

It is quite possible that informants will have considerable difficulty placing a large number of diseases or poor health conditions relative to one another on a rating scale that may run from a level worse than death to complete health, particularly in making distinctions between two quite different, but seemingly undesirable, alternative states, such as diabetes and schizophrenia. To assist in the ordering task and to attempt to assure equal intervals between different sets of conditions, the informants may be asked to put the conditions into several different categories. The worst health condition may go into category 1 and the best health condition may go into category 12. Then other conditions would be put into one of the remaining ten intermediate categories.

Assessment for a Chronic Condition: Better Than or Worse Than Death

When a rating scale is used to rank various health conditions, these conditions would be expected to have certain aspects in common. For example, a group of chronic conditions being ranked would be expected to have the same age at onset and the same length of life after onset. This would be acceptable for conditions clearly more or less desirable than death, and such conditions could be ranked together on the same scale. Chronic conditions that may clearly have different ages at onset and different potential lengths of life after onset would be ranked in another group, however. For example, childhood onset diabetes and adult onset diabetes generally would not be ranked in the same group.

Assessment of Temporary Conditions

Temporary conditions can be ranked on a rating scale just as chronic conditions can, but in general would be ranked against a scale from the worst possible temporary condition to complete health. If this is done, however, establishing the ranking of the worst possible temporary state on a scale that includes chronic conditions ending in death is necessary. Temporary conditions would be ranked in groups for which the age of onset and length of condition would be specified. The assumption would be that after the specified length of time, the person in the state would return to the best state of health.

Paired Comparisons

A modification of rating scales that is similar to the standard gamble or the time trade-off but that may require less conceptual sophistication on the part of informants is the paired comparison. In this strategy for measuring the relative value of health states, each pair of states is compared and the informant is asked to select the state that is preferred for that pair.

In such a comparison, a reasonable expectation is that a transitivity of preference will hold. If condition A is preferred to condition B and condition B is preferred to condition C, condition A will be preferred to condition C. If this property holds, the paired comparisons will produce an ordered set, where one condition will be preferred to all others (e.g., complete health), the next most preferable condition will be preferred to all others except complete health, and so on, to a condition that is preferred to none. Under these circumstances, the number of other conditions that any given condition dominates becomes its score, so that if, for example, twenty conditions are being ranked, the worst condition will have a score of 0 and the best condition will have a score of 19.

In practice, if a large number of comparisons are being made, and particularly if many of the conditions are approximately equal in desirability or lack thereof, informants will not necessarily always exhibit this transitivity of preference. Certain conditions may be preferred to other conditions in a circular, or nontransitive, pattern. If this occurs, some of the conditions will then receive the same scores if they are scored as the number of other conditions that any condition dominates.

Assessment for a Chronic Condition: Better Than or Worse Than Death

There is no reason that chronic conditions of equal age at onset and equal length of life after onset cannot be assessed in the same paired comparison group, whether these are perceived a priori to be states more desirable than death or states less desirable than death. For example, if 20 health states, including complete health and death, and 18 chronic conditions were being assessed by a group of informants, whether a state was preferable to death or not should be determined by the informants. If an informant indicates a preference for death over a given chronic health state, that state is, for that informant, a state worse than death.

The score results of a paired comparison for a single informant will be the numbers ranging from 0 to one less than the number of states being compared. If the desire is to translate these scores to a scale ranging from 0 for death to 1 for complete health, doing so is possible with Equation 14.6:

$$h_i = \frac{s_i - s_d}{s_h - s_d} \qquad (14.6)$$

where h_i equals the score on a scale of 0 to 1 for condition i, s_i equals the original score value for condition i, s_d equals the original score value for death, and s_h equals the original score value for complete health.

If the informant has judged a state or states to be worse than death, the score for these states will automatically be converted into values less than 0. Unless the informant assesses more than half of the states as being worse than death, which is unlikely to occur, this scoring system has the characteristic that $-1 \le h_i \le 1$, for all h_i.

For example, suppose seven conditions are being compared relative to each other: death; health; diabetes; a state that in the paired comparison is judged by the respondent as worse than death; and three other states. Assume that transitivity of preference is displayed by the preferences, and diabetes is preferred over four other conditions. In this case, diabetes would be assigned a raw value of 4. As one state is judged worse than death, death is assigned a raw value of 1. The raw value of complete health is 6. With this information, the value h for diabetes is:

$$h_{diabetes} = \frac{s_{diabetes} - s_{death}}{s_{health} - s_{death}} = \frac{4 - 1}{6 - 1} = .6$$

The value h for the state worse than death is:

$$h_{swd} = \frac{s_{swd} - s_{death}}{s_{health} - s_{death}} = \frac{0 - 1}{6 - 1} = -.2.$$

Assessment of Temporary Conditions

Temporary conditions can also be assessed using paired comparisons in the same way that chronic conditions can be assessed. When this is done, complete health should be one of the comparison options, but death should definitely not be. When the comparisons are done, initial scores can again be assigned to each condition as the number of other conditions, which are less preferable. For example, if seven conditions are being compared, and for one of these four conditions are less preferable, the score for that condition is 4.

In this form, the score of 4 cannot be compared in any meaningful way to a score of 4 for a chronic condition ranked by paired comparison with death as one of the options. It is possible to put the temporary health states onto a scale with chronic health states by first including the least desirable temporary state as a chronic state in a paired comparison with the other chronic states, and then calculating a value for that chronic state using Equation 14.6. The values of the other temporary states can then be scaled comparable to the chronic states using Equation 14.7:

$$h_i = \frac{s_i(1 - h_w)}{s_h} + h_w \qquad (14.7)$$

where h_i equals the score on a scale of 0 to 1 for condition i, s_i equals the original score value for condition i, h_w equals the 0 to 1 scale value for the worst temporary state as determined by assessing it in a paired comparison with chronic states, and s_h equals the original score value for complete health as determined on the temporary condition scale.

To follow the preceding example, imagine seven temporary conditions were being compared, including complete health and six other states, and one of these (e.g., upper respiratory ailment) was preferred to all but complete health, and another (e.g., severe and persistent migraine) was preferred to no others. To convert the raw score of 5 (for upper respiratory ailment) it is necessary first to rate severe and persistent migraine as a chronic condition along with other chronic conditions to obtain a score on a 0 to 1 scale for severe and persistent migraine. Suppose this has been done and the value h_{spm} for severe and persistent migraine was found to be .25. The value h_{ura} for upper respiratory ailment is:

$$h_{ura} = \frac{s_{ura}(1 - h_{spm})}{s_h} + h_{spm} = \frac{5(1 - .25)}{6} + .25 = .875$$

where h_{ura} equals the 0 to 1 scale score for upper respiratory ailment, s_{ura} equals the raw score for upper respiratory ailment, h_{spm} equals the 0 to 1 scale score for severe and persistent migraine (determined in a paired comparison with chronic conditions), and s_h equals the raw score for complete health in the temporary condition comparison.

Development of Consensus Measures of Health States Using Utility Techniques

Thus far, we have presented the concept of utility measures as being assessed by a single informant. In the development of health utility using the techniques discussed here, the rankings would be performed by a number of people (Stiggelbout et al. [1996] report using 68 patients as assessors, Rutten-van Molken et al. [1995] report using two groups of 85 and 144 patients as assessors, Kaplan et al. [1989] report using 44 patients as assessors). The actual rankings of health states would represent the composite of all the informants.

For all the utility measures, the most useful composite of the ratings for representing consensus of informants is probably the mean, although the median has also been used. The median will give less weight to extreme judgments than the mean. In the standard gamble and time trade-off approaches, the value of interest would be the mean or median of the h values assigned to any health state. With the rating scale, the value of interest would be the mean scale position assigned to a given health state. With paired comparisons the mean number of states would be considered less desirable than the one assessed.

In accumulating informants to develop consensus assessments, a question of who the informants should be will arise. There seems to be no clear answer to this. Informants have been groups of clinicians or medical practitioners, healthy people with no particular knowledge of disease states being rated, patients with various conditions being rated, and even policymakers interested in the effect of changes in allocation of resources on health outcomes. In a large-scale utility assessment effort (Murray 1996), physicians were used specifically because they would require the least amount of background information on any health state, and thus be able to make informed assessments in the least amount of time. A major criticism of the utility measure concept is the likelihood that different people have different utilities for various health states depending on their first-hand knowledge of those states.

The development of consensus measures, by any of the techniques discussed here, can also be influenced by the degree to which the health conditions are detailed for the informants. There seems to be disagreement among those who have used the various techniques as to how detailed the descriptions should be. The descriptions may range from a single descriptive name (e.g., diabetes) to a brief description of a condition (e.g., able to walk only short distances with walking equipment, and requires a wheelchair to get around the neighborhood [Boyle et al. 1995]), to a fairly extensive description of a feeling state including both physical impairments and psychological response to those.

Comparison of Utility Measures

The standard gamble, the time trade-off, and the paired comparison are implicit measures of health states. The informants are asked to rank one condition against another and from those comparisons a score is developed that puts all conditions on a scale from (in the case of only conditions more desirable than death) 0 to 1. The rating scale is an explicit measure of health state. This methodology asks the informant to directly and explicitly put the various health conditions into a scale relative to one another (which may range from 0 to 1, but does not need to do so).

A criticism of all these techniques is that people for whom assessed states are hypothetical may assess them differently from people for whom they are more realistic. This problem has been noted particularly by Kind and Dolan (1995), whose work shows clearly that different results may be obtained in valuations of health states based on the current health status of the assessors.

Assessment of the Standard Gamble

One of the most important arguments for the use of the standard gamble as a measure of the utility of a health state is that it is based on the von

Neumann-Morgenstern utility, which fits nicely into the decision theory model as discussed in Chapter 16 on operations research techniques. A second argument is that an element of risk is introduced into the assessment through the standard gamble, and any health situation inherently involves risk.

A number of potential problems exist with the standard gamble as a strategy for assigning a measure to a particular health state, however. One of these is the problem of nonlinearity in the values assigned to states worse than death. Of more difficulty is the concept of probabilities that the standard gamble forces informants to understand and deal with. Not all people are equally comfortable with the concept of probabilities, and their ability to think in terms of probabilities seems to become increasingly difficult as the probabilities become very large or very small.

Assessment of Time Trade-Off

The time trade-off strategy for measuring the value of a given health state seems to be less difficult for informants to understand and thus may be a better alternative to the standard gamble. Such is the case especially when it is not easy to ensure that informants actually grasp the concept of probabilities embodied in the standard gamble. However, the time trade-off is also more complex than either the rating scale or the paired comparison, both of which are relatively easy for informants to understand. The time trade-off also has the same problem as the standard gamble in that scores for states assessed as worse than death do not automatically have a convenient lower limit such as −1.

Assessment of Rating Scales

Rating scales are certainly the easiest of the utility measuring devices for the average informant to understand. Their explicit nature is quickly communicated to the informants. If informants also are told to place the conditions on the rating scale not just in an ordered manner but in a manner that is reflective of an interval measure (i.e., that the distance between conditions should represent the relative degree to which the better placed condition is preferable to the other), they are usually quite able to so.

Rating scales also seem to require somewhat less time in that informants do not seem to agonize so long over the decisions they make. However, several authors (Rutten-van Molken et al. 1995; Mulley 1989; Read et al. 1984) have noted that assessments by patients of their own health states relative to others tend to be lower when assessed on rating scales than when assessed through the standard gamble (and one might assume time trade-offs as well). Unlike both the standard gamble and the time trade-off, however, rating scales provide explicitly for the measures of states worse than death, if such are assessed, to be on a scale where the score of the worst state can still be easily limited to a scale with values no lower than −1.

Assessment of Paired Comparisons

Paired comparisons are an implicit strategy for assessing health states that have some of the simplicity of the rating scale but at the same time allow direct comparisons between states. The paired comparison does have some significant limitations, however.

The standard gamble, time trade-off, and rating scales all have the capability to produce a resulting set of ratings that can be perceived as interval in nature. The paired comparison produces, at best, an ordinal scale. For example, suppose three states have the characteristic in the paired comparison for one informant that one is preferred to seven other health states, one to six other health states and one to five other health states. The raw score for these health states in the paired comparison would be 7, 6, and 5, respectively. No reason exists, however, to believe that the preference for the state with a score of 7 over the state with a score of 6 is the same degree of preference as the preference for the state with a score of 6 over the state with a score of 5. If a large number of informants are asked to compare health states, however, the average preference for each health state across all informants may begin to take on the characteristics of an interval scale.

Another limitation of the paired comparison is the amount of effort required of the informant. For example, if 20 health states (including death and complete health) were being assessed using the standard gamble or time trade-off, it would essentially be necessary to compare each of the assessed states only to death and to complete health for 18 comparisons. If the same 20 states were being assessed using a rating scale, the informant again places 20 conditions along a continuum. If a paired comparison is used to assess the same 20 health states, however, the informant must make a decision on 190 different pairs. While in many cases making a decision is extremely easy (e.g., complete health compared to death), the physical act of assessing 190 pairs remains time consuming. This becomes particularly important when health states are quite similar to each other.

Converting Measures from Individual Scores to Population Scores

As they apply to individuals, utility measures can be useful as a way of assessing the results of a program intervention (e.g., across a range of recipients of the program). Utility measure scores for 30 people who were part of a pilot rehabilitation program may be compared to utility measure scores of 30 people who were not part of the program. Utility measures can also be used to create composite scores for whole populations using the concept of quality adjusted life years (QALYs). The QALY is a manifestation of the desire to equate utility value of years of life for healthy people with the utility value of years of life for people who are less than totally healthy.

Quality Adjusted Life Years (QALY)

The quality adjusted life year (QALY) embodies the concept of assigning the utility of the state in which a person transits a given year of life to the year itself, so that, for example, if a person were in a state of health during the year that was assessed through one of the utility measures as having a value of .75 (on a scale from 0 to 1, or from a negative value to 1), then that person's year of life would be counted as .75 QALYs. If 100 people transited a year of life, some in complete health (score of 1), some in states of health with utility values ranging from negative values to positive proportions of 1, and if the average utility value for all 100 people was, for example, .8, the 100 people would have accounted for 80 QALYs. Similarly, if a single person transited ten years of life, six of them spent in complete health and four of them spent in a state of health having a utility of .6, then that person would have accounted for 8.4 QALYs (6 years × utility of 1 + 4 years × utility of .6).

The use of QALYs in evaluation arises from the desire to compare populations in terms of outcomes of health programs. For example, if one population is provided fee-for-service medical care while another is enrolled in a capitated managed care plan, what is the result in terms of life years for the entire populations adjusted for quality (QALYs)?

From another perspective, suppose one population was made up of 1,200 people who had an average QALY level of .7 for 11 years (a total of 9,240 QALYs) and another population was made up of 1,000 people with an average QALY level of .924 for 10 years (for a total, again, of 9,240 QALYs). From the standpoint of QALYs as an aggregate measure of payoff, both populations (one of 1,200 person living 11 years, and one of 1,000 people living 10 years) are exactly equivalent. Further, if one person lived for ten years with a utility level of .9 (9 QALYs), that would be exactly equivalent to nine people living one year each with a utility level of 1.

For this concept of QALYs to be useful, it is necessary to be able to assign a value during a year or a part of a year to all people transiting that year, regardless of their health state. This requires that the states of health to which utility values are assigned must be readily recognizable, either to an external assessor or to the people under study. If the people under study are making the assessment of their own relative utility states (e.g., by means of a questionnaire that asked them to rate themselves on a variety of dimensions), the assessment tool can be fairly detailed. An example of this questionnaire, the Health Utilities Index—Mark III, is shown in Table 14.1.

TABLE 14.1
Health Utility Index—Mark III Health Status Classification System: Attributes and Functional Level Descriptions

Attribute	Level	Description
Vision	1	Able to see well enough to read ordinary newsprint and recognize a friend across the street without glasses or contact lenses.
	2	Able to see well enough to read ordinary newsprint and recognize a friend across the street, but with glasses.
	3.	Able to read ordinary newsprint with or without glasses but unable to recognize a friend on the other side of the street, even with glasses.
	4	Able to recognize a friend on the other side of the street with or without glasses but unable to read ordinary newsprint, even with glasses.

TABLE 14.1
(Continued)

Attribute	Level	Description
	5	Unable to read ordinary newsprint and unable to recognize a friend on the other side of the street, even with glasses.
	6	Unable to see at all.
Hearing	1	Able to hear what is said in a group conversation with at least three other people without a hearing aid.
	2	Able to hear what is said in a conversation with one other person in a quiet room without a hearing aid, but requires a hearing aid to hear what is said in a group conversation with at least three other people.
	3	Able to hear what is said in a conversation with one other person in a quiet room with a hearing aid, and able to hear what is said in a group conversation with at least three other people with a hearing aid.
	4	Able to hear what is said in a conversation with one other person in a quiet room without a hearing aid, but unable to hear what is said in a group conversation with at least three other people even with a hearing aid.
	5	Able to hear what is said in a conversation with one other person in a quiet room with a hearing aid, but unable to hear what is said in a group conversation with at least three other people even with a hearing aid.
	6	Unable to hear at all.
Speech	1	Able to be understood completely when speaking with strangers or friends.
	2	Able to be understood partially when speaking with strangers but able to be understood completely when speaking with people who know me well.
	3	Able to be understood partially when speaking with strangers or people who know me well.
	4	Unable to be understood when speaking with strangers but able to be understood partially by people who know me well.
	5	Unable to be understood when speaking with other people (or unable to speak at all).
Ambulation	1	Able to walk around the neighborhood without difficulty and without walking equipment.
	2	Able to walk around the neighborhood with difficulty, but does not require walking equipment or the help of another person.
	3	Able to walk around the neighborhood with walking equipment but without the help of another person.
	4	Able to walk only short distances with walking equipment, and requires a wheelchair to get around the neighborhood.

TABLE 14.1 (Continued)	Attribute	Level	Description
		5	Unable to walk alone, even with walking equipment. Able to walk short distances with the help of another person, and requires a wheelchair to get around the neighborhood.
		6	Cannot walk at all.
	Dexterity	1	Full use of two hands and ten fingers.
		2	Limitations in the use of hands or fingers, but does not require special tools or help of another person.
		3	Limitations in the use of hands or fingers, is independent with use of special tools (does not require the help of another person).
		4	Limitations in the use of hands or fingers, requires the help of another person with certain tasks (not independent even with use of special tools).
		5	Limitations in the use of hands or fingers, requires the help of another person for most tasks (not independent even with use of special tools).
		6	Limitations in the use of hands or fingers, requires the help of another person for all tasks (not independent even with use of special tools).
	Emotion	1	Happy and interested in life.
		2	Somewhat happy.
		3	Somewhat unhappy.
		4	Very unhappy.
		5	So unhappy that life is not worthwhile.
	Cognition	1	Able to remember most things, think clearly, and solve day-to-day problems.
		2	Able to remember most things, but has a little difficulty when trying to think and solve day-to-day problems.
		3	Somewhat forgetful, but able to think clearly and solve day-to-day problems.
		4	Somewhat forgetful, and has difficulty when trying to think or solve day-to-day problems.
		5	Very forgetful, and has great difficulty when trying to solve day-to-day problems.
		6	Unable to remember anything at all, and unable to think or solve day-to-day problems.
	Pain	1	Free of pain and discomfort.
		2	Mild to moderate pain that prevents no activities.
		3	Moderate pain that prevents a few activities.
		4	Moderate to severe pain that prevents certain activities.
		5	Severe pain that prevents most activities.

Source: Boyle et al. 1995.

If an external panel of judges were assigning the relative utilities, the assessment tool would generally need fairly gross and easily recognizable categories. An assessment tool developed by Rosser and Kind (1978) uses the combination of two continua with relatively easily recognized categories, one assessing distress (pain), and one assessing disability (limitation of activity). These two continua are shown in Table 14.2. The two dimensions of distress and disability are then combined in a matrix as is shown in Table 14.3.

Rosser and Kind arrived at score values for each of the 32 states by asking selected informants, including medical and psychiatric patients, nurses, physicians, and healthy volunteers, to rate each of the 31 states other than A/I in regard to how much worse the state was than state A/I. Seventy respondents were asked to rate each of the 32 combinations in the matrix, and the median rating was accepted as the scale score. As the ratings indicate, two of the combinations, A/VIII and D/VII were actually rated below 0, indicating that the respondents assessed these conditions as states worse than death.

Numerous criticisms have been leveled at the use of QALYs (see Potts 1992; Richardson 1994). Some of these criticisms arise from:

- the nature of utility functions themselves;
- the difficulty of actually assessing utility through any of the four techniques previously discussed;

TABLE 14.2
Grades of Disability and Distress for Assessment of Utility of Life States

Grades of Disability

Grade I	No disability
Grade II	Slight social disability
Grade III	Severe social disability, slight impairment of performance at work, or both; able to do all except heavy housework
Grade IV	Choice of work or performance at work severely limited, housewives and old people able to do only light housework but able to go out shopping
Grade V	Unable to undertake any paid employment, unable to continue any education; old people confined to home except for escorted outings and short walks and unable to shop; housewives able to perform only a few simple tasks
Grade VI	Confined to chair or wheelchair or able to move only with support
Grade VII	Confined to bed
Grade VIII	Unconscious

Grades of Distress

Grade A	None
Grade B	Mild
Grade C	Moderate
Grade D	Severe

Source: Rosser and Kind 1978.

TABLE 14.3

Matrix for Valuing Combinations of Disability and Distress for Assessment of Utility of Life States

		Distress Rating			
		A	B	C	D
Disability Rating	I	1.001	0.995	0.990	0.967
	II	0.990	0.986	0.973	0.932
	III	0.980	0.972	0.956	0.912
	IV	0.964	0.956	0.942	0.870
	V	0.946	0.935	0.900	0.700
	VI	0.875	0.845	0.680	0
	VII	0.677	0.564	0	−1.486
	VIII	−1.028	N/A	N/A	N/A

Source: Rosser and Kind 1978.

- the likelihood that one person's utility for a particular state will not be the same as another person's, particularly when one has firsthand experience with a given health state while another does not; and
- a number of methodological issues in defining and calculating utilities through any of the methods available.

Some of the criticisms of QALYs stem from their use in cost-utility analysis and the difficulties of defining whose costs are assessed, problems of discounting, and the general question of the desirability of any type of cost-utility analysis. Some of these issues are addressed in Chapter 17.

Some of the criticisms of QALYs are directed at the QALY itself. One such criticism is that the QALY discriminates against older people. A person at age 60 can produce only an average of perhaps 20 more QALYs, even if they remain in perfect health for the remainder of their life, while a person age 30 can produce perhaps 50 QALYs under the same circumstances, so it would seem reasonable to devote costly medical interventions to the 30-year-olds before the 50-year-olds.

Another criticism is that the QALY is indifferent between collective and individual good. An intervention that produces 20 healthy years of life for one person is no different than an intervention that produces one healthy year of life for 20 people. Distributive justice would seem to favor the latter over the former. Finally, the QALY could be used to justify euthanasia. People living in states of negative QALYs could possibly be considered targets for cost reduction for society.

The DALY as a Universal QALY

One form of QALY that has received much attention in the international arena is the disability adjusted life years (DALY). The DALY first gained prominence with the publication of the World Development Report, 1993 (World Bank 1993), where it was used both to demonstrate the world burden of disease, disability, and death and to show the comparative burden of disease, disability, and death among countries. The DALY has been discussed extensively by Murray (1994, 1996).

Like any other QALY, the DALY is a composite measure of years of life adjusted for the utility of the health state in which these years are lived. Unlike QALYs, however, time lost to nonfatal health states are measured on a scale from 0 for perfect health to 1 for death. The consequence of this is that DALYs are expressed as years lost to disease or disability, rather than years limited by disease or disability.

For example, if a person could expect to live ten years with a given chronic condition (e.g., diabetes), and the value normally assigned to diabetes is .75 on a scale where perfect health is 1 and death is 0, the general approach to QALYs would be to multiply 10 by .75 and report the result as 7.5 QALYs. Using this formulation, the person would have lost 2.5 QALYs to diabetes. The approach adopted with DALYs has been to weight diabetes on a scale of perfect health at 0 and death at 1, thus reversing the calculation and automatically producing in the preceding case 2.5 DALYs for diabetes, which corresponds to 2.5 years of life lost.

The benefit of weighting DALYs so that complete health gets a weight of 1 is that the DALYs based on years lost to nonfatal health states can be directly added to DALYs based on years lost to mortality. In general, QALYs have not been used to assess years of life lost to death, but as the DALY concept was developed particularly to provide a mechanism for assessing the global burden of disease and injury based on both death and reduced health states, the addition of years of life lost to mortality is essential to the concept. This means that every measure of DALYs is the sum of years lost to nonfatal health states, whether temporary or permanent, and of years lost to premature death.

To assess DALYs based on nonfatal health states, it is necessary to know how long people have lived or may be projected to live in the various health states. To assess DALYs lost to premature death, it is necessary to know how long a person would have been expected to live if that person had not died at a given point in life. Both types of DALYs require a measure of expected length of life at the onset of a nonfatal but chronic condition, or expected length of life at death.

Murray (1996) makes a strong point of the idea that the DALY has been developed specifically as a common means of assessing burden of disease that would be equivalent for all countries. Because of this, a standard life table with a life expectancy at birth for women of 82.5 years and a life expectancy at birth for men of 80 years is used as the common life expectancy assessment tool. Table 14.4 shows the life expectancies at birth, age one, and five-year age intervals to age 100 used by Murray (1996). This life expectancy table is adjusted for conditions that are chronic nonfatal by a fairly complex process discussed in Murray and Lopez (1996), so that specific chronic conditions generate their own life expectancy tables.

Murray (1996), working with the World Health Organization, developed valuations for 22 specific health states based on a modification of the time trade-off technique known as the person trade-off. Person trade-off is viewed as more appropriate to decisions being made by those setting policy in the healthcare realm than is time trade-off. In the person trade-off employed by Murray, both chronic and temporary health states have been treated in the same assessment.

TABLE 14.4

Standard Life Expectancies of Each Age for Computation of DALYs (Murray 1996)

Age (Years)	Life Expectancy (Years)	
	Females	Males
0	82.50	80.00
1	81.84	79.36
5	77.95	75.38
10	72.99	70.40
15	68.02	65.41
20	63.08	60.44
25	58.17	55.47
30	53.27	50.51
35	48.38	45.56
40	43.53	40.64
45	38.72	35.77
50	33.99	30.99
55	29.37	26.32
60	24.83	21.81
65	20.44	17.50
70	16.20	13.58
75	12.28	10.17
80	8.90	7.45
85	6.22	5.24
90	4.25	3.54
95	2.89	2.31
100	2.00	1.46

For example, severe sore throat was assessed on the same scale as blindness. In Murray's formulation, conditions that may reasonably be considered as worse than death were not assessed. In Murray's view, conditions worse than death may be quite important in decisions about the treatment of individual patients but can be seen as equivalent to death in a policy level assessment such as the DALY.

Given the interest only in assigning a value to health states not considered to be worse than death, and treating temporary conditions identically with chronic ones, the person trade-off could be pictured as shown in Figure 14.10. It can be seen that the person trade-off looks very much like the time trade-off given in Figure 14.6, except that here the vertical dimension is number of people rather than time. The question for the person trade-off in Figure 14.10 would be stated as: If you had the resources to ensure 1,000 completely healthy people one additional year of life, would you be willing to expend the same resources to ensure 1,500 people with diabetes one additional year of life? The number of people in the disease state diabetes is varied until the informant is indifferent between providing a year of life to 1,000 healthy people or to the number of people with diabetes indicated. Computation of the DALY weighting in this case would again be found (as with the case of the time trade-off given in Equation 14.3) by determining the value for diabetes that makes the area under each of the two rectangles equal. Because the person trade-off used in DALY computation

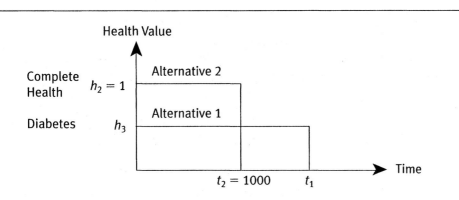

FIGURE 14.10
Person Trade-Off
for Chronic Disease
Diabetes

reverses the direction of the values of health states, however, the value of h_3 is found using Equation 14.8, which is Equation 14.3 (with $h_2 = 1$ and $h_1 = 0$) subtracted from 1, or:

$$h_3 = 1 - \frac{t_2}{t_1} \tag{14.8}$$

where t_2 and t_1 are as given in Equation 14.3. On this basis, if the policy-level informants were indifferent between giving 1,000 healthy people an extra year of life or giving, for example, 1,333.33 diabetics an extra year of life, the value h_3 of diabetes would be .25.

The actual list of conditions valued by Murray and his colleagues in the DALY assessment numbered in the hundreds. Each condition was placed in one of seven categories that were developed in a consultative meeting sponsored by the World Bank and held at the headquarters of the World Health Organization (WHO) in Geneva, Switzerland in August 1995. The consultative meeting assessed 22 specific health states, both temporary and chronic, which were then collapsed into the seven categories. These categories were then assigned disability weights based on the range of the representatives of the 22 categories that appeared in each category. The categories, specific health conditions of the original 22 assessed at the Geneva meeting and the range of weights assigned to each category are shown in Table 14.5.

The computation of DALYs for a person who develops a chronic nonfatal condition at a given age and then dies at a later age but short of the life expectancy at that age would contribute two components to the DALY score. These would include the disability-weighted time for the chronic condition before death (with perfect health scored as 0), plus the number of years lost to premature death.

For example, if a person developed adult onset diabetes at age 45 and died at age 55 the DALY, based on a hypothetical score of .25 for diabetes and life expectancy at age 55 based on Table 14.4, the score for that person would be .25 × 10 + 29.77 = 32.37. The actual computation of DALYs includes additional assumptions about the value of a year of life at a given age and the discounting of future years of life, so that the actual DALY total in the case above

TABLE 14.5

Disability Classes
Used in the
Calculation of
DALYs, Based on
Geneva Meeting of
1995

Disability Class	Severity Weights	Indicator Conditions
1	0.00–0.02	Vitiligo on face, weight-for-age less than two standard deviations
2	0.02–0.12	Watery diarrhea, severe sore throat, sever anemia
3	0.12–0.24	Radius fracture in a stiff cast, infertility, erectile dysfunction, rheumatoid arthritis, angina
4	0.24–0.36	Below-the-knee amputation, deafness
5	0.36–0.50	Rectovaginal fistula, mild mental retardation, Down syndrome
6	0.50–0.70	Unipolar major depression, blindness, paraplegia
7	0.70–1.00	Active psychosis, dementia, sever migraine, quadriplegia

would be substantially less than 32.37. The assumptions about the value of a year of life at a given age and the discounting of future years of life are addressed in greater detail in Chapter 17.

Summary

There are a number of ways in which the utility of health states have been measured. Each way presents problems and provides unique information not available in measures such as mortality or morbidity data. The major difficulty of using utility measures is reaching consensus about what particular disease states mean in terms of utility. Clearly, much work remains before utility measures are as widely available as data on mortality or are as widely accepted in evaluation as data on morbidity.

Discussion Questions

1. What are the various mechanisms for valuing human life and how are they implemented?
2. What problems may arise from the different mechanisms for valuing human life in terms of comparisons among them?
3. What is the benefit of using the mechanisms for valuing human life and what types of decisions might be made with these valuations?
4. What are the possible pitfalls in using these mechanisms for valuing life?
5. What is the nature of QALYs and DALYs and how can these be used for policy decisions, if at all?

15

SAMPLING

S ampling has two main functions: (1) describing a total population on the basis of an examination of only a small part of it; and (2) being certain that results obtained from an experiment reflect its true effect. The objective of this chapter is to apply the principles of sampling to program evaluation. The differences between descriptive sampling and sampling for more analytic evaluation are addressed. Various types of sampling designs are considered, together with external-internal validity, bias, and precision. The chapter concludes with the selection of a sample of health departments to illustrate basic sampling procedures.

Descriptive versus Analytic Sampling

Sampling for descriptive purposes involves populations of interest already defined. Such a population may be all the people served by a health services program, all the people within a geographic area where a new planning program has been instituted, or all the hospitals in a state. It may be too costly or physically impossible to obtain information about all members of a population of interest. Thus, a sample may be drawn on the basis of known and agreed-on criteria to be used as the basis for estimating the characteristics of the total population.

Sampling for analytic purposes is a means to ensure that differences found between an experimental group and a control group can actually be attributed to the experimental intervention and are not a function of other external or unmeasured factors. Sampling, or in this case, random assignment of units under study to experimental or control groups, represents an effective control for factors to be excluded as possible causes of observed differences in outcome measures for the experimental and control groups. In every instance, the units to be included in the sample, or the decision about whether a particular unit is in an experimental or control group, must be the result of a random process or chance.

A sample drawn on a random basis or chance is referred to as a *random sample* or a *probability sample*. This chapter refers to random samples or probability samples more or less interchangeably. The design of a sample involves a number of basic terms and concepts: mean, variance, standard deviation, and standard error of the means. The mean refers to the average value of the variable of interest and is calculated as:

$$\mu = \frac{\sum_{i=1}^{N} X_i}{N} \tag{15.1}$$

where X is the value of the variable of interest and N is the number of observations.

The variance is a measure of dispersion—that is, the extent to which the number of observations differs from one another for a variable of interest. It is calculated as:

$$\sigma^2 = \frac{\sum_{i=1}^{N}(X_i - \mu)^2}{N} \qquad (15.2)$$

The square root of the variance is the standard deviation:

$$\text{Standard deviation} = \sigma = \sqrt{\sigma^2} \qquad (15.3)$$

The *standard error of the mean* (also known as the *standard deviation of the sample mean*) is the square root of the average squared difference between the mean for each sample and the true population value μ and is calculated as:

$$\sigma_{\overline{X}} = SE_{\overline{X}} = \sqrt{\frac{\sum_{i=1}^{k}(\overline{X} - \mu)^2}{k}} = \sqrt{\frac{\sigma^2(N - n)}{n(N - 1)}} \qquad (15.4)$$

where k is the number of samples of size n that can be drawn from a population of size N. Because k is likely to be very large and in any case, the value of the mean for all samples is almost never known, the computation of the standard error of the mean is usually given as the term under the second square root sign in Equation 15.4. Even here, the true population variance is likely to be only rarely known. In most cases, the standard error of the mean is calculated on the sample estimate of the population variance. The use of these concepts and terms is described later in the chapter.

Issues of Sample Design Validity

When a sample is selected for the purpose of evaluating a program, the evaluator must be concerned about two types of validity: external validity and internal validity.

External Validity

External validity deals with the question of whether what is observed from the sample is true of the whole population. For example, if the evaluator finds that the greater proportion of sample program recipients favor the program, is it possible to conclude that the greater proportion of all service recipients are favorable toward it? Suppose that the selection of a sample to be used for evaluation is done on a random or probability basis. If so, sampling statistics or sampling theory provides a means by which to determine the validity of findings from the standpoint of inferences from the sample to the population and, in the case of experimental studies, the internal validity of the results on a sample itself. The critical factor, however, is whether the sample has been selected on a random or probability basis. If it has not (i.e., if the sample is a haphazard one, a sample of convenience, or another nonrandom sample), there is no theoretical basis on which to assess the validity of the results either internally or externally.

Because randomization, or the notion of a probability sample, is so critical to sampling and to the internal and external validity of results obtained from evaluations that involve sampling, discussion of randomization and its characteristics is needed. First consider the question of extrapolating from a sample to the total population—external validity.

Illustration

In drawing a sample to provide data that describe the total population, the evaluator is attempting to estimate, on the basis of the sample, certain important population values or characteristics. Suppose that the evaluator is trying to estimate the level of need in the population for primary healthcare services. The evaluator has available a scale that has been used to measure need in other populations. This scale, which physicians agree is valid, is based on physician examinations and questionnaires directed to the respondents that are capable of classifying people on an interval scale from 10 to 1, which represents high need to low need for personal health services. The evaluator will draw one sample of 100 people from the population. These individuals will complete questionnaires and have physical examinations from the physicians. Using this information, the evaluator will make an estimate of the probable level of need in the population.

Assuming that in the population of 10,000 people for whom an estimate of need is being determined, 1,000 people would actually be recorded by the assessment instrument as being in each of the ten levels. One thousand would be ranked 1, 1,000 would be ranked 2, and so on. In this case, the true mean level of need in the population would be 5.5. If every one of the very large number of possible samples of 100 was drawn from this population of 10,000—the total number of samples of 100 that can be drawn from a population of 10,000 without replacement is 10,000! (factorial)/100! × the quantity 10,000 minus 100!. The distribution of mean values (average assessment of need) for all these samples would be approximately normal with its midpoint at 5.5. The population variance for a set of data consisting of an equal number of values 1 through 10 is 8.25 (Equation 15.2). The standard error of the sampling distribution of the mean can be calculated as:

$$\sigma_{\overline{X}} = SE_{\overline{X}} = \sqrt{\frac{\sigma^2(N-n)}{n(N-1)}} = \sqrt{\frac{8.25 \cdot 9900}{100 \cdot 9999}} = .29 \qquad (15.5)$$

In a normal distribution the standard error of the mean has the interesting property that approximately 95 percent of the means of all the many samples of 100 that can be drawn from a population of 10,000 will be within two standard errors of the population mean. In terms of the present distribution, 95 percent of all possible sample results will show a mean between 4.93 and 6.07.

Using another perspective, because a normal distribution is symmetrical, only 2.5 percent of the samples will have mean values smaller than 4.93 (e.g., a sample in which of the 100 cases selected, all 100 were values of 1), and only 2.5 percent will have mean values greater than 6.07.

What have been described here are population values. The mean of 5.5 is a population value (i.e., a value that pertains to the entire 10,000 cases). The standard error of 0.29 is again a value that applies to the entire set of samples of size 100 that can be taken from these 10,000 cases, and the confidence limits of 4.93 to 6.07 represent population based confidence limits.

The important point, however, for estimating characteristics of a population is that data from a sample will work in almost precisely the same way. If a single sample of 100 cases is selected on a random basis, a standard error of the mean can be calculated by using the variance from the sample as an estimate of the true population variance. An estimate of the standard error of the mean can be calculated from the estimate of the variance, and confidence limits can be established about the estimated means of the population in exactly the same way.

For example, assume that the actual sample of 100 produced a mean value of 5.2 as the point estimate of the level of need, and a standard error for that mean of .33 as the estimate of the true standard error of the mean. We could then be 95 percent certain that the true need mean of the population lies somewhere between 4.54 and 5.86. This means that if we were able to select every sample of the many samples that could be drawn from a population of 10,000, sampling 100 at a time, 95 out of every 100 of those samples would produce a confidence limit of two standard deviations on either side of the estimated mean, which would include the true mean value of 5.5.

This type of statement can be made if sampling is random. If sampling is nonrandom, no statistical method exists to determine the accuracy of the estimate. Random selection provides external validity (i.e., it ensures that an assessment of the validity of the estimate can be made). Nonrandom sampling does not provide external validity.

Internal Validity

Internal validity is concerned with the question of whether the evaluator's observations or conclusions about relationships within the sample drawn actually exist for that sample. Suppose that an evaluator draws a sample of people who have access to a particular health services clinic and from this sample determines that over half the people sampled are satisfied with the services. Here, internal validity would be concerned with the extent to which that statement about the members of the sample is true. In this case, internal validity primarily involves how the determination is made as to whether people favor or do not favor the program. In other cases, the question of internal validity may be a sampling problem, particularly with regard to experiments.

Internal validity is similar to external validity in that it may depend on random sampling, but it is more specifically directed toward the issue of whether what has been observed within the sample is true for that sample, rather than true for a population. The issue of internal validity as it pertains to sampling arises specifically when the evaluation takes an experimental format. In the experimental setting a type of program is provided to one or more experimental groups of recipients while an alternative program or no program at all is provided to another group or groups of people, or other areas that are considered the controls. This ignores the nonexperimental before-after study with no control group, whether it is a panel study or a longitudinal time series analysis.

Assume again that the subject of interest is the level of need for primary healthcare services within a population of 10,000 people. Also assume that the provision of a certain level of primary healthcare services will reduce this need as evaluated by the instrument described in the preceding discussion. One hundred people in the population will be selected to receive these primary healthcare services for a specified period of time. One hundred other people in the population will be selected as controls; these individuals will not receive any special treatment, although they are free to obtain services in any way that they may have obtained them prior to the study.

Illustration

Suppose that every possible sample of 100 people was drawn from this population of 10,000 and compared to every other sample of 100 people in the complete absence of any program. This comparison (or the absolute value of the mean of the first sample minus the mean of the second sample) would produce a distribution with its minimum value at 0, where both samples of 100 people had exactly the same mean score. Its maximum value would be at 9, where everyone in one of the samples had a score of 10 and everyone in the other sample had a score of 1. The distribution would look something like Figure 15.1.

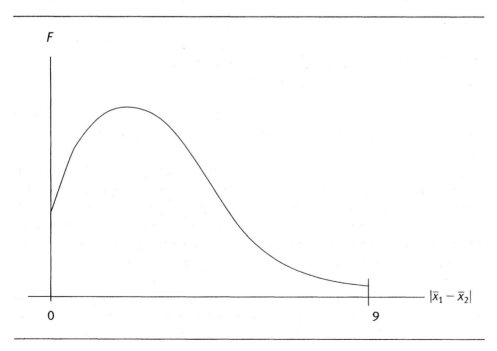

FIGURE 15.1
Hypothetical Distribution of Absolute Difference Between Means of Two Samples of 100

If the difference between the mean in each of the alternative samples being compared is now divided by the average standard error of the two samples, a *t*-test of the difference between the means can be performed. Because the best estimate of the variance for any sample is the population variance of 8.25, the best estimate of the pooled standard error for two samples (from the formula in endnote 1) is 0.071. If the difference between each possible pair of samples is divided by the pooled standard error, the result will be essentially a one-sided *t* distribution. What this means is that 95 percent of all the sample pairs will produce *t* values of less than about 2. There is less than a 5 percent chance of getting a value of a difference between two means divided by the pooled standard error that will be greater than 2.

Consider again the original idea of a single experimental sample and a single control sample. If they are randomly selected, the probability is .95 that at the outset they will have mean values that, when divided by the pooled standard error of the two groups, will produce a *t* less than 2. If, after the experimental group has received personal health services for a period of time, the difference between the groups divided by their pooled standard error is greater than 2, the researcher would conclude that there is a very small probability (.05 or less) that the two samples differed before the onset of the experiment. The researcher then would accept the alternative hypothesis that the experiment made a difference in the level of need.

This conclusion could be drawn even in the absence of any measurement of need before the beginning of the experiment. If such an experimental setting uses random selection to assign people to the two comparison groups, the experiment will have internal validity. If random selection is not used for group assignments, there is no way of assessing the probability that people's status beforehand will not be reflected in the measure of level of need after the experiment and consequently no way of assessing its internal validity.

Possibilities for Improving Internal Validity in the Absence of Random Selection

Often the case in evaluation is that random assignment to an experimental and control group is not possible, perhaps for ethical, political, or practical reasons, or because the evaluator has been brought in after the evaluation intervention has been initiated. In this situation, internal validity cannot be assured by random selection to experimental and control groups. However, an attempt to improve internal validity of an analytic evaluation can be made by using regression analysis to attempt to adjust for major differences between the intervention (experimental) and nonintervention (control) groups. For example, suppose that for practical reasons it is possible to initiate a program only at a county level, so that every person in the intervention county potentially will be affected by the intervention and every person in a nonintervention county will not. The people have not been selected at random for the intervention, so internal validity is threatened. Any difference found between the two counties could just as reasonably be due to preexisting differences on a range of characteristics of the people in the county as to the intervention itself.

The evaluators, however, possibly may determine that the major differences between the two counties prior to the intervention were age and gender distributions and that these differences are closely associated with a level of program output of interest. If the evaluators can use age and gender as independent variables to predict program output, they can then determine whether there is any difference between people in the intervention county and people in the control county when the effect of age and gender have been removed.

Suppose, however, that the evaluators were able to include all variables (i.e., age, gender, race, income, and so on) that may reasonably influence the level of program output. In this case, they could be fairly confident of the internal validity of the result (i.e., any difference between the intervention and the control county would be a function of the intervention). A problem is that it is rarely possible to be totally convincing that all variables on which people in the two counties may differ, and that also may have an influence on the measure of program output, had been included in the control. Nevertheless, if no possibility of random assignment exists, an effort at increasing internal validity using regression should be considered.

Bias, Accuracy, and Precision

Bias, accuracy, and precision are three important characteristics of any sample design. The terms actually refer to the estimates made from a particular sample. In general, these terms are applied to samples drawn for the purpose of making estimates about populations. In that sense, they would refer to samples taken from the survey research strategy or perhaps monitoring or case study approaches. It is also possible, however, to talk about bias, accuracy, and precision of estimates based on experimental sample designs.

In the case of descriptive samples, *bias* refers specifically to whether the expected **Bias** value of an estimator being used is the same as the true value being estimated. Suppose, for instance, that the purpose of an evaluation is to determine the extent of need for a specific type of medical care service within a geographic service area. Using a random or other type of probability sample for which each member of the population has a known and nonzero probability of being selected and using a nonratio estimator to determine the level of need in the population will give an unbiased result. It will be unbiased because every possible sample of an equal size from the population has a known nonzero probability of selection and the mean value of all these estimates would be the true population value. The selection of any single sample by this strategy would result in an unbiased estimate.

However, if the sample did not provide the possibility that every member of the population would have a known and nonzero chance of selection, the resulting estimate would be biased. The expected value or mean of all possible samples drawn in a manner in which every member of the population does not have a chance for inclusion would produce a biased estimate. The most common way in which biased estimates occur is when there is a difference between the target population (the one about which a statement is to be made) and the sampled population (the one actually available for selection).

In an attempt to estimate the need for a certain type of primary healthcare service in a geographic service area, bias could be introduced into the estimate in a number of ways. For example, it is possible that the population actually sampled to determine need is those who come to a clinic for services. If only the people who come to the clinic for services of a certain type are possible selections for a sample to estimate need for the entire service area, the sample will be heavily biased by the fact that people who do not use clinic services have no possibility of being selected.

Other sampling strategies can produce similar problems of bias. Suppose that a city is the service area for a healthcare provider in question; the sample of people in that service area may be drawn by using the telephone directory or tax listing for the community. Either approach, although better than a sample taken from people coming to the clinic, is still likely to produce a biased result. Not every family has a telephone. People with unlisted telephones or new arrivals in the community will not be listed. Not everyone is included on the tax rolls, and gaining access to these rolls is often difficult. Bias, therefore, can be introduced in estimations when either approach is used as the sampling frame.

Similar types of phenomena can occur in experimental work when people or other units of observation, such as organizations, are selected from a larger group to be included either in a control or an experimental group that will ultimately be compared to determine the effect of a program. If a sampling strategy is used for selecting the experimental and the control groups that will result in all possible pairs of samples being selected for comparison to one another, the result of this selection strategy will be an unbiased estimate of the effect of the experiment, at least as far as sampling is concerned. If, however, the sampling strategies used make it likely that only certain people or organizations are selected for the experimental group, while other people or organizations are selected for the control group, the result of the experiment in terms of sampling will be biased. It is as important in experimental work as in surveys or case studies to avoid bias if possible. In particular, if two strategies for sampling are available, of which each is essentially identical in cost, the one that produces the least bias should always be preferred.

Accuracy *Accuracy* refers only to the extent to which the estimate of the population is close to the true population value, regardless of whether the estimating was done on a biased or unbiased sample. Accuracy is basically independent of bias. A sample may produce a relatively accurate or inaccurate estimate and still be unbiased. Alternatively, a biased sample could produce a relatively accurate result. Accuracy is measured by the difference between the sample estimate of the population value and the true population value, but because the true population value is rarely known, the assessment of accuracy is rarely possible.

Precision is a measure of the degree of variation in the estimates that may be made **Precision** on the basis of all possible samples drawn in a particular manner. The best measure of precision is the standard deviation of the sample. If the standard deviation of the sample is large, precision is determined to be relatively low. If the standard deviation is small, precision is assumed to be fairly high.

Clearly, the desirable situation for any sample is one that is unbiased, relatively accurate, and highly precise. Combining all three characteristics is not always possible. In certain circumstances a biased estimate, such as one taken from a sample based on a telephone directory, may be the only estimate available or that the variation in the population is so great that a high degree of precision is impossible to obtain. Nevertheless, basic assumptions of sampling are that bias will be ruled out to the extent possible and that the sample will produce an accurate and precise estimate.

Estimating Optimal Sample Size

In many evaluation settings, the question arises of how large a sample is needed. There is no easy answer in all applications. In many types of program evaluation, the evaluator will be forced to accept a sample size smaller than what would be ideal. Suppose that a certain type of primary care program is being implemented within a number of local governmental jurisdictions and the desire is to compare some overall measures of health between those local jurisdictions and other control jurisdictions over a period of time. In this case, the evaluator must be satisfied with the number of places in which the program is being implemented, plus a number of nonimplementation areas, as the total universe of observations.

In other applications, the determination of an optimal sample size may be nearly impossible. When several variables are to be assessed at one time—for example, when the evaluation may involve something like analysis of covariance or regression—the determination of optimal sample size may be extremely difficult and probably not worth the time and effort of the evaluator. Then, the best strategy for determining sample size is getting as large a sample as feasible, given time and money constraints.

In one setting, however, what may be both desirable and possible is to determine an adequate sample size. Suppose that a certain number of people are to be selected for special treatment of a costly nature and a comparison is to be made afterward between a control group and the treated group to determine if there is a difference between the two groups. If the treatment is costly, selecting as small a sample as possible, while still being able to detect an expected difference of a certain amount, would make sense.

To put this issue in concrete terms, suppose that a traditional rehabilitation program returns 70 percent of eligible stroke victims to full functioning within a six-month time period, while the other 30 percent do not regain full function in that time period. Suppose also that an alternative rehabilitation program is expected to return a higher percentage of eligible stroke victims to full function in the same amount of time. Before adopting the alternative program, however, a trial period is proposed in which the effectiveness of the alternative program is to be tested. After this trial period a decision will be made as to whether to remain with the traditional method or to go to the alternative method. The trial period will last until enough people have gone through the alternative rehabilitation program to determine whether it results in a larger proportion of people returning to full function in a six-month period. Then the question is how many people have to go through the alternative rehabilitation program to say that it returns a higher proportion of eligible stroke patients to full functioning in six months.

This question may be approached many ways; many different information needs may arise depending on the approach. Only one is addressed as a way of considering the issue of optimal sample size, based on a comparison of historical data under the traditional approach to prospective data under the alternative rehabilitation method. Regardless of how the question of sample size is examined, one important issue will be the estimated variance σ^2 of the proportion, which will be necessary for calculating the estimated standard error $(S.E._{\bar{X}})$ of the available data. When proportions are being considered, the estimated variance (see Equation 15.2) is:

$$\sigma^2 = p(1 - p) \tag{15.6}$$

where p is the proportion with a given characteristic (in this case, 70 percent of the stroke victims). The standard error of the proportion would be calculated as Equation 15.4, above, but with the elimination of $(N - n)/(N - 1)$, because the potential universe of stroke victims is very large so that $(N - n)/(N - 1)$ essentially vanishes, and the standard error becomes:

$$S.E._{\bar{X}} = \sqrt{\frac{\sigma^2}{n}} = \sqrt{\frac{p(1 - p)}{n}} \tag{15.7}$$

Suppose we want to compare a new group of stroke victims, treated in the alternative manner, to the history of stroke victims for the past ten years. Perhaps in the past ten years, there have been 500 eligible stroke victims who have undergone the traditional rehabilitation program, out of whom 350 (70 percent) have recovered fully in six months. If all 500 people are used as n for Equation 15.7, the standard error of the proportion is .02. Because about two standard errors on each side of the mean (the proportion, in this case) includes about 95 percent of all possible means of sample size 500, there is a 95 percent certainty that the true population value for the proportion who recover fully from stroke in six months under the traditional method lies between .66 and .74 (assuming the actual 500 treated patients represent a sample of 500 from an unlimited population of potential eligible stroke victims). Clearly, whatever group of eligible stroke victims receive the alternative treatment, the proportion who recover fully in six months will have to exceed .74 or the alternative would not be viewed as being any better than the traditional method. Anything less than .74 would not be considered statistically different from .70.

Now suppose that the alternative program has begun—that 30 stroke patients are followed for the necessary six months, and a discovery is made that 24 of them (80 percent) have recovered fully in the six-month period. The proportion .80 is greater than .74, which is the approximate 95 percent upper limit for a true proportion of .70. Should the conclusion be that the program has been a success? The answer, unfortunately, is no. The reason the answer is no is shown in Figure 15.2, and has to do with sample size.

Figure 15.2 shows the proportion of people from the original 500 observations who recovered in six months, which is .70, and the distribution of possible mean values from a large number of samples of 500 around .70. The figure also shows the proportion of people from the subsequent 30 observations who received the alternative program and who recovered in six months, which is .80, and the distribution of possible mean values of a large number of samples of 30 around .80. The figure also shows the upper .95 limit of .74 for the sample of 500 and a lower .95 limit for the subsequent sample of 30 having a proportion of .80.

As Figure 15.2 shows, the conclusion is that if .80 is the *true* proportion of people who will recover using the alternative treatment method, this proportion is statistically greater than the observed .70 over the last 500 people treated (i.e., because .80 is greater than .74). On the basis of 30 people treated, however, the conclusion cannot necessarily be that the actual proportion who recover fully in six months using the alternative therapy is .80 over the unlimited number of people who may be eligible for the alternative program. The reason is that the standard error of .80 based on a sample of 30 is about .07, which means that two standard errors below .80 would be about .66. There is substantially less than 95 percent certainty that the observed proportion of .80 could not have come from a population in which the true proportion was as low as .70.

A sample size of around 180 is required to have 95 percent certainty that the alternative therapy actually produces a proportion of people fully recovered in

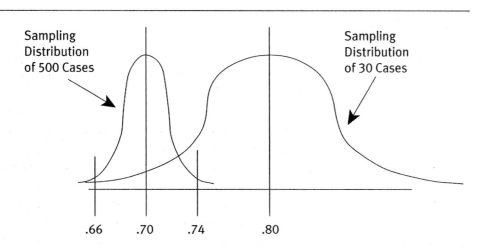

FIGURE 15.2

Sampling Distributions of Traditional Treatment for 500 Observations with 70 Percent Success and 30 Observations with 80 Percent Success

six months that is larger than .74 (the upper limit on the traditional method), given that the data still yield a proportion of .80 fully recovered. The standard error for a sample of 180, given that the proportion is .80, is about .03, and two standard errors below .80 would be about .74. If 180 eligible stroke victims could be followed through treatment and 144 were found to be fully recovered in six months, there would be 95 percent certainty that the new treatment was an improvement over the traditional treatment with $\alpha = \beta = .05$.

Unfortunately, 180 is a fairly large number, given that there have been only 500 eligible stroke victims over the past ten years. A question that may arise, therefore, is whether there is any way to arrive at a useful conclusion with fewer observations. One way would be to not consider the alternative program a useful new program unless it could raise the proportion of people who recover in six months from the current 70 percent to a level higher than 80 percent (e.g., 90 percent). If we made this decision at the outset, it would require that we follow only about 15 eligible stroke victims to determine that the proportion observed (if it was about .90) was larger than .74 with 95 percent confidence. (The standard error of .90 with 15 observations is about .08, so two standard errors below .90 is .74.)

This example points to two truisms in regard to determining sample size. First, the smaller the difference that is to be shown between two groups, the larger the sample must be to show that difference. It requires a larger sample to show that .80 is different from .70 than it does to show that .90 is different from .70.

Second, sample size is determined both by the variation in the control group and the variation in the intervention group. As previously addressed, the variation in the control group based on 500 observations is relatively small. However, even though we observe a proportion in the intervention group larger than the upper limit of the control group, we must still be concerned about whether the true value of the intervention group could be lower than the upper limit of the control group and we must have a sample large enough to assure that the probability of this is acceptably low.

Types of Samples

In general, for analytic evaluations such as the comparison of an innovative treatment modality to a control modality, the sample may be drawn, as was the case in the immediately previous example (i.e., all eligible cases included from the start of the program). The sample also can be drawn through a simple random method of assigning each succeeding case to the experimental or control group on the basis of a random assignment, by using a coin toss, for example. If the coin toss produces a head, the case is included in the experimental group; if the coin toss is a tail, the case is included in the control group.

For descriptive-type evaluations attempting to determine the level of need for services or results of a program on the basis of a case study or a survey, several kinds of sampling strategies may be considered applicable. This is depending on the information available for drawing the sample: simple random sampling, systematic sampling, stratified sampling, cluster sampling, or multi-stage sampling.

Simple Random Sampling

A *simple random sample* is one in which every member of the population, whether people, organizations, geographic areas, or political entities, has an equal probability or possibility of being selected. This distinction is important in comparison to systematic samples: each possible sample has an equal probability of being selected. As the name implies, simple random sampling is conceptually one of the simplest types of samples. In practice, however, it is not necessarily one of the easiest to implement.

Suppose that an estimate of the level of need for primary health services within a healthcare service area were desired, and that a reasonably accurate list of all people living within this area existed. A simple random sample could be drawn to produce an estimate of level of need, assuming the availability of an instrument to assess level of need. Suppose that 20,000 people were in the area under consideration, and that the decision had been made to select 400 as a sample to whom the need assessment instrument would be administered. The decision about the level of need for the entire population would be based on this sample of 400. If this were the case, each person in the population would have a .02 probability of being selected for the sample (400/20,000).

Illustration

Assuming that a numbered, ordered list of all people in the area is made available for sample selection, a strategy for selecting a simple random sample of 400 from the 20,000 people would be to select 400 random numbers in the range 1 to 20,000, and to include in the sample the people who corresponded to these 400 numbers from the numbered, ordered list. If the evaluator has access to a computer spreadsheet program such as Excel, this spreadsheet program could be used to generate a series of 400 random, uniformly distributed numbers between 1 and 20,000. Excel will produce the numbers, which will probably have to be rounded off to whole numbers, and will allow the evaluator to sort the selected numbers into ascending order. The evaluator can then go down the list of random numbers generated and select the person from the numbered and ordered list who corresponds to each random number generated by Excel.

A similar sampling strategy could be employed if the evaluation were concerned with estimating, for example, the level of health services available throughout an entire county. In this case, it may be substantially easier to compile a complete list of eligible sampling units—that is, a complete sampling frame. If an estimate of the primary healthcare services provided by local health departments within a state is to be produced, it would be quite easy to compile a list of all counties in the state. The list would not exceed 254 counties (Texas, the state with the largest number of counties, has 254 of them). From this list a random sample of counties could be drawn.

Limitations   Although simple random sampling is conceptually straightforward, it has two problems when compared to other sampling strategies. The first problem is one of precision. Because in a simple random sample every possible sample has an opportunity to be included, the sampling distribution of the means of simple random samples tends to be relatively larger than the sampling distribution of carefully designed stratified samples (to be discussed later). If a carefully designed stratified sample is possible, precision of the result will be potentially much greater.

The second problem of a simple random sample (and the problem that makes the name *simple* a misnomer in many instances) is the difficulty of obtaining a complete and accurate sampling frame. Even with a problem as small as sampling from an area with a population of 20,000 people, obtaining an accurate list of these 20,000 people to ensure that the target population and the sampled population are the same will likely be difficult. For example, it may be possible only to obtain a list of households that have telephones, or a list of registered voters. Neither list would be likely to include all 20,000 people in the area. To the extent that the target population and the sampled population are not the same, the sample result will be subject to bias.

Even if all 20,000 people in the area were included on an available list, drawing a simple random sample would still require that each name on the list be numbered. When the sample of 400 numbers was identified, the person on the list that corresponded to each of the 400 numbers selected must be found. While possible, this is not a simple task. These problems lead to the desirability of also considering other types of samples.

Systematic Samples

A simple random sample can be difficult to select from a large population, particularly when the large population is difficult to enumerate. A frequently used alternative to the simple random sample is the systematic sample. A *systematic sample* is one in which every member of the population, whether people, organizations, geographic areas, or political entities, has an equal probability or possibility of being selected. However, the systematic sample differs from the simple random sample in that not every sample has an equal probability of selection.

Illustration   Assuming that an estimate of the level of need for primary health services within a healthcare service area were desired and that a reasonably accurate list of all people living within this area existed, a systematic sample could be drawn to produce an estimate of level of need. Again, there are 20,000 people in the area under consideration and a sample of 400 will be selected for the need assessment. Again, each person in the population will have a .02 probability of being selected for the sample (400/20,000). In the systematic approach, however, not every possible sample of 400 has an equal probability of selection. In fact, because of the way in which the systematic sample is selected, only 400 different samples can be selected.

The systematic sample is selected by choosing one random number from the range 1 to 400. This can be done by using a random number table (and choosing only one number—throwing a dart at it would work) or by generating one random number in the range 1 to 400 using Excel. When the number is selected, the observation in the population corresponding to that number and every 400th observation thereafter becomes a member of the sample. For example, suppose that the random number chosen was 237. The 237th person on the list would be selected as the first member of the sample. The 637th would be selected as the second in the sample, the 1,037th person as the third in the sample, and so on, adding 400 each time until the entire sample was filled.

Selecting a systematic sample in this manner would require counting a new group of 400 people each time the next person was selected for the sample. In practice, however, a systematic sample can actually be easier than this. It is not uncommon, if a list of 20,000 people existed and was in a uniform type face, to simply measure with a ruler the space required to record 400 names. On the list, let us say it was 33 inches. Then, after the first person (number 237) was chosen, 33 inches on the list could be measured and the next person chosen, another 33 inches measured and the third person chosen, and so on. While this is not as precise as actually counting, it is an acceptable approach.

Limitations

Systematic sampling if often easier than simple random sampling but has significant drawbacks. One of these is the problem that the systematic sample actually represents a sample of one observation, in that once the first unit in the sample is chosen, all other units are fixed (in the preceding case, they are every 400th person after the first is selected). In terms of formal sampling theory, the systematic sample should be treated as a single observation even though it contains 400 cases. In practice, a systematic sample is generally treated as a simple random sample.

A second drawback of the systematic sample can also be an advantage. This is related to the ordering of the observations in the target population. In the case of the population of 20,000 people, if they were somehow ordered in a way that was actually related to need (e.g., by age) then the estimate using the systematic sample would tend to give a more accurate result than a simple random sample. If the target population was randomly ordered, the systematic sample would tend to give results about as accurate as could be expected from a simple random sample. If the target population was ordered in a repetitive pattern, so that those with least need tended to alternate with those with most need at about the same frequency as the sampling interval, highly inaccurate results could be obtained from a systematic sample. Systematic samples generally should always be avoided when there is evidence of repetitive ordering in the target population.

Stratified Samples

A *stratified sample* is specifically designed to increase precision and hence the probable accuracy of sample results. In stratified sampling the population is divided into two or more strata that are assumed to be closely associated with the characteristic of the population to be estimated. When estimating the need for primary care services, the population may be divided into two strata consisting of those people who had sought services in any of the healthcare agencies in the area during a specified period of time and those people who had not. The assumption would be that people who had sought services would be more likely to have a need for them. An alternative strategy would be to stratify the population on the basis of age on the assumption that perhaps the very young and very old are more likely to need primary care services than people in middle age. Other stratification variables could probably also be useful.

When a decision has been made about the stratification variable, two different approaches can be used to determine the size of the sample to be taken from each strata. Sampling can be based on drawing an equal number from each of the strata defined—generally the best approach when comparisons between strata are to be made. Sampling can also be based on the probability of selection proportional to the size of the strata. In general, when evaluating for descriptive purposes—usually the type done for the purpose of establishing the state of a system or determining the state after an intervention—overall estimates will be needed, and sampling probability proportional to strata size will be most useful. Suppose that the group of people within an area were divided for sampling purposes into those who have visited a clinic and those who have not. Suppose also that 32 percent of all area residents were known to have visited the clinic. Thirty-two percent of the sample should be taken from among the clinic visitors and 68 percent of the sample from among those who are nonclinic visitors. This process will generally give the most efficient sample for estimates of the overall need for services in the population.

Stratified sampling reduces the probability that extreme samples from the population will be selected and so increases the likely precision (and ultimately the accuracy) of the sample results. Assume that the population is divided into two strata, those who have and those who have not sought services from any healthcare facility within the past year. It is agreed that a specified number for the sample will be drawn from each of the two strata.

Suppose that 128 people will be drawn from those who have sought services (32 percent) and 272 from those who have not (68 percent). If people in least need of services were likely to have a low probability of being among those people who have sought services or, alternatively, those people in most need of services have a low probability of being among those who have not sought them in the past year, drawing a sample dominated by people in either group using this stratification technique will be unlikely. Consequently, the probability of obtaining a highly inaccurate or extreme appraisal of the need for services in the population has been reduced. The extent to which precision has increased and the probability of an inaccurate result has decreased is directly related to the extent to which need for services is associated with membership in one of the two stratification groups.

Limitation A major problem of stratified sampling is defining a sampling frame. In the example of the service area and the question of need for primary health services, stratification does simplify definition of the sampling frame for those who have visited the clinic. The frame thus becomes all people who have used clinic services. But it does not simplify the problem of getting a total list of people who have not used clinic services but who are residents, however defined, of the area. Consequently, the problem of ensuring that the target and sampled populations are the same remains, as well as the problem of potential bias resulting from selection of a sample that does not have as its expected value the true population value.

After sample strata have been defined (e.g., those who have used services and those who have not), the actual selection of people from each strata must be done either by simple random sampling or by systematic sampling. For sampling theoretical reasons, simple random may be preferred. For ease of selection, systematic may be preferable.

Cluster Samples

A strategy that may be used to increase the probability that the sampled population and target population are the same and that has certain advantages over either simple random or stratified sampling is the cluster sample. *Cluster sampling* is a technique whereby the sample is drawn in two or more stages. At the first stage the total population to be sampled is divided into several clusters on the basis of a meaningful variable. These clusters will be mutually exclusive and all-inclusive.

To illustrate, a sample representing all people in a state could be drawn, with the first clustering being counties, so that a sample of counties would be drawn from the state at the first stage. In the second and subsequent samples, smaller units within clusters could be drawn, representing the specific units to be sampled. The sampling would end at this point, or would continue with units representing areas smaller than the county (e.g., census tracts, from which individuals could be drawn).

For example, in a study of health departments in North Carolina, one unit of analysis was ultimately to be health department employees. The sample was drawn in two stages. The first stage included as a sampling frame or target population all health departments in the state of North Carolina. From this population, 16 health departments were drawn using simple random sampling at that level (i.e., the 100 health departments in the state were numbered from 1 to 100, 16 random numbers in the range 1 to 100 were selected from a random number table, and the 16 health departments having the selected numbers were included in the sample). At the second stage, employees within these 16 health departments were sampled (also using simple random sampling) to comprise a sample of health department personnel for the entire state.

The advantage of this approach is that a detailed list of health department employees need be drawn up, in general, only for the 16 health departments actually included in the sample at the first stage. No list of employees need be available for health departments excluded from the sample. This process substantially reduces the amount of work required to construct a useful list of people to be sampled.

To consider the example of an estimate of the need for primary care services in a health service area, a cluster sample can make constructing an accurate list of all people in the area unnecessary. As an alternative, it would be possible to use logical divisions, such as census tracts or blocks, postal zones, or another logical set of divisions, and then draw a sample of clusters from them. It would be necessary to construct an accurate list only of those people residing within the clusters selected.

For example, if city blocks were selected as clusters, a relatively accurate list of people to be sampled at the second stage could be constructed simply by going to one or two households on the block and asking who lived in the other households. Alternatively, a sample could be drawn by numbering all the housing in the sampled block and drawing a sample of them.

Cluster sampling can be carried out at more than two stages. For example, a national sample of the United States may begin with a cluster sample of states. Within states, a cluster of counties may be selected; within counties, townships may be selected; and within townships, people may be selected.

While cluster sampling can serve to reduce the possibility of missing potential respondents and hence biasing results, cluster sampling can be useful in reducing such factors as the cost of actual data collection if the data will be collected by interview or by another strategy that requires someone to contact the respondents personally. If a simple random sample of personnel within health departments were selected to produce information about employees working within health departments in a given state, it is quite likely that the majority of health departments would be included so that the evaluator would be forced to visit most health departments to obtain data. If a cluster sample is drawn, it is only necessary to visit those health departments that are included in the initial cluster sample.

Limitation   Cluster sampling has the disadvantage that sample respondents within initial cluster units are likely to be more similar than they are between units. For example, people within health departments would be more likely to be more similar to one another than they are to people in other health departments in many aspects of their responses. This means that relatively high variation between clusters will exist. Although similarity of people within strata is an advantage for stratified sampling, this is a disadvantage for cluster sampling because all clusters are not represented. Consequently, most cluster sample–based estimates of population parameters are likely to be less precise (and thus less accurate) than stratified sample estimates and are frequently less precise than simple random sample estimates.

At each level of cluster sampling, the actual selection of clusters (or at the final level, the selection of individual observations) should be done using a probability method. This would be either simple random sampling or systematic sampling. For example, in certain circumstances when clusters are being selected at a first level, an unequal probability selection may be used so that clusters may be selected with probability proportional to the size (number of possible observations) in the clusters. Selection should always be done on a probability basis, however.

Other Multistage Samples

Cluster sampling is one type of multistage sampling. A second type of multistage sampling similar in execution, although not necessarily in concept, is the kind in which information is desired at two or more levels. For example, in a study of health departments, it may be important to the evaluation to have information about individual employees and their perceptions of departmental activity as well as information about aspects of the health departments themselves. The sample may be drawn, therefore, on the basis of health departments as clusters at the first stage and employees as units of analysis at the second stage. Data, however, will be collected about both the individual employees and the departments within which they are located.

With a sample of this type, estimates can be made about the population of health departments and the employees who work in them; information also becomes available that can be used to describe characteristics of health workers that may be associated with the specific health departments in which they work. When data for evaluation purposes are desired at several different organizational levels, a relatively uncommon mistake—but one that is occasionally made—is the selection of samples independently at different levels. If, for example, an evaluation of communication and coordination between health departments and health department personnel was to be undertaken, it would be highly desirable to be assured that the health departments included in the sample corresponded with the personnel included, and vice versa. Thus, the best approach would be first to sample health departments and then to sample people working within the health departments selected. While this seems obvious, there are instances when evaluators have undertaken such work by selecting independent samples at the organization and at the individual level. In this situation, correspondence between sampled units at each level was essentially a matter of chance. This makes definitive statements about the relationships that exist between the two units much more difficult.

Nonrandom Samples

Not all samples are based on probability. Many samples in evaluation applications are what may be called haphazard samples (i.e., the units observed have been selected on a basis that appears to be random but may not be). One type of haphazard sample is the *sample of convenience.* If something is to be known about all the people who use a particular clinic for a type of service, the sample for obtaining this information may be the first 50 people who arrive at the clinic during a period of one week; it is in no sense a random sample and should not be treated as such. Conclusions drawn from such a sample are generally applicable only to the sample itself.

Another common type of nonprobability or nonrandom sample is the *representative sample.* In such a sample, units are selected because they seem to be representative of the population as a whole. If an evaluation is to be carried out on a program that exists in all counties within a state, the representative sample may include a high-income county, a low-income county, a rural county, an urban county, and so on. Although conclusions drawn from such a sample may be more useful in the long run than conclusions drawn from a haphazard sample or a sample of convenience, they are still able to be generalized to the whole population, but with a great deal of caution.

Sample Selection: An Illustration

Consider the simplest sampling situation, one in which each element (e.g., organization) in the population has an equal probability of entering the sample. Assume that a study of county health departments is being conducted within a state that has 120 counties, each with one health department. Resources are available to draw a sample of 30 health departments from the 120. Each health department thus has 30 chances out of 120, or 1 in 4, of entering the sample.

There was a time when the drawing of a random sample of 30 from a population of 120 would have been done using a printed random number table (e.g., Arkin and Colton 1963). Commonly today, the sample will be drawn using a series of random numbers generated by a computer program. The spreadsheet program Excel has the capability to generate random numbers (actually computer generated random numbers are often referred to as *pseudo-random* numbers because they are generated by an algorithm that will always produce the same set of numbers given the same starting point) with a large number of different distributions (e.g., uniform, normal, binomial, and poisson).

To draw a sample of 30 health departments from the population of 120, the easiest approach would be to begin with the numbers 1 through 120 in a column on an Excel spreadsheet. This column represents the 120 health departments. The random number generation capability (under Tools, Data Analysis, Random Number Generation) can then be invoked to generate 120 random numbers in the column contiguous to the list of 120 numbers (the best distribution option to select is probably normal).

After Excel generates the 120 random numbers (which will range, if the normal distribution option is chosen, from about −4 to +4), the list of 120 numbers can be sorted on the column containing the random numbers (in either ascending or descending order), and the first 30 numbers in the sorted list can then be chosen to be included in the sample. This will produce a random selection of exactly 30 health departments.

The strategy of listing all members of the population will work quite well to select a sample of a specific size from a population of interest when it is relatively easy to enumerate every member of the population and include a number representing each one on a spreadsheet. This is quite easy with 120 health departments. It can also be done fairly easily if the population does not exceed 65,536, which is the number of rows on an Excel spreadsheet (the fill command can be used to generate a list of numbers from 1 to 65,536 in one column and a set of 65,536 random numbers can be generated in a contiguous column).

At a certain level, however, it becomes relatively onerous to list all members of the population. When that happens, it is possible to request that Excel generate a set of random numbers in the range represented by the entire population (e.g., a range 1 to 80,000 if the total population is 80,000), but to generate only the total number of random numbers as are to be included in the sample. If the sample size were to be 400, only 400 numbers would be generated. In this case, the distribution to be used would have to be the uniform distribution. The 400 numbers generated could then be matched with the same number in the population and those cases selected.

A minor problem that arises with the generation of only enough random numbers to fill the sample is that some numbers are likely to be generated twice. The solution to this problem is to generate more random numbers than the actual sample size, and just use the first 400 unique numbers generated.

Sample Design and Evaluation Strategies

If it were possible in any evaluation setting to observe the entire population of interest, sampling would be a subject of little interest to program evaluation. In many evaluation settings, however, it is neither physically possible nor financially feasible to obtain information on or observe the entire population of entities to be evaluated. When less than the total number of units of interest can be observed or measured, sampling becomes a real concern. In many instances, only through the selection of a sample can a reasonable evaluation be conducted.

Monitoring

In most monitoring formats, sampling is not likely to be a major concern. Monitoring is usually applied to a single program or a limited number of programs selected because they are one of a kind or, at most, the several programs that make up the total universe. In such programs, the management may be performing the monitoring, or perhaps the monitors are consultants working directly with the program management. These evaluators or managers generally have access to the entire universe of information about most aspects of the program for which progress information—monitoring data—is useful or necessary. For instance, information for monitoring purposes may include weekly or monthly expenditures of funds or comparisons of funds expended to funds budgeted by time period. It may include information about the daily patient census or services provided each week or quarter.

Still, certain aspects of monitoring data may be available only on a sample basis. If a program is designed to deliver a type of service to clients, one possible aspect of program progress that may concern administrators is the continuing perception of the program in the eyes of its clients. If clients are generally satisfied with the services being received, management may elect to allow the program to continue providing services in more or less the same way. However, if over a period of time clients appear to be dissatisfied with the services or if their satisfaction declines, management may wish to take steps to increase client satisfaction.

Specific information about client satisfaction may be available on a routine basis. Such information as appointments missed may be considered a measure of client dissatisfaction. Missed appointments may be information that is available routinely, but if a more direct measure of client satisfaction is wanted (e.g., answers to a direct question or set of questions on satisfaction with the program), such information may be collected most easily on a sample basis. If the sample were to assess client satisfaction with services, one way to make certain that clients would respond to questions about satisfaction with services would be to query them at the time they received the service. A sample strategy would be needed in which a client could be identified as being in the sample at the time service was delivered and the questionnaire or set of questions could be addressed to that client.

Case Studies

There are two levels at which sampling should be discussed in regard to the case study evaluation format. At one level, the entire issue of sampling may seem irrelevant because the situation selected for case study purposes represents the entire universe. If the specific case is unique and is selected not for the purpose of generalizing to a larger population but for program activity evaluation within the specific example, then there is no need to sample.

To illustrate, an evaluation of how a specific strategic alliance dealt with its hospitals to ensure nonduplication of facilities could be undertaken to gain a better understanding of the process with which the alliance pursued these objectives. The results of such an evaluation—the evaluator's conclusions—would clearly pertain to this alliance alone. However, at the same time there would be a basic assumption that the results may apply reasonably well to other alliances as well. Nevertheless, the particular alliance selected would have been chosen because it had addressed the problem of nonduplication of services in a particular way or because it was an area of interest to the evaluator on another ground. In this sense, the alliance under study is different from all other alliances and to that extent represents the entire universe. This alliance is one of many, however, and its selection may be considered a purposeful selection from a larger population. Still, it is unlikely that selecting any program or organizational form as the subject of a case study—or choosing a particular area in which a larger program or organization is operating as a case study example—should be done on a random basis. Because case studies are exploratory, in many respects, the specific case selected for study should clearly be chosen for a reason other than randomness.

After a specific program or organizational form, such as a strategic alliance, or a political or geographic entity, such as a county, state, or region, has been selected as the subject of a case study, it may be possible to evaluate the program or aspects of it within a given area without considering any type of sample selection. The procedure for evaluating how a particular alliance has worked with its constituent hospitals to ensure nonduplication of services may involve direct interviews with the health services alliance executive officers and officers of the participating hospitals. Given the size of most alliances, the evaluators probably would want to meet and obtain additional information from each executive officer of the alliance and all constituent hospitals. In this case, sampling would be unnecessary for evaluation purposes.

However, part of the evaluation may be assessing the impact of an effort to ensure nonduplication of various hospital services on physicians who use them for their patients within this alliance area or on patients who seek them. If such an interest was included in the evaluation, it may be unreasonable to anticipate the possibility of reaching every physician in the alliance or every patient or potential patient to assess their attitudes toward the alliance's efforts.

In this situation it is not uncommon to see a sample design embedded within a case study. Here, a case study is being carried out on the strategic alliance as a whole, but specific pieces of information about the alliance may be obtained from a sample of people within the alliance on a survey basis. Such an evaluation approach, although part of a case study, is no different from survey research as the overall evaluation tool.

Survey Research

Sampling is a central component of survey research. Survey research as an evaluation tool can be used to assess the state of the system to ascertain its relevance before the program has been undertaken. Surveys can also be used after a program has been in operation to assess at certain levels effectiveness, efficiency, and impact. Survey research can also be used in certain settings to evaluate the relationship between program output and certain aspects of program input. Each situation requires a sample to select information for analysis.

Trend Analysis

As an evaluation tool, trend analysis is generally concerned with data that represent the universe of all data available. Trend analysis may be applied to such data as the hospital cost per patient day before and after the passage of the Medicare bill to assess the impact of Medicare on hospital costs. Or it may be applied to highway death tolls before and after reducing speed limits to 55 mph to assess the impact of that directive on highway deaths. For such an analysis, the entire population of observations would probably be used for the evaluation of impact.

When a long time series is required for assessment of program interventions, however, the entire universe may not be available for study. Data representing more limited geographic areas, such as states, may be readily available to assess the impact of the speed limit reduction. The data set thus becomes a sample of all states in the population selected because it is available to the evaluator and, to be absolutely correct, should be considered its own entire population or universe.

Experimental Design

Experimental design is the most powerful evaluation format. For example, it has been used with considerable success in evaluating the effectiveness of drug treatment through random clinical trials. Experimental design is less applicable, as previously noted, to program evaluation for a number of reasons. One reason is the difficulty of identifying control groups to use in comparison to experimental groups or areas. Still, experimental design as a program evaluation tool should receive consideration in any evaluation context and should depend heavily on sampling or, more specifically in terms of experimental design, on random selection.

In an evaluation based on experimental design, the evaluator's concern is to determine whether the program or project as structured and carried out was the causal factor in producing an observed outcome. How this is done depends on a comparison between one or more experimental groups, programs, or program areas and one or more control groups, programs, or program areas. In such a comparison, the evaluator must rule out any other factors that may have produced a particular observed level of outcome (i.e., produced a difference between the experimental and control programs).

There are two ways to attempt to ensure that any difference between the experimental and control groups is a function of program input and not of another characteristic or set of characteristics. One way is using matching and the other way is using random selection.

In the matching strategy the people or organizations that are the subjects of an evaluation are matched on any characteristics assumed to be associated with outcomes that the program to be implemented may produce. After this matching has been carried out, it is common to randomly select an equal number of people, groups, organizations, or areas from the matched sets for inclusion in the experimental and control categories. Depending on the unit of analysis, matching can be done on basic characteristics that may be considered associated with response to the experimental variable.

After the matching is finished, random selection is almost always used to determine the specific evaluation units to be assigned to the experimental or control group. For example, if matching has been carried out so that every unit in the potential evaluation population has been matched with one other unit, the decision about assigning the two units to either the experimental or control group still should be based on chance. The flip of a coin could be used to determine which one of this matched pair would be a member of the experimental group. If matching is not so complete, it is even more important that units be selected randomly from the two sets of groups.

If matching is not done to control for variables that may influence the results of the evaluation, such variables can still be controlled through the technique of complete random assignment. If this is the case, all units subject to the evaluation would be assigned to the experimental category or the control category on a random basis without regard to whether their characteristics matched or not. If carried out properly, the process of random assignment itself will provide a control for differences among the units to be examined that may be reasonably expected to affect the outcome.

Unfortunately, random assignment can never totally ensure that the possible effects of confounding factors have been controlled. Random assignment is most effective when the number of units to be compared or observed is relatively large (perhaps more than 30 observations in both the experimental and control group). Random assignment is less effective when the number of units to be compared gets small.

For example, if the evaluation is to be an assessment of the impact of a family planning program in a limited number of different regions of a country—perhaps six to eight—random assignment is not a powerful tool in controlling for characteristics that may be related to results of the evaluation. No statistical procedure is likely to be particularly useful with such a small group. Probably the best that the evaluator can do is to match the areas of the country as closely as possible and assign the matched areas to the experimental and control group, respectively.

When random assignment is used, the basic approach is simple random sampling. In an experimental setting, using more complex designs is not necessary (e.g., stratified, cluster, or multistage sampling).

Note

1. The average standard error is generally called the pooled standard error in a comparison between means. It is calculated as

$$
SE_{pooled} = \sqrt{\frac{n_1\sigma_1^2 + n_2\sigma_2^2}{n_1 + n_2}\left(\frac{1}{n_1} + \frac{1}{n_2}\right)}
$$

where n_1 refers to the size of the first sample, n_2 refers to the size of the second sample, σ_1^2 is a variance of the first sample, and σ_2^2 is the variance of the second sample.

Discussion Questions

1. What is the difference between descriptive and analytic sampling? What types of evaluation questions are best answered by each type of sampling strategy?
2. Why is the appropriate sample size so important to evaluation yet so difficult to achieve?
3. Distinguish between a simple random sampling, stratified random sampling, cluster sampling, and nonrandom sampling. What are the conditions that determine their appropriate use in evaluation activities?
4. What is the role of internal and external validity in different types of evaluation strategies, such as monitoring, case studies, survey research, trend analysis, and experimental design?
5. Illustrate the types of evaluation questions appropriate to each type of validity for each type of evaluation strategy.

OPERATIONS RESEARCH TECHNIQUES AND INTERPRETATION

Evaluation techniques are used when the outputs are known but the best method or program design for achieving those outputs is unknown. Evaluation methods, as an aid to cybernetic decision making, can provide the means for continually assessing program outputs and assuring continual improvement of outputs through successively better decisions. In the cybernetic mode, there is no formula or algorithm that leads to the optimal or preferred result, only the availability of information about the result of a particular strategy that is then used to modify the strategy so as to become more effective.

This chapter will again contrast the cybernetic decision-making mode to the mechanistic decision mode and provide illustrations from an outpatient clinic. In the mechanistic decision mode, various operations research techniques are available for making decisions that produce the best result under a defined set of circumstances in exactly the same way as the square root algorithm described in Chapter 2 produces the square root of a number. If a manager applies the technique correctly, there is no need to monitor the progress of the program or compare its outputs to outputs derived through the application of alternative decision strategies. By the nature of the technique, the result will be the best result available under a given set of conditions.

As with other techniques described in this book, the presentation is designed to introduce the techniques and illustrate their application within a health service setting. Selected techniques are presented, including model building, linear programming, queuing theory, and inventory control.

Model Building

A first step in the application of operations research techniques to decision making is almost always the development of a mathematical model of how a given system operates. In the simplest formulation, a mathematical model is the statement in equation form of a relationship between a dependent variable, or a program or process output, and one or more independent variables, or program inputs. In general, program inputs may be divided into two groups: those over which the decision maker has some control, and those that are essentially uncontrollable.

For example, the number of clients who can be served in a clinic may be considered as determined by a minimum of three components: the number of providers associated with the clinic; the number of clients a provider can serve in a given unit of time; and total amount of time available. A mathematical formulation of this is:

$$C = P \times ST \times TT \qquad (16.1)$$

where:

- C = clients served;
- P = number of physicians;
- ST = clients served per unit of time; and
- TT = total time available.

Thus, if a clinic had three physicians, each physician spends 15 minutes with each patient at a rate of four patients per hour, and each physician works for six hours a day, the clinic could serve 72 patients in a day ($C = 3 \times 4 \times 6$).

This mathematical model is so simple that it may seem almost trivial. Yet it can provide information to decision makers about types of decisions that *must* be made in operating the clinic, even if they are not at this stage the decisions that *should* be made.

For example, if an administrator was faced with an increasing demand for services, so that the ability to serve 72 patients per day was not adequate for the needs of the organization, the mathematical model provides direct information about how the problem may be solved. The administrator may consider one of three possible options to increase the number of patients served: increase the number of physicians; increase the number of patients that physicians are able to serve in a given amount of time; or increase the number of hours that physicians work.

A fourth option is also open to the decision maker, which is simply to ignore the increased demand and use the limited service availability as a rationing device. This solution has been adopted widely in the Western world as healthcare costs have risen. From the standpoint of either evaluation or decision making, however, this decision is based essentially in the political realm and cannot be effectively informed by evaluation or operations research techniques, at least as the issue is posed. Assuming that the decision maker will not decide to ignore the increased demand, however, the three decisions available are essentially as previously indicated. The decision maker may have no control over one or all of the inputs to patients served. Inputs may be divided into those that are subject to control by the administrator and those that are not subject to such control. It is also often true that those inputs that are under an administrator's control and those that are not may depend largely on the context.

In the preceding example, all three inputs are potentially controllable. But it may well be that a decision maker may have little or no control over the amount of time a physician spends with a patient. In large part, this is likely to be a matter of practice patterns. An administrator may be able to determine the number of physicians available or the number of hours they are available during a day. In virtually all cases, however, this would require additional resources. A valuable aspect of operations research techniques is their ability to identify the decision that provides the greatest output for a given level of cost or, alternatively, the least-cost alternative for a fixed output.

Illustration: Clinic Staffing

Using the preceding model, an administrator may wish to increase the capacity to serve patients from 72 patients per day to 90 per day. If the assumption is that time spent with a patient is fixed, the only two decision variables are number of physicians and hours that they work per day. To add one physician would increase the capacity of the clinic to 96, which would solve the problem of capacity but would leave an excess capacity of 6 patients. An alternative would be to increase the number of hours worked by physicians to seven and one-half per day. This would increase the capacity of the clinic to exactly 90 patients per day.

On an annual basis, perhaps a new physician may cost $120,000 for a six-hour workday. In addition, there may be a fixed cost of $50,000 per year to add another physician, for examining-room space, administrative costs, support costs, and so on. To increase the amount of time spent by physicians on a daily basis may cost an additional $90,000 at the same hourly rate of reimbursement. A decision to add one physician, therefore, will produce the desired capacity of 90 patients for an additional $37.78 per patient with a slack of 6 patients per day, while the decision to add hours to the workday will produce the desired capacity of 90 patients for an additional $20 per patient.

This is a simple example to illustrate the application of models to decision making. In this case, it is possible to arrive at the optimal solution with little effort. Operations research techniques can assist in making the same type of decisions when the alternative decisions (i.e., variable inputs in the model) and the alternative constraints (i.e., costs associated with various decisions) are much more complex.

Clinic Staffing with a Mechanistic Solution: A Linear Programming Example

Linear programming allows an administrator to arrive at an optimal solution to a management problem in an entirely mechanistic way. After the problem is presented in the proper form, the application of an algorithm known as the *simplex method* will produce the optimal answer (i.e., the best solution) without any feedback. This is much the same as the square root of a number found according to the mechanistic method shown in Chapter 2.

Illustration

A group of administrators is confronted with the need to provide as many hours of clinic care as possible to people coming to their facility. In this sense, the problem is like the one previously mentioned. Assume that not only can physicians provide needed patient care, but in addition, that the administrators have the option of hiring physician assistants to provide care as well. The administrators know from long experience that physicians, on the average, can see and treat four patients per hour. Physician assistants, however, both because they have been trained to spend more time with patients and because they perform many tasks that physicians rely on nurses for, will be able to treat no more than three patients per hour.

The administrators have a budget that provides $1,400 per day for direct patient care salaries, independent of nursing services. They must pay physicians $70 per hour and physician assistants $35. In addition, the clinic has three examining rooms, each of which can practically be used for ten hours per day. The total hours of patient care time by either physicians or physician assistants cannot exceed 30 hours per day. Finally, the administrators know that it will be necessary to have a physician at the clinic at least six hours per day, both for supervision of the physician assistants and because some of the presenting diagnoses cannot reasonably be dealt with by physician assistants.

Also assume that the administrators are operating in a community in which hiring either physicians or physician assistants on an hourly basis is possible. Administrators are thus free to make the decision about how much time during a day either physicians or physician assistants work. This is a highly artificial assumption for many administrators but not unrealistic for others. The question, then, is what mix of physician and physician assistant time should the administrators buy to maximize the number of patients who can be seen at the clinic while remaining within the constraints of time and money.

It is possible to solve this problem in a cybernetic (i.e., feedback) mode. Approaching the problem this way, the administrators could conclude that because physician assistants are cheaper than physicians are, they should use as many hours of physician assistant time as possible. If the administrators were to buy 30 hours of physician assistant time per day, the result would be a capacity for 90 patients. They know, however, that they must have at least six hours of physician time as well, and because they have only space enough for 30 hours of time in total, they can buy no more than 24 hours of physician assistant time. Calculating total patients that can be seen using 24 hours of physician assistant time and six hours of physician time, they see that the clinic capacity is now 96 patients per day. But they also can see that with 24 hours of physician assistant time and 6 hours of physician time, they are expending only $1,260 per day on clinic personnel ($24 \times 35 + 6 \times 70 = 1,260$). They therefore realize that they can increase the number of physicians (who can see more patients than physician assistants) and still remain within their budget.

The administrators may then begin to increase the number of physician hours, for example, in two-hour intervals, to try to reach the maximum number of patients while not exceeding their daily budget. If they contract for eight physician hours and thus 22 physician assistant hours, total patients will increase to 98 and total cost will increase to $1,330. They still have money to work with. If they increase physician time to 10 hours and reduce physician assistant time to 20 hours, total patient capacity will rise to 100 per day and total cost will rise to $1,400, which is the limit available. A little further tinkering with the figures will demonstrate to the administrators that they can do no better with their constraints of money, time, and clinic space than a combination of 10 hours of physician time and 20 hours of physician assistant time.

The administrators have solved this problem in the cybernetic mode. Even though they did not actually put into place a decision to contract for a certain number of physician hours and a certain number of physician assistant hours, they have done essentially the same thing "on the back of an envelope." This is a problem, however, that can be solved directly, in a mechanistic mode without any feedback at all, using linear programming.

To employ linear programming to solve this problem, the administrators must first be able to formulate the problem in the form of a set of mathematical equations that represent the outcomes they are seeking. The primary thing the administrators wish to do is maximize the number of patients who can be seen in a day at the clinic. They know physicians can see four patients per hour and physician assistants can see three. They can state this knowledge in terms of an equation:

$$\text{Maximize: } Z = 4X + 3Y \qquad (16.2)$$

where:

- Z = total number of patients who can be seen;
- X = number of hours worked by physicians; and
- Y = number of hours worked by physician assistants.

The administrators also know that maximizing the preceding function shown is subject to constraints of money to pay for daily salaries and of available examining-room space—and thus total hours during which practitioners can see patients, and the constraint that there must be at least six hours of physician time available during the day. These constraints are shown as the following equations:

$$70X + 35Y \leq 1,400 \qquad (16.3)$$

$$X + Y \leq 30 \qquad (16.4)$$

$$X \geq 6 \qquad (16.5)$$

Equation 16.3 shows that the $70 multiplied by the number of physician hours plus $35 multiplied by the number of physician assistant hours cannot exceed $1,400 each day. Equation 16.4 shows that the total hours worked by both physicians and physician assistants must not exceed 30 hours, and Equation 16.5 shows that there must be at least six hours of physician time each day.

Having cast the problem in this form, the administrators can use the simplex method, a mathematical algorithm, to solve directly for the optimum mix of physician and physician assistant time to maximize patients seen while remaining within the constraints of money and space. The first step in the simplex method is to rewrite the equations in the form shown in Table 16.1.

TABLE 16.1

Simplex Method Formulation for Maximization Problems

	X	Y	S_1	S_2	S_3	A	Z
(1)	4	3	0	0	0	M	0
(2)	70	35	−1	0	0	0	1,400
(3)	1	1	0	−1	0	0	30
(4)	1	0	0	0	−1	1	6

As shown in Table 16.1, the original set of equations can be seen with additional information added. The headings of the table include X, the designator for physician hours, and Y, the designator for physician assistant hours. In addition, S_1, S_2, and S_3 represent slack in the system. There generally will be as many slack variables as there are constraints (in this case, three). The next letter, A, designates an artificial variable that is included to allow the use of a *greater than or equal* to constraint (the third constraint) in the simplex method. The final letter, Z, represents the column in which the final solution will be found.

Line (1) in Table 16.1 represents the expression to be maximized, the objective function. It can be read as:

$$4X + 3Y = 0 \qquad (16.6)$$

The challenge, then, is to change this in a way so that:

$$4X + 3Y = \text{the largest value possible.}$$

The M in column A will not enter into the solution. To ensure this, it is considered to be a very large negative value, such as $-10,000$. Only positive values in the objective function are considered in carrying out the simplex process.

Line (2) in Table 16.1 represents the constraint that the cost of physician hours ($70X$) plus the cost of physician assistant hours ($35Y$) cannot exceed $1,400. The -1 is shown under S_1 to eliminate the *less than* part of this constraint, so that:

$$70X + 35Y - 1S_1 = 1,400 \qquad (16.7)$$

Similarly, line (3) in Table 16.1 represents the constraint that the number of hours available for clinic services (because of the limitation of space) is 30. The -1 under S_2 eliminates the *less than* part of this constraint:

$$1X + 1Y - 1S_2 = 30 \qquad (16.8)$$

Finally, line (4) in Table 16.1 represents the constraint that there must be at least six hours of physician time available during the day. To remove the *greater than* part of this constraint, a -1 is shown under S_3 so that:

$$1X - 1S_3 = 6 \qquad (16.9)$$

In this case, however, it is also necessary to include an artificial variable, A, in the equation shown in the line (4) to assure that any surplus represented by S_3 will be positive, so the final version of the third constraint is:

$$1X - 1S_3 + 1A = 6 \qquad (16.10)$$

As indicated previously, A is an entirely artificial variable that will not appear in the final solution, but that is there only to allow the simplex solution to work.

Now that the form of the simplex method is specified as shown in Table 16.1, it is possible to discuss the algorithm that will produce the maximum number of patients to be seen during any day while remaining within the constraints of time and money available.

To begin the simplex algorithm, it is necessary to identify a *pivot value*. The pivot value is found by first selecting the largest value of the objective function. In Table 16.1, the largest value of the objective function (line 1) is the 4 associated with X, the number of hours of physician time. This identifies a column, the X column, in which the pivot value will be found. The pivot value is selected from the X column by finding the entry, among the constraints (excluding line [1]), that gives the smallest result when the entry in the Z column is divided by the entry in the X column. This will be the pivot value. In Table 16.1, the pivot value is the 1 in line (4), column X ($1,400/70 = 20$; $30/1 = 30$; $6/1 = 6$). The entire row in which the pivot value is located is then transformed by dividing the row by the pivot value. In this case, no change is produced in line (4) and the result is:

	X	Y	S_1	S_2	S_3	A	Z
(4)	1	0	0	0	-1	1	6

The next step in the simplex process is to subtract from each of the other three lines in Table 16.1 a multiple of the transformed line (4) that will reduce the entry in the pivot column (column X) to zero. Thus, for line (1)—the objective function—each value in the transformed line (4) is multiplied by 4 and subtracted from line (1). For line (2), each value in the transformed line (4) is multiplied by 70 and subtracted from line (2). Line (3) is simply subtracted from line (4). These operations produce the result shown in Table 16.2.

The simplex process is continued by finding in Table 16.2 the largest value in the transformed objective function for the next step. This is the value 4 in col-

	X	Y	S_1	S_2	S_3	A	Z
(1)	0	3	0	0	4	M	-24
(2)	0	35	-1	0	70	-70	980
(3)	0	1	0	-1	1	-1	24
(4)	1	0	0	0	-1	1	6

TABLE 16.2
Simplex Method: Step Two

umn S_3. In that column, the pivot value is the value in lines (2), (3), or (4) that gives the smallest result when divided into column Z, only considering positive values in column S_3. This is the 70 in line (2) ($980/70 = 14$; $24/1 = 24$). This is the new pivot value. All values in line (2) are then divided by the pivot value, producing the following as line (2) to be entered as line Z in Table 16.3.

	X	Y	S_1	S_2	S_3	A	Z
(2)	0	0.5	−0.014	0	1	−1	14

Just as in the development of Table 16.2, a transformed line (2) is subtracted from each row in Table 16.2 to produce the result in Table 16.3.

To continue the simplex process, the largest value in the transformed objective function in Table 16.3 is found. This is the 1 in column Y. The same process as followed previously is used to produce the result shown in Table 16.4.

The simplex process is now finished, because no columns exist in the original objective function, which included only X and Y, for which there is a positive value in line (1). The maximum number of patients who can be seen given the constraints of time and money is shown as the negative number under Z in line (1). One hundred patients per day is the maximum that can be seen. Line (4) shows the number of hours of physician time that should be used to achieve that total, ten hours. It is possible to see that these ten hours are associated with physician time because of the value 1 in line (4) under X. Line (3) shows the number of physician assistant hours to use, 20 hours. Again, there is a 1 in line (3) under Y. The 4 under Z in line (2) indicates that the constraint of at least six hours of physician time each day is exceeded by four hours. Thus, four hours of slack physician time appear in the optimal solution. This last constraint, even though it may be very important to the administrators in their decision making to assure that the necessary skills are available in the clinic, has no effect on the optimal solution.

TABLE 16.3
Simplex Method:
Step Three

	X	Y	S_1	S_2	S_3	A	Z
(1)	0	1	0.057	0	0	M	−80
(2)	0	0.5	−0.014	0	1	−1	14
(3)	0	0.5	0.014	−1	0	0	10
(4)	1	0.5	−0.014	0	0	0	20

TABLE 16.4
Simplex Method:
Step Four

	X	Y	S_1	S_2	S_3	A	Z
(1)	0	0	0.028	2	0	M	−100
(2)	0	0	−0.028	1	1	−1	4
(3)	0	1	0.028	−2	0	0	20
(4)	1	0	−0.028	1	0	0	10

This problem can be solved through trial and error, as seen in our earlier discussion in a cybernetic mode. In that sense, one may ask why the simplex approach is necessary. The answer is that the simplex method is a technique for solving a variety of maximization problems that may involve many more terms in the objective function than appear in this example, as well as many more, and more complicated, constraints. Furthermore, linear programming is one of a whole class of mathematical programming techniques that may be used to solve a wide variety of optimization problems.

Until recently, solving linear programming problems required either going through the simplex method step by step, or it required a special computer program dedicated to producing the solution to the simplex. With the advent of spreadsheet computer programs, however, this situation has changed dramatically. For example, linear programming problems can be solved quite easily using the solver add-in that is part of the Excel spreadsheet. While the purpose of this book is not to make the reader an expert in the use of Excel, a brief presentation of the solution of the preceding linear programming problem as solved by Excel may be useful for those who want to explore this further.

To solve a linear programming problem with Excel, it is necessary to specify the objective function and the constraints in the Excel spreadsheet. Figure 16.1a shows an example spreadsheet with the objective function (to be maximized) and the constraints prior to the solution. The entries in column B represent labels for the objective function and constraints. These entries simply provide a reference for the user, but are not part of the calculations. The actual calculations will be done in column C. Column D shows what the calculations in column C actually do.

For example, the objective function as calculated in cell C2 will be equal to 4 multiplied by the value in cell C6 plus 3 multiplied by the value in cell C7. Cell C2 is the function to be maximized. The formulas for the other cells in column C (the constraints) are also shown in the respective rows of column D. There is no formula in D for cells C6 and C7, because these are the cells that will be changed to maximize the objective function. Figure 16.1b shows the solution to the linear programming problem after the application of solver. As shown in

	A	B	C	D
1				
2		4X + 3Y = Max	0	= 4 * C6 + 3 * C7
3		70X + 35Y <= 1400	0	= 70 * C6 + 35 * C7
4		X + Y <= 30	0	= C6 + C7
5		X >= 6	0	= C6
6		X =	0	
7		Y =	0	

FIGURE 16.1a

Example Layout for Excel Solver Solution to Linear Programming Problem: Before the Solution

FIGURE 16.1b

Example Layout for Excel Solver Solution to Linear Programming Problem: After the Solution

	A	B	C	D
1				
2		4X + 3Y = Max	100	= 4 * C6 + 3 * C7
3		70X + 35Y <= 1400	1,400	= 70 * C6 + 35 * C7
4		X + Y <= 30	30	= C6 + C7
5		X >= 6	10	= C6
6		X =	10	
7		Y =	20	

the figure, the results are the same as given by the steps of the simplex method already discussed.

Solver is opened from the tools menu. The target cell, the cell in which the formula for the objective function is placed, is shown as C2. Solver allows the user to specify whether the target cell is to be maximized, minimized, or made equal to a specific value. In this case, it is to be maximized. It also allows the specification of the cells to be changed to reach the solution, in this case, cells C6 and C7. If the cells to be changed are not known, solver can guess. The last box in the screen provides the place to put in the constraints.

The first constraint is that cell C3 must be less than or equal to 1,400 (the total amount of money available for salaries each day). The second constraint is that cell C4 must be less than or equal to 30 (the total number of hours available). The last constraint is that cell C5 must be equal to or greater than 6 (the minimum number of hours of physician time each day). The solution to this linear programming problem using solver can be found much faster than it can be described.

Clinic Staffing from a Different View: A Queuing Solution

The administrator in the preceding example is satisfied that the clinic has been adequately staffed to serve 100 patients during a ten-hour period and that all of the space and money has been used through the combination of ten hours of physician time and 20 hours of physician assistant time. Unfortunately for the administrator, if patients begin to arrive unscheduled at the clinic at an average rate of ten per hour, he or she will soon discover that, despite what is learned from the linear program, queues will begin to form in the clinic and grow to amazing lengths. To see that this will be the case, the administrator can use another operations research tool known as queuing theory.

Queuing theory is a body of knowledge that is useful for examining the nature of waiting lines. It is concerned with what happens to a waiting line when people (or any other units to be served or processed) arrive at a service facility on a random basis and are served at a varying rate.

Queuing theory may be applied to many different types of queues. For example, the simplest queue would be the single arrival line/single server system. This system could be characterized by a single physician working alone in his office, seeing patients as they arrive unscheduled during the day. A somewhat more complex system would be a single arrival line/multiple server system. This is the system thus far discussed if the assumption is that the servers (physicians and physician assistants) are all essentially homogeneous in their service time. A more complex system would be one in which servers are not homogeneous, as previously noted. Still more complicated systems include those in which there may be multiple servers with express lanes for emergency services, multiple arrival lines, or multiple sequential services for each client. In this section, only two types of queues are addressed: those with a single arrival line and a single server, and those with a single arrival line and multiple but homogeneous servers.

Single Server Systems

Suppose there is a single arrival line and a single service source, and all possible people who may need medical care arrive in an unscheduled manner from an essentially unlimited source. The general assumption is that the arrival rate (the average number of people who arrive per unit of time) will follow a *Poisson distribution* and the service time will follow a *negative exponential distribution*. Figures 16.2a and 16.2b show examples of these two distributions with an assumed average arrival frequency of four per hour and average number of people served of four per hour. The Poisson distribution in Figure 16.2a shows a possible distribution of arrivals for 100 hours. During four hours of the 100, there was only one arrival, during ten hours there were two arrivals, during 21 hours there

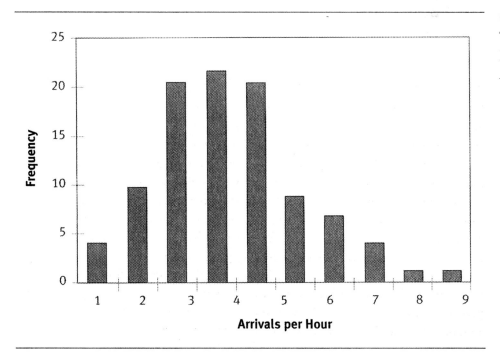

FIGURE 16.2a
Theoretical Distribution of Arrivals

were three arrivals, and so on. The negative exponential distribution in Figure 16.2b shows that if an average of 4 people per hour are being served, about 33 percent of those served will require .1 hours, or six minutes, about 15 percent will require .3 hours, or 18 minutes, and so on.

Under the assumptions in the preceding paragraph, and in a single server system, the following relationships will hold.

1. **The Probability of an Empty Facility, P_0.** The probability that no clients are in the waiting line or being served is

$$P_0 = 1 - \frac{A}{S} \qquad (16.11)$$

where S = average clients served per unit of time (in the previous edition of this book this was designated m), and A = average number of clients arriving per hour (in the previous edition this was designated l).

2. **The Average Number of Clients in the Queue, L_q.** The average number of clients in the waiting line is:

$$L_q = \frac{A^2}{S(S - A)} \qquad (16.12)$$

3. **The Average Number of the Clients in the System, L.** The average number of clients in the total system is:

$$L = \frac{A}{S - A} \qquad (16.13)$$

FIGURE 16.2b

Negative Exponential of Service Time

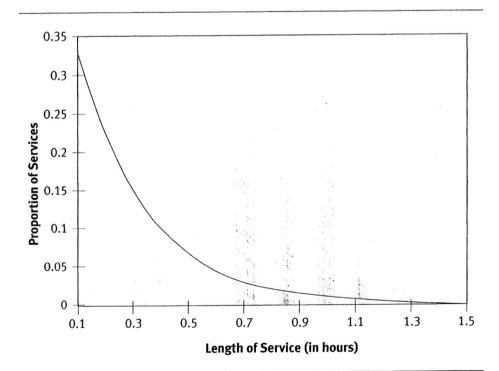

4. **Average Waiting Time in the Queue, W_q.** The average time a client is in the queue is:

$$W_q = \frac{A}{S(S-A)} \qquad (16.14)$$

5. **Average Waiting Time, W.** The average waiting time in the system, both in line and being served, is:

$$W = \frac{1}{S-A} \qquad (16.15)$$

With these relationships given, it is possible to see what may happen in a facility with a single server system. Suppose a physician has set up a private practice as a walk-in clinic (i.e., no appointments) and expects to be able to effectively meet the needs of four patients per hour during the hours that he works. He is not certain how many people will arrive each hour at his walk-in clinic, but he thinks it will be between two and four patients per hour.

The physician wants to know if he will be able to deal with this number of clients. The preceding relationships provide a way of finding out. Table 16.5 shows that if two patients arrive per hour, the average waiting time will be .5 hours or 30 minutes, the number of patients in the queue will be on average .5 people, and the probability of finding an empty facility will be .5, or one chance in two. If three patients arrive per hour, the average waiting time will be one hour, there will be 2.25 patients in the queue, and the probability of finding an empty facility will be .25. The table also shows an interesting characteristic of queues.

As the number of people arriving for services approaches the service limit of the facility, the waiting time and patients in the queue both approach infinite length. As Table 16.5 shows, if the number of patients is 3.999 per hour, the waiting time will be 1,000 hours and there will be 3,998 patients in the queue.

To expect that a real queue at a real walk-in clinic would ever get as long as the theoretical limits is clearly unreasonable. This is because people will refuse to join the queue to wait for services, or the physician would speed up his work if he could, or he would simply close his doors after the queue became too long. But the important point to note is that in a queuing system, given random arrival and

Measure of Performance					
Patients arriving per hour (A), (l)	2	3	3.8	3.999	
Patients served per hour (S), (m)	4	4	4	4	
Average waiting time (W)	0.5	1.00	5	1000	
Average time in queue (W_q)	0.25	0.75	4.75	999.75	
Patients in system (L)	1	3.00	19	3999	
Patients in queue (L_q)	0.5	2.25	18.05	3998	
Probability of empty facility (P_o)	0.5	0.25	0.05	0.0003	

TABLE 16.5
Characteristics of Queue with a Single Physician Seeing Four Patients Per Hour and Variable Numbers of Arrivals

random service times, it will not be possible for a facility to serve the theoretical maximum (in this case, four patients per hour).

Multiple Servers Systems

The system that was examined in the preceding topic of linear programming was actually a multiple servers system, which is somewhat more complex than a single server system. In a multiple servers system, the assumption is still that there is a single arrival line, but any one of several servers can serve this arrival line.

An example that is quite similar to the linear programming problem already discussed would be a walk-in clinic, with unscheduled visits, and with more than one provider. An important simplification to the multiple servers system that will be assumed here is that all servers are capable of providing services at the same average rate. (In the linear programming example, the specific assumption was that physicians provided services faster than physician assistants did.) If this same average rate is not assumed, the problem exceeds the level of complexity that can be addressed here.

In a multiple servers system, the following relationships will hold.

1. **The Probability of an Empty Facility, P_0.** The probability that no clients are in the waiting line or being served is:

$$P_0 = \cfrac{1}{\cfrac{U^K}{K!(1 - \overline{U})} + \sum_{i=0}^{K-1} \cfrac{U^i}{i!}} \tag{16.16}$$

where K = the number of servers in the facility, U = the utilization of one server (A/S), and $\overline{U}$ = the utilization factor for the entire system, so that:

$$\overline{U} = \frac{U}{K} = \frac{A}{KS} \tag{16.17}$$

2. **The Average Number of Clients in the Queue, L_q.** The average number of clients in the waiting line is:

$$L_q = \frac{P_0 U^K \overline{U}}{K!(1 - \overline{U})^2} \tag{16.18}$$

3. **The Average Number of the Clients in the System, L.** The average number of clients in the total system is:

$$L = L_q + U \tag{16.19}$$

4. **Average Waiting Time in the Queue, W_q.** The average time a client is in the queue is:

$$W_q = \frac{L_q}{A} \tag{16.20}$$

5. **Average Waiting Time, W.** The average waiting time in the system, both in line and being served, is:

$$W = W_q + \frac{1}{S} \qquad (16.21)$$

If the physician who plans to start his own walk-in clinic decides that he will not be able to deal effectively with the patient load and decides to bring in a partner, this will not simply halve the waiting lines and waiting times. For example, assume that clients will arrive at an average of 3.999 per hour, which would totally swamp the one-physician clinic. On the basis of the preceding equations, the probability of the facility being empty would be .28 (by Equation 16.16), the average time in the facility for each patient would be .32 hours or about 20 minutes (by Equation 16.21), and the length of the waiting line would be .29 people (by Equation 16.18). Clearly, the addition of a second physician does much more than simply cut the wait and length of the queue in half.

Consider again the situation of the administrator who on the basis of a linear program was satisfied that the clinic had been adequately staffed to serve 100 patients during a ten-hour period. The assumption must now be that all providers work at the same rate for the multiple servers queuing solution to work. If that assumption is made, as well as the assumption that patients arrive in an unscheduled manner, the waiting times and queue length will be as shown in Table 16.6.

As Table 16.6 indicates, if eight patients arrive each hour, the average waiting time will be .62 hours or about 35 minutes, and the average waiting line will be about 2.5 people. If 9.8 arrive each hour, the waiting time will be over five hours and the queue will be about 47 people. Therefore, unless a system of scheduling is adopted, a clinic with enough staff to physically see ten patients per hour will not be able to do so because of the random pattern of arrival.

Linear Programming versus Queuing Theory

How can the results of linear programming, which indicates that ten people can be served per hour, and queuing theory, which indicates that even nine per hour will back up the system, be so different? The difference lies in the assumptions of

Measure of Performance				
Patients arriving per hour (A), (I)	8	9	9.5	9.8
Patients served per hour (S), (m)	3.33	3.33	3.33	3.33
Number of providers (K), (X)	3	3	3	3
Average waiting time (W)	0.62	1.12	2.11	5.11
Average time in queue (W_q)	0.32	0.82	1.81	4.81
Patients in system (L)	4.99	10.05	20.08	50.10
Patients in queue (L_q)	2.59	7.35	17.23	47.16
Probability of empty facility (P_o)	0.056	0.025	0.012	0.004

TABLE 16.6
Characteristics of a Queue with Three Physicians Seeing 3.33 Patients Per Hour and Variable Numbers of Arrivals

linear programming that there is never a wait for the next person to be served, which is not the case with a real queue, and that the service time is always exactly the same, which is not the case in a real service situation. Linear programming in this case provided a general notion about the optimum mix of service providers given certain limited resources. Queuing theory, however, provides a much more realistic picture of the type of burden on the system if the patient load approached the theoretical maximum of the linear programming solution.

Even queuing results will not necessarily adhere to actual events. The mathematically solved queuing solution depends on the basic assumption of a Poisson arrival pattern and a negative exponential service pattern. In real life, providers are likely to work faster as lines become longer, potential clients are likely to leave when lines become too long if they can, and doors are likely to be closed in extreme cases of service lines becoming too long. All these factors take the solution out of the realm of classical queuing and make the results of queuing theory less than wholly applicable. Nevertheless, queuing theory provides a basic understanding of what happens in the service provision setting.

Decision Analysis: Dealing with the Problem of Long Queues

The administrator of the clinic in the preceding situations may decide that it is of substantial concern that the average waiting time for a patient at the clinic may be nearly 50 minutes even if the clinic actually has a client load of 90 patients per day. The administrator may also anticipate that a reasonable possibility exists that the patient load would increase to as much as 110 patients per day. If this latter event occurred, there would be no reasonable way for the existing staff to deal with the patient load.

The administrator knows that adding hours to the time already worked can increase available clinic hours. Assume that two additional hours can be added to the ten hours that the three examining rooms are used. In this case, a service provider (possibly hired on an hourly basis) could be available 12 hours each day in each of three examining rooms.

Alternatively, the administrator knows that it would be possible to hire an additional provider if an examining room was added to the clinic. However, is it better to hire additional provider time on an hourly basis or to add an examining room to the clinic and hire an additional full-time provider? Is this question answered differently if the demand remains constant at 90 clients per day or increases to 110 clients per day? Decision analysis can provide a strategy for such decisions.

Suppose that the administrator believes that regardless of what he or she decides, the same decision will be faced again next year—that is, whether to add a second office or more overtime to cope with possible (but not certain) increases in patient load in the second year.

Decision analysis actually refers to several different mechanisms for arriving at the same basic conclusion. Three of these mechanisms are addressed, one based on a conditional payoff table, and two based on decision trees. While all three mechanisms lead to the same result, they do not all produce the same expected payoffs.

Before going to the discussion of the three mechanisms, it is necessary to specify in somewhat more detail the nature of the decision problem faced by the administrator. The administrator has the option this year of hiring additional medical staff on a part-time hourly basis or of adding an additional examining room to the clinic and the equivalent of an additional full-time person. In either case, the administrator will add six hours daily to clinic time—in the first case extending the hours during which the three existing clinic rooms are used to 12, or in the second case cutting back the time during which the clinic is open to nine hours per day. The total clinic hours in either case will be 36 as opposed to 30 prior to the decision. Regardless of the clinic experience this year, the administrator will be faced with the same type of decision (to add overtime or to add a second office) in the second year.

If the administrator chooses to add an office in either the first or second year, the annual cost will be an additional $50,000 for the office space plus $63,000 for six additional hours of a physician assistant ($35 × 6 hours per day × 300 days per year) for a total of $113,000. If the administrator decides to add overtime, the cost will be only $63,000 per year. The administrator believes that the client demand at the clinic will do one of two things over the coming two years: in either year it will remain at 90 patients per day or will increase to 110 patients per day. The administrator also believes that if an office is added there is a .7 likelihood that the client load will increase and a .3 likelihood that it will remain at 90. However, if only overtime is added, the administrator suspects, because the hours may be more inconvenient for many people, there is only a .5 likelihood that the volume will go to 110 per day and an equal likelihood that it will remain at 90.

A further necessary piece of information for decision analysis is the payoff of these different decisions and possibilities. The administrator expects that if the client load goes to 110, either by increasing office space or by adding overtime, the number of clients seen by the additional medical personnel will average 18 per day. The administrator knows that the average clinic visit returns $50 in revenue, so that the payoff from 18 patients per day would be $270,000 per year. Alternatively, if there is no increase in clients, the administrator expects that the extra medical personnel will see only four to eight people per day, essentially just taking up slack in the system and cutting the waiting times. In this case, however, the payoff from the additional staff would be 0, because the expectation is that all clients would be served by existing staff.

Table 16.7 shows a solution to this decision problem based on a conditional payoff table. The top row of the payoff table shows the four possible decisions that can be made: add an office in each of two years; add overtime in each of two years; or two mixed strategies. The left column of Table 16.7 shows the possible outcomes that can be expected: an increase in patient load in each of two years, the same patient load in each of two years, or two outcomes with one year of increase and one year that remains the same.

TABLE 16.7

Conditional Payoff Table for Adding Office Space or Adding Overtime in Each of Two Years

Possible Outcomes	Possible Decisions			
	Add Office; Add Office	Add Office; Add Overtime	Add Overtime; Add Office	Add Overtime; Add Overtime
Increase; Increase	0.49 $314,000 $153,860	0.35 $364,000 $127,400	0.35 $364,000 $127,400	0.25 $414,000 $103,500
Increase; Same	0.21 $44,000 9,240	0.35 $94,000 $32,900	0.15 $94,000 $14,100	0.25 $144,000 $36,000
Same; Increase	0.21 $44,000 9,240	0.15 $94,000 $14,100	0.35 $94,000 $32,900	0.25 $144,000 $36,000
Same; Same	0.09 −$226,000 −$20,340	0.15 −$176,000 −$26,400	0.15 −$176,000 −$26,400	0.25 −$126,000 −$31,500
Expected Payoff	**$152,000**	**$148,000**	**$148,000**	**$144,000**

The first row in each of the 16 cells of the table is the probability that a given outcome will occur when a particular sequence of decisions is made. Thus, .49 in column one represents the probability that patient load will increase in both years if an additional office is added in each year (.7, the probability that the patient load will increase in the first year if an office is added, times .7, the probability that it will increase in the second year). The second row is the income to be derived from a particular sequence of decisions minus the cost of the decisions. Thus, $314,000 is the income expected to be derived from adding an office each year ($270,000 in each year) minus the cost ($113,000 in each year). The third row in each cell is the first multiplied by the second, which represents the amount of money to be expected from each decision under each outcome situation.

The total expected value of a particular set of decisions is the sum of the values in the third row in each column of the decision table. Thus, adding an office in each year returns an expected payoff of $152,000, adding overtime in each year returns an expected payoff of $144,000, and either mixed strategy returns an expected payoff of $148,000 as represented by the last row of the table. Based on this analysis, and given the assumptions presented, the decision that maximizes the expected payoff is to add office space in both years.

Maximizing expected payoff, however, may not be the best decision in every case, or for every administrator. The decision that maximizes the expected payoff is also the decision, if client load stays the same in both years, with the largest possible loss (at $226,000). In many situations, decision makers may follow a conservative strategy that is "risk averse" (i.e., a strategy that minimizes the maximum possible loss). In such a case, adding overtime in each year would be the strategy that minimizes the maximum possible loss.

The same problem can be examined using the mechanism of a decision tree and the "rollback" method. This mechanism begins with a decision tree representing each possible decision point and chance point. Such a decision tree is shown in Figure 16.3. Decision point 1 is the decision taken in the first year as to adding an office or adding overtime. As shown in the figure, adding an office costs $113,000, while adding overtime costs only $63,000. Chance point 1 represents the possibility that clientele will increase in the coming year (.7 if an office is added, .5 if only overtime is added) or the possibility that clientele will remain constant at its current level (.3 and .5).

Decision point 2 represents both the point at which the second year decision is to be made (to add an office at $113,000 or overtime at $63,000), and the payoff from the first year's decision (a realization of an additional $270,000 or $0). Chance point 2 represents the possibility that clientele will increase in the second year with the same probabilities assumed as in the first year. Payoff 2 represents the amount of money to be realized, again depending on whether patient load increases or remains the same.

The solution to this decision problem using the rollback method begins with the assumption that the process has reached a given end state. At that end state, the value of the decision made to reach that end state is calculated. Then the process moves back to assess the value of the next most proximate decision on the path to a given end state. This continues until the values of all decisions are assessed. In Figure 16.3, the rollback method begins at chance point B1, which represents the decision to add an office in the second year after adding one office in the first year. The expected value (EV) of having taken that decision is calculated as the payoff for each chance path from B1 multiplied by the probability of taking that path, minus the cost of the decision to choose B1. In general terms, the expected value (EV_i) for any decision i using the rollback method is:

$$EV_i = \left\{ \sum_{j=1}^{J} PO_{ij}P_{ij} \right\} - C_i \tag{16.22}$$

where:

- EV_i = the expected value for decision i;
- PO_{ij} = the payoff for decision i and chance event j;
- P_{ij} = the probability that chance event j will occur given decision j $\left\{ \sum_{j=1}^{J} P_{ij} = 1 \right\}$; and
- C_i = the cost for decision i.

The expected value of the decision at decision point 2 that led to chance point B1 is:

$$EV_{B1} = (.7 \times \$270,000 + .3 \times \$0) - \$113,000 = \$76,000 \tag{16.23}$$

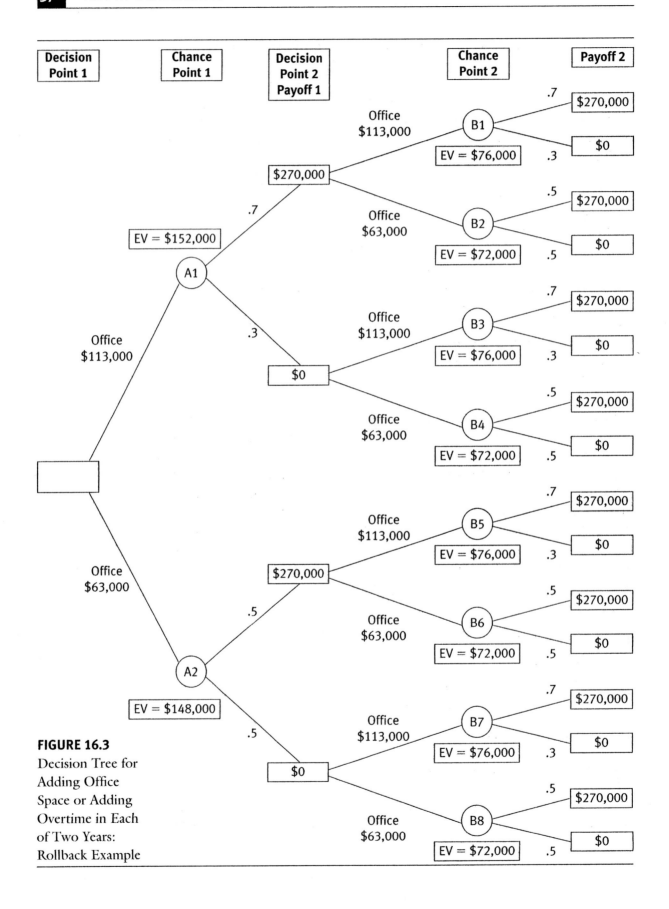

FIGURE 16.3
Decision Tree for Adding Office Space or Adding Overtime in Each of Two Years: Rollback Example

The expected values of the other chance points designated B2 through B8 are found in the same way. As shown in Figure 16.3, all the decisions involving the addition of an office have an expected value at chance point 2 of $76,000, and all the decisions involving the addition of overtime have an expected value of $72,000.

The next step in the rollback method is to examine the value of the decision that was made prior to the decision just assessed. In this case, that is the decision leading to chance points A1 and A2. The assessment of the expected value for chance point 1 is carried out in the same manner as the assessment of the expected value for chance point 2, with one addition. The largest expected value from decision 2 is added to the calculated expected value from decision 1 when the expected value is calculated. Thus, the expected value for chance point A1 is:

$$EV_{A1} = (.7 \times \$270,000 + .3 \times \$0) - \$113,000 + \$76,000$$
$$= \$152,000 \qquad (16.24)$$

Calculated the same way, the expected value for A2 is $148,000. Decision analysis, this time in the form of a decision tree, thus indicates that the optimal decision is to add office space in both years.

The final mechanism for making a decision in regard to additional office space or overtime also relies on a decision tree and is called the forward method in contrast to the rollback method. Figure 16.4 shows a decision tree that presents the forward method. The decision tree in 16.4 is essentially the same as that in 16.3, but with changes that reflect the forward method. The essential difference between the forward method and the rollback method is that the forward method assigns probabilities to the chance points and to the decision points.

As shown in Figure 16.4, there is a probability of .5 that the decision to add office space will be accepted, and an equal probability that overtime will be added. An immediate response to this may be that because this is a decision point rather than a chance point, the administrator can make either decision with certainty or can assign an unlimited number of different probabilities to making one decision or the other. It is possible to show that this does not make a difference in the selection of the best outcome, if all possible paths are assigned all options. The convention adopted here is that all branches at a decision point are assigned equal probability, with the sum of the probabilities at any decision point being equal to 1.

With this convention accepted, a probability of any one of the 16 possible outcome paths in Figure 16.4 occurring over the two-year time period can be calculated. The probability that an outcome will occur is the multiplication of all probabilities in the series of events leading to a particular outcome. In the case of the first outcome in Figure 16.4 (the path that moves from decision point 1 to A1 at chance point 2, to $270,000 at payoff 1[decision point 2], to B1 at chance point 2 to $270,000 at payoff 2) the probability p that this outcome will occur is:

$$p_1 = .5 \times .7 \times .5 \times .7 = .1225 \qquad (16.25)$$

All other probabilities are calculated the same way.

Decision Point 1	Chance Point 1	Decision Point 2 Payoff 1	Chance Point 2	Payoff 2	Probability and Expected Value	Total for Each Decision Set

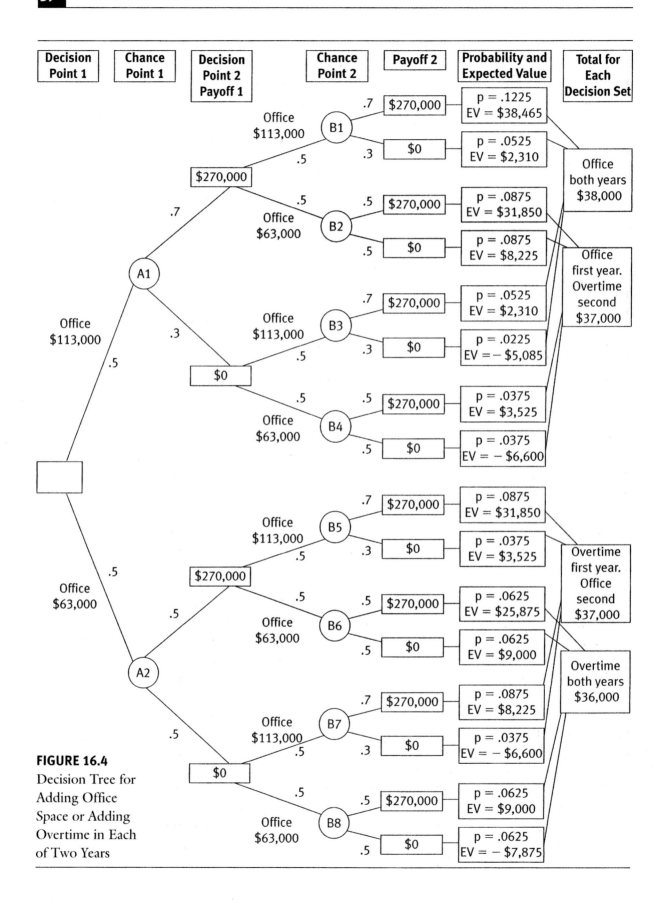

FIGURE 16.4

Decision Tree for Adding Office Space or Adding Overtime in Each of Two Years

The expected value of any outcome is found by multiplying the difference between the total benefits involved in reaching a particular outcome and the costs of reaching a particular outcome multiplied by the probability that it will occur. So in the case of the first outcome, the expected value is:

$$EV_1 = (\$270,000 + \$270,000 - \$113,000 - \$113,000) \times .1225 \quad (16.26)$$

In general, the expected value for any outcome i is:

$$EV_i = \sum_{j=1}^{J} (B_j - C_j) \prod_{j=1}^{J} P_j \quad (16.27)$$

where:

- the subscript i refers to each of i possible outcomes (in this case, 14);
- the subscript j refers to the j possible branch points (in this case 4, two decision points and two chance points);
- B_j = the benefit in dollars associated with each path from each branch point j;
- C_j = the cost in dollars associated with each branch point j;
- P_j = the probability associated with each branch point j;
- Σ = the usual summation operator; and
- Π = the product operator.

Using this formulation, the expected value of outcome 1 in 16.4 is $38,465. Expected values for the other 15 possible outcomes are calculated the same way.

The administrator may actually make only four different combinations of decisions: the decision to add offices in both years; the decision to add an office the first year and overtime the second; the obverse of that decision; and the decision to add overtime in both years. Four outcomes and expected values represent each of these possible decisions. The last column in the decision tree in Figure 16.4 shows the total expected value for each of these four decision sets. As can be seen there, adding an office in both years results in a total expected value of $38,000, while each of the other options results in a lower total value. Thus, this approach to decision analysis results in the same decision as the two preceding methods.

One difference between the decision tree forward method and either the payoff table or the decision tree rollback method is that it apparently results in a different (and substantially lower) expected value for the set of decisions. The expected values found in the latter two methods, however, can be reconstituted from the forward method by dividing each expected total outcome by the probability that that outcome will occur. For example, each of the four decision sets, as the example is set up, has a probability of .25 of occurring. Dividing $38,000 (the EV for the decision to add offices in both years) by .25 gives $152,000, which was the expected value of the same decision set given by the other two methods.

One of the most important issues in the outcome of decision analysis, regardless of the method used to do the actual calculations, is the probabilities assigned to the alternative paths that can be taken from the chance points. If, for example, the administrator thought that regardless of whether office space was added or overtime was added, there was only an equal chance in either year that clientele would increase or remain the same, the result of the decision analysis would be that adding overtime in each year would have a substantially higher expected value ($144,000) than either mixed strategy ($94,000) or adding office space in both years ($44,000). The most important issue in decision analysis, therefore, is to be certain that probabilities assigned to chance events are reasonable.

A second important point about decision analysis, alluded to previously in this chapter, is the point of whether the decision maker is indifferent to risk. Decision analysis shows the decision set that has the highest or the lowest expected net payoff. In many instances, however, when real decisions are being made, the highest expected net payoff may not be the decision criteria that is of most importance to the decision maker. By making the decision with the highest expected value, the decision maker would be following a rational procedure to get the biggest payoff possible. The decision maker is also risking the possibility of taking the biggest loss possible. If office space is added in both years and client load does not increase, he or she will actually be out $226,000. If the decision maker only adds overtime in both years and the client load does not increase, he or she will only be out $126,000—a difference of $100,000. The decision method that administrators will often use in practice is sometimes called the *minimax* method, which is short for, "minimize the maximum possible loss." Using this strategy, the best decision is the one that costs least, which is overtime.

A Different Problem for the Clinic: Inventory

The clinic manager is responsible for maintaining an extensive inventory of supplies and equipment and assuring that these are always available when needed. While the clinic has a part-time pharmacist who handles the pharmaceutical supplies, the manager also feels responsible for being certain that the supplies of pharmaceuticals are always adequate for the everyday needs of the clinic. The manager also knows that placing orders for supplies costs money in terms of time required to decide on the size of the order and staff time needed to fill out and mail order forms. The manager is constantly aware, however, that storage space at the clinic is limited, so that maintaining a quantity of supplies larger than needed actually represents a cost to the clinic in terms of other supplies that cannot be stored, and even in the necessity to rent additional storage space.

Assuming that the manager can determine the cost of placing an order and the cost of holding the inventory, operations research techniques provide a deterministic solution that will arrive at the proper ordering quantity and ordering frequency to assure the minimization of inventory ordering and storage costs.

The basis of this example of the application of operations research techniques is what is referred to as the *economic ordering quantity* (EOQ). The EOQ makes several basic assumptions about the inventory control problem including:

- The demand for the item is constant over time.
- The unit holding and ordering costs are independent of quantity ordered.
- Replenishment is scheduled so that new stock arrives just at the time that the old stock is entirely exhausted.
- Orders for different items are independent of one another.

Illustration

The clinic will see about 90 patients per day—between 28,000 and 29,000 patients per year. Assume that each patient seen requires the physician, on the average, to use two pairs of rubber gloves. This means that the manager must ensure the timely, and most cost-effective, availability of about 57,000 pairs of rubber gloves each year. Assume further that the manager has spent time studying the cost of placing orders for various supply items and has determined that the cost of placing any order for rubber gloves is $7.00. The cost of storage space has been calculated for a box of rubber gloves (100 to a box) as being $.80 per year. Given this trade-off between cost of ordering and cost of storing, and the need to assure constant availability, how often are orders for rubber gloves placed and how many are ordered each time?

The EOQ calculation is generally based on an annual supply cycle, although longer cycles could be assessed. Assume that the concern is with an annual cycle. In this formulation the following parameters can be specified:

- annual demand   (D)   570 boxes
- ordering cost   (K) $7.00
- holding cost   (H) $.80
- quantity ordered   (Q)   to be determined

Within this formulation, annual ordering cost (T_o) is equal to the annual demand divided by the quantity ordered at each order multiplied by the cost of ordering, or:

$$T_o = \frac{D}{Q}K \qquad (16.28)$$

Annual holding cost (T_h) is equal to the average inventory ($Q/2$ if demand is constant) multiplied by the cost of holding one box, or:

$$T_h = H\frac{Q}{2} \qquad (16.29)$$

Then total annual cost (T) is:

$$T = T_o + T_h = \frac{D}{Q}K + H\frac{Q}{2} \tag{16.30}$$

Both calculus and graphic solutions to this problem will show that the minimum value of T is obtained when T_o and T_h are equal, when:

$$\frac{D}{Q}K = H\frac{Q}{2} \tag{16.31}$$

or when:

$$Q = \sqrt{\frac{2KD}{H}} \tag{16.32}$$

With this information, the optimal ordering quantity will be:

$$Q = \sqrt{2 \times 7.00 \times \frac{570}{.80}} = 99.87 \text{ boxes} \tag{16.33}$$

With this number of boxes of gloves, the total inventory cost of rubber gloves for one year will be:

$$T = T_o + T_h = \frac{570}{99.87} \times 7 + 0.80 \times \frac{99.87}{2}$$

$$= 39.95 + 39.95 = \$79.90 \tag{16.34}$$

Of course, it is unlikely that the clinic will be able to buy 99.87 boxes of rubber gloves at one time, so if the quantity is changed to 100, the total cost per year is:

$$T = T_o + T_h = 39.90 + 40.00 = \$79.90 \tag{16.35}$$

In this case, the difference in the price of the next higher number of boxes was not detectable at the level of cents.

This formulation also indicates to the manager how often gloves must be purchased. This will be the number of days in a year multiplied by the quantity purchased at any one time divided by the annual demand, or every 64 days.

The EOQ also provides useful information in the situation where purchasing supplies in exactly the most economic quantities may not be possible. For example, assume that rubber gloves can be purchased by the clinic at a reasonable purchase price only if obtained in lots of 60 boxes (perhaps 60 boxes are packaged in a larger carton). As previously shown, the optimal purchase in terms of inventory costs is approximately 100.

Will it be more efficient for the clinic to purchase gloves as one carton of 60 boxes each time it makes a purchase, or will it be more efficient to purchase two cartons of 60 boxes each, for 120 boxes at each purchase? The EOQ provides the answer. The purchase of 60 boxes at a time will give an annual cost of

$66.50 for ordering and $24.00 for holding, for a total of $90.50. The purchase of 120 boxes at a time will give a total of $33.25 for ordering and $48.00 for holding, for a total of $81.25 (only $1.35 more than the optimal solution). In this case, it is better to buy the larger amount each time, rather than the smaller. This is true because the cost of holding is small compared to the cost of ordering. If the reverse were true, a different solution would have resulted.

This is the simplest of all inventory models. A separate calculation must be done for each item of inventory. More complex models exist, but the purpose here is merely to provide an introduction to the types of decisions that can be made with operations research—in this case, inventory models.

Discussion Questions

1. What is the relationship of operations research techniques to the cybernetic model and decision making?
2. Under what conditions are operations research techniques the method of choice? Illustrate your answer.

COST-BENEFIT, COST-EFFECTIVENESS, AND COST-UTILITY ANALYSIS

Cost-benefit, cost-effectiveness, and cost-utility analysis are the last chapter in the topics covered on the subject of evaluation. In the sense that cost-benefit, cost-effectiveness, and cost-utility analysis are not specific types of evaluation tools per se but are a set of techniques that would be well applied to any evaluation, the position presented in this chapter is logical. To the extent, however, that virtually no evaluation can ignore the issues of cost and the most efficient ways in which to produce a desired result, cost-benefit, cost-effectiveness, and cost-utility analysis should be considered an integral part of any evaluation effort. They specifically address the efficiency element of evaluation discussed in Chapter 1.

Benefit, Effectiveness, and Utility

The first issue to address in a chapter on cost-benefit, cost-effectiveness, and cost-utility analysis is the distinction between the three concepts. All three techniques are concerned with a comparison between program costs and the results of the program or program outputs or outcomes. A program with a lower cost that produces the same level of outputs or outcomes as another program would be considered the more cost-beneficial, cost-effective, and cost-useful. The distinction between the three techniques is that, while all three attempt to assess program inputs in dollar terms, program outputs or outcomes are assessed in dollar terms only in cost-benefit analysis.

In cost-utility analysis, program outcomes are assessed in terms of utility as addressed in Chapter 14. In cost-effectiveness analysis, outcomes are assessed in terms of actual discrete results themselves, without recourse to any effort to reduce these to a common measuring device such as dollars or utility. Before continuing with a discussion of the differences between benefit, effectiveness, and utility, however, consider outputs and outcomes in the context of these three techniques.

The distinction between outputs and outcomes has been addressed elsewhere in the book as the distinction between the immediate results of a program and longer-term results of a program. The output of an immunization program is the immunized children; the output of a nurse-training program is the trained nurses. The outcomes of an immunization program are numerous, but include an accumulation of people no longer at risk (or temporarily not at risk) for certain immunizable conditions, lowered incidence of the condition, and lives saved. The outcomes of a nurse training program are also numerous but may include an increased supply of nursing services, a higher level of quality of nursing services, and more people treated.

In general, cost-effectiveness analysis can deal with outputs as the result of interest or with outcomes as the result of interest. Cost-benefit analysis may also deal with outputs as the result of interest but more frequently deals with outcomes as the result of interest. The nature of utility as a result measure is such that any cost-utility analysis is almost certainly concerned with outcomes as the result of interest.

With certain types of programs (e.g., immunization) the outputs and outcomes are clearly and intimately related. As long as the cold chain is maintained and the vaccine is potent, immunization for polio is directly related to reduced incidence and prevalence of the disease. This relationship is so direct that polio has been targeted for eradication based on the effectiveness of immunization, as was small-pox in the 1960s and 1970s. In a case such as immunization, cost-effectiveness particularly can be addressed as either a relationship between inputs and outputs (immunizations given) or inputs and outcomes (changes in incidence of disease). Cost-benefit can be addressed in regard to immunization programs as a relationship between inputs and a measure of outcomes. These outcomes may be dollars saved in treatment of new cases of immunizable disease, dollar value of productive years of future life, or another dollar measure related to avoidance of disease rather than simply vaccines given. Cost-utility analysis would deal exclusively with the relationship of inputs to outcomes in the sense of the utility of added years of healthy life for children immunized.

Certain types of programs possibly may produce outputs that have little direct effect on the outcomes desired. A classic example is tonsillectomy. In the mid-1930s, the medical value of tonsillectomy was being widely questioned (Glover 1938), but it continued to be a staple of childhood medical intervention well into the early 1950s. This was a procedure the output of which (children no longer burdened with tonsils) has been determined to have little to do with the outcome desired (fewer sickness days, less long-term morbidity).

In a case such as this, it would be meaningless to talk of cost-effectiveness as tonsillectomies performed per unit of dollar input, or to talk of the cost-benefit of tonsillectomies as the dollar value of physicians' time saved in the actual procedure by one method as opposed to another. Cost-utility analysis, by its very nature, requires that a clear relation exist between the inputs and the outcomes (utility). But because cost-benefit and particularly cost-effectiveness analysis can fall into the trap of examining the efficiency of a program where the link between outputs and outcomes is quite tenuous, this chapter will, except where specifically noted, deal with all three concepts in the context of a relationship between inputs and outcomes rather than inputs and outputs.

The differences among the three techniques of cost-benefit, cost-effectiveness, and cost-utility analysis lead to differences in actual application. Cost-effectiveness analysis is most usefully employed when the expected outputs or outcomes of programs to be compared—or of a single program before and after an intervention—are precisely the same. For example, two immunization strategies—one based on routine availability of vaccine at local clinics and the other based on short, intense, centrally directed campaigns—could be assessed in terms of proportion of children effectively immunized as the output of interest. Cost-effectiveness analysis could not be used to compare an immunization program to a program with greatly different outputs or outcomes, such as a nurse-training program.

Cost-benefit analysis can be used when the expected results of two programs to be compared are not necessarily the same. A cost-benefit analysis could compare a program to prevent cigarette use through education with a program of heart bypass surgery in terms of the amount of money each program saved in future medical care costs. The two programs could also be compared on the dollar value of future earnings of the two groups of people. Because the outcomes of the two programs are so different at many levels, cost-effectiveness analysis would be more problematic. Cost-effectiveness analysis could be applied, however, to an outcome measure such as years of life saved or simple mortality.

Cost-utility analysis can be used when the expected results of two programs will not be the same, but when the results of either program should be expected to improve quality of life. A program directed at prevention of cigarette use, for example, may be compared to a program to reduce vehicle accidents, in terms of future quality of life of affected populations. With an agreement on what the quality of life measures should be, these two programs could theoretically be compared on the basis of which one produced the greatest volume of quality of life for the resources (dollars) utilized.

This distinction between these three techniques has important consequences. Cost-benefit analysis would seem to be the most desirable tool to use, because it is, in theory, able to assess a wider range of alternative programs against one another. A program aimed at reducing drug use among inner-city youth may be compared to a program aimed at assuring full immunization levels for infants, or one providing improved bypass surgery for heart patients. The expected results of these programs could all be valued in dollar terms and the program that provided the highest ratio of dollars gained to dollars invested would be determined to be the best program.

But herein lies the problem. The outcomes of interest, increased years of healthy and productive life as a consequence of the three programs, is extremely difficult to value in dollar terms. While authors have valued life in economic terms (Rice and Cooper 1967) as well as explored the difficulties of doing so (Card and Mooney 1977), what is generally believed is that such valuation is fraught with both conceptual and statistical problems (Landefeld and Seskin 1982). The result is that there is little agreement on an appropriate strategy for placing a dollar value on years of life. Assessing the dollar value of medical services averted by putting any of the three programs in place is possible, however. This would be a legitimate cost-benefit analysis. The problem with this approach is that saving money on medical care costs, while not a trivial issue, would probably not be the main reason for the initiation of any one of the programs.

Given that additional productive years of life may represent the ultimate goal of any one of the programs mentioned previously, it is feasible to assess them in terms of cost-utility analysis. Strategies for developing utility measures were addressed in Chapter 14, and it would be reasonable to compare the three programs on the basis of QALYs, for example. In fact, that is precisely the point of the QALY concept. Some of the difficulties inherent in the development of utility measures were also addressed in Chapter 14.

Cost-effectiveness analysis could also be used to compare the three preceding programs, if the expected results were stated in terms of years of life saved or reduced morbidity. While any one of the techniques could be used to assess the three different programs, the assessment may very well produce different and conflicting findings based on the different level of results assessed. Some of these issues are addressed later in the chapter. Prior to this, however, is an examination of the general techniques of cost-benefit, cost-effectiveness, and cost-utility analysis in somewhat greater detail and with examples.

Cost-Benefit Analysis

In the simplest terms, cost-benefit analysis is a comparison of the costs of a program to the benefits to be derived from that program. While all costs are valued in dollar terms, only in cost-benefit analysis are the payoffs of a program valued in dollar terms.

Illustration

If it costs $16,000 in the first year to initiate a program and an additional $1,000 per year to keep it going for four subsequent years, the total cost of the program is $20,000 for five years. Assume that the projected benefits from the program will equal $10,000 in the first year and decline at the rate of $2,000 per year over the life of the program (perhaps this is a training program where fewer people are trained in each year). In this case, the total benefits derived from the program are, in dollar terms, $30,000. The net difference between the costs and the benefits (the net benefit) is a positive $10,000. Thus, initiating the program is a good idea.

Doing further analysis before actually initiating the program may be wise for two reasons. The first is that there may be other programs that will return a greater net benefit for the money invested. The second is that the preceding paragraph assumes that there are no other opportunities lost for the use of the $20,000 invested in the program.

To consider the first issue, suppose that a certain program will cost $4,000 in each year of operation for five years. Unlike the previously described program, there are essentially no start-up costs (the initial year's costs were $16,000). Assume also that this program returns $36,000 rather than only $30,000, but that the benefits are not realized until year 3, when they start at $8,000, followed by $10,000 in year 4 and $18,000 in year 5. If a manager had only $20,000 to invest in a new program, he or she may reasonably decide that the second program, which returns a net of $16,000 for the investment, is more desirable than the first, which only returns a net of $10,000. If the only consideration was the absolute difference between costs and benefits, the second program is superior.

Net Present Value

The fact that the value of money is not constant over time must be considered in cost-benefit analysis. If you are given a dollar today, it is more valuable to you than a dollar that you will acquire one year from now. Even if we disregard inflation that is certain to erode the value of the dollar that you will receive one year from now, making it worth less in buying power than a dollar today, another issue also exists. The dollar you obtain today can be invested at a rate of interest (r) to produce $1 + r$ dollars in one year.

In considering the costs and benefits of any given project, or when comparing one or more projects, it is usually desirable, if not essential, to take into consideration the time value of money. The time value of money is often stated as the net present value (NPV) of a quantity of money that will be obtained at a point in time in the future. If the interest rate (i.e., the *discount rate*) is r, the NPV of a quantity of money, P, to be received one year in the future, is:

$$NPV = \frac{P}{1 + r} \tag{17.1}$$

In particular, if the P is one dollar and r is .05, the NPV of one dollar received in one year is $1/(1 + .05)$, or .952.

If we are interested in the benefits of a program that will be implemented and active over a period of years, t, the NPV of the money invested in the program, costs (C), and the returns from the program, benefits (B), will be:

$$NPV = \sum_{t=1}^{T} \frac{B_t - C_t}{(1 + r)^t} \tag{17.2}$$

Equation 17.2 indicates that the NPV of the program is the sum of the annual difference between the costs and benefits of the program over its lifetime reduced by one, plus the discount rate raised to the power of the number of years that have elapsed since program start-up.

One problem with this cost-benefit formulation is that it assumes a particular discount rate, or rate at which the value of uninvested money would be expected to decline over time. In general, the discount rate can only be estimated. In many cases, the decisions reached through cost-benefit analysis may depend directly on the assumptions about the discount rate. To see this, consider the consequences of alternative discount rate assumptions in regard to the two projects addressed previously, one that returns a net $10,000 for an investment of $20,000 and the other that returns $16,000. Table 17.1 shows a comparison of the two programs in terms of the time value of money.

Table 17.1 shows several different discount rates and the calculation of net present values for the projects in years 1 through 5, based on that discount rate, as well as the total NPV (the last column). At a discount rate of 0, each project has an NPV of exactly the difference between the total investment and the total

TABLE 17.1

Comparison of Two Projects with Comparable Investments

		Year 1	Year 2	Year 3	Year 4	Year 5	NPV
Program A							
Benefits		$10,000	$8,000	$6,000	$4,000	$2,000	
Costs		16,000	1,000	1,000	1,000	1,000	
Discount Rate	0	−6,000	7,000	5,000	3,000	1,000	$10,000
	.1	−5,455	5,785	3,757	2,049	621	6,757
	.2	−5,000	4,861	2,894	1,447	402	4,604
	.3	−4,615	4,142	2,276	1,050	269	3,122
Program B							
Benefits		$0	$0	$8,000	$10,000	$18,000	
Costs		4,000	4,000	4,000	4,000	4,000	
Discount Rate	0	−4,000	−4,000	4,000	6,000	14,000	$16,000
	.1	−3,636	−3,306	3,005	4,098	8,693	8,854
	.2	−3,333	−2,778	2,315	2,894	5,626	4,724
	.3	−3,077	−2,367	1,821	2,101	3,771	2,249

return, making program B more attractive. At a discount rate of .1 (10 percent) or .2 (20 percent), program B is still superior on the basis of the NPV. If a discount rate of .3 is projected, however, program A becomes the one with the higher NPV and remains so at all higher discount rates. A logical consequence of the fact that the two programs shift position with regard to NPV is that a discount rate exists (in this case, approximately .21) at which both programs are equally attractive. If the discount rate is projected to be below that level for the next five years, then option B is preferred. If the discount rate is projected to be above that level then option A is preferred. This is simply an example to illustrate the idea that what is considered the "best" program can be dependent on the discount rate. In general, discount rates may range from as low as .03 to as high as .15, but rarely would a discount rate as high as .3 or even .21, be posited.

Despite the fact that the discount rate at which program A and program B are equal is quite high, the comparison between the programs suggests at least one generalization. Programs with relatively large returns that come late in the program life will tend to be preferred over programs with more modest returns that come early in the program life when a low discount rate is projected. Programs that have early modest returns will be preferred over programs with larger later returns when a high discount rate is projected.

The level of the discount rate will not always determine the desirability of one program over another. It is easy to postulate that one program will be more attractive than another and will dominate the other program no matter what the discount rate. A program with the same stream of investments as that in program A in Table 17.1, but with a stream of returns that was equal to $10,000 in each of the five years of program operation, would be a clear example of such a dominant program. The decision to choose this latter program over program A would be independent of discount rate.

Internal Rate of Return (IRR)

The NPV is generally accepted as the best measure of the value of a program, either as assessed against no program or as assessed against alternative competing programs. Other assessment measures exist, however. The internal rate of return (IRR) is the discount rate at which the NPV of a given project is equal to 0, or the discount rate at which returns from the project will exactly equal outlays. The IRR is defined as that discount rate r that satisfies the equation:

$$0 = \sum \frac{B_t - C_t}{(1 + r)^t} \tag{17.3}$$

The IRR, although commonly employed as a means of comparing one program to another, has several fundamental problems. It is possible to calculate the IRR for programs A and B in Table 17.1 and determine that the IRR for program A is approximately .81, while the IRR for program B is about .47. If no other information was available, the common decision rule would be to select that program with the higher IRR (i.e., program A). The NPV of program B has already been shown to be higher than program A at values of r lower than .21, however.

The IRR has other problems as well. The IRR generally applies easily and clearly only to those programs in which the first years of a program's life are characterized by an investment stream that is greater than the stream of returns, but in which returns exceed investments in later years. As defined in Equation 17.3, the IRR will take on as many values as there are shifts, over the life of the program, between costs exceeding benefits and benefits exceeding costs.

For example, consider a program in which investments exceeded returns early in the life of the program, returns exceeded investments during the middle years of the program life, and then investments again exceeded returns at the end of the program (i.e., two changes of the relative status of costs and benefits). Such a program would have two different values of the IRR that would be equal only by chance. However, if it was possible to implement a program that in the first year would begin to realize benefits greater than costs (e.g., a five-year program that costs \$1,000 per year to initiate and that realizes benefits of \$2,000 per year from year 1), no IRR exists. The IRR would be undefined, because the relative position of benefits and costs never shifts and the sum of the benefit stream will always exceed the sum of the cost stream.

The Benefit-Cost Ratio

The benefit-cost ratio also provides a means of assessing the value of a program. However, it also presents difficulties when comparing programs. The benefit-cost ratio (B/C) is defined as:

$$B/C = \sum \frac{\dfrac{B_t}{(1 + r)^t}}{\dfrac{C_t}{(1 + r)^t}} \tag{17.4}$$

Any program with a B/C greater than 1 will return a net benefit to society, and any program with a B/C less than 1 will be a net loss. But the B/C, when used to compare programs, will not in general yield the same results as the NPV. For example in the case of programs A and B in Table 17.1, the B/C would prefer program B even at discount rates as high as .3, when the NPV of program A is clearly higher. In most cases, it is agreed that the NPV is the measure of choice in assessing costs and benefits, in determining whether a program will be a net benefit to society, or in choosing between two or more competing programs.

Cost-benefit illustration

Windsor and his colleagues (1993) provide a recent example of a cost-benefit analysis of health education methods used to reduce smoking among pregnant women. A randomized trial (see Chapter 12) was conducted in which 814 pregnant smokers attending maternity clinics at the Jefferson County Health Department in Birmingham, Alabama were randomly assigned to an experimental group of 400 and a control group of 414. Self reports and saliva cotinine tests confirmed smoking status at the first visit, at mid-pregnancy, and at the end of pregnancy. The intervention for the experimental group included standardized smoking cessation skills, training and risk counseling, and training in a seven-day smoking cessation guide as well as a buddy contract and a quarterly, one-page newsletter with testimonials from successful quitters, additional risk information, and cessation tips. Both the experimental and control groups received pamphlet material on risks of smoking and a two-minute presentation on smoking risks at first visit.

Analysis of the intervention and control group smoking quit rates indicated that a difference in quit rate of about 12 percent existed between the former and the latter during the period of their pregnancy. The authors estimated that this rate would probably be more likely at about 8 percent in routine use of the intervention by nurses. The difference in percent quitters was statistically significant at the .01 level. Having shown a statistically significant difference in quit rates, the next question was whether this difference was found to be cost-beneficial. This required estimates both of cost and of benefit.

Costs

Windsor and his colleagues (1993) adopted the perspective that the costs of the intervention would be valued only as the recurrent costs (i.e., personnel time and materials) of the intervention. (Ramifications of the decision about what is valued as a cost are explored in more detail later in this chapter.) Thus they did not value as costs the components of the women's time, the capital cost of the facility itself (or cost of rental space to provide the intervention), or the development cost of the program. They assessed personnel time as being $17.31 per hour based on prevailing nurse salaries in the state of Alabama. This was calculated as a $30,000 annual salary plus 20 percent fringe benefits ($36,000), divided by 2,080 hours of work per year. The smoking cessation guide provided to each patient was assessed at $1.20. The authors estimated an additional $0.40 for other materials, reproduction, and labor costs. The actual intervention by the nurse required approximately ten minutes, so the total cost of the program per pregnant woman was estimated to be $4.49 ($17.31 per hour $\times$ ⅙ hour + $1.20 + $0.40), which the authors round up to $4.50.

Windsor and his colleagues (1993) avoid the problems of estimating the dollar value of life or health that plagues many efforts at cost-benefit analysis by the simple expedient of defining benefit only as the amount of money saved by avoiding the medical care costs associated with cigarette smoking related to low birth weight. They accept 1987 Office of Technology Assessment estimates of the medical care costs of low birth weight that, when adjusted for inflation between 1987 and 1990, range from a low of $12,104 to a high of $30,935. These estimates include hospitalization and physician costs at birth and hospitalization in the first year of life, and long-term medical care costs associated with low birth weight.

Windsor and his colleagues (1993) indicate that between 20 and 35 percent of low birth weight is attributable to smoking. In 1990 there were 16,000 pregnant women receiving services in the Alabama public health system. The low-birth-weight rate prevailing in Alabama is about 12.5 percent, so about 2,000 low-birthweight infants were born in that year (.125 $\times$ 16,000). Using the low estimate of the proportion caused by smoking (.20) gives about 400 smoking attributable low-birthweight births in 1990 (.20 $\times$ 2,000). Using the 8 percent difference in quit rates between the experimental and the control groups in their randomized trial, the authors conclude that 32 fewer low-birthweight infants (.08 $\times$ 400) would have been born if the intervention had been employed with all 4,800 smokers among the pregnant women coming to the clinics. The authors fail to acknowledge that among the 32 women who quit smoking, about 12.5 percent would also have low-birthweight infants, which reduces the 32 to about 28. This, however, is not a major factor in the outcome.

Extension to a population of pregnant women in Alabama

The calculation of the cost-benefit ratio for this program is shown in Table 17.2. Based on the assumptions of the authors, the program returns a low estimate of $17.93 and a high estimate of $45.83 in terms of medical services costs saved for each $1.00 invested in the intervention to promote smoking cessation among the women coming to the Alabama Health Department Clinics. On the basis of the concept that any cost-benefit ratio greater than 1 represents a program that returns a net benefit to society, this program would be cost-beneficial. Because the costs and benefits of this program are estimated for one year only, the time value of money is not an issue. The cost of lifetime medical care for low-birthweight infants would be subject to discounting, but this was already contained in the high and low estimates of cost projected by the Office of Technology Assessment.

Cost-Effectiveness Analysis

Cost-effectiveness analysis is a program assessment that does not convert the outputs of the program to dollar terms. In cost-effectiveness analysis the output may be measured in episodes of illness averted, deaths averted, years of life added,

TABLE 17.2

Calculation of Cost-Benefit Ratio for Cigarette Smoking Cessation for Pregnant Women in Alabama Health Department Clinics

Category	Variable	Calculation	
Total births to women in Alabama health department clinics	TB		16,000
Alabama low-birthweight rate	LR		0.125
Probable number of low-birthweight births	TL	TB × LR	2,000
Proportion of low-birthweight births attributable to smoking	AS		0.20
Total low-birthweight births attributable to smoking	SL	TL × AS	400
Increased quit rate as a result of intervention	QR		0.08
Number of additional women quitting with intervention	AQ	QR × SL	32
Low estimate: Cost of low-birthweight infant	LE		$12,104
High estimate: Cost of low-birthweight infant	HE		$30,935
Low estimate: Cost saved (benefit) of intervention	BL	LE × AQ	$387,328
High estimate: Cost saved (benefit) of intervention	BH	HE × AQ	$989,920
Proportion of smokers among women in Alabama health department clinics	PS		0.3
Total number of smokers among women in Alabama health department clinics	TS	TB × PS	4,800
Cost of intervention for one smoker	CI		$4.50
Cost of intervention for all smokers	C	CI × TS	$21,600
Benefit/cost for one year of program intervention			
Low estimate		BL/C	$17.93
High estimate		BH/C	$45.83

doses of vaccine administered, children fully immunized, people served by a water system, or any other set of units that are relevant to the project being assessed. As already discussed, outcome measures such as deaths averted would normally be preferred to output measures such as number of people trained, except in those instances when the relationship between the output (e.g., children immunized) and the outcome (e.g., sickness or death averted) is not problematic.

In general, cost-effectiveness analysis will be concerned with comparing two or more mutually exclusive programs that provide the same benefits at different levels, or provide the same level of benefits at differing costs. For example, a cost-effectiveness analysis may be conducted to assess the relative advantage of an immunization program in a developing country that is based on centrally directed immunization campaigns compared to one based on routinely available vaccine for immunization at local health departments. Less frequently, cost-effectiveness analysis may be used to assess the marginal benefits to be derived from additional program efforts. For example, it may be of interest to assess the cost of a second wave of vaccinations during a vaccination campaign that had already been carried out in a given community area. To better understand cost-effectiveness analysis, consider both examples.

Consider a comparison of centrally directed immunization campaigns to routinely available immunization at local health departments. A country wishes to provide immunization to an area in which 40,000 eligible children are to be immunized every six months. Immunizations can be provided through centrally directed immunization campaigns that involve teams of workers who go out on a semiannual basis to immunize all eligible children in the area, or they can be provided through immunizations routinely available at local health centers. The experience of the Ministry of Health (MOH) indicates that the local availability of vaccine has resulted, in the past, in approximately 13,260 children effectively immunized over a typical six-month period at an estimated total cost of $1,486. The ministry projects that the campaign approach, carried out over a period of two weeks every six months, could result in the equivalent number of children immunized at a cost of $3,060. Table 17.3 compares these two programs in terms of cost-effectiveness.

What is shown in Table 17.3 is a result typical of cost-effectiveness analysis. The campaign program costs about $0.23 for each immunization and $92.31 for each one percent of the eligible population immunized, while the local availability of vaccine costs about $0.11 for each immunization and $44.82 for each one percent of the eligible population immunized. On the basis of these results, campaign approach to immunization appears to be twice as expensive as the local availability of vaccine. If the MOH was satisfied with the status quo in terms of the number of children immunized, it should accept the local availability of vaccine as the preferred approach and not consider the campaign approach.

One reservation about this conclusion, however, is that it is based on a comparison of the two programs assuming a proportion of children immunized as would be expected from an existing program of supplying locally available vaccine. Typically, the costs of realizing a given level of effectiveness will not be linear for a particular program across the entire range of possible program outputs. To illustrate this point, consider Figure 17.1, which shows a hypothetical graph of costs for clinic-based immunization and campaign-based immunization over the range from 0 to 100 percent of eligible children immunized.

	Campaign	Local Availability
Children Immunized	13,260	13,260
Percent Immunized	33.15	33.15
Total Cost	$3,060	$1,486
Cost Per Immunization	$0.23	$0.11
Cost Per Percent	$92.31	$44.82

TABLE 17.3
Cost-Effectiveness of Two Program Strategies for Immunization

As Figure 17.1 shows, the hypothesized cost of both immunization strategies first decreases (economies of scale) and then increases at an increasing rate as the proportion of children immunized increases. This is to be expected because as a larger proportion of the eligible children are immunized, it becomes increasingly difficult and costly to identify and locate the remaining children and to obtain agreement for immunization from their parents. Curves for both programs go off the chart before reaching 100 percent based on the not unreasonable expectation that complete coverage in most circumstances is almost prohibitively expensive. Figure 17.1 also shows the reasonable expectation that at low proportions of children immunized, there will be a higher cost that represents the fixed costs associated with any level of program activity.

A second and more important point in cost-effectiveness terms that is made in Figure 17.1 is that the preferred program in terms of cost-effectiveness may actually, and quite reasonably, depend on the level of effectiveness to be achieved. After initial start-up costs, the cost per immunization increases for either program approach. While the cost of clinic-based immunization is less expensive than campaign-based when the level to be achieved is below 50 percent, clinic-based becomes increasingly more expensive as the proportion of children immunized exceeds 50 percent. Thus, if the MOH planned to produce immunization levels above 50 percent it would seem logical to go to a campaign-based approach.

Figure 17.1 also provides initial and somewhat approximate information for assessing the marginal benefits to be derived from additional program efforts. For example, suppose that a campaign approach was utilized and it was carried out

FIGURE 17.1

Comparison of the Cost of Two Immunization Programs

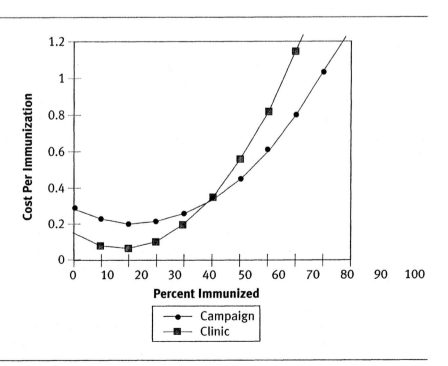

over a period of time necessary to immunize approximately 60 percent of eligible children (in an area with 40,000 such children, this would be 24,000 children). In this case, the cost would be approximately $0.46 per immunization, totalling $11,040. If the program had set out to immunize 80 percent of the children initially, the cost per immunization would have been about $0.80 per immunization, or $25,600. The reasons for this difficulty in accessing the remaining eligible children and gaining permission from their parents (which translates into more time in the field) have been previously indicated. The difference between the two total figures gives a good working figure for the cost of launching a second wave of immunizations to increase the proportion of children immunized to 80 percent when a first wave immunized only 60 percent. Under these circumstances it would be reasonable to estimate that each additional immunization will cost approximately $1.82. The cost of immunizations in a second wave thus would be almost four times as much as the cost of immunizations in the first wave.

One remaining point must be made in regard to this presentation of cost-effectiveness as a comparison between two different types of programs that are aimed generally at producing the same end result. The locally available vaccine approach to immunization and the campaign approach are not necessarily mutually exclusive. It is quite possible that an MOH could adopt both strategies, making immunization routinely available at local clinics and also undertaking periodic campaigns. In this case, the cost of each strategy would have to be reestimated. One result, however, would be almost certain: the cost of completed immunizations for the campaign-based strategy would increase, because it would be more difficult, and hence more costly, for campaign workers to identify eligible children in the field. Many of the children they would see would have already received immunizations at local clinics.

Cost-Effectiveness Illustration

Wasley and his colleagues (1997) provide a recent example of a cost-effectiveness analysis of two strategies for assisting people to quit smoking. The methods are a short counseling session by a physician and a nicotine transdermal patch in addition to the short counseling session. The authors contrasted the cost-effectiveness of the two methods with two hypothetical cohorts of 400 people, one that received both counseling and a prescription for a nicotine transdermal patch as the hypothesized intervention (group I), and the other that received only the counseling session (group II). The authors proceeded to estimate, on the basis of current literature, the proportion of people who would be likely to be permanent quitters of smoking under each scenario and the cost of each scenario. The effectiveness measure was years of life saved for each group. The authors present evidence that physician counseling alone is more cost-effective than counseling combined with the use of the transdermal patch.

Costs

Wasley and his colleagues (1997) use a number of assumptions from the current literature to estimate the costs of the transdermal patch. The basic assumption is that only about 25 percent of people who receive such a prescription will actually fill it, of whom only 50 percent will purchase the entire course of treatment, and the other 50 percent will purchase half the course of treatment. They also estimate that an entire eight-week course of treatment with the transdermal patch costs $224, and half the course of treatment costs half as much. On this basis, the authors estimate that of a cohort of 400 people receiving prescriptions for the transdermal patch, the actual cost of the prescriptions will be $16,800 (400 people × .25 acceptor rate = 100 acceptors; 50 acceptors × $224 (full course) + 50 acceptors × $112 (half course) = $16,800). In addition to the cost of the transdermal patch, each of the 400 in group I also received the short counseling session, which the authors estimate as costing $11.64 for each person, or a total of $4,656. The people in group II who received no transdermal patch prescription received only the counseling, for a total cost for group II of $4,656.

As with the previous example of cost-benefit analysis, Wasley and his colleagues did not value the time of the patients as costs; for example, time involved in counseling or travel time to obtain prescriptions. The authors also did not value any of the facility space required for counseling. While these are probably minor items, they do have costs that are ignored in the assessment.

Effects Wasley and his colleagues are extremely careful and conservative in estimating effects, which they estimate as years of life saved (YLS) for either group. Based on existing literature, they estimate that 4.5 percent of group II will abstain from smoking for 12 months as a result of the physician counseling alone. They further estimate that only 65 percent of 12-month abstainers will be lifetime quitters. Of the 400 people in group II, they estimate that 11.7 (400 × .045 × .65 = 11.7) will actually be lifetime quitters. Based again on current literature, the authors estimate that the transdermal patch in conjunction with counseling will improve the 12-month abstinence rate by 391 percent, but that the lifetime abstinence will remain at 65 percent of the number who are 12-month abstainers. Thus, the number of lifetime quitters in group I due to the use of the transdermal patch will be 11.4 (100 acceptors × .045 × 3.91 × .65 = 11.4). In addition, the authors estimate that of the 300 people in group I who do not elect to use the transdermal patch, 4.5 percent will quit as a result of the counseling session alone. This adds an additional 8.8 people to the quitters in group I (300 × .045 × .65). The total quitters in group I is estimated to be 20.2.

Wasley and his colleagues then use life tables for smokers and non-smokers to estimate the additional number of years a typical cohort of people in each group would live based on 20.2 lifetime quitters in group I and 11.4 in group II. As an example, they say that a male quitter between age 35 and 39 would live an additional 5.08 years over a non-quitter. The authors also discuss the discounting of years lived in future years exactly in the same manner as discounting dollars acquired in future years. With a discount rate of .05, they indicate that 5.08 years gained by quitting smoking would be reduced to only .99 discounted years. While the authors do not give the formula they use for arriving at the 5 percent discounted years of life added as a result of smoking cessation, it is almost certainly something like that shown in the Equation 17.5:

$$YLS_{discounted} = \sum_{t=1}^{T_1} \frac{1}{(1 + r)^t} - \sum_{t=1}^{T_2} \frac{1}{(1 + r)^t} \qquad (17.5)$$

where YLS is years of life saved (discounted), r is the discount rate, T_1 is the expected number of years lived without smoking, and T_2 is the expected number of years lived with smoking.

Based on 5 percent discounting, the authors conclude that the average discounted cost per YLS for males and females who receive the patch ranges from a low of about $965 to a high of $2,360, while for brief counseling alone, the average YLS ranges from $362 to $884. On the basis of this analysis, the conclusion is that the counseling alone, with a maximum cost of $884 for one discounted year of life saved, was more cost-effective than the counseling with transdermal patch with a minimum cost of $965 for one discounted year of life saved.

Cost-Utility Analysis

Cost-utility analysis is a program assessment that converts the outputs of the program to a measure of utility. In cost-utility analysis the output is most likely to be measured in quality adjusted life years (QALYs), disability adjusted life years (DALYs) (Murray 1994, 1996), or healthy-years equivalents (HYEs) (Mehrez and Gafni 1991; Rittenhouse 1997).

Chapter 14 provides a discussion of utility measures, including QALYs and DALYs. If a reasonable and accepted measure of utility can be established using one of the techniques addressed in Chapter 14 or another acceptable technique, cost-utility analysis is quite similar to cost-benefit analysis. A program that could be seen to return 10,000 QALYs (the measure of utility) for $14,000 (the measure of cost) would be preferable to a program that could be seen to return 10,000 QALYs for $16,000. But it is important to recognize that cost-utility analysis almost always treats utility in exactly the same way dollars are treated in cost-benefit analysis; that is, the present value of utility is discounted when a measure of utility is received in the future. In consequence, a unit of utility (e.g., a QALY) received now would be valued in cost-utility analysis more highly than a unit of utility that is to be received next year, or in 10 or 20 years.

While the preceding discussion of discounting years of life may seem somewhat cold, the logic is clear. For example, suppose that a person was at a portion of a QALY (e.g., .3 QALYs). That person's health state could improve to full health, and this improvement could be realized this year for a single year, or 20 years from now for a single year. The amount of money that person would be willing to pay today for that improvement to occur today would in all likelihood be greater than the amount of money that person would be willing to pay today for that improvement to occur 20 years from today. The difference between the two amounts represents the consequence of the effective discount rate.

To see the effect of discounting utility, assume that a program that returns 10,000 QALYs does so with an expenditure in year 1 of $14,000 by which 1,000 people who would otherwise die would live, on average, 20 years in a state of health with a utility level of .5 (where death has a utility level of 0 and full health a utility level of 1). Assume also that another program that returns 10,000 QALYs does so with an up-front expenditure of $16,000 by which 1,000 people who would otherwise die would live, on average, 10 years at a utility level of 1 (full health).

This scenario is shown in Table 17.4. Discounting utilities at a rate of 0, the program that returns 1,000 people to a utility of .5 for 20 years has a cost-utility ratio of $1.40, while the other program has a cost-utility ratio of $1.60. The 20-year program is still preferable at a discount rate of .02. At discount rates above approximately .029, however, the cost-utility ratio for the two programs is equal. At higher levels of discounting, the $16,000 program has a cost-utility ratio that is lower (and therefore better) than the $14,000 program. For example, at a discount level of .04, the $14,000 program has a cost-utility ratio of $1.98 and the $16,000 program has a cost utility ratio of $1.90.

Either of the programs described in the preceding paragraphs probably would not simply have front-end costs but would have recurrent costs as well.

TABLE 17.4

Comparison of Utility for a 20-Year Program and a 10-Year Program, Each Returning an Undiscounted 10,000 QALYs, at 0, .02, and .04 Discount Rates

Discount Rate	0		0.02		0.04	
Year/Cost	20-Year Program $14,000	10-Year Program $16,000	20-Year Program $14,000	10-Year Program $16,000	20-Year Program $14,000	10-Year Program $16,000
0	500	1,000	500	1,000	500	1,000
1	500	1,000	490	980	481	962
2	500	1,000	481	961	462	925
3	500	1,000	471	942	444	889
4	500	1,000	462	924	427	855
5	500	1,000	453	906	411	822
6	500	1,000	444	888	395	790
7	500	1,000	435	871	380	760
8	500	1,000	427	853	365	731
9	500	1,000	418	837	351	703
10	500		410		338	
11	500		402		325	
12	500		394		312	
13	500		387		300	
14	500		379		289	
15	500		372		278	
16	500		364		267	
17	500		357		257	
18	500		350		247	
19	500		343		237	
Total QALYs	10,000	10,000	8,339	9,162	7,067	8,435
Cost per QALY	$1.40	$1.60	$1.68	$1.75	$1.98	$1.90

Suppose that both programs realized their costs as cost streams of equal annual costs ($700 per year over 20 years for the program costing $14,000 and $1,600 over ten years for the program costing $16,000). In this case, the program costing $14,000 produces a lower cost-utility ratio at discount rates as high as .2, and hence is preferable. The formula that can be used for calculating cost-utility ratios for any level of discounting is given in Equation 17.6:

$$C/U = \frac{\sum_{t=1}^{T} \dfrac{C_t}{(1 + r)^t}}{\sum_{t=1}^{T} \dfrac{U_t}{(1 + r)^t}} \tag{17.6}$$

where C/U is the cost-utility ratio, C_t is the annual cost, U_t is the annual utility, and r is the discount rate.

Cost-Utility Illustration

The DALY (Murray 1994, 1996) was presented in Chapter 14 as an attempt to create a universal QALY. The DALY represents a composite of years of life lost to early mortality and years of life lived with differing levels of disability as assessed on a seven-category scale that ranges from .02 for the least disabling health conditions (e.g., weight-for-height below 2 standard deviations from the mean) to .7 or greater for the most disabling health conditions (e.g., active psychosis, severe migraine, quadriplegia). Because the DALY accumulates years lost to death and years lived with disabilities, it inevitably raises the issue of discounting. In its use by the World Bank for the World Development Report (1993) and in subsequent discussion of the DALY by Murray (1994, 1996) the discounting of years to be lived in the future is an intensely discussed issue. The decision explicitly made by the bank is that in the construction of DALYs, future years and partial years will be discounted at 3 percent (.03) per year. This decision is extensively addressed and the final decision to discount is made explicit so that the construction of the measure of the DALY will be as transparent as possible to readers and users.

The effect of this discounting is shown in Figure 17.2. Keeping in mind that the DALY is a measure of years lost, assume that a male dies at age 40. According to the life expectancy table used for construction of the DALY (see Table 17.5) that male should have expected to live an additional 40.64 years. The value of those years in DALYs will decrease *as a result of discounting alone* as indicated in Figure 17.2. The value, for example, of the fifth year after the death will be reduced to approximately .86 of a year, the tenth year after the death .74 of a year, and the twentieth year after the death .55 of a year. The cumulative value of the years in this example will be discounted to only about 24 DALYs rather than 40.64.

In addition to the discounting of years (or weighted years, depending on the degree of disability), the DALY also incorporates an additional weighting of years that is related to the age of the person at death or at the onset of a particular disability. Again, Murray has devoted extensive discussion to the pros and cons of differential value of years of life for people at different ages. However, the decision reached by the developers of the DALY is to value years of life for people in

FIGURE 17.2

Value of a Year of
Life at Year in the
Future Based on
Discount Rate
of 3 Percent—
Calculation of
DALYs

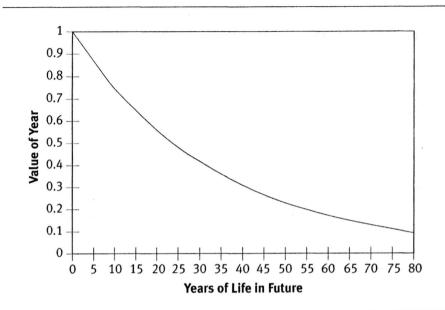

productive years (approximately ten to 55) more highly than years of life for people in younger or older ages. The logic of this is essentially that until a certain age
a person is not productive and after a later age becomes increasingly less so. The
actual expression of this for the DALY is the function:

$$Cte^{-\beta t}$$

where $C = .1658$, $\beta = .04$, and t represents the year of life. This function creates
a curve as shown in Figure 17.3. The value imputed to a year of life before about

FIGURE 17.3

Value of Year of
Life at Age Used in
the DALY

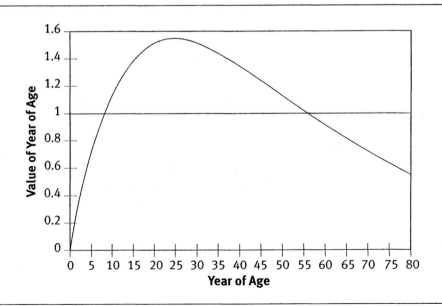

age ten is less than 1 (beginning at 0 for 0 years of age) and also less than 1 for years following about age 55. In between the value of a year of life is greater than 1.

With both the discounting of years of life lost (as well as discounting of years lived with disability in the future) and with differential weighting of the value of a year of life based on the preceding function, the actual equation that describes the number of DALYs given death at any age, or given the onset of disability at any age, is given by Murray (1996, 65–66) and is shown in Equation 17.7:

$$DALY = D\left\{ \frac{Ce^{ra}}{(r+\beta)^2} \left[e^{-(r+\beta)(L+a)} \left[-(r+\beta)(L+a) - 1 \right] - e^{-(r+\beta)a} \left[-(r+\beta)a - 1 \right] \right] \right\}$$

$$(17.7)$$

where D = disability score (from 0 for complete health to 1 for death), $C = .1658$, $\beta = .04$, $r = .03$, and L is the standard expectation of life at age a. It should be noted that L and a have different interpretations if the DALY is being computed for years of life lost to death or years of life lived with disability. In the former, L represents life expectancy at age a, while for a chronic condition not resulting in death L represents the expectation of life *for a person in that condition* with onset at age a. For temporary health states, L represents years of life lived in the temporary health state given age of onset at a.

Table 17.5 shows the result of the application of Equation 17.6 for a death at ages 0, 1, and five-year age intervals to age 80 as given in Murray (1996, 17).

Age (Years)	Life Expectancy (Years)		DALYs Lost to Death at Each Age	
	Females	Males	Females	Males
0	82.5	80	33.13	33.01
1	81.84	79.36	34.07	33.95
5	77.95	75.38	36.59	36.46
10	72.99	70.4	37.63	37.47
15	68.02	65.41	36.99	36.80
20	63.08	60.44	35.24	35.02
25	58.17	55.47	32.78	32.53
30	53.27	50.51	29.92	29.62
35	48.38	45.56	26.86	26.50
40	43.53	40.64	23.74	23.32
45	38.72	35.77	20.66	20.17
50	33.99	30.99	17.69	17.12
55	29.37	26.32	14.87	14.21
60	24.83	21.81	12.22	11.48
65	20.44	17.5	9.75	8.95
70	16.2	13.58	7.48	6.69
75	12.28	10.17	5.46	4.77
80	8.9	7.45	3.76	3.27

TABLE 17.5

Standard Life Expectancy Table and DALYs Lost to Death at Each Age

This table indicates that for death for a male or female at any age, the DALY total is incremented by the amount given in the two columns "DALYs Lost to Death at Each Age."

For example, if a male dies at age 20, rather than adding 60.44 years to the DALY total (the expectation of life for a male at age 20), the discounting and differential weighting of years of life adds only 35.02 to the DALY total. The same type of table for years lived with a chronic disability would have to be computed on the basis of individual life-expectancy tables for each separate disability.

For example, a person who was living with a disability such as infertility (given a rating of .177 for the calculation of DALYs) may reasonably be expected to have a life expectancy with infertility equal to someone in complete health, while a person suffering from angina (which has a DALY rating of .231) may have a reduced expectation of life due to the potential onset of other heart problems. A similar table computed for years lived with a temporary disability would have to be calculated on the basis of a table of average time in the temporary condition for each disability. The probable time in a health state of severe sore throat (which has a DALY rating of .082) is likely to be shorter than probable time in a health state of fractured radius in a stiff cast (which has a DALY rating of .107).

Assessing Costs

Cost-benefit analysis relates costs in dollar terms to results measured in dollar terms. Cost-effectiveness analysis relates costs in dollar terms to results measured in kind. Cost-utility analysis relates costs in dollar terms to results measured as utility. The topics of how costs may be valued and of how benefits may be valued briefly have been addressed. This section addresses much more explicitly how costs may be valued and what the consequences of alternative valuation decisions will be on the overall analysis, whether it is cost-benefit, cost-effectiveness, or cost-utility. In the process, we will also say a few words about valuing benefits in dollar terms.

The first step in assessing costs and benefits is to understand what they are and where they may arise. To take the latter point first, consider again the simple program diagram shown as Figure 17.4. This figure is an excellent starting point for discussing an assessment of costs and benefits. Costs of a program are to be found in the box labeled "inputs." Benefits (or effects or utility) are to be found in the two boxes labeled "outputs" and "outcomes."

The notion that cost-effectiveness should be concerned primarily with the link between input and outcomes has already been addressed briefly. In particular, the effectiveness of a program should be assessed in terms of what it is trying to

FIGURE 17.4

Simple Diagram of Program Flow

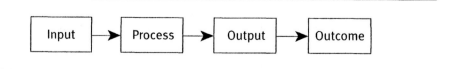

accomplish (e.g., in improved health status) rather than in terms of what it produces (e.g., immunizations given). But the distinction is not always made, nor does it always need to be made. A program to reduce cigarette smoking may have as its outputs people who have quit. The ultimate outcome is improved health. The link between smoking and health is so clear that a cost-effectiveness analysis can be conducted that may use smoking quitters as the measure of effectiveness and two programs could reasonably be compared on the ratio of costs to quitters (inputs to outputs). In other areas, the link between outputs and outcomes may not be so clear and cost-effectiveness analysis should be concerned with the relationship between inputs and outcomes. Because of the way that utility is measured, cost-utility analysis is specifically about the relationship between inputs and outcomes.

Program Costs

To return to the notion of valuing costs, anything that represents a program input is a cost. A case may be made that program costs could also be identified in the process box in Figure 17.4. For example, a committee may require a period of time to reach a decision, part of the program process. But the time of the members of the committee can also be valued as an input, as can any other opportunities lost because of the time taken for the decision. Thus, this discussion of costs will be limited only to the input box.

There are various ways of determining what should be included as program inputs. Bainbridge and Sapirie (1974) see the program inputs that will make up the components of the costs of a program as including salaries and expenses, transportation, space, supplies and equipment, capital equipment, consultative or contractual services, training, publication, and miscellaneous. Drummond (1980, 27–29) classifies inputs to healthcare, particularly, as:

1. health service resources, including land, buildings, personnel, equipment, and consumable supplies;
2. other support services (outside the health services); and
3. patients' (and their families') resources, including personal time, drugs and dressing provided by the family, transportation, home adaptation, special diets, and other expenditures.

In establishing the relevant inputs for assessing the cost of any specific program, it will almost certainly be necessary to draw up a list of program costs from the beginning, rather than assuming that it will be possible to rely on a predetermined list of inputs. In particular, it will be necessary to determine which inputs are actually going to be considered as important. Certainly in the overall societal assessment of costs of a given program, patient time may be considered as an important input. A program manager may not be too concerned about patient time when considering whether a centrally directed immunization campaign is more cost effective than one in which vaccine is available through local health clinics. To know what items should be valued and included as part of the costs of a program, however, a reasonable place to start is with the broadest set of definitions possible.

Illustration

To examine in somewhat more detail the issue of program costs, consider the assessment of the cost of a campaign-based approach to immunization. The Ministry of Health (MOH) anticipates that it will use four teams of five people each for the campaign. An initial assessment of the input categories for such an immunization effort may be as listed in Table 17.6. This table also shows those items that will be explicitly valued because they are direct costs to the MOH, and those items that will be ignored because they are costs either to external donors or to patients themselves.

In any analysis, there are two levels of costs: those that accrue directly to the person or organization that is the decision maker with regard to the conduct of the program, and those that accrue to the larger society. Frequently, the decision maker, in this case the MOH, is disinterested in costs to the larger society because these do not affect the decision that the campaign approach is more or less costly than an alternative program (e.g., locally available immunization). If the MOH decided to launch an immunization campaign lasting eight and one-half days (the estimated time required to immunize 33.15 percent of eligible children), the MOH assessment of costs based on Table 17.6 would be $2,295.

TABLE 17.6

Program Inputs for a Centrally Directed Immunization Campaign

	Valued by MOH	Not Valued by MOH
Project Staff		
Salaries		
Team leaders	4 at $5.50/day	
Team members	12 at $5.25/day	
Drivers	4 at $5.25/day	
Expenses (daily)		
Meals	40 at $1.65/day	
Lodging	20 at $1.40/day	
Transportation		
Vehicle costs		Use MOH vehicles
Gasoline, oil	$30.00/day	
Supplies (tires)	$340	
Space for Immunization		Use local clinics
Supplies and Equipment		
Syringes		USAID
Vaccine		USAID
Sterilizing equipment		USAID
Clerical supplies		Use existing MOH
Technical Assistance		UNICEF/WHO
Patient Time		
Travel time		Not valued
Waiting time		Not valued

However, $2,295 is an understatement of the total cost of the campaign. This is an understatement for two reasons: first, it ignores costs not accrued to the ministry; and second, it ignores certain costs accrued to the ministry but for which the ministry does not have to make a cash payment at the time of the immunization campaign.

Cost as Payment or Resource Use

Before continuing with a discussion of the two sources of cost that are not valued in Table 17.6, it will be useful to spend a little time discussing the nature of valuation of cost in general. Costs can be considered in two ways, as payments made for a particular input or as resources used in supplying the input. The Ministry of Health, as shown in Table 17.6, has placed a dollar value on the time of its personnel that in all likelihood refers to the actual amount of money that the ministry must pay for that personnel time on a daily basis. In essence, this is the payment method of valuing inputs. The alternative approach to valuing personnel as an input would be to consider it as a resource that can be used in many alternative ways. The cost of using the personnel for immunization is essentially equivalent to the best alternative use of the same resources. In economic terms, this is the concept of *opportunity cost*. The opportunity cost of using a person as part of an immunization team for a day is equal to the next best alternative use of that person's time that will be forgone during the same day because the person is part of the immunization team.

A colleague, while working with an international technical assistance organization, was part of a survey assessment of primary healthcare services in Sri Lanka, organized in part by the assistance organization. The assessment lasted three weeks and involved about 40 people, mostly Sri Lankans. At the end of the assessment, our colleague submitted a report to the organization that included an estimate of the cost of the activity. As part of the estimate, he included the cost of his time, as paid by the international technical assistance organization at what were essentially U.S. salary levels (the payment method of valuing inputs). This was significantly higher than costs for other people who were involved in the assessment (paid at the prevailing salary levels for health personnel in Sri Lanka) and which greatly inflated the overall cost of the assessment. The deputy director at the assistance organization recommended that he remove the estimate of his time from the estimate of assessment costs because it inflated the cost of the activity so much. The deputy further pointed out that if their colleague had not been involved in the primary healthcare services assessment, he would simply have been sitting in his office (the opportunity cost method of valuing inputs).

There was without doubt an element of politics in the recommendation of the deputy director. The assessment appeared very costly with the inclusion of the technical assistant's time, and that time was valued at a much higher level than the time of host country personnel. At the same time, however, a very clear element of logic existed. In many cases, the alternative uses of a particular resource at a particular point in time—the opportunities forgone because of the use of that resource in a particular way—may be 0. If not for the program, the resource would not be used at all. If not for the immunization program, the MOH personnel may simply sit in their offices for the 8.5 days. In this sense, the cost of using these people in the immunization program is, in fact and in practice, 0 because no alternatives are forgone.

However, it may well be true that the use of a particular resource in a particular way means that other opportunities are indeed forgone. If the MOH personnel are not engaged in the immunization program, they may be providing much needed well-baby care or prenatal care, care that will be unavailable while they are participating in the immunization program. If so, the cost of their time in the immunization program is the value of the medical care forgone.

While the idea of opportunities forgone, or alternative use of resources, is intuitively appealing as a measure of cost, in practical terms, the value of an alternative use of a particular resource may be very difficult to establish. Further, most people would intuitively agree that the value of a resource in any alternative use is exactly what one would have to pay for it to use it in that way. Finally, the idea of a payment for a resource is relatively easy for program managers to grasp when compared to the concept of alternative resource uses. Consequently, the cash or payment basis for valuing inputs is more likely to be seen than the resource use basis.

The Value of All Inputs

As indicated previously, the actual cost of the program as laid out in Table 17.6 is not the $2,295 recognized by the MOH, but another amount that may be substantially more. It may even be more for the ministry itself. As an example, consider costs incurred by the ministry that are not valued and costs incurred by sources other than the ministry.

Costs to the ministry not valued by the ministry

There are two clear sources of costs (i.e., inputs) that accrue directly to the ministry but are not valued by the ministry in their calculation of $2,295. Probably the larger and more important of these will be the four vehicles needed to take the immunization teams to the immunization sites each day. The ministry will use vehicles already owned by the government, and so have assigned no cost to their use. However, these vehicles indeed represent a cost to the ministry. That cost may be viewed as large or small (or as is the case in Table 17.6, as 0) depending on how the value of the vehicles is assessed. The vehicles could be valued at least three alternative ways:

1. as a resource that may be used in an alternative way;
2. as equivalent to the cost of alternative rented transportation; or
3. as a capital expenditure depreciated over an expected operational life.

The possibility that the alternative may be no use at all has already been addressed. In this case, the value of the alternative is 0 and the use of the vehicles is free. If this were not the case, any valuation of the use of the vehicles probably would have to fall back on one of the two other methods.

Taking the second alternative, the MOH could rent transportation, along with a driver. It would not be unreasonable to expect that the cost of a vehicle and driver for one day in a typical developing country would be as high as $150. In this case, the value of the vehicles would be $150 per day minus the cost of the driver, which at about $10 per day would make the cost of the vehicles $140 per day, or $4,760 ($140 × 4 teams × 8.5 days)—an amount greater than all other program costs.

Finally, if the third alternative is chosen, the estimation may be that an MOH vehicle may last five years under the conditions that prevail on the roads of the country under discussion. The ministry may assume that a straight-line depreciation of the value of the vehicles from purchase at $20,500 each for the five-year period, thus making the use of the vehicles equivalent to $4,100 per year. If a working year were considered to be 260 days, this would make the use of the vehicles equal to $15.77 per day, for a total cost of about $536, substantially less than the $4,760 when valued as rental vehicles, but still a significant program cost. However, the MOH likely originally received the vehicles as donations from an international assistance agency, and thinking in these terms, that the vehicles were free to begin with, rather than in terms of the replacement value of the vehicles, may still be justified in valuing them at 0.

The second clear area of cost to the ministry not valued by the ministry is the category of clerical supplies. This may be a small item but would probably be best represented not as a no-cost item, but at the replacement cost value of the supplies that will be used.

The second realm of costs that will accrue as part of this program that are not explicitly valued by the ministry are all inputs provided to the program from other sources. These include:

Costs to others not valued by the ministry

- the use of local clinics as immunization sites;
- the syringes, vaccine, and sterilizing equipment being donated through USAID;
- the technical assistance being provided through UNICEF/WHO; and
- the time being provided by the people who will bring children for immunizations, and even the time of the children themselves.

These costs do not need to be addressed in detail. The concept of alternative uses of the resources as well as cash value of the resources have been previously addressed. If local clinic space were not being used for the immunization campaign, however, the clinic space likely would be serving a useful alternative. The value of this may be assigned on the basis of a reasonable local rental price for space. If the immunization supplies and equipment were not being used in this campaign, it may be used in a different immunization program in a different country entirely. In this case, it represents a resource forgone by the other country and a cost that may be best estimated by the price of the equipment and supplies on the international market. If, however, the supplies and equipment are earmarked as the property of the country and the question is simply whether they are used in the campaign approach or through locally available immunization, then the cost of the supplies and equipment is 0.

Technical assistance from UNICEF/WHO is a potentially valuable commodity, which when assessed at the salary level of a person providing such assistance, plus travel and housing for the time of the program, may easily be at the level of $650 to $750 per day. Such a level would make this the most costly component of the campaign.

Finally, the costs to the people who come for the service may be valued. This is in no way a cost of the campaign either to the MOH, to the local clinics, or to the other sponsoring agencies. However, it clearly represents a cost to the society in terms of lost production and resources that must be used in this way as opposed to an alternative way. Just as an estimate, suppose that each person who brings children for immunization must travel two hours round trip and wait one hour for the immunization. In a developing country context, such travel and waiting times are not an unreasonable expectation. Suppose further that travel costs are equivalent to $0.25. Finally, suppose that each person brings two children, on average, for immunization. The total cost to the society for this activity may reasonably be estimated as $4,000 to $4,500, based on an average annual income of about $250 and assuming a working year of 230 to 250 days. This may seem like little for the time of all these people, but depending on how vehicles are valued, it may still represent the single largest program cost after the technical advisors.

Valuing Benefits

The preceding section has concentrated on the valuation of inputs, or costs. Now we will consider the valuation of outputs, or benefits. With regard to cost-benefit analysis, dollar values are actually assigned to the outputs, or at least to those outputs that are the primary interest of program decision makers. With regard to cost-effectiveness and cost-utility analysis, results are valued either in kind (e.g., immunizations performed, hospital discharges, neonatal deaths, and so on), or as utility measures. With this in mind, the valuation of outputs in dollar terms is applicable only to the case of cost-benefit analysis.

The conscious dollar-based valuation of healthcare or social welfare programs is an extremely difficult task. For example, what is the dollar value of an immunization? Is it the positive value of the cost of treating a disease that if not immunized against may occur? Windsor and his colleagues (1993) take this approach in the valuation of benefits of health education for pregnant smokers by valuing the cost of medical treatment for low birth weight. Or is it the amount of money that the average person will be willing to pay for immunization, or willing to pay to be treated for the disease that the immunization is aimed at preventing? Willingness to pay has become an increasingly popular method for valuing benefits (Donaldson and Shackley 1997; Ryan, Ratcliff, and Tucker 1997; Ryan 1996; Weaver et al. 1996).

From another perspective, is it the value of a productive life that may be terminated by disease in the absence of the immunization? Is it useful to try to assess the dollar value of pain and suffering? Depending on how benefits are valued, the results of the same program may be quite different in benefit terms. Moreover, the dollar level assigned to benefits under differing valuation strategies will also differ substantially from one culture to another. For example, the average person may be willing to pay little for immunizations in one culture but may be willing to pay a significant amount in others. The value of each additional year of productive life in a western culture may be many thousands of dollars, while in a less developed society may be only a few hundred dollars.

These problem issues in valuing benefits of health programs have plagued those who have sought to carry out cost-benefit analyses of health programs. The problems associated with valuing the outputs of an immunization program are equally problem issues in attempting to value, for example, an early cancer screening program, a renal dialysis or a kidney transplant program, an infant-feeding program, or any other type of program that has improved health states as the primary outcome. In regard to such valuation efforts, they will always be subject to a level of controversy over whether a valid dollar figure has been applied. Where two different types of programs producing similar results are being valued, the specific valuation strategy may not be too important because both programs may be assessed under specified and similar conditions.

However, programs may produce different types of results (e.g., one program produces additional years of life for middle-aged adults, while another improves nutritional status for children). They may take place in substantially different settings (e.g., one program may be directed toward hypertension screening among urban poor populations, while another may be concerned with breast self exams by middle-class women). In these cases, the dollar valuation becomes extremely difficult. This is particularly problematic, because these are precisely the types of situations in which cost-benefit analysis should be able to provide the most useful information. Because valuation of health outcomes in ways that enjoy widespread acceptance and agreement remains an unattained goal, cost-benefit analysis applied to health programs is less useful than it may otherwise be.

Discussion Questions

1. Distinguish between cost-benefit, cost-effectiveness, and cost-utility analysis. What type of program decisions are appropriate to each type of analysis?
2. Discuss the advantages and disadvantages of the market value and willingness-to-pay approaches to assigning values to program outputs. Under what conditions may each be the preferred approach?
3. What is discounting?
4. Why is discounting so important to decision making regarding health service programs—and particularly health promotion and disease prevention programs?

GLOSSARY

Accuracy. The extent to which the estimate of the population is close to the true population value, regardless of whether the estimating was done on a biased or unbiased sample.

Analysis of covariance. A mechanism for comparing two groups or two areas, or sets of groups or areas, when the effects of differences in other characteristics of the groups or areas are held constant.

Analysis of variance. A test or an assessment of whether two distributions in total can be considered different from one another.

Analytic surveys. Surveys concerned chiefly with describing relationships between real-world phenomena. *See also* Descriptive surveys.

Association. The notion that as one measure, phenomenon, or attribute changes, another measure, phenomenon, or attribute will change.

Autocorrelation. Correlation of error terms across individual observations, usually associated with time series data.

Bias. The extent to which the expected value of an estimator being used is not the same as the true value being estimated.

Case study. The selection and observation of a single unique activity, organization, or entity (or of one example from a number of activities,

organizations, or entities), and the formation of conclusions based on the observations.

Categorical data. Data consisting of variables assessed in terms of their belonging, or not belonging, to certain specified categories. *See also* Continuous data.

Cause-and-effect diagram. A graphic tool used to display all the factors that may produce a given effect; often referred to as an Ishikawa diagram.

Checklist. A form providing an exhaustive list of items for recording data.

Chi-square statistic. A statistical test that measures variation from expectation. The larger the chi-square value, the less likely that a particular distribution is a chance occurrence.

Cluster sampling. A sampling technique whereby the sample is drawn in two or more stages: in the first stage the total population to be sampled is divided into several clusters (mutually exclusive and all-inclusive) on the basis of some meaningful variable; in the second and subsequent stages, smaller units within clusters are drawn. Sampling is random or systematic at each stage. *See also* Simple random sampling; Stratified sampling.

Cohort changes. Systematic changes associated with one particular age group of the population.

Communality. The portion of the variance in each of the variables in a data set that is shared with one or more other variables.

Community clinical oncology program (CCOP). A community-based research network involving hospitals, physicians, and support staff funded by the National Cancer Institute.

Composite measure. A single numerical value derived by combining two or more constituent measurements.

Content analysis. A technique for making inferences by objectively and systematically identifying specific characteristics of written and oral communications.

Content validity. An assessment of whether the measure being used to describe some real-world phenomenon seems to be *prima facie* describing that phenomenon.

Contingency table. The tabular joint array of two or more frequency distributions showing the number of cases falling simultaneously into a category of each distribution.

Continuous data. Data consisting of variables that can take any numerical value within a given interval. *See also* Categorical Data.

Control chart. An extension of the run chart that includes a statistically determined upper and lower limit for the normally expected variation.

Correlation. The joint relationship of two variables; the extent of correlation is generally assessed by a correlation coefficient such as Pearson's *R*.

Cost-benefit analysis. A comparison of the costs of a program to the benefits to be derived that converts all benefits (outputs) to dollar terms. *See also* Cost-effectiveness analysis.

Cost-effectiveness analysis. A comparison of costs of a program to benefits derived that does not convert the benefits of the program to dollar terms. *See also* Cost-benefit analysis.

Criterion validity. An assessment of whether the current measure of a phenomenon produces results that are closely related to other reasonable or accepted independent measures of the same phenomenon.

Critical path. In PERT and CPM, the sequence of activities and events that defines or determines the longest time from the start of a project to its end.

Critical path method (CPM). A method for scheduling the component parts of a complex project, similar to PERT, but with the addition of information about a critical path. *See also* Critical path; Program evaluation and review technique.

Cybernetic decision making. Decision making where information about the state of a program is used to make decisions that bring the program closer to the verifiable ends desired (no accepted process; ends verifiable).

Cybernetics. The science of program control based on program information.

Disability adjusted life years (DALY). A utility measure expressing the number of years lost in a defined population as a result of disease or disability, as compared to a control (healthy) population. *See also* Quality adjusted life years (QALY).

Decision mode drift. A tendency for decision making to drift to the random walk model or the traditional model.

Degrees of freedom. The number of observations in a set of observations that remain free to vary when some subset is fixed. For example, the sequence: $2 + ? + ? = 11$ has one degree of freedom because when either question mark is determined, the other is fixed.

Delphi technique. A data collection technique involving an iterative series of questionnaires and feedback reports to a designated panel of respondents; usually associated with forecasting and larger surveys, but of use also in providing structure to case studies.

Dependent variable. A variable whose particular value is assumed to be determined by, and is dependent on, the values of some set of other independent variables.

Descriptive surveys. Surveys concerned with producing as accurate a picture as possible of a real-world situation. *See also* Analytic surveys.

Dichotomous evaluation outcomes. Outcomes assessed only in terms of a single choice between two options, such as the presence or absence of some condition. Examples of dichotomous evaluation outcomes would include whether a patient lived or died, whether a laboratory test was positive or negative for a particular trait, and whether a patient agreed to sign an advance directive or not.

Double-blind experiment. An experiment conducted so that neither the subjects nor those conducting the experiment nor the evaluators know which subjects are members of the experimental group and which subjects are members of the control group.

Dummy variable. A dependent or independent variable that takes on only two (or occasionally three) values (i.e., 1, 0).

Durbin-Watson test. A common test for autocorrelation.

Economic ordering quantity. A technique for determining the size of an order that results in the lowest inventory cost given some specific assumptions about storage and use.

Effectiveness. The degree to which program results meet predetermined objectives, with an emphasis on program outputs or the immediate results of program effects and whether these outputs are as expected.

Efficiency. The degree to which program results are obtained as inexpensively as possible.

Efficiency tests. Determination of whether the specific means employed is the most efficient means for producing the ends desired; critical to the mechanistic model.

Evaluability assessment. The determination of whether program objectives are well-defined and plausible and whether the intended uses of evaluation information are well defined.

Evaluation. The collection and analysis of information by various methodological strategies to determine the relevance, progress, efficiency, effectiveness, and impact of program activities.

Evaluation research. As typically defined, results based not on the evaluator's judgments but on the scientific method.

Expert bias. Predetermined notions that many experts may have about what the actual problem or solutions to the problem may be.

External validity. The issue of whether what is observed from the sample is true of the whole population. *See also* Internal validity.

Face validity. *See* Content validity.

Factor analysis. A technique for finding composite weights involving a certain empirical logic for determining the weights and at the same time ensuring that the resulting weighted scores will not be such that midpoint values are ambiguous.

Factor loadings. In factor analysis, the values of the vector or vectors that best reproduce the original correlation matrix.

Flow diagram. A graphic representation of the flow of all actions involved in a given process, providing a detailed picture of specific activities involved in the process under study.

Formative evaluation. Evaluation of activities associated with the ongoing operations of a program, with an emphasis on decisions to improve the program and its management. *See also* Summative evaluation.

Frequency distribution. The one-dimensional array of the categories of a variable, showing the number of cases falling into each category.

F-test. A statistical test associated primarily with regression or analysis of variance that shows whether results could be expected by chance or not.

Gantt chart. A visual means of indicating the sequence of events or activities that make up a project as it proceeds through time.

Guttman scaling technique. A technique based on the assumption that dichotomous attributes can be ordered in such a way that, for the least common attribute to exist or to have a positive value for a given respondent or organization, all other attributes will also exist or will be positive responses for the same respondent or organization; for the next less common attribute to exist, all attributes except the least common are assumed to exist, and so forth.

Hawthorne effect. The tendency for people to act differently when they know that they are part of an experiment, thus obscuring the expected effects of interventions.

Impact. The long-term outcomes of a program.

Incidence. The number of persons (scaled to an appropriate base, such as percentage or per 100,000) who succumb to a disease within a given time range. *See also* Prevalence.

Independent variable. A variable that serves to determine the value of some dependent variable, but is not itself determined by some other variable.

Inputs. The resources and guidelines necessary to carry out a program.

Instrumental tests. Determination of whether in the broad sense it is possible to demonstrate empirically that the means employed produces the ends desired; primarily appropriate within the cybernetic model.

Interactive problem solving. The resolution of problems by actions rather than by thought.

Internal rate of return. The discount rate at which the net present value of a given project is equal to zero.

Internal validity. The issue of whether the evaluator's observations or conclusions about relationships within the sample drawn actually exist for that sample. *See also* External validity.

Interval scale. A scale where the points are ordered and spaced at equidistant intervals.

Interview. An instrument or schedule that an interviewer administers.

Ishikawa diagram. *See* Cause-and-effect diagram.

Item-to-scale correlation. A method used for the accumulation of dichotomous, interval, and ratio-scale response items by first converting items to a standard scale (such as a Z score), then analyzing the correlation between each item's score and the summed standard scores for the categories of interest.

Likert scale. A statement or series of statements made in either a positive or negative manner, concerning which respondents are asked to check one category—from among several categories of answers—that best represents their feeling about or belief in the statement.

Linear programming. A quantitative technique for maximizing some program output subject to program constraints.

Management by objectives (MBO). A management technique that focuses on objectives rather than process.

Mean. Average value of the variable of interest found by summing all values and dividing by the number of values.

Mean square. The total sums of squares divided by the degrees of freedom for the sums of squares.

Measurement. The assignment of one set of entities—generally numerical values—to another set of entities—generally some empirical fact or phenomenon.

Mechanistic decision making. Decision making where the ends are verifiable and the appropriate decision process is known and accepted.

Model specification. The description or elucidation of a causal model of how program inputs and process produce program outputs and outcomes.

Monitoring. The continuing comparison between a program process or results and expectations, with the aim to improve the quality of the program.

Multidimensionality problem. The problem that occurs in interpreting a single numerical value assigned to a particular phenomenon as if that value reflected a point along a single real world measurement scale, when in fact the value resulted from a compromise or other combination of scores derived from additional, and possibly conflicting, measurement scales. *See also* Unidimensionality.

Multiple regression. A technique for regressing a single dependent variable simultaneously on two or more independent variables.

Needs assessment. The process of determining the nature and extent of the problems that a program is designed to address; the first stage in program implementation.

Net present value. The value today of an amount of money to be received or expended at sometime in the future.

Nominal group technique. A technique used to generate data systematically within a case study format, involving a structured group meeting in which individuals are given a specific task.

Nominal scale. A scale where only a distinction between similar or dissimilar items is made.

Nonresponse. The unwillingness or the inability of persons selected for the sample to cooperate in answering either the questionnaires or interviews.

Operations research. The study and application of a variety of quantitative methods for management and decision making.

Opportunity cost. A term used to denote the loss of opportunities to use resources in ways alternative to a specific use strategy.

Ordinal scale. A scale in which the categories are ordered by magnitude.

Ordinary knowledge. Knowledge that does not owe its origin, testing, degree of verification, truth status, or currency to distinctive professional social inquiry techniques but rather to common sense, causal empiricism, or thoughtful speculation and analysis.

Ordinary least square. A mathematical technique for solving regression problems.

Outputs. The products of the program, which consist of direct outputs, intermediate effects, and long-run or ultimate effects or outcomes.

Pareto chart. A bar graph used to arrange information in such a way that priorities for managerial action can be established.

Pattern matching. A process in which empirically based patterns are compared with predictor patterns, and data from each case are assessed to determine if they support a set of theoretical propositions that are formulated as questions.

Perception measures. Any of the broad range of attitudes, beliefs, knowledge, and agreements that can be used in program evaluation.

Poisson distribution. A statistical distribution that provides the likelihood of outcomes for rare events.

Precision. A measure of the degree of variation in the estimates that may be made on the basis of all possible samples drawn in a particular manner.

Prevalence. The number of persons at any time (scaled to an appropriate base, such as percentage or per 100,000) who actually show evidence of a disease. *See also* Incidence.

Probability sample. *See* Random sample.

Process. The specific set of activities, their sequencing, and timing for the sequencing, which actually represents program operation.

Program evaluation and review technique (PERT). An evaluation technique that (1) divides a project into self-contained activities; (2) develops a precedence table for them; (3) produces a network of circles representing discrete events and arrows representing activities; and (4) determines a critical path of activities and events.

Progress. The degree to which program implementation complies with the plan for it.

Quality adjusted life years (QALY). A utility measure derived by assigning a utility value to the total remaining years of life of a defined population in order to compare the utility (quality) of those years with those of a control (healthy) population. *See also* Disability adjusted life years (DALY).

Questionnaire. An instrument or schedule for collecting data that the respondent self-administers.

Queuing theory. A body of knowledge useful for examining the nature of waiting lines.

Random sample. A sample drawn on a random basis.

Random walk decision making. Making decisions through a random process (no accepted process; ends nonverifiable).

Rate. A ratio of two measures.

Ratio scale. A scale in which the points are ordered by magnitude and spaced at equidistant intervals and that has a true zero point.

Reactiveness. The effect of knowledge of a situation on subsequent measures of the situation. *See also* Self-fulfilling prophecy.

Regression. A technique for describing the relationship between two continuous variables, one considered as dependent and the other as independent, associated with one another in a linear fashion.

Regression coefficients. A number, found by regression, that describes the amount of change in a dependent variable associated with a one-unit change in the independent variable.

Regression discontinuity. A point of change in a regression line or the slope of the line associated with a change in a program variable.

Regression to the mean. The tendency for any time-related data to "regress," or come back, to the long-term trend line.

Relevance. The necessity of a program or service.

Reliability. The extent to which a measurement device will produce the same result when used more than once to measure precisely the same item.

Representative sample. A nonrandom sample where units are selected because they seem to be representative of the population as a whole.

Reproducibility. The extent to which a given researcher or evaluator can reproduce measures used in one setting to apply to the same phenomenon in other settings.

Run chart. A simple display of the average time of the occurrence of the event of interest displayed over time.

Sample of convenience. Sample chosen by selecting units that are conveniently available.

Scale. *See* Interval scale; Nominal scale; Ordinal scale; Ratio scale.

Self-fulfilling prophecy. An initial preconception concerning the way a program may work or its relative success that becomes one of the findings of an evaluation, even though it may not be true. *See also* Reactiveness.

Sensitization. *See* Hawthorne effect.

Sentinel events. Medical conditions and stages of conditions that indicate a lack of access to acceptable quality primary care.

Significance test. A statistical exercise designed to determine the probability that a particular observed incident occurred not by chance alone.

Simple random sampling. A sampling technique where every sample of a given size from a population has an equal probability of being selected. *See also* Linear programming.

Social learning. The actual participation in ongoing social phenomena through which individuals learn new behavior.

Social tests. Determination of whether the means employed meets relevant social criteria; appropriate to the random walk and traditional decision-making models.

Split halves. A reliability test, where the results of half of the measurements are correlated or compared with the results of the other half.

Spurious relationship. An apparent relationship between two variables that can be shown to be a result of their relationship to a third variable.

Standard deviation. The square root of the variance.

Standard deviation of the sample mean. *See* Standard error of the mean.

Standard error of the mean. The average squared difference between the mean for each sample and the true population value.

Standard gamble. The method described by Neuman and von Morganstern (1953) of measuring preferences based on the indifference of informants to two alternatives, the first of which involves the possibility of extreme outcomes, the second of which involves an assured intermediate state.

Stratified sampling. A sampling technique where the population is first divided into two or more strata that are assumed to be closely associated with the characteristic of the population to be estimated, and then sample members are drawn from every strata. *See also* Cluster sampling; Simple random sampling.

Structured observations. The development of categorical schemes during and after observation.

Summative evaluation. Evaluation of activities associated with outputs and outcomes of a program. *See also* Formative evaluation.

Sums of squares. The summation of the squared difference between each observation and the mean of all observations.

Survey research. An approach to knowledge that uses information collected through questionnaires or interviews directed to a sample of persons drawn from some population of interest.

Time series analysis. *See* Trend analysis.

Tracer condition. A particular disease entity around which observations in data collection efforts are structured that is used to characterize a range of diseases or treatment of these diseases.

Traditional decision making. Decision making where a decision process has become accepted process will produce a verified desired end.

Transferability. The extent to which other researchers or evaluators can use a measurement tool in similar settings or in other settings.

Trend analysis. A general evaluation strategy that depends on data analyzed over a series of discrete points in time.

t-test. A statistical test that two values are different from one another, usually applied to results of experiments.

Type one error. The finding of a program result when none actually exists.

Type two error. The finding of no program result when one actually exists.

Type three error. The assumption that a program was implemented, when in fact it was not.

Unidimensionality. The assurance that a numerical value assigned to a particular phenomenon reflects a point along one and only one real world measurement scale. *See also* Multidimensionality.

Utility measures (also referred to as **trade-off measures**). As used in health evaluation, these refer to techniques that assess the full range of possible health states experienced by entire populations or subsets of populations based upon the perception of informants about the relative desirability of each state.

Validity. The extent to which a measurement device actually represents reality. *See also* Content validity; Criterion validity; External validity; Internal validity.

Variance. A measure of the extent to which a number of observations differ from one another for some variable of interest.

BIBLIOGRAPHY

Aldrich, J. H., and F. D. Nelson. 1984. *Linear Probability, Logit and Probit Models.* Sage series: Quantitative Applications in the Social Sciences no. 45.

Appleby, C. 1997. "Organized Chaos." *Hospitals & Health Networks* (July 20): 51–52.

Arkin, H., and R. R. Colton. 1963. *Tables for Statisticians.* New York: Barnes and Noble.

Bainbridge, J., and S. Sapirie. 1974. *Health Project Management: A Manual of Procedures for Formulating and Implementing Health Projects.* Geneva: World Health Organization.

Bastos, P. G., X. Sun, D. P. Wagner, W. A. Knaus, and J. E. Zimmerman. 1996. "Application of the APACHE III Prognostic System in Brazilian Intensive Care Units: A Prospective Multicenter Study." *Intensive Care Medicine* 22 (6): 564–70.

Batalden, P. B., and P. K. Stoltz. 1993. "A Framework for the Continual Improvement of Health Care: Building and Applying Professional and Improvement Knowledge to Test Changes in Daily Work." *The Joint Commission Journal on Quality Improvement* 19 (10): 424–45.

Berelson, B. 1952. *Content Analysis in Communications.* Glencoe, IL: The Free Press.

Berwick, D., A. Godfrey, and J. Roessner. 1990. *Curing Health Care: New Strategies for Quality Improvement.* San Francisco: Jossey-Bass.

Bhrolchain, C. M., and S. J. Shribman. 1995. "A New Method of Evaluating Selective School Entry Medicals." *Public Health* 109 (2): 117–21.

Blumenthal, D., and A. C. Scheck (eds.). 1995. *Improving Clinical Practice: Total Quality Management and the Physician.* San Francisco: Jossey-Bass.

Boyle, C. 1989. "The Challenge to Operationalize Research Methods from a Management Perspective." *Journal of Health Administration Education* 17 (3): 557–66.

Boyle, M. H., W. Furlong, D. Feeny, G. W. Torrance, and J. Hatcher. 1995. "Reliability of the Health Utilities Index—Mark III Used in the 1991 Cycle 6 Canadian General Social Survey Health Questionnaire." *Quality of Life Research* 4 (3): 249–57.

Browne, A., and A. Wildavsky. 1987. "What Should Evaluation Mean to Implementation." In *The Politics of Program Evaluation*, edited by D. Palumbo, 146–72. Beverly Hills: Sage Publications.

Bunker, J. P., H. S. Frazier, and F. Mosteller. 1994. "Improving Health: Measuring Effects of Medical Care." *Milbank Quarterly* 72 (2): 225–58.

Burns, L. R., G. S. Lamb, and D. R. Wholey. 1996. "Impact of Integrated Community Nursing Services on Hospital Utilization and Costs in a Medicare Risk Plan." *Integrated Community Nursing Services, Inquiry* 33 (1): 30–41.

Campbell, D. T. 1969. "Reforms as Experiments." *American Psychologist* 24 (4): 409–29.

Campbell, D. T., and J. C. Stanley. 1963. *Experimental and Quasi-Experimental Designs for Research*. Chicago: Rand McNally.

Card, W. I., and G. H. Mooney. 1977. "What Is the Monetary Value of Human Life?" *British Medical Journal* 2 (6103): 1527–29.

Carey, T., L. Kinsinger, T. Keyserling, and R. Harris. 1996. "Research in the Community: Recruiting and Retaining Practices." *Journal of Community Health* 21 (5): 315–26.

Cochrane, A. 1972. *Effectiveness and Efficiency*. London: The Nuffield Provincial Hospitals Trust.

Cook, T. D., and D. T. Campbell. 1979. *Quasi-Experimentation: Design and Analysis Issues for Field Settings*. Chicago: Rand McNally.

Davidson, H., P. H. Folcarelli, S. Crawford, L. J. Durat, and J. C. Clifford. 1997. "The Effects of Health Care Reforms of Job Satisfaction and Voluntary Turnover Among Hospital-Based Nurses." *Medical Care* 35 (6): 634–45.

Delbecq, A. L., A. E. Van de Ven, and D. H. Gustafson. 1975. *Group Techniques for Program Planning: A Guide to Nominal Group and Delphi Processes*. Glenview, IL: Scott, Foresman.

DeLuca, J. M., and R. E. Cagan. 1997. *The CEO's Guide to Health Care Information Systems*. AHA Publications.

Deming, W. E. 1986. *Out of Crisis*. Cambridge, MA: Massachusetts Institute of Technology.

Deming, E. 1993. *The New Economics for Industry, Education, Government*. Cambridge, MA: MIT Center for Advanced Engineering Study.

Denzin, N. K. 1978. *The Research Act: A Theoretical Introduction to Sociological Methods*. New York: McGraw-Hill.

Deutsch, K. W. 1968. "Toward a Cybernetic Model of Man and Society." In *Modern Systems Research for the Behavioral Scientist*, edited by W. Buckley, 387–400. Chicago: Aldine Publishing Company.

Donaldson, C., and P. Shackley. 1997. "Does 'Process Utility' Exist? A Case Study of Willingness to Pay for Laparoscopic Cholecystectomy." *Social Science and Medicine* 44 (5): 699–707.

Drummond, M. F. 1980. *Principles of Economic Appraisal in Health Care*. Oxford: Oxford University Press.

DuRant, R. H., E. S. Rowe, M. Rich, E. Allred, S. J. Emans, and E. R. Woods. 1997. "Tobacco and Alcohol Use Behaviors Portrayed in Music Videos: A Content Analysis." *American Journal of Public Health* 87 (7): 1131–35.

Fetterman, D. M., S. J. Kaftarian, and A. Wandersman. 1996. *Empowerment Evaluation: Knowledge and Tools for Self-Assessment and Accountability*. Sage Publications.

Fischer, L. R. 1998. "Quality Improvement in Primary Care Clinics." *JCAHO Journal of Quality Improvement* 24 (7): 361–70.

Flexner, B. 1995. "Designing and Facilitating OptionFinder-Supported Meetings." Mendota Heights, MN: Option Technologies, Inc.

Fraisier, P. Y., P. Slatt, V. Kowlowitz, D. O. Kollisch, and M. Mintzer. 1997. "Focus Groups: A Useful Tool for Curriculum Evaluation. *Family Medicine* 29 (7): 500–507.

Freeman, H., and P. Rossi. 1981. "Social Experiments." *Health and Society: Milbank Memorial Fund Quarterly* 59 (3): 340–73.

Friedlob, A. 1997. *Case Study: Los Angeles County Department of Health Services*. Atlanta, GA: Centers for Disease Control and Prevention, Public Health Practice Program Office.

Ghoshal, S., and C. A. Bartlett. 1995. "Changing the Role of Top Management: Beyond Structure to Processes." *Harvard Business Review* Jan–Feb: 86–96.

Gitlow, H., S. Gitlow, A. Oppenheim, and R. Oppenheim. 1989. *Tools and Methods for the Improvement of Quality*. Richard Irwin, Inc.

Glover, J. A. 1938. "The Incidence of Tonsillectomies in School Children." *Proceedings of the Royal Society of Medicine* 31: 1219–39.

Goldberg, H., and H. McGough. 1991. "The Ethics of Ongoing Randomization Trials: Investigation Among Intimates." *Medical Care* 29 (7): 41–48.

Goldberg, H. E., S. Wagner, S. Fihn, D. Martin, C. Horowitz, D. Christianson, A. Cheadle, P. Diehr, and G. Simon. 1998. "A Randomized Control Trial of Academic Detailing Techniques and Continuous Quality Improvement Teams: Increasing Compliance with National Guidelines for the Primary Care of Hypertension and Depression." *JCAHO Journal of Quality Improvement* 24 (3): 130–42.

Grembowski, D., L. Fiset, P. Milgom, D. Conrad, and A. Spadafora. 1997. "Does Fluoridation Reduce the Use of Dental Services Among Adults?" *Medical Care* 35 (5): 454–71.

Grindel, C. G., K. Peterson, M. Kinneman, and T. L. Turner. 1996. "The Practice Environment Project, a Process for Outcome Evaluation." *Journal of Nursing Administration* 26 (5): 43–51.

Gujarati, D. N. 1988. *Basic Econometrics*. 2d ed. New York: McGraw-Hill.

Gurel, L. 1975. "The Human Side of Evaluating Human Services Programs: Problems and Prospects." In *Handbook of Evaluation Research, Volume II*, edited by E. L. Struening and M. Guttentag, 11–28. Beverly Hills: Sage Publications.

Hage, G. 1974. *Communication and Organizational Control: Cybernetics in Health and Welfare Settings*. New York: Wiley.

Halverson, P. 1995. "Davidson County: Agenda or Health Project Final Report." University of North Carolina at Chapel Hill, School of Public Health.

Halverson, P., A. Kaluzny, and C. McLaughlin (eds.). 1998. *Managed Care and Public Health*. Aspen.

Health Care Advisory Board. 1993. *Line of Fire: The Coming Public Scrutiny of Hospital and Health System Quality*, Washington, DC.

Holsti, O. R. 1968. "Content Analysis." In *The Handbook of Social Psychology, Volume 2*, 2d ed., edited by G. Lindzey and E. Aronson, 596–692. Reading, MA: Addison-Wesley.

Jackson, R. S., L. S. Leininger, R. P. Harris, and A. D. Kaluzny. 1994. "Implementing Continuous Quality Improvement in Primary Care: Implication for Preventive Services." *Journal of Ambulatory Care Management* 17 (3): 8–14.

Johnson, S. P., and C. P. McLaughlin. 1994. "Measurement and Statistical Analysis in CQI." In *Continuous Quality Improvement in Health Care: Theory, Implementation, and Applications*, edited by C. P. McLaughlin and A. D. Kaluzny, 70–101. Gaithersburg, MD: Aspen Publishers.

Kahan, J., D. Kanouse, and J. Winkler. 1984. "Variations in the Content Style of NIH Consensus Statements: 1979–83." RAND note (November).

Kaluzny, A. D., R. Harris, and V. Strecher. 1991. "North Carolina Cancer Early Detection Program." NCI/DCPC-funded research. Chapel Hill, NC: University of North Carolina.

Kaluzny, A., T. Ricketts, R. Warnecke, L. Ford, J. Morrissey, D. Gillings, E. Sondik, H. Ozer, and J. Goldman. 1989. "Evaluating Organizational Design to Assure Technology Transfer: The Case of the Community Clinical Oncology Program." *Journal of the National Cancer Institute* 81 (22): 1717–25.

Kaluzny, A. D., and J. E. Veney. 1980. *Health Services Organizations: A Guide to Research and Assessment.* Berkeley: McCutchan.

Kaluzny, A., O. Brawley, D. Garson-Angert, J. Shaw, P. Godley, R. Warnecke, and L. Ford. 1993. "Assuring Access to State-of-Art Care for Minority Populations." *Journal of the National Cancer Institute* 85 (23): 1945–50.

Kaluzny, A., R. Warnecke, and Associates. 1996. *Managing a Health Care Alliance: Improving Community Cancer Care.* San Francisco: Jossey-Bass.

Kaluzny, A., H. Zuckerman, and T. Ricketts (eds.). 1995. *Partners for the Dance: Forming Strategic Alliances in Health Care.* Chicago: Health Administration Press.

Kanouse, D. E., J. D. Winkler, J. Kosecoff, S. H. Berry, G. M. Carter, J. P. Kahan, L. McCloskey, W. H. Rogers, C. M. Winslow, G. M. Anderson, L. Brodsley, A. Fink, L. Meredith, and R. H. Brook. 1990. *Changing Medical Practice Through Technology Assessment: An Evaluation of the NIH Consensus Development Program.* Chicago: Health Administration Press.

Kaplan, R. M., J. P. Anderson, A. W. Wu, W. C. Mathews, F. Kozin, and D. Orentstein. 1989. "The

Quality of Well-Being Scale: Applications in AIDS, Cystic Fibrosis, and Arthritis." *Medical Care* 27 (3): s27–43.

Katz, D., and R. L. Kahn. 1978. *The Social Psychology of Organization.* New York: Wiley.

Kerlinger, F. N. 1986. *Foundations of Behavioral Research.* 3d ed. NY: Holt, Rinehart & Winston.

Kerlinger, F. N., and E. J. Pedhazur. 1973. *Multiple Regression in Behavioral Research.* NY: Holt, Rinehart & Winston.

Kessner, D. M., C. K. Snow, and J. Singer. 1974. *Assessment of Medical Care for Children.* Washington, DC: Institute of Medicine.

Kierkegaard, S. 1967. *Journals and Papers.* (1843, vol. 1.) H. V. Hong and E. H. Hong (trans.).

Kilpatrick, K. 1995. "Evaluation of the Primary Care Education (PRIME) Initiative in the Veterans Health Administration." Proposal funded by the Veterans Administration, Office of Academic Affairs.

Kilpatrick, K. 1997. "Draft Summary of the VISN 6 Site Visit Reports." Chapel Hill, NC: University of North Carolina, School of Public Health, Department of Health Policy and Administration.

Kind, P., and P. Dolan. 1995. "The Effect of Past and Present Illness Experience on the Valuations of Health States." *Medical Care* 33 (4): AS255–63.

Kinsinger, L. S., R. Harris, B. Qaqish, V. Strecher, and A. Kaluzny. 1998. "A Randomized Trial of an Office System Intervention to Increase Breast Cancer Screening in a Community Primary Care Practice: Results from the North Carolina Prescribe for Health Study." *Journal of General Internal Medicine* (in press).

Kizer, K. W. 1995. *Vision for Change: A Plan to Restructure the Veterans Health Administration.* Department of Veterans Affairs.

Knaus, W. A., E. A. Draper, D. P. Wagner, and J. E. Zimmerman. 1986. "An Evaluation of Outcome from Intensive Care in Major Medical Centers." *Annals of Internal Medicine* 104 (3): 410–18.

Kotch, J., A. Kaluzny, and J. Veney. 1991. "The Performance-Based Management System to Reduce Prematurity and Low Birthweight in Local Health Departments: Final Report." Submitted to the Association of Schools of Public Health and the Centers for Disease Control.

Kritchevsky, S. B., and B. P. Simons. 1991. "Continuous Quality Improvement: Concepts and Application in Primary Care." *Journal of the American Medical Association* 266:1817–23.

Krueger, R. A. 1994. Focus Groups: *A Practical Guide to Applied Research.* 2d ed. Thousand Oaks, CA: Sage Publications.

Landefeld, J. S., and E. P. Seskin. 1982. "The Economic Value of Life: Linking Theory to Practice." *American Journal of Public Health* 72 (6): 555–66.

Lave, J. R., D. G. Ives, N. D. Traven, and L. H. Kuller. 1996. "Evaluation of a Health Promotion Demonstration Program for the Rural Elderly." *Health Services Research* 31 (3): 261–81.

Lawler, E. E., III. 1985. "Challenging Traditional Research Assumptions." In *Doing Research That Is Useful for Theory and Practice*, edited by E. E. Lawler, III, A. M. Mohrman, Jr., S. A. Ledford, Jr., and G. E. Cummings and Associates, 4–17. San Francisco: Jossey-Bass.

Leape, L. 1990. "Practice Guidelines and Standards: An Overview." *Quality Review Bulletin* 16 (2): 42–49.

Leininger, L., R. Harris, R. Jackson, V. Strecher, and A. Kaluzny. 1994. "CQI in Primary Care." In *Continuous Quality Improvement in Health Care: Theory, Implementation and Application*, edited by C. McLaughlin and A. Kaluzny. Gaithersburg, MD: Aspen Publishers.

Lieu, B. 1976. *Quality of Life Indicators in U.S. Metropolitan Areas.* New York: Praeger.

Lindblom, C. E., and D. K. Cohen. 1979. *Usable Knowledge: Social Science and Social Problem Solving.* New Haven, CT: Yale University Press.

Lohr, K. N. 1988. "Outcome Measurement: Concepts and Questions." *Inquiry* 25 (1): 37–50.

Macnee, C. L., and R. Penchansky. 1994. "Targeting Ambulatory Care Cases for Risk Management and Quality Management." *Inquiry* 31 (Spring): 66–75.

Margolin, B. 1996. "Averting Disaster: A Conversation with the Los Angeles County 'Health Czar.'" *Health Affairs* 15 (1): 86–91.

Marshall, C., and G. Rossman. 1989. *Designing Qualitative Research.* Beverly Hills: Sage Publications.

Mays, G., C. A. Miller, and P. Halverson. 1999. *Local Public Health Practice: Trends and Models.* American Public Health Association.

McGlynn, E. A. 1997. "Six Challenges in Measuring the Quality of Health Care." *Health Affairs* 16 (3): 7–21.

Mehrez, A., and A. Gafni. 1991. "The Healthy-Years Equivalents: How to Measure Them Using the Standard Gamble Approach." *Medical Decision Making* 11 (2): 140–46.

Miles, M. B., and M. Huberman. 1994. *Qualitative Data Analysis.* 2d ed. Thousand Oaks, CA: Sage Publications.

Miller, D. C. 1991. *Handbook of Research Design and Social Measurement.* 5th ed. New York: Sage.

Miller, R., and H. Luft. 1997. "Does Managed Care Lead to Better or Worse Quality of Care." *Health Affairs* 16 (5): 7–25.

Mintzberg, H. 1987. "Crafting Strategy." *Harvard Business Review* 87 (4): 66–75.

Mintzberg, H. 1989. *Mintzberg on Management.* New York: The Free Press.

Mitchell, L., S. Fife, A. Chopthia, D. Leona, S. Dixon, A. Airola, J. Stickney, J. Mueller, R. Ruvalcaba, and L. Neuman. 1996. "Three Teams Improving Thrombolytic Therapy." *JCAHO Journal of Quality Improvement* 22 (6): 379–90.

Morrisey, M. A., J. Alexander, L. R. Burns, and V. Johnson. 1996. "Managed Care and Physician/Hospital Integration." *Health Affairs* 15 (4): 62–73.

Mulley, A. G. 1989. "Assessing Patients' Utilities. Can the Ends Justify the Means?" *Medical Care* 27 (3): s279–81.

Murray, C. J. L. 1994. "Quantifying the Burden of Disease: The Technical Basis for Disability-Adjusted Life Years." *Bulletin of the World Health Organization* 72 (3): 429–45.

Murray, C. J. L. 1996. "Rethinking DALYs." In *The Global Burden of Disease,* edited by C. J. L. Murray and A. D. Lopez, 1–89. Harvard School of Public Health.

Murray, C. J. L., and A. D. Lopez. 1996. "Global and Regional Descriptive Epidemiology of Disability: Incidence, Prevalence, Health Expectancies and Years Lived with Disability." In *The Global Burden of Disease,* edited by C. J. L. Murray and A. D. Lopez, 201–46. Harvard School of Public Health.

Neuhauser, D. 1998. "Parallel Providers, Ongoing Randomization and Continuous Improvement." *Medical Care* 29 (7): 5–8.

Neuhauser, D., J. E. McEachern, and L. Headrick (eds.). 1995. *Clinical CQI: A Book of Readings.* Oakbrook Terrace, IL: Joint Commission on Accreditation of Healthcare Organizations.

Nie, N. H., D. H. Bent, and C. H. Hull. 1975. *SPSS: Statistical Package for the Social Sciences.* New York: McGraw Hill.

Palumbo, D. (ed.) 1987. *The Politics of Program Evaluation.* Beverly Hills: Sage Publications.

Park, R. E., A. Fink, R. Brook, M. Chassin, K. Kahn, N. Merrick, J. Kosecoff, and D. Solomon. 1986. "Physician Ratings of Appropriate Indications for Six Medical and Surgical Procedures." *American Journal of Public Health* 76 (7): 766–72.

Petasnick, W. 1989. "Expectations of What an Entry-Level Manager Should Know about the Application of Health Service Research Methods: Perspectives of an Administrator of a University Teaching Hospital." *Journal of Health Administration Education* 17 (3): 567–72.

Plsek, P. E. 1992. "Tutorial: Introduction to Control Charts." *Quality Management in Health Care* 1 (1): 65–74.

Potts, S. G. 1992. "The QALY and Why It Should Be Resisted." In *Philosophy and Health Care,* edited by E. Matthews and M. Menlowe. Aldershot, United Kingdom: Avebury.

RAND. 1988. *Health Insurance and the Demand for Medical Care: Evidence from a Randomized Experiment.* Santa Monica, CA.

Ransohoff, D., R. Harris, L. Kinsinger, and A. Kaluzny. 1997. "Cancer Prevention in Primary Care: Practice

Activation. NCI/DCPC funded research. Chapel Hill, NC.

Read, J. L., R. J. Quinn, D. M. Berwick. 1984. "Preferences for Health Outcomes: Comparisons of Assessment Methods." *Medical Decision Making* 4 (3): 315.

Rice, D. P., and B. S. Cooper. 1967. "The Economic Value of Human Life." *American Journal of Public Health and the Nations Health* 57 (11): 1954–66.

Richardson, J. 1994. "Cost Utility Analysis: What Should Be Measured?" *Social Science Medicine* 39 (1): 7–21.

Rittenhouse, B. E. 1997. "Healthy Years Equivalents Versus Time Trade-Off: Ambiguity and Uncertainty." *International Journal of Technology Assessment in Health Care* 13 (1): 35–45.

Roethlisberger, F. J., and W. J. Diskson. 1939. *Management and the Worker.* Cambridge, MA: Harvard University Press.

Rogers, E. M. 1995. *Diffusion of Innovations.* 4th ed. New York: The Free Press.

Rosenthal, R., and L. Jacobson. 1968. *Pygmalion in the Classroom.* New York: Holt, Rinehart & Winston.

Rosser, R., and P. Kind. 1978. "A Scale of Valuations of States of Illness: Is There a Social Consensus?" *International Journal of Epidemiology* 7 (4): 347–58.

Rutten-van Molken, M., C. Bakker, E. van Doorslaer, and S. van der Linden. 1995. "Methodological Issues of Patient Utility Measurement: Experience from Two Clinical Trials." *Medical Care* 33 (9): 922–35.

Ryan, M. 1996. "Using Willingness to Pay to Assess the Benefits of Assisted Reproductive Techniques." *Health Economics* 5 (6): 543–58.

Ryan, M., J. Ratcliffe, and J. Tucker. 1997. "Using Willingness to Pay to Value Alternative Models of Antenatal Care." *Social Science and Medicine* 44 (3): 371–80.

Savitz, L., and A. Kaluzny. 1998. *Assessment of Dissemination of Clinical Process Innovations in an IDS Environment.* University of Washington: Center for Health Care Management Research.

Schaefer, M. 1987. *Implementing Change in Service Programs: Project Planning and Management.* Sage Publications.

Scheirer, M. A. 1989. "Implementation and Process Analysis in Worksite Health Promotion Research." In *Methodological Issues in Worksite Research.* Bethesda, MD: National Heart, Lung and Blood Institute.

Schaefer, M. 1987. *Implementing Change in Health Service Programs: Project Planning and Management.* Sage Publications.

Schriefer, J. 1995. "Managing Critical Pathway Variances." *Quality Management in Health Care* 3 (2): 30–42.

Scott, W. R. 1998. *Organizations: Rational, Natural and Open Systems.* 4th ed. Upper Saddle River, NJ: Prentice Hall.

Scriven, M. 1967. "The Methodology of Evaluation." In *Perspective of Curriculum Evaluation,* edited by R. W. Tyler, R. M. Gagne, and M. Scriven. Chicago: Rand McNally.

Senge, P. M. 1990. *The Fifth Discipline: The Art and Practice of the Learning Organization.* New York: Doubleday Publishing.

Smith, T. A., H. E. Lyon, D. Hardison, and B. Bogi. 1995. "Using a Delphi Technique in a Needs Assessment for an Innovative Approach to Advanced General Dentistry Education." *Journal of Dental Education* 59 (3): 442–47.

Solberg, L,. G. Isham, T. Kottke, S. Magnan, A. Nelson, M. Reed, and S. Richards. 1995. "Competing HMOs Collaboration to Improve Prevention Services." *JCAHO Journal of Quality Improvement* 21 (11): 600–601.

Solberg, L., T. Kottke, and M. Brekke. 1998. "Will Primary Care Clinics Organize Themselves to Improve the Delivery of Preventive Services? A Randomized Control Trial." *Preventive Medicine* (in press).

Solberg, L. I., T. E. Kottke, M. L. Brekke, C. A. Calomeni, S. A. Conn, and G. Davidson. 1996. "Using CQI to Increase Preventive Services in Clinical Practices: Going Beyond Guidelines." *Preventive Medicine* 25 (3): 259–68.

Stearns, S. 1991. "Preliminary Drafts of Survey Instruments to Obtain Information Relevant to Costs for the North Carolina Prescribe for Health." University of North Carolina at Chapel Hill.

Stiggelbout, A. M., M. J. C. Eijkemans, G. M. Kiebert, J. Kievit, J.-W. H. Leer, and H. J. De Haes. 1996. "The 'Utility' of the Visual Analog Scale in Medical Decision Making and Technology Assessment: Is It an Alternative to the Time Trade-Off?" *International Journal of Technology Assessment in Health Care* 12 (2): 291–98.

Succi, M. J., S. Lee, and J. A. Alexander. 1997. "Effects of Market Position and Competition on Rural Hospital Closures." *Health Services Research* 31 (6): 679–99.

Suchman, E. A. 1967. *Evaluative Research.* New York: Russell Sage Foundation.

Swartz, K. 1997. "Changes in the 1995 Current Population Survey and Estimates of Health Insurance Coverage." *Inquiry* 34 (Spring): 70–79.

Tedaldi, M., F. Scaglione, and V. Russotti. 1992. *A Beginner's Guide to Quality in Manufacturing.* ASQC Quality Press, 156–63.

Thompson, J. D. 1967. *Organizations in Action.* New York: McGraw-Hill.

Torrance, G. W. 1986. "Measurement of Health State Utilities for Economic Appraisal, a Review." *Journal of Health Economics* 5: 1–30.

Torrance, G. W., and D. Feeny. 1989. "Utilities and Quality-Adjusted Life Years." *International Journal of Technology Assessment in Health Care* 5 (4): 559–75.

Torrance, G. W., W. H. Thomas, and D. L. Sackett. 1972. "A Utility Maximization Model for Evaluation of Health Care Programs." *Health Services Research* 7 (2): 118–33.

Vaughn, D. 1996. *The Challenger Launch Decision: Risky Technology, Culture and Deviance at NASA.* Chicago: University of Chicago Press.

Veney, J. E., and J. W. Luckey. 1983. "A Comparison of Regression and ARIMA Models for Assessing Program Effects: An Application to the Mandated Highway Speed Limit Reduction of 1974." *Social Indicators Research* 12 (1): 83–105.

Veney, J., P. Kory, J. Barnsley, and A. Kaluzny. 1991. "Designing Clinical Protocols for Optimal Use: Measuring Attributes of Treatment and Cancer Control Trials." *Journal of Medical Systems* 15 (5–6): 335–44.

Veney, J. E. 1993. "Evaluation Applications of Regression Analysis with Time-Series Data." *Evaluation Practice* 14 (3): 259–74.

Veney, J. E., and P. Gorbach. 1993. "Definitions of Program Evaluation Terms." Working paper. The EVALUATION Project, Carolina Population Center.

von Nuemann, J., and O. Morgenstern. 1953. *Theory of Games and Economic Behavior.* New York: Wiley.

Wasley, M. A., S. E. McNagny, V. L. Phillips, and J. S. Ahluwalia. 1997. "The Cost-Effectiveness of the Nicotine Transdermal Patch for Smoking Cessation." *Preventive Medicine* 26 (2): 264–70.

Weaver, M., R. Ndamobissi, R. Kornfield, C. Blewane, A. Sathe, M. Chapko, N. Bendje, E. Nguembi, and J. Senwara-Defiobona. 1996. "Willingness to Pay for Child Survival: Results of a National Survey in Central African Republic." *Social Science and Medicine* 43 (6): 985–98.

Weiner, N. 1948. *Cybernetics, or Control and Communications in the Animal and Machine.* New York: Wiley.

Weiss, C. H. 1975. "Evaluation Research in the Political Context." *In Handbook of Evaluation Research, Volume I*, edited by E. L. Struening and M. Guttenag, 13–26. Beverly Hills: Sage Publications.

Weiss, C. H. 1989. "Congressional Committees as Users of Analysis." *Journal of Policy Analysis and Management* 8 (3): 411–31.

Wennberg, J. E. 1994. "Health Care Reform and Professionalism." *Inquiry* 31 (Fall): 296–302.

Westphal, J., R. Gulati, and S. Shortell. 1997. "Customization or Conformity? An Institutional and Network Perspective on the Content and Consequences of TQM Adoption." *Administrative Science Quarterly* 42: 366–94.

Wholey, J. S. 1979. *Evaluation: Promise and Performance.* Washington, DC: Urban Institute.

Windsor, R. A., J. B. Lowe, L. L. Perkins, D. Smith-Yoder, L. Artz, M. Crawford, K. Amburgy, and N. R. Boyd. 1993. "Health Education for Pregnant Smokers: Its Behavioral Impact and Cost Benefit." *American Journal of Public Health* 83 (2): 201–06.

Winer, B. J. 1991. *Statistical Principles in Experimental Design.* New York: McGraw-Hill.

The World Bank. 1993. *World Development Report 1993: Investing in Health.* Oxford University Press.

World Health Organization. 1981. "Health Programme Evaluation: Guiding Principles, Health for All, Series No. 6." Geneva.

World Health Organization. 1984. *World Health Statistics Annual: 1984.* Geneva.

Wortman, P., A. Vinokur, and L. Sechrest. 1982. "Evaluation of NIH Consensus Development Process, Phase I: Final Report." Ann Arbor, MI: Center for Research on Utilization of Scientific Knowledge, Institute for Social Research, University of Michigan.

Young, G. J., M. Charns, J. Daley, M. Forbes, W. Henderson, and S. Khur. 1998. "Patterns of Coordination and Clinical Outcomes: A Study of Surgical Services." *Health Services Research* (in press).

Zuckerman, H., D. Hilberman, R. Anderson, L. Burns, J. Alexander, and P. Torrens. 1998. "Physicians and Organizations: Strange Bedfellows or a Marriage Made in Heaven?" *Frontiers of Health Services Management* 14 (3): 3–34.

INDEX

ABOUT THE AUTHORS

The authors, both of whom are professors of health policy and administration at the School of Public Health of the University of North Carolina at Chapel Hill, have extensive experience in research and evaluation in the domestic and international arenas. Dr. Veney has been the director of research for the National Blue Cross Association, has taught courses in research and evaluation for a number of years, and has directed a program to train postdoctoral fellows in program evaluation techniques in mental health programs. Dr. Veney has also spent time as a technical specialist with the World Health Organization Southeast Asia Regional Office in New Delhi, where he worked specifically in helping country health planning units to improve this program evaluation efforts. During that time he worked with health planning personnel in India, Burma, Nepal, Sri Lanka, and Thailand. From 1984 to 1989 he was the evaluation officer for the program for International Training in Health at the University of North Carolina, a United States Agency for International Development project for training of family planning personnel in Africa and Asia that involved him in field-based evaluation efforts in several countries of sub-Saharan Africa and South Asia. Dr. Veney has been the principal in investigator for a project funded by the National Institute of Allergy and Infectious Diseases (NIAID) to develop an evaluation design to assess the NIAID Community Program for Clinical Research on AIDS. Most recently Dr. Veney has been an active consultant to the World Health Organization in their efforts to assess progress toward global health goals for the year 2000. He is presently director of the doctoral program in the department of health policy and administration.

Dr. Kaluzny has been involved with various domestic and international evaluation research activities. He is a consultant to various federal and state government agencies, as well as a number of private research corporations. His evaluation and research efforts have included work with the National Cancer Institute (NCI), the Joint Commission on Accreditation of Healthcare Organizations (JCAHO), the Veterans Administration, the Agency for Health Care Policy and Research (AHCPR), and the Institute for Medicine as well as with the United States Agency for International Development, the Ford Foundation, Project HOPE, and the United Nations. Dr. Kaluzny has been the principal investigator of the NCI-funded contract to evaluate the Community Clinical Oncology Program (CCOP) and most recently is the principal investigator of an NCI grant to evaluate methods to increase the use of cancer detection regimens among primary care physicians.

Drs. Veney and Kaluzny have collaborated on a number of research and evaluation efforts. They have been coprincipal investigators of one of the early studies of innovation in hospitals and health departments funded by the National Center for Health Services Research and an evaluation of drug treatment centers in North Carolina funded by the National Institute for Mental Health. They have recently collaborated on research in local health departments, where they have carried out evaluations of state-imposed standards and primary care programs and the implementation and evaluation of performance evaluation systems to prevent low birth weight and prematurity. Most recently, Drs. Veney and Kaluzny, and other colleagues from the University of North Carolina at Chapel Hill, have collaborated on an AHCPR-funded project assessing the attributes of clinical protocols as part of the larger NCI-funded CCOP evaluation.

Printed in the United States
42289LVS00005BA/7